TWENTY LESSONS IN
THE SOCIOLOGY OF FOOD
AND AGRICULTURE

Oxford University Press Lessons Series

Series Editors: Kenneth A. Gould and Tammy L. Lewis

The Lessons Series aims to introduce undergraduate students to sub-fields in sociology in an accessible and engaging manner. The editors bring together leading scholars who are also excellent teachers to produce unique contributions designed to expose students to the range of ideas, concepts, theoretical approaches, and empirical research in a subfield. This approach enables students to cover a lot of ground without requiring them to read a large number of individual books, nor highly technical articles written by sociologists for sociologists. The contributors for the series are writing for students. Our hope is that you will find these collections accessible, engaging, and beneficial.

We have partnered with Oxford University Press, a not for profit publisher. They have committed to keeping the cost of their books as low as possible for students.

The series editors welcome proposals.

Books in Series

Ten Lessons in Introductory Sociology
Edited by Kenneth A. Gould and Tammy L. Lewis

Twenty Lessons in Environmental Sociology
Edited by Kenneth A. Gould and Tammy L. Lewis

Twenty Lessons in the Sociology of Food and Agriculture
Edited by Jason Konefal and Maki Hatanaka

TWENTY LESSONS IN
THE SOCIOLOGY
OF FOOD AND
AGRICULTURE

Jason Konefal
Sam Houston State University

Maki Hatanaka
Sam Houston State University

New York   Oxford

OXFORD UNIVERSITY PRESS

Oxford University Press is a department of the University of Oxford.
It furthers the University's objective of excellence in research, scholarship,
and education by publishing worldwide. Oxford is a registered trade mark of
Oxford University Press in the UK and certain other countries.

Published in the United States of America by Oxford University Press
198 Madison Avenue, New York, NY 10016, United States of America.

© 2019 by Oxford University Press

Library of Congress Cataloging-in-Publication Data

Names: Konefal, Jason, author. | Hatanaka, Maki, author.
Title: Twenty lessons in the sociology of food and agriculture / Jason
    Konefal, Sam Houston State University, and Maki Hatanaka, Sam Houston
    State University.
Description: New York, NY : Oxford University Press, [2019] | Series: Lessons
    in sociology | Includes bibliographical references and index.
Identifiers: LCCN 2018027012| ISBN 9780190662127 (pbk.) | ISBN 9780190662141
    (eISBN)
Subjects: LCSH: Food habits–Social aspects. | Agriculture–Social aspects.
Classification: LCC GT2850 .K67 2019 | DDC 394.1/2–dc23
LC record available at https://lccn.loc.gov/2018027012

9 8 7 6 5 4 3 2 1
Printed by Sheridan Books, Inc., United States of America

Table of Contents

Annotated Table of Contents

Introduction
Jason Konefal and Maki Hatanaka

This introduction outlines why food and agriculture are important topics of sociological inquiry. The first part introduces the relationship between food, society, and the environment, including the ways social structures and relations affect what people eat, how politics and economics affect the kinds of foods produced, and who, where, how, and by whom food is produced. The social and environmental problems associated with food and agriculture are also introduced. In the second part, an overview of sociology and the sociological imagination is provided. In the third part, a snapshot of the world today is presented. The emphasis is on three of the defining forces in society today, neoliberalism, globalization and inequality, all of which greatly affect food and agriculture. In the last part, the approach, aim, and organization of the book are briefly sketched out.

Part 1   Consuming Food

1. Consuming Food
Maki Hatanaka

This lesson examines the consumption of food using a sociological lens. While the consumption of food is an everyday practice and hence often taken for granted, it is a crucial component to understanding who we are, how we interact with the environment, and what kind of society we are part of. In particular, this lesson emphasizes the "interlocking" character of food production, distribution, and consumption and argues that our consumption practices are both influenced by and shape the food and agriculture system. The lesson poses three questions. First, what do people tend to eat today? In this section, the ways that food is becoming increasingly globalized, corporatized, standardized, processed, and disconnected are examined. Second, why do people consume what they consume? Specifically, the ways that our food choices are affected by institutional arrangements are discussed. Third, can consumers transform the food and agriculture system using their purchasing power? This last section analyzes the idea of ethical consumerism and its transformative capacity.

2. Food, Culture, and Identity
Janine Kay Gwen Chi

This lesson identifies ten essential lessons on the interrelated concepts of food, culture, and identity. Focusing on the sociological underpinnings of how and why we eat what we eat, the chapter utilizes a multilevel analysis that examines the relationship between food and representative politics on micro, meso, and macro levels. The lesson begins at the micro level with the social construction of taste, proceeds with a discussion of how the concept of authenticity has been deployed in recent food trends, and concludes on the macro level by examining the recent rise of culinary tourism in the context of globalization.

3. Food, Diets, and Industrialization
Anthony Winson and Jin Young Choi

This lesson brings a focus to the structural factors underpinning population-wide increases in body weight in nations across the globe—the so-called obesity crisis—and considers why it occurred so rapidly and at this point in human history. Specific attention is given to the role of the American food industry in transforming food environments over the past one hundred years and promoting the industrial diet. The concept of the dietary regime is used to understand dietary changes throughout human history and how the emergence of a profit-oriented food industry since the mid-nineteenth century has degraded the quality of the foods we eat through the processes of simplification, speed-up, and adulteration. This lesson also discusses how highly processed, nutrient-poor edible products, or *pseudofoods*, have been diffused in food environments to the point where we can speak of a pervasive industrial diet.

4. Food and Nutrition
Aya H. Kimura

Nutrition science is increasingly powerful in shaping our relationship with food. We often decide what to eat based on the nutritional knowledge of calories, vitamins, and minerals and their purported health effects. This lesson examines how nutrition science is influenced by social relations and highlights the important influence of class, race/ethnicity, and gender on nutrition interventions. Key concepts in the lesson such as nutritionism, charismatic nutrients, and nutritional fix help the readers to critically understand normalized assumptions and blind spots of nutrition-centered interventions and campaigns.

Part 2   Producing Food

5. The Industrialization of Agriculture
Douglas H. Constance

The lesson provides a historical perspective on the industrialization of agriculture, the outcome of long-term processes of technological and cultural innovation, which supported agricultural extensification and intensification. Extensification refers to bringing more lands into agricultural production and intensification refers to increasing yields on those lands. Increased yields created food surplus, which allowed a growing division of labor and the emergence of horticultural and agricultural societies. The Industrial Revolution accelerated this process, resulting in an agrifood system where a very small percentage of farmers produce enough food to feed the world. While industrial agriculture is very productive, in recent years it has come under increasing criticism for its negative ecological, economic, and social impacts.

6. Science, Technology, and Agriculture
Leland L. Glenna and Daniel Tobin

Scientists, politicians, and development specialists have long promoted agricultural science and technology to address food shortages around the world and are increasingly advocating their use as a strategy to address social problems like poverty. This perspective is seductive because there are historical examples where this seems to occur. However, a more careful analysis of these examples reveals that social conflicts over how to apply these agricultural science and technology outputs are common and that the resulting benefits and harms from these outputs tend to be unequally distributed. This lesson reviews several prominent examples of agriculture science and technology to illustrate the potential benefits and pitfalls of relying on agricultural science and technology to address social and economic problems. The goal of this lesson is to challenge the portrayal of agricultural science and technology as inherently good or bad and to indicate that maximizing social benefits is contingent on a more equitable social context from which agricultural science and technology are generated and diffused.

7. Increasing Corporate Control: From Supermarkets to Seeds
Philip H. Howard

The US food system can be compared to an hourglass, with approximately two million farmers at the top and over three hundred million people who eat at the bottom, but a much smaller number of corporations controlling the stages that connect farmers to everyone else. This lesson explores key links in the food chain and their levels of corporate control, including retailing, distribution, packaged food manufacturing, commodity processing, farming, and farm inputs. In each of these stages the focus is on more specific markets or products, such as those involving cow's milk or soybeans. The role of changing government actions in increasing the power of dominant firms is explored. The potential for these trends to continue is also discussed—growing awareness of the negative impacts of greater corporate control of food has motivated a diverse range of movements to oppose it.

8. Globalization of Food: The World as a Supermarket
J. Dara Bloom

This lesson introduces the concept of globalization in agriculture and the food system. Applying food regime theory, theories of governance, and global commodity chain analysis, we explore the history and origins of the current globalized agrifood system, as well as points of resistance and future trajectories.

9. Governing Agriculture: Public Policy and Private Governance
Elizabeth Ransom

Trade in agriculture and food has always been global, but the scale and scope of international trade have grown enormously, and with this growth has come a transformation in how we govern our food system. The transformation has included a shift from governments overseeing the food supply to what we will refer to as governance of the food supply by a multitude of actors. Four types of governance in our food system are discussed in this lesson: multinational (quasi-public) governance, private retailer governance, non–governmental led sustainability governance, and alternative agrifood governance. These four types of governance challenge readers to consider why the governance of our food system should be of great interest to anyone interested in power, inequality, and creating a more just and sustainable food system. Governance regulates both humans and nonhumans and, in doing so, governance has political and moral significance.

10. From Ocean to Plate: Catching, Farming, and Eating Seafood

Rebecca Clausen, Stefano B. Longo, and Brett Clark

Billions of people around the world rely on seafood as a direct source of nutrition and a means of income. In this lesson, we first discuss the social context of catching seafood by exploring how fishing practices have changed over time and outlining the ecological impacts of overfishing. Second, we examine fish farming and its growth as a significant source of seafood. We introduce questions about the ecological and social effects of transitioning from wild-capture to farm-raised seafood. Third, we explore the social and ecological conditions regarding how seafood is traded around the world, who works in the seafood industry, and how people's consumption of seafood has changed over time. Throughout these discussions, we contend that decisions about seafood and the sustainability of marine systems must address issues related to who controls the production of seafood, what type of knowledge about marine systems is prioritized, what is the larger ecological context of the fishery, who will benefit from seafood production, and who may be harmed. In short, we contend that discussions regarding global seafood must include considerations of global justice.

Part 3   Food, Equity, and Environment

11. Food and Labor

Margaret Gray

Food workers are some of the poorest paid workers in the United States and their jobs are insecure. This lesson focuses on farmworkers and food processing workers and explores the structural factors that shape worker inequality and lead to labor abuses. Weaving together contemporary data, history, a look at labor laws, and interviews with Hudson Valley farmworkers, this lesson explores some of the factors related to worker exploitation including ethnic succession and paternalism. Furthermore, it examines deficiencies in government regulation and describes current collective action efforts to activate consumer campaigns and improve worker conditions.

12. Food and the Environment

Sean Gillon

Food systems are inseparable from the global environments in which food is produced, processed, transported, sold, consumed, and wasted. Food systems are shaped by and shape biological, ecological, and other environmental processes. This lesson explores food system–environment relationships, situating environmental questions as fundamentally social to better understand the environments food systems produce and pathways for positive change. The lesson discusses the biological and ecological foundations of industrialized food systems, explaining how attempts to minimize or evade these components of food production have resulted in environmental problems in the same categories. Key topics discussed include global land use change, soil erosion, water quality and availability, pesticide use, livestock production, and energy use and climate change. Throughout, the lesson explores the social dynamics that underpin our food system and result in both hunger and food waste at tremendous social and environmental cost. The lesson concludes by noting efforts to improve the sustainability and equity of food systems.

13. Food and Hunger

Justin Sean Myers

Hunger is a pervasive and persistent problem in the United States, as well as around the world. Tens of millions of people domestically, and hundreds of millions globally, face food insecurity and hunger on a daily basis, most of whom are poor, are economically marginalized, and labor in the food system growing, processing, preparing, and serving our food. This lesson focuses on the structural conditions of the economy and the food system that produce hunger as a normal outcome of how society distributes income and therefore access to food. It will shed light on both charitable and government efforts to combat hunger, the tensions between these private and public programs, and how economic and political policies have increased, as well as decreased, hunger in the United States and the world. Additionally, it will emphasize several ways that governments can work to reduce food insecurity both domestically and internationally.

14. Food and Obesity

Melina Packer and Julie Guthman

National health statistics in the United States that indicate a rise in the prevalence of obesity between the early 1980s and 2000s, along with distinct patterns of obesity in relationship to race, gender, and income status, have galvanized a significant public response. Shunning punditry that suggests that obesity reflects a failure of personal responsibility—people making the wrong choices—many scholars and public health professionals have argued for a food system perspective on obesity, one that accounts for the external conditions that shape food choices. Although the food system perspective appropriately draws attention to public policy and business behavior, it still treats obesity as if the connections between food intake and weight are clear and uncontested. This lesson critically interrogates four key assumptions that link food and obesity, namely that obesity results from: (1) an excess of calorie intake relative to calorie expenditure, (2) a built environment that encourages consumption of nutritionally vacuous foods, (3) national agriculture policy, which subsidizes certain crops that go into cheap, nutritionally inferior foods, and (4) what people purposely ingest as food, as opposed to other ingestions or exposures. The lesson shows a lack of scientific consensus for each of these claims based on countervailing evidence and argument. In sum, this lesson suggests that weight gain may be about not only what people eat, but also the toxic exposures and stresses that permeate environments, especially those inhabited by low-income people and people of color. Obesity, then, may be better treated by deeper engagements with policy, especially policies relating to chemical regulation and income inequality.

Part 4 Food, Justice, and Sustainability

15. Organics

Brian K. Obach

You have probably seen products labeled *organic*. If you are like most Americans, you have probably eaten at least some organic goods as well. In the United States today most of these products include a green and white USDA seal indicating official approval by the federal government. But what does organic mean? The definition of organic has evolved over several decades and the particulars of what constitutes organic methods have been debated throughout. Even today, some would say that the organic seal represents the highest standard of healthy sustainable agricultural practices, while others would argue that it is essentially meaningless. The place of organic agriculture in our society has also changed dramatically. Once the province of fringe countercultural radicals seeking to subvert the dominant social order, today organic has been accepted by the most powerful institutions, from the federal government to multinational corporations. This lesson will trace the evolution of organic and consider some of the debates that continue to shape the social meaning of this agricultural practice.

16. Fair Trade
Daniel Jaffee

The fair trade movement was founded almost thirty years ago to rectify the unfair economic conditions faced by small farmers in the global South who grow primary agricultural commodities such as coffee. Fair trade is both a social movement and an alternative market system, and it aims to use the structures of global markets to reverse some of the injustices they generate. This chapter discusses the dynamics behind the structural inequity in the global trade in agrifood products. It briefly describes fair trade's history, the basic mechanisms of the fair trade model for food products, and the current state of fair trade. Two case studies of fair trade in action—coffee farmers in Mexico and hired tea pickers in India—illustrate the social benefits that participating in this alternative market can generate for producers, as well as the limits to fair trade's impact and the contradictions that can arise. The chapter examines several controversies that have caused major divisions within the fair trade movement and market, including the entry of large corporate firms into fair trade and the role of plantation agriculture. It ends with some reflections on the future of fair trade and its ability to transform the global market.

17. Food and Localism
Clare Hinrichs

Since the mid-1990s, localism has become a dominant theme within discussions about developing alternatives to the mainstream conventional industrial food and agricultural system. As a concept, localism is not new. Its growing application to food and agriculture, however, presents some distinctive manifestations. This lesson critically examines the idea and appeal of local food. Reconnecting food producers and consumers through direct market interactions is central to food localism, as evident in the signature institutions of farmers markets and community-supported agriculture. However, limitations in these two types of food localism have led to initiatives to *scale up* local food, with the aim of increasing local food supply and extending benefits of local food markets to more farmers, benefits of local food access to a wider range of food consumers. The lesson presents the history, performance, and varied benefits and drawbacks of food system alternatives centered on local food. It concludes by considering some emerging alternatives that build on, but move beyond, a strong focus on local food, including place-based food systems, regional food systems, and integrated food systems.

18. Getting to Food Sovereignty (Locally?) in a Globalized World

Hannah Wittman

The idea of food sovereignty has gained considerable momentum in global food policy debates, bringing together a coalition of agrarian, indigenous, environmental, and antihunger movements across the globe in discussions of how to feed the world sustainably and equitably. Food sovereignty is concerned with the rights of local peoples to have a voice in their food system. The food sovereignty framework enables a critical discussion about the roles and responsibilities of farmers, indigenous peoples, fisherfolk, the state, civil society, consumers, environmentalists—in short, all global citizens—in constructing a new global food system from the ground up. The food sovereignty movement goes beyond a food security framing that simply mandates the right to have enough food to eat to include the right for people to shape the political and social processes governing the ways that foods are cultivated, distributed, and shared. This lesson will examine the idea of food sovereignty and the ways it challenges the current global food and agriculture system. After discussing the recent history of the food sovereignty movement through the development of a transnational advocacy network and the relationship between the concepts of food sovereignty and food security, the lesson provides examples of new policy approaches to food sovereignty in Ecuador and Brazil.

19. Urban Food Production

Joshua Sbicca

Urban agriculture is spreading globally as more people move to cities. As a social practice, ecological, economic, political, and cultural conditions structure and reflect who grows food, what food is grown, and why and where people grow food. In brief, urban agriculture reflects a matrix of power relations. Economic and racial inequities present opportunities and obstacles for social change. Cultural traditions manifest in interstitial city spaces. Historical contingencies and environmental conditions influence the expansion of urban agriculture. These relations reflect the complication of growing food in cities. To address this diversity, this lesson discusses urban agriculture within the history of capitalism and urbanization, drawing on Ebenezer Howard's garden cities and Karl Marx's social metabolism and metabolic rift. It then offers examples from the United States to discuss some of the key values informing urban agriculture, namely, building community, connecting to nature and expanding green space, fostering social connectivity, and democratically agitating for social change. Nevertheless, growing food in cities must navigate neoliberalism and the ongoing legacy of institutional racism. Social boundaries, inequities in land access and use, and labor challenges present distinct obstacles to the development of socially just urban agriculture. This lesson helps to tease apart these entanglements to teach the importance of critically interrogating the successes and failures of urban agriculture.

20. Food and Justice
Alison Hope Alkon

Food justice can be defined as the struggle against racism, exploitation, and oppression taking place within the food system that addresses inequality's root causes both within and beyond the food chain. The term was originally used by community-based organizations seeking to expand opportunities for farmers and gardeners of color and to provide better access to fresh produce in low-income communities and communities of color. More recent food justice initiatives have linked it to farmworkers' and food workers' rights campaigns and to a variety of social justice movements.

Conclusion: Toward More Sustainable Food and Agriculture
Maki Hatanaka and Jason Konefal

The preceding twenty lessons have provided sociological analyses of the food and agriculture system, the challenges associated with it, and movements and initiatives working to address these challenges. In the conclusion, we use the idea of sustainability to tie together these diverse analyses. First, we introduce the idea of sustainability and examine its contested meaning and different interpretations. Next, we provide an overview of three different approaches to food and agricultural sustainability: community based, standards and certification, and sustainable intensification. We end with a discussion of ways that you can take action and get involved in decision-making regarding the food and agriculture system.

Acknowledgments

The idea for this book has long been percolating in our minds. It was Kenneth Gould and Tammy Lewis and their *Twenty Lessons in Environmental Sociology* that provided us the inspiration to finally actualize this project. We are indebted to Ken and Tammy for their encouragement and support to use the *Twenty Lessons* model to develop this volume on food and agriculture.

Needless to say, we are tremendously thankful to all the contributors of this volume. They have taken the time to write lessons that are informative, stimulating, and provocative. We are honored to work with such an excellent group of scholars.

We would also like to thank all our current and previous students at Utah State University and Sam Houston State University for motivating us to develop a stimulating and engaging book about food, agriculture, and society. We are also grateful to the many wonderful professors and colleagues from who we have learned, and continue to learn the power of teaching and research. They include Lawrence Busch, Craig Harris, Laura Raynolds, Carmen Bain, Keiko Tanaka, Allison Loconto, Michael Mascarenhas, Elizabeth Ransom, Alan Rudy, Christopher Oliver, Rita Gallin, Peggy Petrzelka, Douglas Constance, Emily Cabaniss, and Bart Stykes, among many more.

Lastly, we owe a debt of gratitude to the reviewers of this volume for their thoughtful comments and suggestions: Timothy W. Cameron (Johnson & Wales University), Walter F. Carroll (Bridgewater State University), Ginny Garcia-Alexander (Portland State University), Jessica Goldberger (Washington State University), Stella Grigorian (University of Houston), Deborah Harris (Texas State University), Jill Harrison (University of Colorado-Boulder), Stephanie Holcomb-Kreiner (Campbellsville University), Jeff London (Hunter College), Gerad Middendorf (Kansas State University), Jennifer Rogers-Brown (Long Island University-Post), and Deric Shannon (Emory University). We also thank Sherith Pankratz and Meredith Keffer from Oxford University Press for patiently working with us to make this volume a reality.

About the Contributors

Alison Hope Alkon is an associate professor of sociology at the University of the Pacific, as well as a cofounder of their San Francisco–based master's program in food studies. She is the author of *Black, White, and Green: Farmers Markets, Race, and the Green Economy* and coeditor of *The New Food Activism* (with Julie Guthman) and *Cultivating Food Justice* (with Julian Agyeman).

J. Dara Bloom is an Assistant Professor and Local Foods Extension Specialist at North Carolina State University. In this role, she provides training to Cooperative Extension agents about developing community-based local food projects and educating the general public about food and farming systems. Dara's research takes a value chain approach to analyzing issues of consumer access to local food systems, including how to address the core challenge of designing food systems that benefit both farmers and consumers.

Janine Kay Gwen Chi, associate professor of sociology, has worked at Muhlenberg College since 2003. Her research and teaching interests have circulated around issues of culture, identity, and nationalism. She has taught a wide range of courses that include sociology of food, sociology of diasporas, and political economies of Chinese societies. Besides teaching in the classroom, she has taught and led students on study-abroad experiences to China, England, and Cuba.

Jin Young Choi is an associate professor in the Department of Sociology at Sam Houston State University. Based on her interdisciplinary academic training in sociology and public health, her research has focused on immigrant and minority health and health policy, the nutrition transition and dietary change, obesity, and occupational health in the food industry. She has published in several leading journals and books in the social sciences, health, and food studies. Currently she is working on a monograph that brings a novel focus to the issue of dietary change as the product of military occupation, manmade and natural disasters, and ensuing domestic and international migration by examining the twentieth-century experiences of the Marshall Islanders who have been subject to invading armies, large-scale nuclear testing (sixty-seven nuclear tests between 1946 and 1958), destructive tropical storms, and now rising sea levels.

Brett Clark is an associate professor of sociology and sustainability studies at the University of Utah. His research focuses on the political economy of global environmental change and the philosophy, history, and sociology of science.

Rebecca Clausen is an associate professor of sociology and environmental studies at Fort Lewis College. Her work focuses on the intersection of social justice and global sustainability.

Douglas H. Constance is a professor of sociology at Sam Houston State University in Huntsville, Texas. His degrees are in forest management (BS), community development (MS), and rural sociology (PhD), all from the University of Missouri–Columbia. His research area is the impact of the globalization of the conventional agrifood system and alternative agrifood systems. He has written numerous journal articles, book chapters, and books on these topics. His most recent coedited book is *Alternative Agrifood Movements: Patterns of Convergence and Divergence* (Bingley, UK: Emerald Group, 2014). He is past president of the Southern Rural Sociological Association (2003) and the Agriculture, Food, and Human Values Society (2008) and past vice president of the Rural Sociological Society (2013). He is also past editor in chief of the *Journal of Rural Social Sciences*. Dr. Constance currently serves as the quality-of-life representative and chair of the administrative council of the USDA/Southern Sustainable Agriculture Research and Education Program.

Sean Gillon, PhD, is an assistant professor of food systems and society and serves as the chair of the Department of Interdisciplinary and Applied Liberal Arts at Marylhurst University near Portland, Oregon. His research includes work on agrarian political economy, biofuel production, agriculture, conservation and climate change, agroecological science and practice, and social–environmental politics and policy in the US food system and beyond.

Leland L. Glenna is an associate professor of rural sociology and science, technology, and society in the agricultural economics, sociology, and education department at Pennsylvania State University. His research interests are in the areas of social and environmental impacts of agricultural science and technologies, the role of science and technology in agricultural and natural resource policymaking, and the social and ethical implications of democratizing science and technology research.

Margaret Gray is an associate professor of political science at Adelphi University. Her book *Labor and the Locavore: The Making of a Comprehensive Food Ethic* (Berkeley: University of California Press, 2014) about New York farmworkers and food won the 2014 Best Book Award from the Association for the Study of Food and Society and the 2014 Best Book Award from the Labor Project of the American Political Science Association.

Julie Guthman is a geographer and professor of social sciences at the University of California at Santa Cruz where she teaches courses primarily in global political economy and the politics of food and agriculture. Her publications include two multi-award-winning books: *Agrarian Dreams: The Paradox of Organic Farming in California* and *Weighing In: Obesity, Food Justice, and the Limits of Capitalism*. She has been a recipient of the excellence in research award from the Agriculture, Food, and Human Values Society, as well as fellowships from the Radcliffe Institute and the Guggenheim Foundation.

Maki Hatanaka is an associate professor of sociology at Sam Houston State University. Her research examines economic globalization and efforts to regulate it in the areas of food, agriculture, and the environment. In particular, her interests focus on forms of governance and the possibilities they hold for promoting sustainability and justice. She has published in numerous edited volumes and journals, including *Science, Journal of Rural Studies, Food Policy,* and *World Development*, and co-edited *Contested Sustainability Discourses in the Agrifood System* (London: Earthscan, 2018).

Clare Hinrichs is a professor of rural sociology at Pennsylvania State University. Her current research interests center broadly on sustainability transitions in food, agriculture, and energy systems. She teaches undergraduate courses on food systems and on environment and society, as well as graduate courses on sustainability and on qualitative research methods. Her interest in food and localism dates back to the year she took off from college to live and work on a small organic farm. She has belonged to her current community-supported agriculture system in central Pennsylvania for thirteen years and makes a point of visiting farmers markets wherever she travels.

Philip H. Howard is an associate professor of community sustainability at Michigan State University. He is the author of *Concentration and Power in the Food System: Who Controls What We Eat?* (New York: Bloomsbury Academic, 2016) and a member of the International Panel of Experts on Sustainable Food Systems. He was president of the Agriculture, Food, and Human Values Society from 2015 to 2016 and is a member of the editorial board of *Agriculture and Human Values*. He teaches undergraduate and graduate courses on food and agricultural systems, as well as a graduate course on the political ecology of food.

Daniel Jaffee is an associate professor of sociology at Portland State University. His research examines the politics of fair trade, agrifood certification, social movements around food and agriculture, and contestation over the commodification of drinking water in the global South and North. He is the author of *Brewing Justice: Fair Trade Coffee, Sustainability, and Survival* (Berkeley: University of California Press, 2007) and winner of the C. Wright Mills book award.

Aya H. Kimura is an associate professor at the University of Hawai'i–Mānoa. She is the author of an award-winning book, *Hidden Hunger: Gender and Politics of Smarter Food* (Ithaca, NY: Cornell University Press, 2013), as well as *Radiation Brain Moms and Citizen Scientists: The Gender Politics of Food Contamination after Fukushima* (Durham, NC: Duke University Press, 2016). She has also published on food education, farming and disaster, food standards, and consumer cooperatives and edited *Food and Power: Visioning Food Democracy in Hawai'i* (Honolulu; University of Hawaii Press, 2016; coeditor with Krisnawati Suryanata).

Jason Konefal is an associate professor in the Department of Sociology at Sam Houston State University. His research examines the relationship between political economic structures and practices and opportunities for social change. Specifically, he is interested in how neoliberalization affects governance processes and possibilities for equality, justice, sustainability, and democracy in food and agriculture. Dr. Konefal's publications have appeared in the *Journal of Rural Studies*, *Agriculture and Human Values*, and *Organization & Environment*. He is also co-editor of *Contested Sustainability Discourses in the Agrifood System* (London: Earthscan, 2018).

Stefano B. Longo is an associate professor of sociology at North Carolina State University. His research and teaching focus on environmental sociology and social theory.

Justin Sean Myers is an assistant professor of sociology at California State University, Fresno. He received his PhD in sociology from the Graduate Center, City University of New York, his MA in sociology from San Diego State University, and his BA in sociology from Sonoma State University. His research utilizes historical and qualitative methods to examine how marginalized communities are organizing against environmental and food inequities. His work has documented how food justice organizations are challenging cultural assimilation, mass incarceration, and gentrification through urban agriculture programs as well as how community mobilizations for unionized grocery stores are working to address the structural roots of inequities in food access through demand-side politics. This scholarship has been published in *Agriculture & Human Values*, *Environmental Sociology*, and *Geoforum*. He is currently writing a book on the food justice movement in New York City.

Brian K. Obach is a professor of sociology and director of environmental studies at the State University of New York at New Paltz. He specializes in the study of social movements, environmental sociology, the sociology of food and agriculture, and political economy. He is the author of *Organic Struggle* (Cambridge, MA: MIT Press, 2015), an examination of the sustainable agriculture movement, and *Labor and the Environmental Movement* (Cambridge, MA: MIT Press, 2004), an analysis of cooperation and conflict between labor unions and environmentalists. He sings and plays guitar in the all-faculty rock band Questionable Authorities.

Melina Packer is a PhD candidate in the Department of Environmental Science, Policy, and Management at the University of California–Berkeley. Her dissertation research explores how US chemical science and regulation reflects and reproduces social anxieties and oppressions concerning sex, gender, and race.

Elizabeth Ransom is an associate professor of international affairs and senior research associate in the Rock Ethics Institute at Pennsylvania State University. She received her Ph.D in sociology. Her areas of expertise include international development and globalization, the sociology of agriculture and food, and social studies of science and technology, and her research focuses on red meat production in southern Africa, gender and development, and science and technology related to food. She has published articles in journals such as *Gender & Society*, *Journal of Rural Studies*, and *Rural Sociology* and coedited *Rural America in a Globalizing World: Problems and Prospects for the 2010s* (with Leif Jensen and Conner Bailey).

Joshua Sbicca is an assistant professor of sociology at Colorado State University. His work focuses on the intersections between food politics, social movements, and inequalities. He is the author of *Food Justice Now!: Deepening the Roots of Social Struggle*.

Daniel Tobin, PhD, is an assistant professor in the Department of Community Development and Applied Economics at the University of Vermont. He teaches interdisciplinary courses on international agriculture and conducts research in both the United States and the Andean region. His research interests include value chain development, climate change adaptation and mitigation, and livelihoods analyses of smallholder farmers.

Anthony Winson is a professor in the Department of Sociology and Anthropology, University of Guelph. He has written about agriculture, food, agrarian development, and politics and the state in the context of Canada, the United States, and the Third World and, more recently, the political economic determinants of diet and nutrition in Canada and globally. His books include *Coffee and Democracy in Modern Costa Rica* (Houndmills, Basingstoke, Hampshire: Macmillan, 1989); *The Intimate Commodity: Food and the Development of the Agro-Industrial Complex in Canada* (Toronto: Garamond, 1993); *Contingent Work, Disrupted Lives: Labour and Community in the New Rural Economy* (Toronto: University of Toronto, 2002, with Belinda Leach, which has won the John Porter book prize of the Canadian Sociology Association); *Critical Perspectives in Food Studies* (Don Mills, Ontario, Canada: Oxford University Press, 2016, with coeditors Mustafa Koc and Jennifer Sumner);

and *The Industrial Diet: The Degradation of Food and the Struggle for Healthy Eating* (Vancouver: UBC Press, 2013).

Hannah Wittman is the director of the Centre for Sustainable Food Systems at the UBC Farm and an associate professor in the Institute for Resources, Environment and Sustainability at the University of British Columbia. She received her PhD in development sociology from Cornell University and conducts community-based research related to food sovereignty, agrarian reform, and urban agriculture in Canada and Latin America. Her work contributes to a critical discussion of grassroots and policy pathways toward agroecology, agrarian citizenship, and health equity. Her recent edited books include *Environment and Citizenship in Latin America: Natures, Subjects and Struggles; Food Sovereignty: Reconnecting Food, Nature and Community;* and *Food Sovereignty in Canada: Creating Just and Sustainable Food Systems.*

Introduction

Jason Konefal and Maki Hatanaka

Food is an essential part of society. Most fundamentally, people need to eat and acquire nutrition to survive. However, food is much more than a basic need. Food is also part of people's identity and a marker of status. Have you heard the phrase "you are what you eat"? What you eat says something about you. Among other things, the foods you eat may reflect your social location, including your class, gender, ethnicity, and religion. Thus, the foods you eat can distinguish you from others and are often one criteria people use to judge you. For example, how do you perceive a person who eats at five-star restaurants with $300 fifteen-course tasting menus? Alternatively, what about a family who goes to Applebee's for a special dinner? How about a couple who only eat organic fruits and vegetables or a person who is strictly vegan? We tend to make different assumptions about these various people.

Many of you likely do not put much thought into the foods you eat. Many of you probably go to the campus dining hall and choose from the abundance of prepared food items on display. Some of you likely prefer fast-food restaurants. Perhaps some of you live off campus, shop at a supermarket, and cook your meals. Regardless of where you eat, an important question is how you decide what eat. That is, in deciding what to eat, what factors influence your decision? Do you take into consideration cost, convenience, taste, quality, nutrition, and/or health? Furthermore, how do you decide what foods are nutritious and which are not or whether food is safe? When different factors come into conflict, how do you decide which to prioritize?

While it seems that food just appears on supermarket shelves or on our plates, food has to come from somewhere. Let's consider this briefly. First, where does your food come from? Does it come from farms near where you live? Or does it perhaps come from farms in Mexico, Chile, or China? Second, who gets your food from the farm to your plate? In other words, who are the farmers who grow it, the workers who harvest and process it, the truck drivers who transport it, the stockers who place it on supermarket shelves, and, if you are eating out, the cooks who prepare it? Third, who are the businesses that employ all these workers from farm to plate? Are they small businesses or multinational corporations? Fourth, what practices and technologies are used to produce your food? Was it farmed with synthetic chemical inputs or organically? Does it include genetically modified ingredients? Did it undergo irradiation to reduce microorganisms? As such, while food seems to just appear on supermarket shelves or on our plates, food production is highly complex and diverse.

Moreover, the food and agriculture system today is highly contested and besieged by a plethora of pressing issues. For example, while most of you probably know that hunger is a problem globally, did you know that it is also a problem in many of the industrialized countries, such as the United States? In fact, approximately 42.2 million Americans are food insecure today (Coleman-Jensen et al. 2015)! Despite such a high prevalence of hunger, obesity has also become an issue of increasing concern in many nations across the world. In the words of the American Heart Association (2016), obesity is everywhere nowadays.

If we move back up food and agriculture supply chains, from our plate to the farms and factories that produce our foods, we find a wide range of other social and environmental issues. For instance, farm work, as well as many processing jobs, is not only low paying but also dangerous. To provide just one snapshot, in the *New Yorker* article "Exploitation and Abuse at the Chicken Plant," Michael Grabell (2017) chronicles how meat processing is among the most dangerous work in America. To provide one grim statistic, since 2010, in poultry, meat, and seafood processing in America, "more than seven hundred and fifty processing workers have suffered amputations" (Grabell 2017). Even worse working conditions are found in much of the global South, where labor regulations are often laxer.

The food and agriculture system is also a significant contributor to environmental degradation. For example, agriculture is a significant source of greenhouse gas emissions, particularly methane resulting from livestock operations. Through deforestation, chemical pollution, and monocultures, agriculture is a key contributor to a potential sixth mass extinction (i.e., a massive loss of plant and animal species) (Kolbert 2014). Agriculture runoff is also responsible for massive annual dead zones in water bodies around the world, including in the Gulf of Mexico, which usually tops six thousand square miles (larger than the state of Connecticut!).

As this brief introduction illustrates, the contemporary food and agriculture system is quite complex and contested. Using a sociological lens, the lessons in this book explore the food people eat and why, how it is produced, and the social and environmental issues associated with food and agriculture. Before we jump into the lessons on food and agriculture, we want to use the remaining parts of this introduction to introduce sociology and key social forces at work in the world today.

SOCIOLOGY: A BRIEF INTRODUCTION

We have compiled this volume in the spirit of public sociology (Burawoy 2013). This means that this book takes a wide array of scientific findings and sociological perspectives on food and agriculture and makes them understandable and relevant to sociologists and nonsociologists alike. Because not all readers of this book will be sociologists, let us first briefly introduce sociology.

The **sociological imagination** impels us to examine the "relationship between personal experience and wider society" (Mills 1959). Put differently, what sociology does, more so than perhaps anything else, is encourage people to think critically and question all those things they tend to take for granted. To borrow from the sociologists Kenneth Gould and Tammy Lewis (2013, 7), sociology drives people to "move beyond their private orbits to examine how history and institutions affect us all." Thus, as you work your way through the lessons, the aim of this volume is to spur you to think about who you are, what you eat, and the implications of your eating. In other words, we want you to reflect on your personal actions and think about the ways they affect society, other groups, and the environment.

At its core, sociology analyzes the relationship between people and the larger world. That is, sociology starts from the premise that people are part of a larger world and that there is a dialectical relationship between people and the larger world. This means that people both affect and are affected by the larger world. Let's briefly explore this dialectical relationship between people and the world they are part of.

When talking about the larger world, sociologists use several different concepts. A general term sociologists often use is **social structure**. Social structure refers to the relatively durable parts of society, most notably **culture**, **institutions**, and organizations. A **structural approach** in sociology examines how the parts of society affect people. For example, a structural sociologist might examine how public policies affect particular groups of people. From a structural perspective, the structure of society is seen as both enabling and constraining people's opportunities and activities. If we take culture as an example, all societies have a set of norms that guide people in terms of how to act and not act. It is also important to note that a structural approach often includes an analysis of the relationship between the natural environment and people. For instance, structural analysis can be used to examine the impact of climate change on people's lives.

As the lessons in this book illustrate, there is a long tradition of structural analysis in the sociology of food and agriculture. Structural analysis directs our attention to the ways that the food and agriculture system is organized. For example, there is increasing economic consolidation at the input (e.g., seeds and pesticides), processing, and retail levels of the food and agriculture system. This has had consequences for not only the foods people eat, but also how they are produced. Furthermore, the food and agriculture system is part of a whole series of other interlocking institutions. These institutions—the economy, government, science, and culture—also affect the food people eat and how it is produced. Thus, to understand food and agriculture, it is also necessary to examine the larger society.

While there is substantial focus on how structures affect people in sociology, sociologists also emphasize that people have **agency**. That is, people can also affect the larger world—by voting, going against norms, and partaking in collective action, to name just a few ways. Sociologists who take an **inter-actional approach** focus on the ways that people's actions affect other people as well as social structures. Examining agency is particularly important to understanding **social change**. Societies change. If we look at the United States, we see significant changes over the past century that are, at least in part, the result of people taking action. Well-known examples include the end of formal racial segregation in the US South and the extension of the right to marriage to same-sex couples in a growing number of countries.

In looking at food and agriculture, an interactional approach draws our attention to the ways that the decisions and actions of people affect the food people eat and how it is produced. For example, some farmers' rejection of chemical-dependent forms of agriculture helped give rise to organic agriculture. Consumer demand for fair trade products (e.g., farmers receive fair prices for what they produce) has spurred the growth of an alternative market system. Thus, people taking action has affected how (some) foods are produced and has given rise to new institutional arrangements in food and agriculture.

Although everyone has some degree of agency, not all people have equal amounts. Sociologists have long documented that some people have greater **power** than others. Power can take many shapes and forms, but generally refers to the ability of an actor to influence others. Often one's power is tied to his or her position in the social structure and/or the amount of resources he or she has. For example, some people in leadership positions at large corporations or in governments make decisions that may affect millions of people. Take the case of Walmart, which has stores in twenty-eight countries. Decisions made by Walmart executives affect a vast number of people across the world. Comparatively, most other people have much less power, as we will see in the ensuing lessons.

A sociological lens helps us pay attention to structure, agency, and issues of power. Each of these concepts is useful in comprehending food and agriculture in today's world. As you read through the twenty lessons in this volume, we suggest you keep in mind the following questions: (1) how does the structure of the food and agriculture system affect the ways that food is grown, processed, distributed, and consumed? (2) To what extent are individuals and groups, such as farmers, workers, consumers, and social movement groups, able to exert their agency in the food and agriculture system? (3) Who has power in the food and agriculture system and who does not, and how do such power relationships (re)produce (in)equalities and (un)sustainability?

THE WORLD TODAY: NEOLIBERALIZATION, GLOBALIZATION, AND INEQUALITY

As discussed previously, sociology impels us to look at the structures that make up society. This means that to understand why we eat the way we do and the implications of how we eat, we must understand the world we live in today. Three defining developments of the past forty years have been neoliberalization, globalization, and an explosion in class inequality, and each of these developments has significantly impacted food and agriculture, in addition to affecting us as individuals. Let us briefly sketch these developments.

Beginning in the late 1970s, public policies in much of the world began to be changed to fit the ideas of neoliberalism. Geographer David Harvey (2005, 2) succinctly summarizes neoliberalism as a political economic system that is based on the belief that "human well-being can best be advanced by liberating individual entrepreneurial freedoms and skills within an institutional framework characterized by strong private property rights, free markets, and free trade." In other words, for supporters of neoliberalism, the best way to organize society is to allow individuals freedom to pursue their self-interest in the marketplace.

To make neoliberalism a reality, three big policy shifts have been necessary. First, regulations needed to be reduced or removed to free up the economy. As a result, in many countries there has been a weakening or elimination of regulations, including in the areas of labor and workplace safety, financial and banking, environment, and social welfare. It is important to note that today, even after more than thirty years of deregulation in some places, the push to deregulate continues across much of the world. This is, perhaps, most visible in the Trump administration's massive effort to roll back regulations in the United States.

A second key part of implementing neoliberal practices has entailed removing barriers to trade (i.e., liberalization). The objective of liberalization is to make the world one giant market, in which people and companies compete against each other on a global scale. Trade liberalization is evident in the immense proliferation of trade agreements over the past three decades. The result is that goods are sourced more globally than ever before, money flows across the world instantaneously, and many companies now recruit highly skilled workers from a global labor market. Last, neoliberalization entails shifting responsibilities that were once managed by the government to private entities. This has included the privatization of regulatory oversight, security operations, and utilities, among other things. The logic underlying such privatization is that private companies can more efficiently and effectively carry out such tasks.

Importantly, social scientists have pointed out that neoliberal ideas have not only led to changes in political and economic practices, but also become part of people's everyday understanding of society. One of the most pervasive effects of neoliberalization on culture is a strong belief in individualism. Strong notions of individualism deny the ways that social structures affect a person's opportunities and agency. In other words, it is the belief by people that they have complete control over their lives. One important consequence of this way of thinking is that it tends to reduce social issues and problems to solely individual problems. For example, from such a strong individualistic perspective, poverty is a result of bad decision-making, such as laziness or irresponsible spending. Such views are now found among politicians, particularly conservatives, as the following remark by a recent Republican presidential candidate and the US secretary of housing and urban development, Ben Carson, illustrates.

> *I think poverty to a large extent is also a state of mind. You take somebody that has the right mindset, you can take everything from them and put them on the street, and I guarantee in a little while they'll be right back up there. (DelReal 2017)*

Although such views on poverty and individuals are not supported by scientific research, the fact that they are pervasive in society, including among some politicians, means they have real effects on society.

At the same time that much of the world has been subjected to neoliberalization, the world has also become much more globalized. In brief, globalization is the increased interconnectedness of much of the world in terms of economics, politics, and culture. A defining characteristic of globalization is time and space compression. Simply put, this means that time and space represent less of a barrier than they used to. For example, many of us can Skype with people across the world, buy products made outside of our home countries on a daily basis, and stream shows produced in other countries on our televisions.

The sphere of society where globalization has been greatest is the economy. Today, supply chains are increasingly global in that they often span multiple countries. Thus, raw materials may come from one country, a good may be processed in a different country, and consumption may take place in a third country. As economic practices have scaled up, the need for regional and global regulations has increased. The result is the development of global regulatory bodies, such as the World Trade Organization, which seeks to facilitate global trade. For example, the World Trade Organization has the authority to declare a national regulation a barrier to trade and order a country to change it. There has also been widespread globalization of culture. The clearest example is the spread of Western media and consumer goods across much of the world. For instance, American movies, stores, and products are now ubiquitous in many countries.

Together, neoliberalization and globalization have produced winners and losers. The most obvious winners have been the wealthy and multinational corporations. For example, there are more plutocrats (i.e., the superrich) today than ever before. In 2017, Forbes counted 2,043 billionaires globally with a total net worth of $7.7 trillion (Kroll and Dolan 2017). Not surprisingly, corporate wealth and profits have also significantly increased with neoliberalization and globalization.

While some have benefited from neoliberalization and globalization, for many the outcome has been much more mixed or negative. Most notably, over the past three decades much of the industrialized world has experienced increased economic inequality and social polarization. In fact, in the United States, economic inequality continues to be at or near an all-time high (Piketty 2014). At the same time, much of the global South continues to be plagued by underdevelopment, massive inequality, and poverty. While it is clear that the further down people are on the social class ladder the fewer opportunities they have, the effects of inequality are much more pervasive. Indeed, there is now a large body of research indicating that societies with higher levels of inequality tend to have more social problems, such as lower educational performance, higher rates of teenage pregnancy, drug addiction, mental health problems, and lower life expectancies (Wilkinson and Pickett 2009).

As the ensuing lessons in this book demonstrate, there are a myriad of connections between neoliberalization, globalization, and inequality and food and agriculture. For instance, one significant outcome of neoliberalization in food and agriculture is that deregulation of antitrust legislation has resulted in ever-larger transitional food corporations globally. The result is that large corporations, like Walmart and Unilever, are able to exert even greater control over the food people eat and how it is produced today. Another effect of neoliberalization has been the rollback of social welfare programs aimed at combating hunger in many nations. For example, in the United States, programs such as the Supplemental Nutrition Assistance Program and Women, Infants, and Children are under continual attack by proponents of neoliberalism. They are often seen as costing too much and enabling people to be lazy and not work.

Globalization has also significantly impacted food and agriculture. While food and agriculture have long had international components, in the past two decades they have rapidly globalized. Food is now sourced and consumed globally. The foods on your dinner plate may come from a handful of different countries. In fact, the prominent sociologist Philip McMichael (2009) argues that a key characteristic of the food and agriculture system today is **food from nowhere**. By this he means that for many people across the world, such things as geography, climate, and seasonality matter little in terms of what they eat. For such people, food appears on their supermarket shelves or on their plates at restaurants. Another effect of globalization has been the further conversion of agricultural lands in the global South to cash crops for exports. In fact, **land grabs** have become increasingly commonplace in the global South as corporations, investors, and the governments of industrialized nations have begun buying up large tracts of land. These land grabs often result in a change in agricultural production to nonfood crops, such as biofuels. As a result, globalization may be contributing to food insecurity in some parts of the world.

Inequalities in society are also intertwined with food and agriculture. Perhaps the most obvious way is in terms of hunger. As Lesson 13 explains, hunger is a result not of a shortage of food, but of people's inability to afford food. Put differently, having enough food to eat is first and foremost a social class issue. Thus, growing class inequality directly affects people's ability to eat. In addition, the agriculture sector also exploits and reproduces inequalities in society. Most notably, Latinos continue to do the bulk of farm work in the United States, which is low paying and dangerous. Similarly, racial and ethnic minorities are also disproportionately employed in meat processing plants in the United States, again some of the lowest paying and most dangerous work. In other words, agriculture and food processing lock many poor racial and ethnic minorities into low-paying and dangerous work that offers little possibility for social mobility.

As this brief discussion indicates, neoliberalization, globalization, and inequality are transforming society, as well as food and agriculture, in profound ways. As sociology focuses our attention on the relationship between people and society, it is a useful tool for understanding these changes and their implications. Specifically, the notion of social structure is helpful for understanding the new organizational forms and relationships resulting from neoliberalization and globalization. Thus, a key sociological question is, how is the structure of the food and agriculture system changing with neoliberalization and globalization? Specifically, are there changes in where, by whom, and how food is produced, distributed, and consumed? This leads to a second important sociological question: What are the implications of such changes for people throughout the system, including farmers, workers, and consumers? In other words, how are such changes in the structure affecting the agency of actors in the food and agriculture system? And do people have the ability to influence or resist such changes? Last, as the food and agricultural system undergoes transformations, how, if at all, is the distribution and exercise of power affected? In today's increasingly neoliberalized and globalized food and agriculture system, who decides what foods people eat and how it is produced? Is it consumers, farmers, governments, or corporations?

THE LAYOUT OF THE BOOK

In putting together this book, our objective is to get you critically thinking about food, agriculture, and society. To help you do this, the lessons in this volume are not written in the standard academic format that you find in scholarly publications, but in a style that is more accessible and engaging. The lessons in this book were written for students, not other professors. Specifically, leading scholars in food and agriculture studies were asked to write their lesson as if they were delivering their best undergraduate lecture. Our hope is that this book will not only expose you to a wide breadth of ideas, concepts, theories, and data about food and agriculture, but also stimulate you to care about the food you and others eat, how it is produced, and the people who produce it.

The first part of the book, "Consuming Food," examines the ways that eating is socially mediated. We start with consumption, because this is how many of you are likely to be most directly connected to food and agriculture. Although we choose what we eat, these decisions are embedded in a larger set of social structures and relations that influence the decisions we make. Lesson 1 examines the interlocking character of food production, distribution, and marketing and the ways this affects the foods people eat. Lesson 2 examines the relationship between food, identity, and culture. Lesson 3 discusses changes in diets over time and the role of the food industry in developing and marketing food products, particularly highly processed, nutrient-poor edible products. Lesson 4 looks at how nutritional knowledge affects what people eat and the ways that what counts as nutritious is often contested. Running throughout these lessons is a focus on the interplay between people's agency and the larger food system.

The second section of the book, entitled "Producing Food," examines agriculture, the processing, and the retailing of food. The focus is primarily on the **conventional food and agriculture system**, which supplies most people in the world with their food. Large farms and transnational corporations, heavy reliance on technological innovations, and global supply chains are the defining characteristics of the conventional food and agriculture system. Lesson 5 examines the development of agriculture over time, with emphasis on its increasing industrialization. Lesson 6 examines the multitude of technologies used in growing and processing food today, as well as the ways that such technologies are developed, adopted, and diffused. Lesson 7 examines corporate concentration and control in food and agriculture, while Lesson 8 examines the globalization of food and agriculture. Lesson 9 looks at how public policies and private governance affect food and agriculture. Lesson 10 examines seafood. While seafood historically has been one of the few non-domesticated sources of food that is widely eaten, today it is increasingly farmed. All the lessons in Part 2 have an emphasis on the **political economy** of food and agriculture. This means that they highlight the ways that the food and agriculture system is organized and governed and who has power in this system. Thus, they pay particular attention to the effects of neoliberalization and globalization on food and agriculture.

The third section, "Food, Equity, and Environment," investigates the social and environmental issues associated with food and agriculture. While the conventional food and agriculture system has been tremendously successful in terms of productivity, it is also implicated in a host of social and environmental problems. Lesson 11 examines workers in food and agriculture, both on farms and in factories. Lesson 12 examines the relationship between agriculture and the environment. Specifically, it focuses on the ways that the industrialization of agriculture has increased the negative environmental impacts of agriculture in terms of global climate change, air and water pollution, biodiversity loss, and soil erosion. Lesson 13 examines hunger in the world today, while Lesson 14 looks at obesity. Throughout the lessons in this section there is a common focus on the ways the food and agriculture system and inequalities in society intersect.

The last section, "Food, Justice, and Sustainability," examines efforts to make the food and agriculture system more just and sustainable. Today, there is a burgeoning set of initiatives and movements seeking to change the way food is grown, processed, distributed, and consumed. The most notable are organic agriculture, fair trade, local food initiatives, urban food production, and the food sovereignty and food justice movements. Lesson 15 examines the development of organic agriculture from its beginnings as a countercultural movement to an increasingly mainstream component of the food and agriculture system. Lesson 16 looks at the ability of fair trade initiatives to use an alternative market system to bring about more just and fair livelihoods for small farmers and farmworkers in the global South. Lesson 17 discusses the meaning of eating locally, as well as the viability of local food systems. Lesson 18 examines the food sovereignty movement in the global South and ways for local people to have a voice in their food system. Lesson 19 examines the capabilities of urban food production to not only provide food for urban populations, but also build community and foster green spaces. Lesson 20 examines the ways that food and agriculture continue to be rife with class, racial, gender, and ethnic inequalities and movements and initiatives seeking to counteract such inequalities. While these various movements and initiatives represent forms of food and agriculture that are more just and sustainable, they also face a myriad of challenges. Hence, running through all the lessons in the section is also a discussion of the challenges, contestations, and limitations facing the different movements and initiatives.

References

American Heart Association. 2016. "Understanding the American Obesity Epidemic." Last modified March 9, 2016. http://www.heart.org/HEARTORG/HealthyLiving/WeightManagement/Obesity/Understanding-the-American-Obesity-Epidemic_UCM_461650_Article.jsp#.WWPoZv_yuiA

Burawoy, Michael. 2013. "Public Sociology: The Task and the Promise." In *Ten Lessons in Introductory Sociology*, edited by Kenneth A. Gould and Tammy L. Lewis, 219–50. New York: Oxford University Press.

Coleman-Jensen, Matthew P. Rabbitt, Christian Gregory, and Anita Singh. 2015. *Household Food Security in the United States in 2014*. Economic Research Report No. ERR-194. Washington, DC: US Department of Agriculture, Economic Research Service.

DelReal, Jose A. 2017. "Ben Carson Calls Poverty 'a State of Mind' during Interview." *The Washington Post*, May 24, 2017. https://www.washingtonpost.com/news/post-politics/wp/2017/05/24/ben-carson-calls-poverty-a-state-of-mind-during-interview/?utm_term=.d6b3ddfd9359

Gould, Kenneth A., and Tammy L. Lewis. 2013. "The Sociological Imagination." In *Ten Lessons in Introductory Sociology*, edited by Kenneth A. Gould and Tammy L. Lewis, 3–30. New York: Oxford University Press.

Grabell, Michael. 2017. "Exploitation and Abuse at the Chicken Plant." *The New Yorker*, May 8, 2017. http://www.newyorker.com/magazine/2017/05/08/exploitation-and-abuse-at-the-chicken-plant

Harvey, David. 2005. *A Brief History of Neoliberalism*. New York: Oxford University Press.

Kolbert, Elizabeth. 2014. *The Sixth Extinction: An Unnatural History*. New York: Holt.

Kroll, Luisa, and Kerry A. Dolan. 2017. "Forbes 2017 Billionaires List: Meet the Richest People on the Planet." *Forbes*, March 20, 2017. https://www.forbes.com/sites/kerryadolan/2017/03/20/forbes-2017-billionaires-list-meet-the-richest-people-on-the-planet/#12da53c462ff

McMichael, Philip. 2009. "A Food Regime Genealogy." *The Journal of Peasant Studies* 36:139–69.

Mills, C. Wright. 1959. *The Sociological Imagination*. New York: Oxford University Press.

Piketty, Thomas. 2014. *Capital in the Twenty-First Century*, translated by Arthur Goldhammer. Cambridge, MA: Belknap Press of Harvard University Press.

Wilkinson, Richard, and Kate Pickett. 2009. *The Spirit Level: Why Greater Equality Makes Societies Stronger*. New York: Bloomsbury Press.

PART 1

CONSUMING FOOD

Shopping at a supermarket. (Photo by Kai Konefal.)

Consuming Food

Maki Hatanaka

E veryone consumes food. Because consumption of food is an everyday practice, many of us tend to take it for granted and do not put much thought into what we eat. However, sociologically speaking, consumption is a crucial component to understanding who we are, how we interact with the environment, and what kind of society we are part of. How so? Can you explain the connections?

Many of you may not realize that you are part of a larger food and agriculture system. For example, when you hear about farmworker conditions in California that violate basic human rights or the use of child labor at a cocoa farm in Ghana, you may feel sorry for the laborers. You may also feel resentful of the use of unethical practices in raising cattle, chicken, or swine at concentrated animal feeding operations. You may be shocked to hear about the ever-diminishing rainforest in Sumatra, Indonesia, that is being clear-cut for palm oil production. You may also be confused why approximately eight hundred million people are suffering from hunger globally, while about one-third of food—approximately 1.3 billion tons per year—is wasted globally (FAO 2011). You may also wonder why, at the same time, obesity is becoming a global epidemic. These things are not directly or immediately connected to many of you, and they may seem a distant reality. However, this assumption is incorrect. Unless you are a farmer who grows all your own food, people like you and me are the consumers who eat the foods that are produced and distributed in the contemporary food and agriculture system. This means that just like farmers, workers, and corporations, we as consumers are essential components of the food and agriculture system, and hence, we are also partly responsible for the problems associated with it.

This lesson examines the consumption of food using a sociological lens. Not surprisingly, class, race, ethnicity, and gender differences influence one's food consumption in a myriad of ways (see Lesson 20). Despite such differences, the objective of this lesson is to examine more general trends that characterize consumption as usual. With this as our goal, first, we explore contemporary consumption trends, such as what we consume today and how our consumption practices are implicated in the food and agriculture system. Second, we analyze why we consume what we consume. In particular, we examine the set of institutional arrangements that influence our food choices. Last, we discuss the idea of ethical consumerism and investigate whether people can change the food and agriculture system through their consumption practices.

WHAT DO WE TEND TO CONSUME TODAY?: CONSUMPTION AS USUAL IN THE FOOD AND AGRICULTURE SYSTEM

A vast diversity of food choices is available today. When I go to the local H-E-B supermarket in my neighborhood, there are several varieties of apples—Gala, Granny Smith, Braeburn, Golden Delicious, Jazz, Fuji, Honeycrisp, and Pink Lady. Furthermore, some of these varieties include organic or locally grown options. When I proceed to the tomato sauce aisle, I see a long and spacious shelf filled with jars and cans of tomato sauce from a plethora of brands, including Bertolli, Barilla, Prego, Ragu, Newman's Own, Classico, Hunt's, and Emeril's. Each of these brands also offers a variety of different flavors, such as classic, tomato, marinara, tomato and basil, fresh mushroom, garlic, Italian sausage, and cheese. In addition to these options are ever more options, such as organic, low calorie, healthy, all natural, fresh from the garden, and homemade. Indeed, choices abound to the point of nearly being endless!

A half century ago, people would not have had so many choices. While not fully local, the production and consumption of food were not globalized to the extent they are today. Among other things, this means that there were fewer options and seasonality mattered more. In addition, there were significantly fewer processed foods. Given the vast array of options and processed foods available to many people today, it is obvious that our food consumption practices have drastically changed over time. Importantly, these consumption trends are not isolated phenomena, but feed into each other. Let us briefly discuss the trends that characterize consumption practices today.

Globalized Food

Today, much of the food we consume is often not produced near us. For example, the beef you enjoyed recently might have come from Texas. The salmon you ate the other night might have been farmed in Norway. The avocado and tomato in your sandwich might have traveled from Florida or Mexico. The table grapes you munched on might have come from Chile. And the apple juice you drank this morning might have come from China. Did you know that the average plate of food on an American table now travels between 1,500 and 2,500 miles to get to the dining table (World Watch Institute 2017)?

The globalization of food and agriculture began during European colonization (1870–1914), but its *globalized* nature accelerated with more recent international politics and policies, such as structural adjustment policies and neoliberal free trade policies (see Lesson 8). In addition to these trade policies, innovation in food processing techniques and advancements in transportation and information technologies enabled food companies and retailers to source food on a global scale. As a result, for many of the consumers across the world who can afford to shop at supermarkets and eat in restaurants, such things as geography, climate, and seasonality no longer matter much in terms of what they eat.

Corporate Food

Who grows the food you eat? Who turns agricultural products into the foods at your table? Who sells you your food? For most people in industrialized nations, as well as in many middle-income nations, the answer is corporations, and increasingly just a handful of them. Today, large corporations control nearly all aspects of food and agriculture, including agricultural inputs (e.g., seeds, fertilizers, and pesticides), processing (e.g., grain elevators and manufactured foods), and retail (e.g., supermarkets and restaurant chains) (see Lesson 7).

Today, a typical supermarket in the United States carries 39,500 products on its shelves (Food Marketing Institute 2017). While there appears to be an abundant and diverse selection of foods, much of the food on supermarket shelves is produced by a small number of companies. Sociologist Phillip Howard (2016) uses examples of margarine and bread to explain food system concentration (see also Lesson 7). At a typical grocery store in the United States, you find multiple brands of margarine, including Becel, Blue Bonnet, Country Crock, I Can't Believe It's Not Butter, Imperial, and Promise. However, if you look closely at each product's package, you will find that the vast majority is owned by either Unilever (accounts for 51.2 percent of sales) or ConAgra (accounts for 16.9 percent of sales). Similarly, two firms—Grupo Bimbo and Flowers Foods—control about half of the US bread market, with each firm owning more than a dozen leading bread brands. Not surprisingly, such consolidation of the food system is not confined to margarine and bread. The situation is the same for many other food products.

Standardized Food

Much of the food we consume today is also characterized by standardization. Increases in the volume and varieties of food products produced, traded, and consumed globally pose new economic and health risks. To address these issues, retailers have begun to impose a wide range of standards on their suppliers. Such standards are developed by a variety of organizations, including international bodies, such as the Codex Alimentarius and the International Organization for Standardization, civil society organizations such as the Fairtrade Labelling Organisation, and conglomerations of retailers and processors, such as GLOBALG.A.P.

Additionally, global supermarket chains, such as Walmart and Carrefour, often have their own standards (see Lesson 9).

What does standardization mean to consumers? Standardization sorts out the nearly infinite varieties that can be found in the natural world and permits only a limited number that conform to the required standards. As a result, much of the food on supermarket shelves today is fairly uniform. For example, when you go to a supermarket, you see pears that are largely standardized in terms of their size, shape, and color. You see almost no flaws from the crowns to the bases and they have a consistent color. They likely taste similar as well, because varieties of pears that are visually appealing and ship well have been selected. Pears that do not meet these standards are likely excluded from supermarkets altogether (and are likely only found at alternative markets, such as farmers markets or specialized niche stores).

Processed Food

Consumers in most industrialized countries, and increasingly in developing countries, are consuming more and more processed foods. By definition, processed foods are any food that has been altered from its natural state, for example, frozen, canned, baked, dried, pasteurized, washed, cut, and pre-packaged. Contrary to what is typically assumed, not all processed foods are unhealthy. Processed foods can vary with regard to the amount of processing, ranging from minimally processed products such as bagged spinach and precut apple slices, to foods with ingredients added for flavor and texture such as yogurt, sodas, and granola bars, to heavily processed products such as frozen pizzas and microwavable dinner meals.

With a few exceptions—mainly minimally processed foods—the majority of processed foods contain two ingredients: corn and soybeans. These two crops are abundantly produced, cheaply available, and fungible. Soybean oil, corn oil, and high-fructose corn syrup are used in thousands of processed foods. Moreover, food scientists are researching and adopting corn and soy varieties in diverse ways to improve the texture, taste, consistency, and other features of processed food products (Busch 2016). Consequently, regardless of whether you are aware, many of us are likely consuming a considerable amount of corn and soybeans through eating processed foods. For example, CNN news reported in 2007, "If we are what we eat, Americans are corn and soy!" What is largely unknown is the fact that over 90 percent of corn and soybeans grown in the United States is genetically modified (Fernandez-Cornejo et al. 2014). Do you know what this means? Apparently, many of us are eating genetically modified food! In fact, it is estimated that up to 75 percent of processed foods on supermarket shelves—soda, soup, crackers, cereals, ice cream, salad dressings, bread, fried foods, pasta, and snacks, to name a few—contain genetically modified corn and soy ingredients in the form of oils, sweeteners, proteins, amino acids, vitamins, and flavoring (Center for Food Safety 2017).

Disconnected Food

Do you know where the food you ate last night or this morning came from and whether it is in season in your locale? Typically, consumers today know very little about the food they consume. Sociologist Philip McMichael (2009) argues that in much of the world people now consume **food from nowhere**. By this he means that for many consumers, the food they eat simply shows up at their nearby supermarkets or on their plates at restaurants, and they have very little knowledge of the life of the food prior to its arrival.

Indeed, this disconnectedness between production and consumption is a prominent characteristic of the contemporary food and agriculture system. Put differently, farmers tend to have little knowledge of who eats their crops or livestock once they leave the farm. At the same time, the vast majority of consumers know very little about the food they eat. This is precisely what Karl Marx referred to as **commodity fetishism**. For Marx, this disconnectedness is a result of a capitalist market system that obscures the social relationships involved in production—including who makes what, who works for whom under what conditions, and how workers are compensated for their work—and emphasizes only economic relations in terms of the exchange of money and commodities in market transactions. As with many other commodities, our food is also largely *fetishized* in the marketplace today, and hence, producers and consumers only know each other abstractly in the form of money and commodities.

Thus far, this lesson has discussed key trends in contemporary food consumption. In many instances, we do not think about the implications of our consumption practices. However, as discussed at the beginning of this lesson, our consumption practices make us part of the food and agriculture system. Thus, as much as our consumption practices are influenced by the food and agriculture system, they also shape that system. Because most of us consume globalized, standardized, corporatized, processed, and disconnected foods, we play an important role in maintaining the status quo of the food and agriculture system, which increasingly poses many challenges (albeit its efficiency and productivity). Among other things, these challenges include labor exploitation, resource depletion, unethical animal welfare practices, uneven access to healthy and nutritious foods by race and class, hunger, and increasing obesity (see other lessons in this volume). Clearly, it is sociologically important to investigate consumption and our role as consumers in the food system. Most notably, why have we come to consume the foods that we do? Are today's consumption patterns coincidental? Are there other forces that shape our consumption practices? Answering these questions requires us to examine the internal workings of the food and agriculture system, which are highly political in nature and largely hidden from consumers.

WHY DO WE CONSUME WHAT WE CONSUME?: INSTITUTIONAL ARRANGEMENTS IN THE FOOD AND AGRICULTURE SYSTEM

Why do you eat the food you eat? This question is posed by prominent food studies scholar and public health activist Marion Nestle at the opening of her acclaimed book, *Food Politics*. Using the meal you ate last night or this morning, consider this question: Why did you eat the particular foods that you ate? Is it because of taste, cost, convenience, religious reasons, environmental or labor concerns, or some combination of these? Was the choice of what you ate completely your decision? That is, did you solely determine what you ate, or was the choice embedded in a larger set of structures that enabled some decisions and constrained others?

From a sociological perspective, how and what we consume are always, at least partially, affected by more than just an individual's preferences. For example, it is hardly a coincidence that certain foods are more readily available to you or vigorously advertised. You likely see certain food products more often than others on your grocery store shelves. Put differently, our consumption choices are embedded in a set of institutional arrangements that often channel our food choices in specific directions.

In exploring some of the institutional arrangements, consider the following narrative.

> *Weekly, Mia does grocery shopping for her family. She usually passes multiple supermarkets nearby and drives a bit farther to a particular Kroger because it has fresher produce and a larger selection. On her way in, she grabs a large shopping cart and then proceeds to push the cart from aisle to aisle looking for particular products she needs. As she makes her way through the store, she finds a box of blueberry breakfast bars. She has just read an article online that describes the health benefits of blueberries. While breakfast bars were not on her grocery list, she grabs the box and tosses it in the cart. When she reaches the dairy section, she remembers that her son requested a particular brand of strawberry-flavored yogurt. He had seen a television commercial in which his favorite cartoon character was happily eating it. She finds the brand, but is not so sure about the product. But then she sees the label, "natural," and notes that the brand was made by a large food company that has been around for ages and makes other products that her family eats. So she decides to give it a try. After spending thirty to forty minutes in the store, she has checked everything off her list for the week. She gets in the long cashier line and pays for her groceries. She makes sure to use her loyalty card and receives some coupons for her next trip to the grocery store.*

Many of you are likely to find this scenario similar to your or your parents' regular grocery shopping experience. In this scenario, Mia's grocery shopping takes place within a series of institutional arrangements.

Can you identify how? Many institutional arrangements are taken for granted, and as a result, most people do not give them much thought. Building on Mia's experience, in the following I elaborate on the institutional arrangements that are *normalized* to most people and hence largely go unnoticed, although they considerably affect people's consumption practices. While many people tend to assume consumer autonomy, in actuality, *many choices are already made for them before they grab something off a supermarket shelf.*

Choice Editing

Today, a majority of consumers in industrialized countries, and increasingly in middle-income countries, purchase most—if not all—of their groceries at a national or global supermarket chain such as Walmart, Kroger, Costco, Carrefour, Target, Safeway, Albertsons, Royal Ahold, Whole Foods, and/or Trader Joe's. Have you ever wondered who decides what food products are on supermarket shelves and how such decisions are made? Whereas in the not too distant past supermarkets were regional chains or independent operations, contemporary supermarket chains tend to operate nationally or globally. The growth in size and revenue of large supermarket chains has resulted in oligopoly conditions in many cities and nations (i.e., a few chains controlling most of the market). One outcome is that while these chains used to purchase whatever was being offered from wholesalers, they now exercise significant power and control over not only what to purchase, but also entire supply chains. For instance, the world's largest supermarkets—both individually and collectively—are requiring suppliers to abide by particular product standards, including ones for food safety and quality. Increasingly, these private standards cover nearly all aspects of agricultural production and food processing, including product quality and safety, packaging, shelf life, traceability, and on-farm practices, such as sustainability and animal welfare (see Lesson 9). Not surprisingly, foods that do not meet these standards are excluded from supermarket shelves.

Do you think the same supermarket chain offers the same line of products at all their stores? Not necessarily. In addition to determining which and whose products and how much they purchase for their chains, supermarkets also tailor their offerings according to a store's geographical location. It is not surprising that supermarkets are highly strategic as to what products and how much of the products should be placed in which stores to maximize their profits. For instance, stores in wealthier residential areas typically offer a greater selection of healthier foods, a greater diversity of fresh produce, and more niche product options (e.g., organic, locally grown, and fair trade). Moreover, the residents of these areas often have many stores to choose from for their grocery shopping. Conversely, low-income and largely racial minority communities typically have fewer stores and a smaller selection of products in those stores. Some low-income and/or predominantly racial minority urban communities lack supermarkets altogether. Instead, residents in such areas are dependent on convenience markets for much of their food. Food scholars refer to such areas as **food deserts** or **food swamps** (see Lesson 13). Additionally, because there is less competition between stores in these residential areas, many products also tend to be more expensive. To return to the short vignette about Mia's experience, her ability to choose supermarkets is clearly made possible by her class position.

Brands and Labels

With the globalization of food and agriculture, the distance between a production site and where food is consumed has expanded. As a result, it has become more challenging for food companies and industry to develop personal relationships with consumers. To address this issue, food companies and retailers strive to develop successful brands or labels to effectively communicate with consumers, catch their attention, and win their trust. With the abundance of food products in the market today, and especially given the aforementioned standardization trend in size, shape, color, and flavor, a successful brand or label plays a crucial role for food manufacturers and supermarkets to distinguish their products from those of their competitors.

If you are to purchase ketchup and you have the option to choose Heinz or a no-name company's brand with not much price difference, which would you choose, and why? Perhaps many of you would choose Heinz because you have known the brand for a long time and thus you trust it more. How about a bag of lettuce? A label "fresh from the farm" or "crispy" may catch your eye and hence the product may become more appealing to you. This is the power of brands and labels. They seek to shape consumer perception about products and in doing so influence people's food choices.

As such, brands and labels are very important business tools for manufacturers and supermarkets and a tremendous amount of resources are allocated to their development and maintenance. One key question concerns how the brands and labels are regulated. For instance, consider Mia's experience in the previous vignette. Originally, Mia was not sure about the new yogurt product, but she trusted the brand, and the "natural flavor" label helped put her at ease. However, what exactly does *natural flavor* mean? Food journalist Eric Schlosser (2002) explains the differences between natural and artificial flavor labels in his book, *Fast Food Nation*. He notes that "both are man-made additives that give most processed food most of its taste" (120), and the only difference is a matter of the method used to add flavor. In fact, in many instances, both flavors—*natural* and *artificial*—contain the same chemicals. Did you know that the Food and Drug Administration does not regulate what natural means and a food labeled natural may contain numerous preservatives and such ingredients as high-fructose corn syrup? Did you know that labels such as fat free, grass fed, local, and free range also do not have agreed-on definitions? Not surprisingly, consumers are confused about the meaning of labels in many instances, and such consumer confusion often works to the advantage of food businesses in helping them to maximize sales.

Food Marketing and Advertising

In thinking about our food choices, we must also consider the food marketing and advertising we are exposed to. Similar to brands and labels, marketing and advertisements by food companies are very influential in shaping consumer perceptions of food. Research finds that advertising affects not only the brands of food consumers buy, but also their eating patterns. For instance, one experiment found that television advertisements for snacks often resulted in greater snacking (Harris et al. 2009).

Research finds that children have been a prime target of food and beverage company marketing, and the ways these companies advertise can affect children's nutritional knowledge, food preferences, consumption patterns, and health (Cairns et al. 2013). Food and beverage companies spend $10 to $15 billion a year marketing their products to children and adolescents; the vast majority of commercials are dedicated to food products that are high in sugar, fat, and/or sodium (Gottlieb and Joshi 2010). It is not surprising that food and beverage companies are strategic in advertising such food products to children. As was the case with Mia's son in the previous vignette, these companies often use cartoon characters and promotions with the latest blockbuster animation. Recently, they have also extended their marketing to social media platforms.

The Magic of Shelving and Tracking Data

Are goods randomly placed in a supermarket? Absolutely not! Not surprisingly, the design of supermarkets is highly strategic. If you walk into a typical supermarket store, around the edges you will find necessity products, including produce, meat, dairy, and baked goods. Nearly the entire center of the store is dedicated to processed foods. Thus, shoppers must walk past many other products to get their necessities. To return to Mia's experience, for example, the supermarket design led her to buy a box of breakfast bars, which she originally did not intend to purchase. Furthermore, the shelving process has become much more sophisticated at many supermarket chains. In many instances, supermarket chains employ category managers whose job is to experiment with different ways of placing various products to maximize sales. For example, should the tortilla chips be placed next to other chips or by the salsas? Should the salad dressing be placed next to the lettuce and mixed greens or by the other condiments? While these may seem like trivial decisions, such decisions do affect what people buy and, thus, a supermarket's profits (Busch 2016).

When you go to the supermarket, have you ever wondered why there are often big displays for Coke, Lay's potato chips, and Nestlé-branded ice creams (e.g., Häagen-Dazs, Edy's, and Skinny Cow)? This is because many supermarkets charge *slotting fees*, which are essentially fees paid by product manufacturers to retailers for the rental of shelf space in the supermarket (Busch 2016). Large companies are often able to pay these fees more easily than smaller manufacturers and rent the "best" shelf space, which results in their products being more prominently displayed. This process is often hidden from the consumer. For example, at the supermarket where I shop, there is a "beer of the month" display. However, I have noticed that the beer of the month is almost always a brand owned by Anheuser Busch. This is not coincidental.

Some of you may also have a supermarket loyalty or reward card. These cards sometimes yield lower prices on some products. But did you know that these cards also collect data on your shopping habits? In other words, they allow supermarkets to compile data on consumer preferences. Hence, these cards enable supermarkets to analyze whether people also tend to purchase salad dressing when they buy lettuce. Such data may in turn lead to supermarkets redesigning product location and placing salad dressing in the produce section. Furthermore, in some instances, loyalty cards may also result in shoppers receiving coupons tailored to their preferences. Thus, while people are free to fill their cart however they like, supermarkets work to steer people to shop in specific ways.

In sum, while people appear to choose what they eat, their decisions take place within a complex set of institutional arrangements. Food companies are constantly seeking to innovate these arrangements, and these arrangements channel people's consumption decisions in specific directions. But do consumers need to adhere to such prescribed patterns of consumption? As many of the lessons in this volume illustrate, the contemporary food and agriculture system is plagued by significant inequality, injustice, and environmental unsustainability. Do consumers have to be part of such a food and agriculture system? Or can people consume differently and, in doing so, begin to change the food and agriculture system? In the final section, I briefly explore the idea of ethical or political consumerism, which conceptualizes consumption as a potential act of social change.

CAN CONSUMERS TRANSFORM THE FOOD AND AGRICULTURE SYSTEM?: ETHICAL CONSUMERISM

Do you know that consumption, and in particular the act of shopping, has long been used as a way to make a difference in our society? One of the earliest forms of consumer activism is the boycott. Historically, the boycott has been used by unions and social movements to express and enact their political stance in public. Among the most prominent in US history is the table grapes strike and boycott organized by the United Farm Workers from 1965 to 1970. In seeking to improve farmworker's labor conditions, United Farm Workers used a grape boycott to connect middle-class families throughout the United States with poor grape farmworkers and their families in California. More recently, from 2001 to 2005, the Coalition of Immokalee Workers advocated for a Taco Bell boycott to improve the wages of tomato farmworkers in Florida. The coalition enrolled students, who are among Taco Bell's prime target consumers, to boycott Taco Bell products and were able to successfully change the fast-food chain's policy.

Starting in the late 1980s, shopping began to be seen as a tool of social changes in ways that go beyond boycotts. Specifically, today, some consumers take part in **buycotts** in which they support specific causes by buying certain products. Have you heard of the idea of **ethical consumerism** or **ethical consumption**? Sometimes the terms **political consumerism** and **political consumption** are used instead.

While many consumers are largely unreflexive in their food consumption practices, advocates of ethical consumerism argue that if consumers become conscientious as to their food choices and begin to consume responsibly, they have the power to influence the food and agriculture system. Put differently, if people are to consume more foods that are less processed and produced in ways that are socially just and environmentally sustainable, farmers and companies will respond to such consumer demands and change their production and distribution practices. Hence, consumers like you and me can "vote with our dollars" to bring about positive social and environmental changes in the food and agriculture system. Political scientist Michele Micheletti (2003) refers to ethical consumerism as a movement where ordinary consumers use everyday consumption practices as a way to enact citizenship ideals.

Let's consider an example of ethical consumption. Typically, when a person goes shopping his or her decision on what to purchase tends to be based on one's needs and interests, such as price, taste, and convenience. For instance, when shopping for hamburgers, you may choose bulk pre-made hamburgers because they are affordable, require little preparation, and likely taste good. However, if you are an ethical shopper, other criteria such as the environmental impact, labor conditions, and animal welfare associated with cattle production may also enter into your calculations. Suppose conserving the environment is important to you. You may choose to stop purchasing beef that is from cattle produced in a large-scale concentrated animal feeding operation and instead decide to purchase organic beef. The argument of ethical consumption supporters is that if enough consumers begin to eat more responsibly, there will be heightened demand for organic beef, and more ranchers will shift their livestock production practices to organic.

It is worth emphasizing that the idea of ethical consumerism fits very well with today's neoliberal economy. Hence, it is not surprising that ethical consumerism has been widely promoted as an innovative solution to many of the ongoing problems and concerns in the contemporary food and agriculture system. Specifically, with the neoliberalization of society, the relationship between the state and its citizens is increasingly displaced into the market and reconceptualized in terms of business–consumer relations. Put differently, whereas in the past citizens worked to *collectively* pressure the state to work on their behalf, in today's environment there has been a shift toward consumers *individually* pressuring firms in the marketplace to fulfill **corporate social responsibilities**. In alignment with this larger shift to market-based approaches, ethical consumerism uses market and consumer purchasing power—over state policies—to try to regulate the food and agriculture system. Hence, the assumption is that if and when consumers commit to purchase ethical commodities, farmers and companies whose practices conform to ethical values—notably, just, fair, and sustainable values—will be rewarded, and those actors whose practices are not congruent with such values will be penalized in the marketplace. The purported outcome would be a reform of the food and agriculture system toward more ethical practices.

Beginning in the 1990s, there have been a variety of food choice campaigns mobilized by civil society organizations and activists. Typically, these campaigns, such as sustainable seafood (see Lesson 10), inform consumers which food products are ethically and politically good or bad and, in doing so, encourage consumers to engage in responsible consumption practices. Additionally, some prominent food movements, such as organic (see Lesson 15), fair trade (see Lesson 16), and local food (see Lesson 17), have also made ethical consumerism a key component of their efforts. The demand for ethical products has grown considerably, which indicates that more and more products are being ethically produced. Hence, it appears that in using our purchasing power, consumers like you and me can address a wide array of problems associated with the contemporary food and agriculture system, including industrialized food production practices, exploitation of small-scale farmers and plantation workers in the global South, unfair trade practices, and overfishing and depletion of marine animals.

Or can we? Can we or should we as consumers bear such a heavy burden? Can we "shop our way" to social change? Remember, the key to good sociological analysis is critical thinking—that is, refusing to take things for granted and posing questions. How would you analyze ethical consumerism and its transformative capacity?

There has been much heated discussion among both scholars and activists as to the transformative capacity of ethical consumerism. I want to specifically discuss two of the tensions that are relevant to the topic of this lesson—consumption. First, one might point to the flimsiness of the idea of **citizen-consumer**. The success of ethical consumerism relies on consumers to act as citizens in the marketplace. However, what does it mean for consumers to act as citizens in their everyday consumption practices?

Sociologist Josée Johnston (2008) emphasizes that consumers and citizens have competing demands. Specifically, whereas consumerism is about maximizing individual self-interest through prioritizing individual choice and variety, citizenship is about adopting collective responsibilities and solutions to social and ecological problems (by limiting individual choice and variety). Thus, a key question is, how can we—individual consumers—reconcile the competing demands of consumerism and citizenship in the marketplace?

Moreover, not all consumers can afford to purchase ethical products. Ethical products tend to be more expensive, because producing foods in ways that ensure farmers are fairly compensated, workers are paid fair living wages, and environmental degradation is minimized tends to cost more than industrialized forms of mass food production. The United States, as well as most other nations, has very high levels of economic inequality. For people struggling to put food on the table, choosing more ethical products is often a second priority. Hence, one unintended outcome of ethical consumerism might be greater inequality (Szasz 2007). Specifically, those people who are able to afford it can have access to a diverse marketplace that includes ethical and sustainable foods, while those who cannot afford such foods have little choice but to eat what they can afford, which tends to be industrialized and processed foods.

The unstable idea of citizen-consumer points to a second tension. This second tension not only applies to ethical consumerism, but also concerns market-based solutions and initiatives more generally. Concurrent with neoliberal thinking, market-based approaches disproportionately highlight individualism, in particular, individual food choices in the marketplace, as a viable solution to problems with the food and agriculture system. For instance, regarding the issue of obesity, it is the responsibility of those who are obese to do something about it, that is, educate themselves about what foods are (un)healthy, eat modest portions, and have an active lifestyle.

However, is it reasonable to expect individual consumers to make responsible food choices and, in doing so, to correct all the wrongdoings and concerns that currently exist in the food and agriculture system? What is largely overlooked in this line of thinking is that as much as the ways we consume can affect the food and agriculture system, the structure and practices of the food and agriculture system also influence what we eat. As we examined in the first parts of this lesson, consumers and their consumption practices are often steered by powerful institutional forces toward particular products and ways of eating. If this is the case, how can individual consumers be expected to exercise autonomy from institutional arrangements and, in doing so, alleviate a wide array of problems and concerns in the food and agriculture system?

Externalizing responsibilities to individual consumers and asking them to change their food choices is easier and more practical than intervening and restructuring the institutional arrangements and practices that are largely controlled by powerful corporations and industry. However, we must acknowledge that there is a paradox within the logic of ethical consumerism, as well as many other market-based approaches. That is, they are trying to address problems and concerns that are outcomes of the marketization and neoliberalization of food and agriculture (e.g., unequal food access, unsustainable agriculture, "race-to-the-bottom" business practices, aggressive promotion of highly processed food) through yet another set of neoliberal marketized solutions. British fair trade pioneer Michael Barratt Brown nicely summarized this conundrum facing market-based approaches to social change as trying to be "in and against the market."

In short, consumption, and in particular the act of shopping, can certainly become a site of social change. Indeed, ethical consumerism has brought about, and will likely continue to bring, some positive social change. However, it is dubious to expect it alone to solve the wide array of problems and concerns with the food and agriculture system. Ethical consumerism, and more generally market-based approaches, is not a panacea, but it is one tool of many that can be used to address issues in food and agriculture.

Conclusion

The contemporary food and agriculture system offers many people substantial benefits. Consumers in many nations have seen a reduction in the price of food over time. The diversity of available food products has grown. For many people, the most frightful problems related to food safety have been reduced. However, there are also problems with the contemporary food and agriculture system. These include continued food insecurity, a lack of food sovereignty, increased obesity, and environmental degradation, to name just a few.

Our food and agriculture system is argued to be at a crossroads. Given that we as consumers are an integral part of the food and agriculture system, we need to ask ourselves, which path should we take and in which directions should we move? There is no easy, clear, and definite solution to any of the complex problems associated with the current food and agriculture system. Food scholars David Goodman and Melanie DuPuis (2002) propose the idea of **reflexive consumerism**. That is, people need to be aware and critical of the ways that the food and agriculture system influences what we eat, as well as the ramifications of our own consumption practices. First and foremost, this means posing questions to yourself regarding your consumption choices. For instance, just because the price is affordable and because it is what you have long consumed, are your usual consumption choices the best ones you can make? Just because corporations are large and powerful and you are a single individual, are you going to close your eyes and ignore the negative consequences associated with the food you eat? If the answer is yes, food companies will interpret this as demand for business as usual in the marketplace and continue to operate accordingly.

Alternatively, if you want to be part of a food system that is more just and sustainable, you must be critical of the "normalized" practices of the food and agriculture system and rethink your consumption choices. I end this lesson by listing several questions that can help you become a more reflexive consumer. Why does the food we consume tend to be affordable and available all year? What are the consequences of (producing) such foods for farmers, workers, and the environment? Why is there so much food waste while there are hundreds of millions of people who are hungry? Is it okay to continue to exhaust limited natural resources to support materialist lifestyles and culture? Should we consume food in ways that are radically different from the ways we do today? And can we, or should we, not only act as consumers but also reinsert our ethics and politics into other facets of our lives?

Discussion Questions

1. Reflect on what you ate last night or this morning. Discuss what you know (or do not know) about the food you ate. How much do you know about the food you ate and why is this the case? Do you think it is important to know about your food? Why/why not?
2. Identify some problems and concerns with the contemporary food and agriculture system. Discuss whether your consumption practices contribute to these problems and concerns? How so?
3. How do you evaluate the shift of our politics from the realm of citizenship and the state to consumption and the market? What are the implications of the shift? Discuss both benefits and concerns that entail the shift.

Exercise

Create a detailed food diary for a week. Record what you eat, where you eat, how much you eat, the cost of what you eat, and the time that is required to prepare/cook what you eat. Then, write a reflective essay on your food consumption practices. Can you identify patterns in your food consumption? How do you think your consumption choices affect the farmers, food and agricultural laborers, companies, the environment, and your community? What do you like or dislike about your food consumption choice, and why? What would you change about your food consumption, if anything? Why?

Additional Materials

Readings

Jones, Ellis. 2015. *The Better World: Shopping Guide.* Gabriola Island, British Columbia: New Society.

Pollan, Michael. 2009. *In Defense of Food: An Eater's Manifesto.* New York: Penguin Press.

Websites

Consumer Federation of America, https://consumerfed.org/
Food Marketing Institute, https://www.fmi.org/
Good Guide, https://www.goodguide.com/
Seafood Watch, https://www.seafoodwatch.org/

Video Clips

ETalks: "The Secrets of Food Marketing," https://www.youtube.com/
watch?v=mKTORFmMycQ

References

Brown, Michael Barratt. 1993. *Fair Trade: Reform and Realities in the International Trading System*. London: Zed Books.

Busch, Lawrence. 2016. "Individual Choice and Social Values: Choice in the Agrifood Sector." *Journal of Consumer Culture* 16 (1): 124–43.

Cairns, Georgina, Kathryn Angus, Gerard Hastings, and Martin Caraher. 2013. "Systematic Reviews of the Evidence on the Nature, Extent and Effects of Food Marketing to Children. A Retrospective Summary." *Appetite* 62 (1): 209–15.

Center for Food Safety. n.d. "About Genetically Engineered Foods." Accessed April 2, 2017. http://www.centerforfoodsafety.org/issues/311/ge-foods/about-ge-foods#.

Fernandez-Cornejo, Jorge, Seth Wechsler, Mike Livingston, and Lorraine Mitchell. 2014. *Genetically Engineered Crops in the United States*. Economic Research Report No. 162. February 2014. Washington, DC: US Department of Agriculture Economic Research Service.

FAO (Food and Agriculture Organization of the United Nations). 2011. *Global Food Losses and Food Waste: Extent, Causes and Prevention*. Rome: FAO.

Food Marketing Institute. n.d. "Supermarket Facts." Accessed April 4, 2017. http://www.fmi.org/research-resources/supermarket-facts.

Goodman, David, and Melanie DuPuis. 2002. "Knowing Food and Growing Food: Beyond the Production–Consumption Debate in the Sociology of Agriculture." *Sociologia Ruralis* 42 (1): 5–22.

Gottlieb, Robert, and Anupama Joshi. 2010. *Food Justice*. Cambridge, MA: MIT Press.

Harris, Jennifer L., Jennifer L. Pomeranz, Tim Lobstein, and Kelly D. Brownell. 2009. "A Crisis in the Marketplace: How Food Marketing Contributes to Childhood Obesity and What Can be Done." *Annual Review of Public Health* 30:211–25.

Howard, Philip H. 2016. *Concentration and Power in the Food System: Who Controls What We Eat?* London: Bloomsbury Academic.

Johnston, Josée. 2008. "The Citizen-Consumer Hybrid: Ideological Tensions and the Case of Whole Foods Market." *Theory and Society* 37 (3): 229–70.

McMichael, Philip. 2009. "A Food Regime Genealogy." *The Journal of Peasant Studies* 36:139–69.

Micheletti, Michele. 2003. *Political Virtue and Shopping*. New York: Palgrave Macmillan.

Schlosser, Eric. 2002. *Fast Food Nation: The Dark Side of the All-American Meal*. New York: Perennial.

Szasz, Andrew. 2007. *Shopping Our Way to Safety: How We Changed from Protecting the Environment to Protecting Ourselves*. Minneapolis: University of Minnesota Press.

World Watch Institute. n.d. "Globetrotting Food Will Travel Farther Than Ever This Thanksgiving." Accessed April 7. 2017. http://www.worldwatch.org/globetrotting-food-will-travel-farther-ever-thanksgiving

Street Food Yasothon (Photo © Takeaway / Wikimedia Commons / CC BY-SA 3.0)

Food Market in Cork (Photo © Jessica Spengler / Flickr / CC BY 2.0).

2

Food, Culture, and Identity

Janine Kay Gwen Chi

There is a common saying, "You are what you eat." This shortened version of the original quote from French gastronome Brillat-Savarin, who wrote in 1826 "Tell me what you eat and I will tell you what you are," originally referred to the idea that one's health condition depends on what one eats. However, it has also been used to refer to the deep connection between one's cultural identity and food preferences or tastes. For example, Japanese food is almost always associated with sushi just as Italian food is synonymous with pasta. Similarly, the Chinese are believed to be a rice-centric society just as the French are renowned for their bread. Clearly, who we are and our cultural identities influence what we eat and how we eat it. But are these food preferences innate? Why do we eat what we eat? Why is food an essential part of any cultural identity? What accounts for the recent popularity of food trucks and street food? And how and why have food trends changed over time?

This chapter considers the sociological underpinnings of how and why we eat what we eat and explains how food consumption can be understood as **politics of representation**. First, dispelling the notion that food tastes are innate and biological, this discussion examines the ways in which tastes are **socially constructed**. By focusing on the prevalence of ethnic food and a rise in popularity of street food, the chapter then proceeds with an examination of how the search for an authentic taste reflects society's organization. Finally, the chapter concludes with an analysis of the ways in which **globalization** through the form of culinary tourism has influenced a reinterpretation of *local* and resurgence of *national* cuisines.

THE SOCIAL CONSTRUCTION OF TASTE

One of the more popular myths about food preferences and tastes is that what we like or dislike is biological and innate. Parents are often overheard referring to their child as a picky eater, remarking on their child's reluctance to eat anything green or mushy; there are even numerous websites and blogs on helping new parents address food aversions for their toddlers and school-age children. Allergic reactions to food items notwithstanding, many of these eating habits are often deemed to be from birth or a function of personality traits. The first lesson on the topic of food and culture is that taste is not solely a biological function; rather, tastes and food preferences are **socially constructed**. Not only are eating practices the result of social structure, but also they reflect a social group's attempts to distinguish themselves from others. There is little dispute that food serves a nutritional purpose necessary for living (see Lesson 4), but seemingly individualistic mundane eating preferences are indelibly tied to more general cultural patterns, political economic processes, and social life.

As sociologist Pierre Bourdieu wrote in *Distinction* (1984, 1), taste functions "as markers of class." Now, there are certain genetic predispositions to taste and smell; studies have shown how some people's aversion to cilantro stems from an odor-detecting gene that recognizes the soapy aromas in the herb (Doucleff 2012). However, as scholars like Sidney Mintz (1996), Mary Douglas (1972), and Norbert Elias (1978) have argued, food systems and eating practices reflect a society's social structure and an individual's social standing in society. From his ethnography on French culture, Bourdieu (1984) identified two distinct categories of taste: one of necessity, "which favors the most 'filling' and most economical foods," and the other of "liberty or luxury," which emphasizes presentation and form of eating (6). For example, hand-held meat pies are often seen as a working person's meal because they are portable and filling, that is, they are functional and relatively economical. In contrast, the dish lobster thermidor represents a taste of luxury because it entails a complicated multistep preparation with a dramatic presentation of creamy lobster meat in an expensive brandy sauce stuffed into a lobster shell. Unlike consumers of the meat pie, who are not necessarily concerned with its presentation, consumers of the lobster dish relish its extravagant preparation and presentation; whereas meat pies are often eaten quickly on the go, lobster thermidor is often eaten in restaurants with other diners present. Bourdieu showed that these antithetical sets of practices not only reflect class or privilege statuses, but also indicate social boundary markers and group distinction. In particular, consumers have eating habits and develop taste preferences that reflect their social status and social identity. Furthermore, Bourdieu demonstrated that taste was not simply a result of money or material wealth, but rather included the attainment of cultural knowledge as a form of capital. Using the concept of **cultural capital**, he thus developed a more nuanced explanation of social inequality by showing how education and the transmission of cultural capital reproduced social inequality through "tastes."

Based on Bourdieu's ideas, we can then begin to understand why we eat what we eat. Not only is it a matter of what is available in our immediate food systems and environment, but also it concerns issues of identity and culture. What and how we eat is a function of how we choose to represent ourselves to others. The second lesson is that food—from its preparation to its consumption—is an essential symbol of culture and identity. As such, food habits and eating practices convey traditions, beliefs, norms, and values; they serve to form the core of who we are and how we identify. Besides an emphasis on how certain foods taste (as they approximate a certain ideal), there is an equally important emphasis on its history and production.

Relatedly, the third lesson is that food conveys meaning; it allows us to make sense of who we are and why we do the things that we do. This is the reason why food becomes a central feature of celebrations of births, weddings, and New Year's. An essential food item on any Chinese New Year menu must include a fish dish (preferably with its head and tail intact) because it conveys the meaning of abundance; the Chinese character for abundance (*yu*) sounds like the word for fish in Chinese. Similarly, the dish Hoppin' John is typically eaten on New Year's Day in the southern United States because the peas represent coins, and eating the dish is thought to bring a prosperous year. Not only consumed under celebratory circumstances, food is also a key feature in times of grief and absence. Feasting during funerals and wakes is a common practice to generate memories of the deceased and the past. In addition, food offerings are also used to commemorate the dead and are especially common in cultures that practice ancestor worship. Ironically, such food traditions offer relief and comfort for the grieving because they provide respite and represent tribute for the dead. Hindu funerals include rituals of placing rice in the mouth of the deceased, followed by monthly food and prayer offerings for the departed. Given that specific food items and ingredients are symbolic and contain culturally specific meanings, food has the ability to represent and often operates as a floating signifier.

A key point to highlight here is that the ability for food to convey meaning is not only associated with immigrant cultures. Rather, the fourth lesson is that there is an intricate relationship between food and memory; whether it is in the form of nostalgia or (dis)location, hunger or abundance, food serves as a vehicle of memory and the embodiment of experience (Holtzman 2006). For example, food products like Korean kimchi and Spanish jamón Ibérico represent more than simply a product of food preservation in the form of fermented vegetables and salted meat. For many, the narrative behind the production and making of these products carries much more historical and cultural weight; the products represent local tradition, memories of family and friends, and the observance of social norms and rituals. In the movie *Le Grand Chef 2: Kimchi Battle*, viewers watch two Korean chefs (sister and stepbrother) travel to different local towns and villages to find the best ingredients for developing the best kimchi dish for a national competition; one of the chefs is known for modern fusion Korean cuisine while her stepbrother's (and competitor) cooking style is steeped in tradition. The film showcases regional variations and local specialties of this popular national dish, calling attention to the apparent clash between traditional methods and modern interpretations. More important, in several scenes characters recall with great emotion memories of "the taste." Invariably, these recollections often included using local ingredients grown using traditional methods, food preparations made by loved ones, and eating with family members.

Although the general principle behind the making of any dish can be widely shared, it is not unusual to hear of regional differences, or even family variations, on recipes that have been passed down from generation to generation. I once overheard a tour guide in Bologna, Italy, say that there may be as many recipes for Bolognese or ragu sauce as there are Italian nonnas (grandmothers). Such family recipes are often fiercely guarded by family members; it is with unwavering loyalty that family members consider their family recipe the best tasting or, simply, the best. Interestingly, these memories are often gendered; it is the women in the family who often play the role of handing down family recipes, and women thus become "carriers of tradition" and "agents of memory" in the realm of food and cooking (Blend 2001; Holtzman 2006). Much of this familial or cultural devotion has to do with the nostalgic or romanticized notions of the past. Consider the number of times you have heard someone say that he or she remembers making a particular dish with a specific family recipe at a family gathering. Such food memories often serve to reify localized and familial associations that are idealized and self-affirming. On those occasions, grandmothers, aunts, and mothers become valorized members of the family and often are charged with the responsibility of continuing family traditions, culture, and identity.

Now, you may ask, if there are multiple recipes for one dish, how do we determine which recipe is the right one or the authentic one? What is the *true* or *original* taste of something? Given that food has the ability to represent all forms and levels of sociocultural identities, this question of authenticity can become highly charged and heavily contested. This debate takes on additional concerns if one begins to consider the person preparing the food and even the place where the food is prepared. Does sushi taste less authentic if the sushi chef preparing it in front of you is not Japanese? Or what about the claim that bagels taste better when made in New York City? The following section discusses the ways in which claims of authenticity are made and deployed within the context of specific food trends.

THE SEARCH FOR AUTHENTICITY: ETHNICITY, CULTURE, AND PLACE

A discussion of food, meaning, and memory requires consideration for an **authenticity of taste**. According to philosopher Charles Taylor (1991, 17), "authenticity is defined as being that which is believed to be accepted or genuine or real: true to itself." Labeling a food item *authentic* means that it should originate from a specific culture, entailing a process of **cultural legitimation**. Food packages and bottles often include the term authentic to attract and let buyers know that they are getting the "real stuff." Even restaurants engage in a performance of authenticity by using culturally appropriate decorations and sometimes requiring wait staff to dress in culturally appropriate costumes to create a certain atmosphere. The goal is to fulfill patrons' expectations and provide them with what they think is a genuine cultural experience. An instance of this is Mexican restaurants, which are often decorated with bright red and yellow colors that connote warmth and contain traditional architectural designs like adobe walls and curved archways with strings of chili peppers hanging on the wall. The idea is that the ambience and design of the restaurant fulfills the consumer's expectations of achieving a true taste of Mexican culture, thereby enhancing the realness of the eating experience. Just as many fans of ethnic foods often use authenticity to rank their dining experience, tourists express similar desires to "see the life as it is really lived, even to get in with the natives" (MacCannell 1973, 592).

However, the reality is that authenticity is contingent and malleable, and there is no objective criterion by which an authentic experience or taste can be determined. The search for authenticity reflects the combination of marketing strategies that are informed by historically constructed ideas of identity and culture as well as current political economic processes. The fifth lesson of this chapter is that the success of this marketing strategy, which is based on appeals of authenticity regarding "real" culture, has much to do with the rise in popularity of ethnic foods among middle-class Americans; ethnic foods have served to stave off America's hunger for culinary voyeurism. To be clear, the presence of *ethnic* restaurants within the American dining scene is not a recent phenomenon: it is one that mirrors historical patterns of immigration and settlement for various groups. According to Gabaccia (1998), popular ethnic foods like spaghetti, tamales, and chow mein were already popular in the 1920s and 1930s. Although initially introduced by immigrants as a form of adaptation to their new surroundings, ethnic foods began to slowly become integrated into the American diet as immigrants assimilated into American society. Increased tourism by Americans to other countries, growing levels of international trade, and expanded opportunities to dine outside urban and suburban homes have further increased the popularity of ethnic foods among America's middle class. In addition, perceived to be a healthy alternative to the typical meal of burgers and fries, certain ethnic foods provided diners with more vegetarian options and low-fat preparations. As diners looked for more favorable attributes like price and value, service and courtesy, fresh ingredients, and authentic environment, consumer perceptions toward ethnic restaurants have become increasingly positive (Lee, Hwang, and Mustapha 2014, 5).

While ethnic foods have become embedded within the American diet, the reality is that much of what is served at many ethnic restaurants has been adapted and altered to meet the parameters of the American palate. For example, the ubiquitous General Tso's chicken—a dish that has become a must-have for thousands of Chinese restaurants all over the country (and even other parts of the world)—is a Chinese American invention. Or consider the long-standing favorite at many Mexican restaurants, fajitas, served on a sizzling platter; originally referring to a specific cut of beef, this Tex-Mex dish now includes chicken or pork strips and even shrimp and salmon. In their research on Chinese restaurants, Lu and Fine (1995, 539) point out that there are "seemingly contradictory requirements for ethnic food—ideally, it should be authentic; practically, it should be Americanized." Conducting interviews with owners, cooks, and customers from four Chinese restaurants in Athens, Georgia, the authors found that not only the preparation of dishes is constrained by costs and availability of ingredients, but also the presentation and structure of the meal. The widespread use of broccoli and carrots in several different stir-fry dishes serves dual purposes: first, to replace more traditional vegetables that are more expensive with more affordable vegetables and, second, to use ingredients that are more familiar to the average American diner. Similarly, in terms of the structure of the meal, although the typical Chinese meal includes several dishes served alongside steamed rice shared among several diners, Chinese American restaurants have taken to serving individual dishes as a meal to accommodate more individualized American eating habits.

Interestingly, as Lu and Fine point out, although customers in their study voiced a preference for authentic rather than Americanized Chinese food, only a few were able to articulate the basis for their judgment (1995, 544). While it may be a surprise to many, Chinese restaurants often offer a second menu to diners in the know that includes more traditional dishes prepared with ingredients that may be more typical to the cookery and cuisine. These menus, often written in Mandarin, target customers with more extensive cultural capital; such diners usually have had previous experience and knowledge of the cuisine and culture. However, this does not necessarily mean that this alternative menu is more authentic than the regular menu; it means that ethnic restaurants are invested in meeting the expectations of a different set of diners, thus attracting a wide range of customers. Just as the average American diner seeks to have an authentic eating experience, ethnic restaurant owners and chefs deploy a range of strategies that meet diners' range of expectations.

Herein lies the sixth lesson: just as there are different groups and types of diners, the market of ethnic restaurants is also variegated into niches within one single ethnic category. This means that, especially in the case of large urban metropolitan cities, one can find at least two or three different types of Japanese restaurants that cater to different crowds with varying definitions of authenticity. The difference between the types of ethnic restaurant is not necessarily accounted for in terms of specialty food items or regional cuisines within one ethnic or national culture. Rather, it is an appeal to different kinds of diners. For instance, a sushi restaurant that emphasizes efficiency and speed with rotating dishes of sushi on a conveyer belt and one that seats only a handful of diners at any given time with an omakase (chef's choice) menu attract very different clientele. Both are technically sushi restaurants, but in the former case, diners tend to be attracted to the affordability and variety of items, as well as the speed with which they are offered. In contrast, in the latter case, diners are motivated by the individualized attention and attention to detail to the exclusive dining experience. By and large, these two types of Japanese sushi restaurants offer different dining experiences—the former is based on efficiency and calculability because diners can have more personalized control, while the latter allows the chef to have full reign over the diner's experience. More important, even though conveyer belt sushi and omakase sushi restaurants offer markedly different dining experiences, both experiences draw on diners' shared associations between sushi and Japanese culture and are deemed authentic by diners, albeit on different terms.

Lest you think that the search for authenticity refers mostly to ethnic foods in America, it also applies to food items that are often marketed and sold widely all over the world where producers must adhere to strict guidelines and employ traditional methods of production to preserve original tastes. Italy's King of Cheeses Parmigiano-Reggiano, Japan's infamous Kobe beef, and England's noble Blue Stilton are just some food products that have gained worldwide recognition for being the best representation of their respective food category. However, these food products share one thing in common: they all have references to a specific territory or place. Not only are all producers of the three food items mentioned above licensed and audited by their respective national agencies to ensure that their production follows prescribed techniques, but also the items must be produced in certain regions and specific locations. For example, Parmigiano-Reggiano must be produced with local unpasteurized milk in the province of Parma, Reggio Emilia, or Modena; Kobe beef must come from the Tajima strain of Wagyu cattle that has been raised in Hyogo Prefecture (with the city of Kobe as the capital); and Stilton can only be made from local pasteurized milk in three counties (Derbyshire, Leicestershire, and Nottinghamshire) in England. Similar products that are produced outside the prescribed locations cannot legally be called by the same names. This leads us to the seventh lesson, that territory or place provides a physical conduit between food and culture by conveying notions of origin and source. Referencing the French concept of *terroir*, food items, such as wine, cheese, coffee, and tea, are thought to possess the qualities of the earth or soil from which they are grown or produced (Trubeck 2008). Given that culture is often conceptualized as an adaptive product of human social engagement with their physical environment, if a food item is thought to be originally from a specific place or territory, especially if it is literally from the earth and soil of the land, then the food item becomes undeniably representative of the culture that is of that place.

In particular, regional designations like the Denominazione di Origine Controllata in Italy or the Appellation d'origine Controlee in France that were initially set up by the European Union as a mechanism to regulate, protect, and control the reputation and production of regional foods are prime examples of how place and location have become central features in the discourse on authenticity. In many ways, these designations legitimate the authenticity of food products, including wines and certain spirits. For example, a bottle of champagne can only be referred as such if it is produced in the French region or appellation of Champagne, and the Spanish version, called cava, can only be named as such if it adheres to a traditional method of production; all other effervescent wine, including those produced in California, must be called *sparkling wine*.

The rise of big food corporations and the rapid global expansion of food markets in the 1990s presented certain sociopolitical and economic threats to many of the farmers and producers of these food items; many of these businesses are traditionally small and family-based operations that can only produce limited quantities of a certain product. For example, while super-market shelves all over the country can carry different bottles of balsamic vinegar from different producers, only those that carry the stamp DOP (De-nominazione di Origine Protetta) produced in Modena and the wider Reggio Emilia region with cooked grape juice as the only ingredient can be called traditional balsamic vinegar. Sometimes known as liquid gold, traditional balsamic vinegar has gained a superartisanal status because of its required minimum aging of twelve years and its limited production; it also carries a hefty price tag, with most costing over a hundred dollars for a one-hundred-milliliter bottle. In fact, producers must apply for the designation yearly and meet the strict standards for every step of its production—from the type of grapes used to the shape of the bottle the vinegar is sold in. This physical rooting of food products to a specific territory appeals to a primordial, if not romanticized, sense of culture and can instigate strong emotional attach-ments. Chinese author Lin Yutang (1937) once asked, "What is patriotism but the love of good things we ate in our childhood?" Michaela DeSoucey (2010) uses the concept of **gastronationalism** to better understand how these regional and origin designations and policies that label particular foods as nationally owned can generate nationalist sentiments. Unable to compete with large-scale productions and fearing the loss of tradition, these regional and place-based designations are seen as protecting small family-based businesses and national culture with authenticity becoming their battle cry.

Along with the legal and political economic reorganization of food pro-duction came a concomitant change in the culture of food consumption in the late 1980s. A slow food movement began to take hold as a reaction to the dominance of the fast-food industry. Originating in Italy, the slow food movement gained rapid popularity worldwide among environmentalists, chefs, foodies, farmers, and grassroots community activists. Central to the organization is the focus on the preservation of local heritage food cultures along with ethical and sustainable food production. As part of its message, the slow food movement emphasizes what they call *food and taste education* by celebrating the *gastronomic traditions* through a program called Ark of Taste. This preservation program is designed to draw attention to food items that may fall under the threat of extinction because of its small-scale production and peripheral cultural status. One criterion for foods to be included in this program is that "products must be linked to a specific area, to the memory and identity of a group and to local traditional knowledge" (http://www .slowfood.com). In essence, the slow food movement has reoriented diners toward idealized notions of authenticity (Lindhom and Lie 2013). This socio-political and cultural movement challenges the domination of large multi-national food corporations that are heavily invested in genetically modified industrial food sources that homogenized food cultures.

Calling attention to heritage breeds and heirloom seeds, the slow food movement has contributed to the rejuvenation of public interest in small-scale farming as well as traditional, local, and artisanal forms of food production and has refocused answers to the questions on how, what, and why we eat what we eat. For many restaurants, the current trend is to list their dishes in terms of ingredients; integral to the listing is the fact that many of these ingredients are known by where they are sourced. For example, a pork chop dish would include the term *Kurobata*, indicating that the pork is a heritage breed from Japan (commonly known as black pig), or something as common as a potato would include its variety and name, like Maine's Kennebac and the United Kingdom's Maris Pipers. Having successfully drawn diners' and consumers' attention to place-based food sourcing and production as a form authenticity, the slow food movement has legitimated the high pricing of specialty food items. Even supermarkets have begun identifying local farms with specific food items and produce as a marketing tool. For example, regional supermarket chains like Wegmans in the Northeast or national supermarkets like Kroger have begun featuring fresh produce from named local farms, especially during the summer season.

During the 1990s, as chefs all over the world took up the cause of eating locally and sustainably, eating locally became (re)associated with healthy eating, and chefs also took on the cause of fighting obesity and unhealthy foods. The popular television chef Jamie Oliver began a public campaign to change school lunches to include fewer processed foods and provide more vegetable- and fruit-based options for schoolchildren. The Farm to School program in the United States, beginning in the 1990s, has gained celebrity chef and national attention and received government recognition and support. In fact, in 2015, the Obama administration awarded Edible Schoolyard founder Alice Waters of Chez Panisse the National Humanities medal. Established in 1995, the Edible Schoolyard in Berkeley, California, is designed to function as an organic garden and kitchen classroom for urban public school students; integrating gardening and cooking into the school curriculum, the project developed what is known as an *edible education* that utilizes food production to teach lessons on the environment, civic and community responsibility, and cultural awareness (http://edibleschoolyard.org). This program has now spread to several other cities like New Orleans and New York City. In addition, award-winning chefs in more exclusive restaurants have introduced menus specially featuring ingredients found locally (typically within a one-hundred-mile radius); some of these restaurants have even stopped using olive oil in place of butter and other sources of fat as a testament to locavorism.

As scholars, activists, and even the former first lady Michelle Obama have pointed out, although eating organically, locally, and sustainably is a laudable goal, it remains out of reach for many Americans on a consistent basis irrespective of urban or rural areas (Guthman 2013; Piontak and Schulman 2014). In fact, much of what is hailed as natural, traditional, artisanal, and slow food is a product of nostalgia, colonialism, historical mythology, and savvy marketing (Laudan 2001). As it turns out, race and class have a lot to do with access to healthy food options (see Lessons 14 and 20). According to

Miller, Middendorf, and Wood (2015, 358), "blacker (and poorer) inner city neighborhoods generally have less and lower quality food available within close proximity of their residences." This discussion of recent food trends leads us to the eighth lesson in this chapter: food choices are not simply a function of culture writ large, but rather are a product of structural factors that affect accessibility and availability.

Besides being criticized for being elitist, faithful gentrified followers of the local organic farmer's market food scene have also been accused of driving up the prices of previously affordable local food products. There is a common joke that shopping at the gourmet supermarket chain Whole Foods will require your whole paycheck. Although the culture wars in the 1990s have mostly referred to debates between conservatives and liberals on sociopolitical issues like abortion, gun control, recreational drug use, and homosexuality, food choices and consumption have not escaped this divide. Accused of snobbery and elitism, gentrified urbanites' disdain for saturated fat–laden processed *junk food* in favor of healthier organic vegetarian (or even vegan) options has attracted the ire of conservative politicians who lament the loss of a meat-and-potatoes culture. To a large extent, how and what we eat reflects the fact that food has become a form of representation and identity politics.

Unfortunately, the discourse on authenticity reifies essentialist notions of culture with ethnicity and place and poses an inherent tension between cultural chauvinism and global cosmopolitanism ideals. In the third and final section of this chapter, we examine the dynamics of culinary tourism and consider how it has affected the idea of national iconic foods and dishes.

CULINARY TOURISM AND FOOD AS NATION BRANDING

Conveying information about cultural difference through food is a popular and heartwarming idea; if there is one thing that all societies and cultures share, it is that we all have to eat. As such, for many, eating becomes a convenient, popular, and pleasant way of engaging with social difference and politics. The popular food writer and former chef Anthony Bourdain had a series, *Parts Unknown*, on CNN where the different and the unknown in foreign countries are introduced to mainstream America through eating practices and food cultures. *Top Chef* winner Michael Voltaggio, accompanied by journalist Mariana van Zeller, taps on the ideal that food has the ability to unite amid strife and unrest in their show, *Breaking Borders*, where he creates a dinner for conflicting parties in places like Sarajevo or Lebanon, hoping that food can serve as a common ground toward reconciliation and understanding. If one watches any amount of food television, such as the Food Network, the Cooking Channel, or Bravo's hit series *Top Chef* and *Master Chef*, the idea that the world, at least the food world, is becoming smaller and more intimate is obvious and apparent. Andrew Zimmern, in his shows *Bizarre Foods* and *Delicious Destinations* on the Travel Channel, transports viewers to different cultures in strange lands with exotic eats. Glossy magazines with well-framed and colorful photographs of nicely composed dishes are another medium for the food entertainment industry to make different foods approachable. Through the food entertainment industry, we are thus able to engage in voyeuristic consumption of strange ingredients and foreign cuisines from a relatively safe distance.

By no means is it surprising, then, that the entertainment industry through television shows, magazines, and various food blogs has led to the rapid growth of culinary tourism. Because of the compelling relationship between culture and food, tourists are now basing their points of destination on eating and drinking adventures. A recent article in the *Huffington Post* reported that the "percentage of US leisure travelers who travel to learn about unique dining experiences grew from 40% to 51% between 2006 and 2013" (Parmar 2015). To be clear, the emphasis on good eating and drinking among tourists has always been strong; from wine tours in Italy, to visits to chocolate artisans in Belgium, to cheese tours in France, gastronomic delights have always featured heavily in any well-planned tour. However, there has been a shift in the ways in which food and national culture are being understood. Whereas many tourists previously focused on luxury gourmet dining, current trends now include local everyday dining, from street food to home cooking, food markets, and local farms.

Lesson nine is that, more than ever, food in the form of iconic dishes has become a form of nation branding—a technique often used by government agencies to articulate a country's distinctive and collective national identity (Aronczyk 2013). Governments recognize that tourism, a viable and lucrative industry, can help a country develop economically, and food, as a persuasive symbol of identity and culture, becomes integral in representing the country to outsiders as a cohesive national whole. Of course, there can never be truly one dish or recipe that represents a cuisine, much less that of an entire country. But, just as there are iconic tourist attractions as must-sees for most visitors in many major cities, like London's Tower of London or Paris's Eiffel Tower, iconic dishes have become must-eats for visitors trying a national cuisine. One only has to think of Vietnam's pho, Korea's kimchi, Spain's paella, Ethiopia's injera, Brazil's feijoada, Mexico's tostadas—this list of iconic dishes goes on. In fact, iconic dishes are not just for tourists and visitors; typically, they are also dishes popular among locals and often gain iconic status because of their perceived undeniable association with local culture and eating habits. Clearly, a reflexive relationship exists between iconic national dishes and culinary tourism. Just as the presence of iconic national dishes enhances and promotes the country as a gourmet dining foodie destination, tourists and visitors are keen on trying and tasting dishes that are representative of the local cuisine.

It is no longer surprising or noteworthy to have French steak frites in Shanghai or Italian pasta in Tokyo. Facilitated by the global movement of goods and services, rapid advances in food technology and cultural exchanges have aided the expansion of food markets so that previously specialized food items like fish sauce from Phu Quoc, Vietnam, or Morocco's spice blend Ras el hanout are also now available in supermarkets and specialty food stores in large metropolitan cities around the world. Given that many well-traveled middle-class home cooks can make full use of the availability of food products from all over the world, the traditional meaning of dining at an expensive restaurant has changed. Formal opulent definitions of lavish fine dining have become gauche and clichéd; rather, influenced by food trends of the 1990s, symbols of locality and authenticity encapsulated by what is locally foraged and indigenous and/or previously ignored and forgotten have become highly valued. This does not mean that fine dining has ceased. There continues to be a demand for high-end exclusive award-winning cookery, and the high prices ensure that the diners are a selective group. A cursory glance at the price for a typical tasting menu at the world's top ten restaurants in 2015 reveals a range from $74 to $307 in US dollars (Myers 2015). A more detailed examination of these tasting menus reveals that the current culinary trend in high-end dining is the creation of new flavor profiles and new dishes with less familiar ingredients and different cooking techniques. For example, previously named one of the best restaurants in the world by *Restaurant* magazine, Noma, in Copenhagen (now closed), is renowned for reintroducing and elevating Nordic cuisine through an emphasis on local foraging and traditional methods of pickling. Recently, food critic Sam Sifton described how one of Australia's best chefs was reintroducing and integrating indigenous ingredients from aboriginal history and culture into Australia's more recent immigrant Chinese, Greek, and Polish food cultures to form a national Australian cuisine (Sifton 2017). What is important to note here is that the nature of gourmet restaurant dining has changed: today's fine-dining establishments, rather than importing expensive ingredients, pursue the use and application of local ingredients. Often through the reinvention and reinterpretation of local cuisine with a refocusing on local seasonal ingredients, celebrity chefs have remained steadfast in highlighting flavors, ingredients, and recipes that hail from their own historical and ecological backyard. The highlighting and celebration of local ingredients, especially those grown and harvested from the country's territory, appeal to narratives that celebrate the bounty of the land and nation.

Essentially, local food items, as national and territorial products, become a source of national pride. As such, national tourist promotion government agencies, recognizing the destination potential of local food markets, have redeveloped these markets to become more accessible to visitors and tourists. In some instances, these markets have been labeled heritage sites, which enhance their attractiveness to visitors. In fact, night markets in cities have become popular tourist attractions as visitors sample local delicacies along with locals and their families. Beijing's Wangfujing Snack Street, Marrakech's Night Market in Djemaa el Fna Square, and Mexico City's La Merced are all prime examples of how local food markets have become important iconic food destinations for culinary tourists. The fact that each street food vendor specializes in one dish or specialty item means that customers can snack from stall to stall. Gourmet foodies and food adventurers alike believe that experiencing affordable and everyday local food allows them to engage more deeply with an authentic, unique local culture. Having to navigate local markets teeming with locals in a foreign language provides for a less touristy experience and suggests a less orchestrated and more realistic mode of travel. More educated and well-traveled tourists have become disdainful of the constructed tourist experience where people are led through deliberately manufactured experiences and sanitized sights. Part of the allure in experiencing everyday local food is that there are promises of spontaneity and surprises. Indeed, as Lisa Heldke (2003) points out, the unfamiliar and the strange are integral to experiencing the exotic "Other." There is a sense of bravado and achievement when one gets to try unknown dishes with esoteric ingredients in a foreign land; it is almost as if there was a merit badge to be earned.

Although largely available today in outdoor markets, street food has had a long history and presence in many cities across the world. Referring to cheap, ready-to-eat food and drink that is sold from a portable food booth, cart, or truck, street food has come to represent everyday local food made for "regular" working people. The ability of street food to symbolize locality, ethnicity, and affordability is also why it has been able to capture the attention of so many young, middle-class American urbanites. Mostly located in farmer's markets and food trucks, street food in America has become the hip new culinary find and has found a faithful following among office workers, young professionals, college students, and anyone looking for good, cheap eats. There have been several food truck competitions on mainstream television, including the Food Network, and the use of social media has been significant in expanding and deepening the food truck scene in America's culinary landscape. Los Angeles's Roy Choi has been extremely successful with his Korean taco food truck, Kogi, which has led to television shows, restaurants, and celebrity chef status. Fusing his Korean family culinary traditions with his adopted city's popular Mexican flavors, Choi is credited with single-handedly elevating the lowly food truck to cult-like gourmet status. In fact, the movie *Chef* (2014), directed by Jon Favreau, was loosely inspired by Choi's experiences; Choi was a coproducer and served as a technical advisor on the film. Not all food trucks offer gourmet treatments of specialty food items; while gyros and falafel trucks dominate the scene in New York City, the ubiquitous hot dog or pretzel cart, for many Americans, continues to form the heart and soul of American street food.

Today, the presence of gourmet food trucks is almost synonymous with gentrification. As less desirable and "troubled" neighborhoods in urban cities become redeveloped and transformed into residential loft apartments with fashionable boutiques, funky art galleries, dive bars, and gourmet food markets, gourmet food trucks offer gentrified residents an imagined bohemian experience, where a portable form of eating and drinking offers a welcome break from homogenized chain eateries and cafes (Zukin 2010). Also, food trucks offer a nostalgic and romanticized association with a plebeian style of living. Given that many food trucks specialize in ethnic street food, it is easy to see how food trucks can satiate the hipster demand for cultural diversity, grungy urban living, and progressive class politics. In so doing, the politics of urban displacement amid gentrification is often ignored.

Globalization has made the world of food, cookery, and cuisine more accessible, less foreign, and less contentious. Food magazines like *Gourmet* (no longer in press), *Bon Appetite*, and *Food and Wine* frequently include recipes using items like Japanese red miso and the Middle Eastern spice za'atar; they also feature chefs who are breaking new ground with their use of traditional cooking techniques applied to nontraditional ingredients or vice versa. Award-winning American chefs like Grant Achatz and Wylie Dufresne have made a name for themselves reconstructing old favorites into postmodern masterpieces with dishes like hot potato, cold potato and peanut butter noodles. The universality of eating (and drinking) appeals to the ideals of cosmopolitanism, where fractious debates and hostile politics are erased in the spirit of good food and happy eating. Indeed, when one visits a fully stocked spice market or a busy farmers' market, the sights, sounds, and smells of abundance and variety can lure one into a semicomatose state of nirvana. For a quick moment, it is easy to see and hear Disney's lyrics to "It's a Small World" come to life. This discussion, thus far, leads us to our tenth and final lesson: a closer examination of cosmopolitan ideals of food reveals that predeterminations of celebration and bliss are perhaps misleading and misconstrued. Instead, identity politics remains deeply entrenched in something as universal as food consumption.

Our human appetite for new flavors, interesting tastes, and gastronomic experiences masks the complex, and often uneven and disparate, **power** relations that undergird access and use of indigenous ingredients and local culture. Culinary tourism has heightened our appetites for culture and identity; it gives us the illusion that we can know something about a culture just by consuming its local food. Striving for authenticity, we tell ourselves that food will teach us something real about a place, its people, and their identity. The argument that food has the ability to convey culture and identity may well be correct, but it would be ahistorical, and even essentialist, to assume that food, as a symbol of cultural representation, is unchanging and stagnant. Rather, as states and governments become increasingly invested in culinary tourism as a form of revenue and branding, food becomes subject to debates of authenticity, ownership, and increasing politicization. In 2014, CNN reported on seven of the world's "fiercest food feuds" between different countries (Lahrichi 2014); the list included legal and political fights over hummus, feta cheese, and the dessert pavlova. While these "fights" might initially appear amusing, they begin to take on a more serious and somber tone when one considers issues of sovereignty and political (and economic) rights of claim to cultural items that are socially significant and meaningful for a population.

Moreover, valid questions about who a food item represents or who gets to be represented by a national food raise sensitive topics on the politics of inclusion and belonging. For example, David Thompson, an Australian chef with award-winning Thai restaurants in London and Bangkok, relies on the unpublished cookbooks of former chefs in the Royal Thai court for recipes and techniques in an effort to revive Thai cuisine. In fact, one of the controversies over Thompson's restaurant in Bangkok, Nahm, was whether a foreign chef would be able to convince local well-heeled Thais that they should pay for a fine-dining experience when they could very well get the same flavors and dishes at home or at their favorite local neighborhood restaurant or food stall (Fuller 2010). In this example, it is important to note that the former chefs in the Royal Thai court on whom Thompson relies for his culinary research and cultural legitimacy remain largely unnamed and unrecognized. It is also noteworthy that diners tend to be more willing to pay higher prices for food in fine-dining restaurants with foreign chefs, who tend to be white European men; these foreign chefs are often credited for "rediscovering" indigenous ingredients or "reinterpreting" traditional recipes. Unfortunately, status inequalities and colonial tendencies continue to plague a seemingly celebratory united food world.

Conclusion

Returning to the quote from the beginning of this chapter, "You are what you eat," reveals deep sociological implications about the interwoven relationships between food, family, culture, and nation. At its most basic level, food has the ability to conjure deep-seated emotions and stir up memories while satiating all our sensory needs. As a cultural product, food is a double-edged sword because it appeals to parochial inclinations toward familiarity and comfort and, at the same time, whets the progressive appetite for cultural diversity and difference. Given that the topic of food, culture, and identity is worthy of an entire book discussion, this chapter discussion thus far remains decidedly incomprehensive. However, this discussion does begin the consideration for the multiple ways in which food entails representational politics within different levels of analysis. As such, it would be appropriate to echo Jacques Pépin on PBS: "Happy eating."

Discussion Questions

1. Identify an iconic dish for America. How does it represent America? What about America does it represent?
2. What are some of our expectations when you go to an ethnic restaurant? What types of decorations do you expect? What kinds of sounds and smells do you anticipate? Why?
3. How are recent food trends like molecular gastronomy, raw foods, and food preservation (pickles and fermented foods) related to other sociopolitical movements in environmentalism, sustainability, and global justice? Are there similarities and differences in the goals and objectives between food-based trends and these other movements?
4. What are some of your family's food traditions? Who does it include? Who is responsible for the food preparation? Are there specific stories or narratives that accompany the occasion?

Exercise

Document a visit to a site of food consumption (dining room, restaurant, festival) and a site of production (kitchen, factory, grocery store), respectively. Make sure that you pay attention to your choice of site; it should not only address the respective (consumption, production, display) process, but also include sociological variables of class, race, gender, etc. Besides observing details about the food, be sure to consider the surroundings of the site, including the behavior or actions of other patrons or participants.

Additional Materials

Films

Big Night
Eat Drink Man Woman
Jiro Dreams of Sushi
Le Grand Chef
Like Water for Chocolate
The Search for General Tso

Video Clips

TED Talk: Dan Barber, "A Fois Gras Parable," https://www.ted.com/talks/dan_barber_s_surprising_foie_gras_parable

TED Talk: Jennifer 8. Lee, "The Hunt for General Tso," https://www.ted.com/talks/jennifer_8_lee_looks_for_general_tso

The Mind of a Chef, PBS, http://www.pbs.org/food/shows/the-mind-of-a-chef/

References

Aronczyk, Melissa. 2013. *Branding the Nation: The Global Business of National Identity.* Oxford: Oxford University Press.

Blend, Benay. 2001. "'I Am an Act of Kneading': Food and the Making of Chicana Identity." In *Cooking Lessons: The Politics of Gender and Food*, edited by Sherrie Innes. Lanham, MD: Rowman & Littlefield.

Bourdieu, Pierre. 1984. *Distinction: A Social Critique of the Judgment of Taste.* London: Routledge & Kegan Paul.

DeSoucey, Michaela. 2010. "Gastronationalism: Food Traditions and Authenticity Politics in the European Union." *American Sociological Review* 75 (3): 432–55.

Doucleff, Michaeleen. 2012. "Love to Hate Cilantro? Its in Your Genes and Maybe, in Your Head." *NPR.* September 14, 2012. http://www.npr.org/sections/thesalt/2012/09/14/161057954/love-to-hate-cilantro-its-in-your-genes-and-maybe-in-your-head

Douglas, Mary. 1972. "Deciphering a Meal." *Daedalus* 101 (1): 61–81.

Elias, Norbert. 1978. *The Civilizing Process.* New York: Urizen Books.

Fuller, Thomas. 2010. "Thais Bristle at Australian's Take on Thai Cuisine." New York Times. September 23, 2010.

Gabaccia, Donna. 1998. *We Are What We Eat: Ethnic Food and the Making of Americans.* Cambridge, MA: Harvard University Press.

Guthman, Julie. 2013. "Fast Food/Organic Food: Reflexive Tastes and the Making of 'Yuppie Chow.'" In *Food and Culture: A Reader,* edited by Carole Counihan and Penny Van Esterik. New York: Routledge.

Heldke, Lisa. 2003. *Exotic Appetites: Ruminations of a Food Adventurer.* New York: Routledge.

Holtzman, Jon. 2006. "Food and Memory." *Annual Review of Anthropology* 35:361–78.

Lahrichi, Kamilia. 2014. "7 of the World's Fiercest Food Feuds." *CNN Travel.* Last modified September 30, 2014. http://edition.cnn.com/travel/article/food-fights/index.html

Laudan, Rachel. 2001. "A Plea for Culinary Modernism: Why We Should Love New, Fast, Processed Food." *Gastronomica* 1 (1): 36–44.

Lee, Jee Hye, Johye Hwang, and Azlin Mustapha. 2014. "Popular Ethnic Foods in the United States: A Historical and Safety Perspective." *Comprehensive Reviews in Food Science and Food Safety* 13:2–17.

Lin, Yutang. 1937. *The Importance of Living.* New York: William Morrow.

Lindholm, Charles, and Siv Lie. 2013. "You Eat What You Are: Cultivated Taste and the Pursuit of Authenticity in the Slow Food Movement." In *The Culture of the Slow,* edited by Nicholas Osbaldiston. Basingstoke, Hampshire: Palgrave Macmillan.

Lu, Shun, and Gary Alan Fine. 1995. "The Presentation of Ethnic Authenticity: Chinese Food as a Social Accomplishment." *The Sociological Quarterly* 36 (3): 535–53.

MacCannell, Dean. 1973. "Staged Authenticity: Arrangements of Social Space in Tourist Settings." *American Journal of Sociology* 79: 589–603.

Miller, Michael, Gerad Middendorf, and Spencer D. Wood. 2015. "Food Availability in the Heartland: Exploring the Effects of Neighborhood Racial and Income Composition." *Rural Sociology* 80 (3): 340–61.

Mintz, Sidney. 1996. *Tasting Food, Tasting Freedom: Excursions into Eating, Culture, and the Past.* Boston: Beacon Press.

Myers, Margaret. 2015. "How Much Does It Cost to Eat Dinner at the 10 Best Restaurants in the World?" *PBS Newshour.* June 4, 2015. http://www.pbs.org/newshour/rundown/cost-eat-10-best-restaurants-world/

Parmar, Parmjit. 2015. "How Culinary Tourism Is Becoming a Growing Trend in Travel." *Huffington Post.* Last modified June 17, 2016. http://www.huffingtonpost.ca/parmjit-parmar/the-rise-of-culinary-tourism_b_7596704.html

Piontak, Joy Rayanne, and Michael D. Schulman. 2014. "Food Insecurity in Rural America." *Contexts* 13 (3): 75–77.

Sifton, Sam. 2017. "'This Is Your Country's Food': One of Australia's Best Chefs is on a Mission to Redefine Its Cuisine." New York Times, June 13, 2017. https://www.nytimes.com/2017/06/13/dining/chef-ben-shewry-melbourne-attica-restaurant.html?ref=dining&_r=0

Taylor, Charles. 1991. *The Ethics of Authenticity.* Cambridge, MA: Harvard University Press.

Trubeck, Amy. 2008. *The Taste of Place: A Culinary Journey into Terroir.* Berkeley: University of California Press.

Zukin, Sharon. 2010. *Naked City: The Death and Life of Authentic Urban Places.* New York: Oxford University Press.

Pseudofoods at a supermarket. (Photo by Anthony Winson.)

3

Food, Diets, and Industrialization

Anthony Winson and Jin Young Choi

R apid and dramatic changes in the body composition of humans across the globe have occurred in just the past few decades. These changes have been captured by the phrase *the obesity crisis* and they have been most evident in developed countries. In the developing world, the reality of undernourishment, starvation, and related infectious diseases still plagues some countries. Today, however, this reality is quickly being replaced by a new reality: overweight, obesity, and associated chronic diseases. This **epidemiologic transition** is well documented as the leading cause of death around the world. According to the World Health Organization (WHO 2017), degenerative and chronic diseases such as heart disease, cancers, stroke, and diabetes cause 70 percent of deaths worldwide. They account for 37 percent of deaths in low-income countries and up to 88 percent in high-income countries. Why, then, is this happening now and why so quickly? Seeking explanations to this question is the principal focus of this lesson.

There is increasing recognition of the importance of *diet* and the contents of *food environments*—those sites where food is sold and/or consumed—in producing this crisis of overweight and obesity, which now has global dimensions. Many people believe that their diet is determined largely by their individual choices and taste preferences. We will challenge these ideas and other assumptions in the sections that follow. We shall argue that far from simply being the product of individual choice, our diet is shaped in complex and often somewhat incomprehensible ways. Moreover, the multiple food environments where we obtain what we eat every day are themselves carefully organized, shaped, and controlled by powerful actors that rarely have your nutritional needs as a priority. This is not to say that individuals bear no responsibility for the foods and beverages they consume. It is to say that in our society today, individual responsibility receives the primary emphasis, while social forces that shape an individual's choices tend to be ignored or downplayed. This chapter seeks a more balanced approach to understanding why diets are the way they are.

CONCEPT OF INDUSTRIAL DIET

To comprehend population-wide weight gain and its related various adverse health outcomes, it is essential to examine the forces that have rapidly transformed food environments and promoted the *industrial diet*. The

industrial diet refers to a mass diet characterized by the consumption of a wide variety of highly processed, nutritionally compromised edible products (Winson 2013). Literally thousands of products can be associated with this diet, but they have some basic features in common. They are typically made with highly processed or engineered ingredients like refined white flour, high-fructose corn syrup, or other cheap sweeteners made from corn and are often loaded with salt. In the supermarket, entire aisles are devoted to soda products, salty snacks, cookies and confectionaries of all kinds, and high-sugar, high-fat dairy dessert products. Elsewhere, high-sugar presweetened breakfast cereals dominate the breakfast food aisle, while juice products loaded with added sweeteners dominate the juice section. Similar nutrient-poor products characterize much of the menu at fast-food outlets.

These products are themselves the result of a complex of agricultural and food technology processes employed by profit-seeking food enterprises since the late nineteenth century. These products have been diffused throughout food environments in the developed world and increasingly in the global South with the aid of the highly sophisticated technologies of mass marketing and product distribution.

To understand the transformation of food environments, the concept of **dietary regimes**, which focuses on the *structural* factors that shape food environments and the choices people make around diet, is useful. Essentially, the dietary regime concept helps us understand the murky "black box" that exists between those who produce our food, on the one hand, and the consumers of food—all of us—on the other hand. The dietary regime concept explains how our diet has been transformed over time and how the industrial diet became "normal" by examining the business of processing, marketing, and retailing of food and food-like products. Two trends characterize dietary change in our world today: (1) the degrading of the quality of whole foods through the processes of **simplification**, **speed-up**, and **adulteration** over the past one hundred years or so; and (2) the diffusion of a host of nutrient-poor food-like products, or what we call **pseudofoods**, into all manner of food environments (see Figure 3.1). These together have had the effect of creating *obesogenic* (obesity-promoting) food environments that contribute to the undermining of our health.

The concept of dietary regimes builds on the pioneering work by sociologists Harriet Friedmann and Philip McMichael (1989) on food regimes,

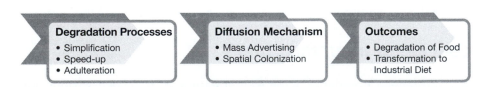

Figure 3.1 Development of the Industrial Diet.

which has provided a useful conceptual frame for understanding the global food economy at different points throughout the industrial era (see Lesson 8). While food regimes focus on the agricultural production side of the food commodity chain, the concept of dietary regimes brings attention to how our contemporary diet came into existence, what our food environments look like, and why. In other words, it analyzes the black box between producers and eaters.

The dietary regime concept shows that diets are ultimately social and political projects. Diets reflect the material conditions of a particular society and specific social and economic arrangements, as well as the structures of political domination, regulation, and control. Dietary regimes can be examined throughout recorded history. However, here we are most concerned with the period of industrial capitalism and, in particular, the past 150 years.

EARLY AGRARIAN SOCIETIES: INEQUALITY AND DIETS

Predating the emergence of agriculture, an exceptionally long period of human evolution known as the Paleolithic era occurred during which humans evolved on diets that were the result of a hunting-and-gathering existence. Basic foods that we consider essential today, especially grains and dairy foods, were not eaten at all, although a wide variety of wild plants and animals were consumed. The Paleolithic diets of this period provide us with a useful benchmark—as diets that we evolved as a species to thrive on— to gauge contemporary diets and understand their impacts on health (Winson 2013).

The domestication of several plant and animal species for human usage, what has been referred to as the Neolithic revolution, was pivotal in the evolution of the human species. The Neolithic revolution began about ten to twelve thousand years ago. It inaugurated the beginning of fairly dramatic changes in diets for the mass of humanity. We have evidence of the earliest domestication process with respect to plants (wheat, peas, olives) from the Fertile Crescent area of the Middle East (present-day Iraq, Syria, Lebanon, Turkey, Israel, and Jordan) (see Lesson 5). Other notable geographical areas of plant domestication are known to have existed in China (rice, millet), Meso-America (corn, beans, and squash), the Andes and Amazonia (potato and manioc), and the eastern United States (sunflower, goosefoot) (Zohary, Hopf, and Weiss 2012; Diamond 1997).

The Neolithic revolution had a twofold impact on diets. First, the *content* of diets changed dramatically as a few cultivated grains, principally wheat, corn, and rice, came to replace animal protein and wild plants. Second, as agriculture came to replace hunting and gathering to meet food needs, sedentary settlements, urbanization, some technological development, and trade began to emerge as well. Sedentary human existence is associated with the rise of social hierarchies, as certain groups of people within society came to control more of the wealth made possible by agricultural surpluses.

These elite groups were instrumental in establishing bureaucratic instruments of governance and control, including judicial systems and standing armies, to preserve and enhance their socioeconomic and political power. These emerging social realities inevitably affected the diets of the mass of the citizens in these ever more hierarchical societies. Diets increasingly reflected a person's social class position as social hierarchies more and more determined who got what to eat. While there is limited historical evidence on mass diets in ancient times, historians have found some useful clues. For most people a grain-gruel diet seems to have been the norm, which indicates a much less diverse diet than that of hunting-and-gathering peoples before the advent of agriculture. However, evidence suggests elites had much more diverse diets (Montanari 2000).

This divergence in diets had certain health outcomes. Evidence from present-day Mexico and Central America has provided relatively rich archaeological documentation of the effects that early forms of social hierarchy had on health. Fossil evidence from teeth and bones provides fascinating clues. For example, in the ancient city state of Teotihuacan found in central Mexico and the Mayan city states of Copan and Tikal farther south that had emerged about 2,000 to 1,500 years ago, inhabitants of what is believed to be a lower-class section of the cities suffered significantly from poor nutrition. They had lower stature, high levels of anemia, and growth disruptions among juveniles, as well as high infant mortality (Danforth 1999).

In more recent times, the boom in long-distance trade in the early modern era between Europe and the New World (North and South America) after 1500 inaugurated what Alfred Crosby (1972) termed the *Columbian exchange*, a broadly based exchange of plants and animals between the two continents. Sugar cane, citrus fruits, banana, and such vegetables as cabbage and lettuce, along with several animal species including cattle, sheep, pigs, and horses, were introduced to the New World. Such foods as cacao, maize, potato, tomato, capsicum peppers, cassava, squashes and pumpkin, peanut, and several bean varieties, along with such fruits as the pineapple, avocado, guava, and papaya, were introduced to Europe from the New World colonies. This trade brought important changes in diet as well, which were forced on many by profound developments in the social organization of European economies.

THE TRANSITION TO INDUSTRIAL FOODS

From the end of the fifteenth century until approximately the latter part of the eighteenth century, then, diets in much of Europe and the New World may be said to be in a state of flux. At this time, an uneven transition to a more decidedly industrial economy based on the factory system was slowly beginning to take shape. This occurred first in Britain and later with much vigor in the United States and elsewhere. During this time, the emergence of agrarian capitalism in Britain and then elsewhere produced tremendous dislocation among the rural population. One serious consequence of this was that the standards of living of large masses of people in the British Isles and in parts of continental Europe, especially eastern Europe, went into decline and so did the quality of their foods. These far-reaching social disruptions occasioned by this development opened the door much wider for the use of cheaper, but less nutritious food such as the potato and later sugar in the diets of increasingly large masses of European peoples (Gibson and Smout 1993).

It was during the period of agrarian capitalism, and most dramatically in the context of England, that the rural domestic household that produced most of the food it consumed was increasingly undermined. This process was initiated by the powerful landowning class who sought new ways to increase their incomes. Landlords used their power in Parliament, and with the local judiciary and police, to displace rural smallholders and transform their farms and the common lands they depended on into sheep pasture for the landlords' private use and profit (Mantoux 1961). As they were dispossessed of their land, the rural folk crowded into the emerging cities where the beginning of industrialization was taking hold. Without land to produce their food, this desperately poor and newly urbanized population suffered from poor diets. They could not afford nutritious food because of their low wages, and factory work left them much less time to prepare food. As one historian has noted in the Scottish context,

> nutritional standards declined further and sharply when the wife went out to work. "When the mother is at work there is not time to prepare porridge or broth in the 'diet hour' . . . usually breakfast and dinner become bread and butter meals." . . . Pressure on the housewife's time was in itself a sufficient explanation of the choice of an inferior diet. The need to save time rather than the need to economize or to maintain nutritional standards determined the choice. Most noticeable was the increased consumption of bread. . . . The cooking of vegetable broth was neglected in the cities (Campbell, quoted in Mintz 1985, 30).

THE FIRST INDUSTRIAL DIETARY REGIME: 1870–1949

While many things were produced under the factory system of production from the seventeenth century onward, food was not typically produced in such a way. This finally began to change in the latter half of the nineteenth century, especially in the United States. The development of integrated internal markets in the United States with the completion of an extensive railroad network greatly aided entrepreneurs who were intent on establishing business enterprises that could manufacture a growing range of processed foodstuffs. Industrialization came to the realm of food in several different ways. In the meat processing sphere, the mechanized *disassembly* line in large factory establishments emerged. In the fruit and vegetable sphere, the evolution of mechanized canning technology made possible the preservation of fruits and vegetables on a large scale so that they could be consumed out of season. In fact, about thirty million cans of food were being processed by 1870 in the United States (Young 1989). Likely the most far-reaching industrial process applied to food occurred in the flour milling industry. Technological changes in that industry had an especially significant impact on the quality of diets, as we will see later in this lesson.

The milling companies of North America producing wheat flour played a pioneering role in the transformation of food production from a small-scale artisanal type of operation to modern factory methods after about 1870. Several factors led to the conversion of small-scale stone milling of grain to industrial milling utilizing new roller milling technology (see Figure 3.2). These factors included the possibility of opening the West to wheat farming, the availability of new hard wheat varieties that grew best there, the invention of new milling technology needed to successfully process them, the construction of an extensive network of railroads and the boost this gave to establishing a national market, rapid urbanization, and the expanding print media. These all spurred the large-scale industrialization of flour milling.

With the advent of new sifting and roller milling technology, wheat flour was transformed. Before this new technology, wheat was stone ground in small mills and the resulting whole wheat flour would only keep for short periods because of the perishable crushed wheat germ that formed part of the flour. Roller milling extended the flour's shelf life by extracting and eliminating the wheat germ from the flour entirely, along with the outer bran. Removing the bran and germ of the wheat removed most of the valuable nutrients as well. This novel *patent* flour was turned into a relatively durable food commodity that could be stored for considerable periods. This made possible its marketing on a much larger geographical scale utilizing some of the emergent **mass advertising** opportunities that the print media offered by the latter part of the nineteenth century. Wheat flour became a pioneering branded commodity by the late nineteenth century and was increasingly sold on a regional and then national scale by large milling companies.

With the industrialization of food processing, another central characteristic of the first industrial dietary regime is the marketing innovations employed by the leading processing firms. Flour milling firms such as Pillsbury were pioneers in marketing a food product on a national scale. Entrepreneurs in a related sector, ready-to-eat breakfast cereal, were the real innovators in the new enterprise of *mass marketing*. This new product was shaped, cooked, dried, and packaged by the processor. A few breakfast cereal entrepreneurs, notably C. W. Post and the Kellogg brothers, used the emerging technologies of mass marketing to create nationally branded products in the very early decades of the twentieth century. Such products as Post Grape-Nuts, Kellogg's Corn Flakes and Rice Krispies, and General

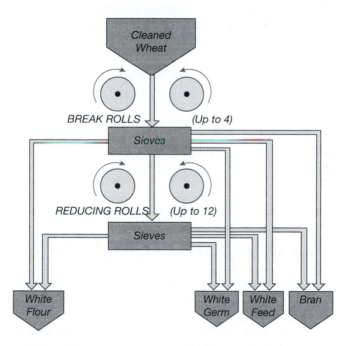

Figure 3.2 Stone Milling Versus Roller Milling of Grain.

Mills' Wheaties were soon marketed nationwide in the United States and not long afterward in Canada as well. These products were differentiated, in marketing terms, in that they were no longer run-of-the-mill food commodities such as wheat flour or oatmeal, but through some extra processing and, notably, extraordinary expenditures (for that period) on advertising, they were *differentiated* in the minds of consumers as qualitatively distinct and superior. As a result, their manufacturers could command higher prices. The marketing efforts of these breakfast cereal entrepreneurs were successful in destroying the traditional American breakfast and replacing it with various forms of processed grains instead (Levenstein 1988, 33). These food industrialists were able to integrate the explosive productive potential of the factory system with strategies that dramatically boosted the demand for their products. The companies they established came to dominate food environments for generations to come.

Once processed food products were adopted by an ever wider public, an **industrial diet** became increasingly commonplace. For this to happen, such processed food had to be *normalized*, because it had not been part of food environments up to that time. Early mass advertising campaigns made novel processed foodstuffs desirable by delivering on promises of convenience and time saving, by claims of purity, and by suggestions that consumption of certain products would confer social status. Over time, a diet that was a radical and disturbing departure from traditional foods was made socially acceptable, indeed desirable. The early establishment of the industrial diet was not in any real sense a natural process. It was consciously orchestrated by a relatively few food processing entrepreneurs savvy to the power of the new technologies of mass advertising and with an eye to maximizing the profit of their businesses.

The first industrial dietary regime lasted until the Second World War and was notable for the industrialization of food processing and the role of mass marketing in the process that we have termed the normalization of the industrial diet. The postwar period inaugurated new developments in the world of agriculture and food.

SECOND INDUSTRIAL DIETARY REGIME (1950–80)

The period following World War II inaugurated a qualitatively new phase of the global food system. In the realm of agriculture, rapid mechanization and a virtual chemical revolution resulted in a dramatic intensification of production with substantially higher yields (see Lesson 5). Mirroring these changes in agriculture, this period marked a qualitative shift in food environments and mass diets as well. There was continuation of an industrial diet that had been given form and developed in the years prior to World War II, but with a notable intensification. Fundamentally, it involved the increasing per capita consumption of a host of manufactured edible products that today we understand to be nutritionally compromised in significant ways. The processes that undermined the nutritional benefits of our food are discussed in a later section.

Why did this intensified consumption of industrial foods occur? The answer to this question is somewhat complex because it is intimately related to broader changes to the structure of society and not only to actors within the food system. In fact, change began during World War II when large numbers of men and women were in the armed forces and millions of women left the home to work in factories to bolster arms production. On the one hand, companies such as Coca-Cola and the Hershey chocolate company had access to the troops through their proprietary agreements to supply army canteens with their snack foods and beverages, which undoubtedly helped create a market for snack food consumption after World War II. On the other hand, working women with serious time restrictions were aggressively marketed to by processors manufacturing time-saving convenience foods (Levenstein 1988).

There were profound *technological* changes as well. The postwar period saw massive state-sponsored highway projects, which gave a boost to the use of the automobile and intensified the phenomenon of car culture. This and the dramatic expansion of the suburbs provided fertile conditions for the explosion of fast-food enterprises in the second half of the twentieth century. While fast-food corporations invented their own edible products, they also promoted established nutrient-poor products such as certain soft drink brands to complement their meal offerings.

Significant *demographic* changes took place at this time as well, and most notable was the decline in the number of farm families and their migration to the cities and suburbs. Without any ties to the land, these migrants were no longer able to engage in self-provisioning and were much more vulnerable to the dietary influences of food corporations. By the 1960s, middle-class women in particular were once again entering the workforce. Both time pressures and growing desire to be free of onerous domestic duties were factors in opening the door to the growing acceptance of fast foods and so-called convenience foods. As time would tell, many of these products were nutritionally problematic and would play a central role in the rise of the epidemic of obesity in years to come.

The intensification of the consumption of industrial foods was most dramatic in North America, with European countries following this pattern decades later. For example, in the United States the consumption of novel processed foods, such as frozen vegetables and processed potatoes, principally frozen French fries, soared from miniscule amounts in the early 1950s to over 50 pounds per person by 1970 (OECD 1979, 118). As foods and beverages became industrialized, there was a significant rise in the amount of fats and sweeteners in people's diets. Fat consumption in the United States rose over 50 percent to an annual 71 pounds per person from the end of World War II to the early 1990s. Sweetener consumption, already high by the 1940s in the United States, increased almost 30 percent over this period to a staggering 147 pounds per person (Winson 2004).

THIRD INDUSTRIAL DIETARY REGIME: 1980S AND AFTER

What is unique to the period after 1980 in terms of the nature of food environments and mass diets? We believe several key developments mark this period as a qualitatively distinct dietary regime. The first development involves changes to food environments in the developed world. While the features of industrial foods remain essentially the same, their impact on diets was magnified by such phenomena as the supersizing of restaurant meals by corporate restaurant chains. Another development was the intensive penetration of industrial edible products and fast foods into *new* institutional domains, including public-sector institutions such as schools, airports, and hospitals, as well as nontraditional private institutions, such as gas stations and even banks.

A central feature of the third industrial dietary regime has been the rapid *globalization* of the industrial diet to the developing world. Throughout the global South dramatic socioeconomic and political changes have opened the door to powerful corporate actors with a strong vested interest in shifting mass diets in this geographical context. Foremost among these factors has been accelerating rural to urban migration. No longer able to grow their own food once they have migrated to the city, masses of people in the global South have become dependent on purchasing their food from urban food environments that are rapidly becoming saturated with nutrient-poor products. Increasing disposable income among the emerging middle classes in a variety of countries has been crucial as well. Finally, during the debt crisis experienced by many developing countries in the early 1980s, such countries were forced by international money lending agencies, in particular the World Bank, to open their domestic markets to transnational food corporations.

The penetration of highly processed industrial foods into the global South has occurred via *three principal vectors*. The first of these vectors is multinational snack food corporations. Companies like Nestlé, Kraft, PepsiCo, and Kellogg's all control several branded *pseudofood and junk food* products that are highly processed and nutrient poor, such as high-sugar juice beverages that contain little real fruit juice, salty snacks, presweetened breakfast cereals, high-fat/high-sugar dairy desserts, and all manner of confectionary products. With saturated markets in North America and western Europe, these companies began looking to Latin America, Asia, and now Africa for profitable opportunities and in recent years have been aggressively marketing their products in these contexts. A second powerful vector of the industrial diet is American fast-food corporations. Companies such as Yum! Brands (KFC, Taco Bell, Pizza Hut) and McDonald's have each spent hundreds of millions of dollars in China alone expanding their outlets since the year 2000 (McDonald's Corporation 2015; Yum! Brands 2015).

The third principal vector for the diffusion of the industrial diet is the entry of supermarket and convenience chain store corporations into the global South. Supermarket chain stores are very quickly transforming traditional forms of food retailing, such as farmers' markets, all over the global South. The takeover of food retail by supermarket chains has occurred much faster than it did in developed countries. For example, in Mexico there was only one supermarket in the nation's second largest city, Guadalajara, in 1979. Approximately twenty-five years later, there were fifty-eight (Harner 2007). Moreover, in many countries local supermarket operations come to be controlled by global supermarket chains (e.g., Walmart, Carrefour) based in the United States or Europe (Reardon et al. 2003). Why are supermarkets a significant force in transforming diets? The chief reason is that they are major suppliers for a host of nutrient-poor, highly processed edible products novel to food environments in developing countries. These products are now being heavily advertised in these countries as well.

Another form of contemporary retailing that has accelerated the diffusion of junk foods and pseudofoods in these countries is the rapid expansion of corporate convenience chain store operations. They typically offer a food environment that is highly saturated with nutrient-poor edible products. This type of food outlet is often the only easily accessible option in poorer neighborhoods.

Snack food corporations, fast-food corporations, and global supermarket chain corporations have a symbiotic relationship, in the sense that each type of corporation has a mutually beneficial relationship with the others (see Figure 3.3). For example, fast-food chains sell well-known snack food and beverage brands and increase the sales for snack food companies. At the same time, these familiar snack food brands enhance the appeal of fast-food chains as places to eat and hence make them more profitable. The relationship of the Coca-Cola Company and McDonald's is a case in point. Similarly, food retail corporations sell large volumes of well-recognized snack food brands in their stores, which makes their stores more attractive

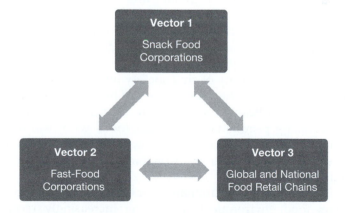

Figure 3.3 Globalization of the Industrial Diet: Three Vectors and their Symbiotic Relationships.

to consumers who seek out these products. For their part, snack food corporations benefit from selling in the supermarket retail food environment where most people in developed countries go to buy food. Moreover, some major supermarket chains now incorporate major fast-food operations into their stores, such as Walmart and McDonald's. Hungry shoppers may appreciate the convenience of ready-to-eat foods available in the supermarket, while the supermarket benefits from rents received from the fast-food corporation.

As food environments are being transformed in the global South, health impacts are becoming increasingly visible there too. Populous countries such as China and Indonesia are experiencing increasing rates of overweight and obesity that are comparable to the highest rates in the developed world. A study led by Popkin (Popkin, Adair, and Ng 2006) of women ages twenty to forty-nine showed that the prevalence of overweight exceeds underweight among women in both urban and rural areas of dozens of poorer countries. Among young children in China in the ten years after 1989, the prevalence of overweight doubled, while the prevalence of obesity has increased about ten times in this period (Luo and Hu 2002).

Not surprisingly, the incidence of chronic disease associated with dramatic weight gain is rising rapidly in the developing world. In the developed world outside the United States, where the American food and beverage companies have had a longer existence, as in Japan, the incidence of type 2 diabetes among school-age children increased ten times between 1976 and 1996. Now we are witnessing a rapid development of the same phenomenon in developing countries like Thailand, the Middle East, sub-Saharan Africa, India, and Southeast Asia (WHO 2003; Wild et al., 2004; Pinhas Hamiel and Zeilter 2005). While weight gain and attendant chronic disease in these societies cannot be blamed solely on the transformation of diets promoted by the actions of foreign food and beverage corporations, there is considerable evidence that the impact of the **nutrition transition** (Popkin, Adair, and Ng 2012) is greater and more thoroughgoing than is commonly appreciated.

A fourth and very significant feature of the third dietary regime is the growing *resistance* to the industrial diet in the developed countries and an emerging struggle for healthy eating. This resistance has taken various forms. They include a variety of civil society interventions, which include efforts to relocalize food, the preservation of heritage foods and culinary traditions, and, significantly, struggles to reform school food environments by replacing pseudofoods and fast foods with healthier options. These various creative initiatives have been characterized as alternative agriculture and food movements (Constance, Renard, and Rivera-Ferre 2014) (see Part 4).

Today, in the context of dramatic population-wide changes to body composition, food environments are being increasingly recognized by some governments as being *obesogenic*, or obesity promoting, and a threat to public health. Moreover, there is a growing recognition of the financial

Table 3.1 Industrial Dietary Regimes

First regime: 1850–1939, normalization	Second regime: 1950–80, intensification	Third regime: post-1980, globalization
• Beginning of industrial processing in canning, milling, and meatpacking sectors • Diffusion of industrial food via novel **mass advertising** campaigns in magazines, newspapers, electric signs, and later radio advertisements • Substantial uptake of processed edible products among urban population • Early degradation of whole foods via industrial processes, for example, *patent* or branded refined flours stripped of vitamins, minerals, and fiber	• Intensification of consumption of industrial edible products • Further normalization of industrial diet, especially in North America • Proliferation of away-from-home fast foods • Mass advertising of industrial food intensified with television • American wheat exports to developing world as food aid, stimulating dietary transition to industrial diet there	• Globalization and rapid transformation toward industrial diet in developing countries via transnational food and retail corporations • Nutrient-poor edible products in new institutional domains in developed countries • More intensive consumption of nutrient-poor edible products in developed countries • First signs of resistance to industrial diet in developed countries • Emergence of healthy-eating initiatives; challenge to legitimacy of nutrient-poor edible products

burden that this situation poses to state budgets, now and in the future. An ever-broader spectrum of state actions has emerged, from local school boards banning the sale of soft drinks in schools (in the United States) to sweeping new guidelines on what can be served in schools (Canadian provinces), nationwide taxes on soft drinks (Mexico), and bans on advertising nutrient-poor edible products on television programs aimed at children and teens (Britain). While there is emerging evidence that these initiatives have some positive effects, they are limited in scope. Indeed, the forces that produced the industrial diet over the past century still dominate our food environments. Food corporations have been responding to threats to their bottom line with new products that are marketed as healthy, but may in fact be of limited benefit to health (Simon, 2006) (see Lesson 4). In this third dietary regime, the industrial diet is increasingly contested as grassroots initiatives and some government actions seek to transform food environments in healthier directions. At the same time, the corporate food sector lobbies hard to undercut more comprehensive healthy eating initiatives by governments and maintain their long-standing dominance in determining what we eat. Table 3.1 summarizes the key features of each dietary regime we have discussed above.

MECHANISMS OF DIETARY TRANSFORMATION

The industrialization of food within the context of for-profit economic organization has taken place through three interrelated processes that have had the effect of degrading food and undermining our health. These processes are (i) simplification, (ii) speed-up of agricultural and transformative (processing) activities, and (iii) adulteration. Coupled with the diffusion mechanisms—mass marketing and spatial colonization (discussed in the next section)—these processes have given rise to the degraded industrial mass diets that characterize our times.

Simplification has two principal dimensions. The first entails a radical reduction in the complexity of whole foods that occurs with industrial processing. The second involves a dramatic reduction in the varietal diversity of foods in food environments because of the economic imperatives of the contemporary food system. Both dimensions of simplification negatively impact the nutritional benefit of the food we eat.

With respect to simplification of whole foods via industrial processing, a classic example is the case of refined wheat flour that has formed the basis of many food products for decades. With the invention of roller milling in the late nineteenth century, the bran and the germ were extracted from grains. Highly refined white flour was favored because it was much less prone to spoilage and could be marketed on a much wider basis (Kuhlmann 1929). According to Weaver (2001), refined white wheat flour has less than 40 percent of such essential nutrients as vitamin E, riboflavin, niacin, thiamin, folic acid, and iron and less than 20 percent of potassium, zinc, and fiber compared to whole wheat flour, where the nutrient-rich wheat germ and bran have not been removed. Another study has documented that industrial milling technology leads to the loss of a group of nutritionally valuable phytochemicals that are only found in whole grains (Adom, Sorrells, and Liu 2005).

In the agricultural sphere there has been a drastic reduction in the varieties available for a wide range of fruits, vegetables, and grains. Many growers switched years ago to mechanical harvesting of crops such as tomatoes to reduce labor costs. As a consequence, older varieties have been abandoned in favor of a variety that will withstand the rigors of mechanical harvesting machines (Friedland et al., 1981) (see Lesson 6). Powerful actors further along the supply chain, such as supermarkets, favor just a few varieties of fruits and vegetables to sell because they last longer in storage and are cosmetically attractive. Examples of this abound and can be illustrated by examining any neighborhood supermarket. In the case of apples, for example, several thousand varieties exist (Browning, 1998), but the typical supermarket will only stock six to eight. The rising popularity of the French fries promoted by fast-food corporations has also had its own impact on varietal simplification, as French fry processors favor only one or two varieties, principally the Russet Burbank potato (Martin, 2017). Many thousands of varieties have been identified in their place of origin in the Andean region of South America (International Potato Center, 2013).

Why be concerned with this varietal simplification? Besides the loss of culinary traditions and taste, we believe it may be limiting the protective health benefits of whole foods. Recent science has found different concentrations of essential nutrients in the same species of fruits, vegetables, and grains. For instance, the protein content of rice can vary among its varieties between 5 and 13 percent, and the carotenoid content of different cultivars of sweet potato can vary by a factor of sixty or more, while one variety of apricot can represent 1 percent and another 200 percent of the recommended daily intake for vitamin A (Heywood 2013). Significant nutritional differences within the same species of livestock exist as well (Hoffmann and Baumong, 2013).

Recent research has also suggested that there is very wide variation in the presence of beneficial phytochemicals among different varieties. Phytochemicals are nutrients that are believed to enhance the immune system, mediate hormones, and have antioxidant effects and benefit digestion. These phytochemicals also may play a key role in inhibiting the development of malignant tumors. With cancer becoming a major scourge in developed countries, a radical reduction in the varieties of fruits, vegetables, and grains available to us is very likely impoverishing the phytochemical components of food that may be keeping cancer at bay (Winson 2013).

A further process degrading our diet is the **speed-up of food production**. Speed-up refers to "pressures within a market-based industrial food system to reduce the time necessary to produce an edible commodity ready for sale" (Winson and Choi 2017). The shorter the turnover time of capital—the time from initial investment to final sale of the product—the greater the *accumulated profits* over a given period (Harvey 2010). The beef cattle industry illustrates the process of speed-up. Cattle breeds are chosen for how rapidly they lay on fat, while the use of hormone implants speeds growth of the animal and the use of industrial corn-based feeds in feedlots is designed to fatten the cattle as quickly as possible. Unfortunately for consumers, in nutritional terms this process results in excessive amounts of saturated fat in the meat and an unhealthy balance of good and bad fats compared to that found in cattle raised on the grasses they evolved to thrive on. This process also changes the vitamin content of the meat and promotes pathogenic bacteria, in particular the deadly *Escherichia coli* O157:H7 that can make its way into the meat we buy with devastating consequences.

Adulteration refers to a set of systematic practices by food processors to increase the palatability of highly processed foods but also to increase shelf life, make processed foods cosmetically more appealing, and lower the manufacturer's cost to produce them. Such adulteration has the effect of degrading foods by compromising their nutritional quality. The main adulterants added to manufactured food today are sugar, salt, fats, especially dangerous hydrogenated fats, and a very extensive range of chemical food additives. Responding to pressure from health authorities, some manufacturers have opted to reduce or eliminate some of these adulterants, in particular trans fats. However, they continue to be added in unhealthy amounts to many of the processed edible products we eat. Adulterants are also very much a part of the meal offerings of restaurant chains and fast-food outlets (Kessler 2009). Such adulterants may be perceived as a benefit to consumers because they may enhance the flavor and texture of highly processed edible products that would otherwise be unpalatable (Schlosser 2001). Nevertheless, these perceived advantages come at a cost to our health.

DIFFUSION OF THE INDUSTRIAL DIET

We have discussed how whole foods have been degraded in various ways by a profit-oriented food economy. However, how were highly processed, nutrient-poor edible products diffused in food environments to the point where we can speak of a pervasive *industrial diet*? In our discussion of the first industrial dietary regime we saw how *mass advertising* had created an interest in these novel products. Mass advertising was an essential step in normalizing these products and making them acceptable, even though they constituted an often-dramatic departure from traditional foods. However, advertising alone was not sufficient to ensure their widespread diffusion. Another factor played an essential role: spatial colonization.

Spatial colonization is a way to ensure that a processed product is *available and visible* in as wide a variety of food environments (e.g., supermarkets, fast-food outlets) as possible, in addition to making products widely recognized through advertising. How this is accomplished depends on the food environment. In the all-important supermarket context, shelf placement of products at eye level and special displays for better visibility are key to sales (Chevalier 1975) and processors pay for these favored locations (Matas, 1987 and Federal Trade Commission 2003).

With respect to fast food, spatial colonization is achieved in another way. The leading fast-food companies have come to dominate food environments by securing the most desirable high-traffic locations in new and existing suburban and urban areas, to the point where they have essentially saturated the market with their outlets in many developed countries. McDonald's, by far the leading fast-food chain store operator/franchisor globally, had over thirty-six thousand outlets in 199 countries by 2015. They have aggressively pursued new market opportunities in emerging economies like China, with up to five hundred new outlets planned there in 2016 alone (McDonald's Corporation 2015). The second largest global fast-food corporation, Yum! Brands (Taco Bell, KFC, and Pizza Hut), had fifteen thousand outlets by 2015 and had plans to open six hundred new ones in China in 2016 (Yum! Brands 2015).

Why is spatial colonization worthy of our attention? The answer is simple: it is a mechanism by which nutrient-poor edible products—pseudofoods—are coming to dominate food environments. Pseudofoods tend to be one of the most profitable edible products in our food system. This brings us to the concept of **differential profits** that helps us understand the widespread diffusion of pseudofoods that make up the industrial diet. In our food system, some products produce higher rates of profit for sellers than others. As it turns out, pseudofoods achieve some of the highest margins for processors and retailers. Salty snacks, soft drinks, and presweetened cereals, to name some of the most important examples, are among the most profitable products in the supermarket (Stuckler et al. 2012). These exceptional profits explain why it is so attractive for processors, and for retailers, to have pseudofoods spatially colonized throughout the supermarket and other food enviroments as well (Bird 2011; Winson 2004). The profitability of such products has been strikingly noted by a representative of PepsiCo's Frito Lay salty snack division who claimed that the company's products accounted for some 11 percent of operating profits and 40 percent of profit growth of the average US supermarket, although they represented only 1 percent of supermarket sales (Wellman 1999).

Conclusion

In this lesson we have considered how the processes of simplification, speed-up, and adulteration have degraded whole foods since the latter part of the nineteenth century. We have argued that from the first industrial dietary regime, mass advertising has served to normalize the industrial diet and diffuse it to most of our food environments. In the second industrial dietary regime the industrial diet was intensified by the spatial colonization of highly profitable, nutrient-poor pseudofoods into new institutional food environments (schools, hospitals, airports, etc.) and by the dramatic flourishing of fast-food chain store operations. The industrial diet has been globalized more recently in the third industrial dietary regime. As a consequence, in more and more countries around the world food environments are nothing less than obesogenic or obesity promoting. They are associated with high rates of overweight and obesity and other nutrition-related negative health outcomes. In particular, growing income inequalities in this period have impacted health in unequal ways because cheap, nutrient-poor edible products are more prevalent in food environments in poorer neighborhoods and are often the ones that the poor can afford to purchase (see Lesson 13).

To deal with the health calamity provoked by the obesity epidemic, we must understand the fundamental realities of the industrial diet and then challenge the corporate forces reproducing it. Fortunately, many positive initiatives to establish healthy food environments have been undertaken around the world in recent years, especially at the level of civil society organizations. To successfully confront the damage to human health triggered by the industrial diet and make healthy eating a normal part of daily existence, it will take much more forceful government policy initiatives and a wide variety of civil society organizations pressing for change to the existing food system.

Discussion Questions

1. Many people believe that diets are mainly the result of individual choices. How does this lesson challenge this view?
2. What are the main features of the industrial diet? Give some examples to illustrate your answer.
3. What are the key features of each of the three industrial dietary regimes?
4. In this lesson the authors argue that three main processes underlie the degradation of food. Describe these three processes and give an example of each.
5. What are the three main vectors by which the industrial diet is currently being diffused in developing countries?

Exercises

1. *Consumption of the industrial diet.* Construct a food log for three days where you record everything you eat and drink. Indicate whether each food that you consume could be considered a pseudofood and/or junk food and count the number of times each day you consume pseudofoods and/or junk foods. Also note the location where you purchased and consumed each of these pseudofoods and junk foods.
2. *Spatial colonization.* Obtain a map of your university campus and plot out your campus food environment (e.g., school cafeteria, snack bar, store, vending machines). Visit each one and record the types of foods being sold there, with particular attention to pseudofoods, junk foods, and fast foods. Identify what strategies are used to increase the visibility of pseudofoods, junk foods, and fast foods. Regarding vending machines, note the locations of vending machines in the building and record the total number of products on display and the total number of junk food products. Calculate the average percentage of junk foods of the total food products displayed in all the vending machines you survey.

Additional Materials

Readings

> Moss, Michael. 2013. *Salt, Sugar, Fat: How the Food Giants Hooked Us.* New York: Random House.
> Nestle, Marion. 2013. *Food Politics: How the Food Industry Influences Nutrition and Health.* Berkeley: University of California Press.
> Nestle, Marion. 2015. *Soda Politics: Taking on Big Soda (and Winning).* New York: Oxford University Press.
> Schlosser, Eric. 2012. *Fast Food Nation: The Dark Side of the All-American Meal.* New York: Mariner Books.
> Winson, Anthony. 2013. *The Industrial Diet: The Degradation of Food and the Struggle for Healthy Eating.* New York: New York University Press.

Films

> *Fed Up,* 2014
> *Food Inc.,* 2008

Food Fight: Bullies Poisoning the 'Hood Get Splattered!, 2013
Supersize Me!, 2004

References

Adom, K. K., M. Sorrells, and R. H. Liu. 2005. "Phytochemicals and Antioxidant Activity of Milled Fractions of Different Wheat Varieties." *Journal of Agricultural Food Chemistry* 53 (6): 2297–306.

Bird, Jo. 2011. "The Retail Dominance of Supermarkets in Australia: A Growing Geography of Pseudo-foods and Its Implications for Obesity." *International Journal of Liability and Scientific Inquiry* 4 (3): 265–80.

Browning, Frank. 1998. *Apples*. New York: North Point Press.

Chevalier, Michel. 1975. "Increase in Sales due to In-Store Display." *Journal of Marketing Research* 12:426–31.

Constance, Douglas, Marie-Christine Renard, and Marta G. Rivera-Ferre. 2014. *Alternative Agrifood Movements: Patterns of Convergence and Divergence*. Bingley, UK: Emerald Group.

Crosby, Alfred. 1972. *The Columbian Exchange*. Westport, CT: Greenwood Press.

Danforth, Marie Elaine. 1999. "Nutrition and Politics in Prehistory." *Annual Review of Anthropology* 28 (1): 1–25. https://doi.org/10.1146/annurev.anthro.28.1.1

Diamond, Jared, 1997. *Guns, Germs and Steel: The Fates of Human Societies*. New York: W. W. Norton.

Federal Trade Commission. 2003. "Slotting Allowances in the Retail Grocery Industry: Selected Case Studies in Five Product Categories." November 2003. https://www.ftc.gov/sites/default/files/documents/reports/use-slotting-allowances-retail-grocery-industry/slottingallowancerpt031114.pdf

Friedland, William, Amy Barton, and Robert Thomas. 1981. *Manufacturing Green Gold: Capital, Labor, and Technology in the Lettuce Industry*. New York: Cambridge University Press.

Friedmann, Harriet, and Philip McMichael. 1989. "Agriculture and the State System: The Rise and Decline of National Agricultures, 1870 to the Present." *Sociologia Ruralis* 29 (2): 93–117. https://doi.org/10.1111/j.1467-9523.1989.tb00360.x

Gibson, A. J. S., and T. C. Smout, 1993. "From Meat to Meal: Changes to Diet in Scotland." In *Food, Diet and Economic Change Past and Present*, edited by C. Geissler and D. J. Oddy. Leicester: University of Leicester Press.

Harner, John. 2007. "Globalization of Food Retailing in Guadalajara, Mexico." *Journal of Latin American Geography* 6 (2): 33–53.

Harvey, David. 2010. *The Enigma of Capital: And the Crisis of Capitalism*. New York: Oxford University Press.

Heywood, Vernon H. 2013. "Overview of Agricultural Biodiversity and Its Contribution to Nutrition and Health." In *Diversifying Food and Diets: Using Agricultural Biodiversity to Improve Nutrition and Health*, edited by J. Fanzo, D. Hunter, T. Borelli, and F. Mattei, 35–67. New York: Routledge.

Hoffmann, Irene, and Roswitha Baumung. 2013. "The Role of Livestock and Livestock Diversity in Sustainable Diets." In *Diversifying Food and Diets: Using Agricultural Biodiversity to Improve Nutrition and Health*, edited by J. Fanzo, D. Hunter, T. Borelli, and F. Mattei, 68–87. New York: Routledge.

International Potato Center. 2013. *Facts and Figures about the Potato*. Accessed October 12, 2016. http://cipotato.org/potato/facts/

Kessler, David A. 2009. *The End of Overeating: Taking Control of the Insatiable American Appetite*. Toronto, Canada: McClelland & Stewart.

Kuhlmann, Charles Byron. 1929. *The Development of the Flour Milling Industry in the United States*. New York: Houghton Mifflin.

Levenstein, Harvey A. 1988. *Revolution at the Table: The Transformation of the American Diet*. New York: Oxford University Press.

Luo, Juhua, and Frank B. Hu. 2002. "Time Trends of Obesity in Pre-school Children in China from 1989 to 1997." *International Journal of Obesity* 26 (4): 553–58.

Mantoux, Paul. 1961. *The Industrial Revolution in the Eighteenth Century*. New York: Harper Torchbooks.

Martin, Ralph C. 2017. "All for the Sake of Long, Skinny, White Fries." *Guelph Mercury Tribune*, February 9, 2017, 7.

Matas, Robert. 1987. "Stocking Shelves Has a Hidden Cost." *Globe and Mail*, February 12, 1987, B1.

McDonald's Corporation. 2015. *Annual Report*. Accessed October 12, 2016. http://www.aboutmcdonalds.com/content/mcd/investors/financial-information/annual-report.html

Mintz, Sidney W. 1985. *Sweetness and Power: The Place of Sugar in Modern History*. New York: Viking Books.

Montanari, Massimo. 2000. "Food Systems and Models of Civilization." In *Food: A Culinary History from Antiquity to the Present*, edited by J-L. Flandrin and M. Montanari, 77–78. New York: Penguin Books.

OECD (Organisation for Economic Co-operation and Development). 1979. *Impact of Multinational Enterprises on National Scientific and Technical Capacities: Food Industry*. Paris: OECD.

Pinhas Hamiel, Orit, and Philip Zeilter. 2005. "The Global Spread of Type II Diabetes Mellitus in Children and Adolescents." *Journal of Pediatrics* 146 (5): 693–700.

Popkin, Barry M., Linda S. Adair, and Shu Wen Ng. 2012. "The Global Nutrition Transition and the Pandemic of Obesity in Developing Countries." *Nutrition Reviews* 70:3–21.

Reardon, Thomas, C. P. Timmer, C. B. Barrett, and J. Berdegué. 2003. "The Rise of Supermarkets in Africa, Asia, and Latin America." *American Journal of Agricultural Economics* 85 (5): 1140–46.

Schlosser, Eric. 2001. *Fast Food Nation: The Dark Side of the American Meal*. New York: Houghton Mifflin.

Simon, Michele. 2006. *Appetite for Profit: How the Food Industry Undermines our Health and How to Fight Back*. New York: Nation Books.

Stuckler, D., M. McKee, S. Ebrahim, and S. Basu. 2012. "Manufacturing Epidemics: The Role of Global Producers in Increased Consumption of Unhealthy Commodities Including Processed Foods, Alcohol, and Tobacco." *PLoS Medicine* 9:e1001235.

Weaver, Glen L. 2001. "A Miller's Perspective on the Impact of Health Claims." *Nutrition Today* 36:115–18.

Wellman, David. 1999. "The Big Crunch." *Supermarket Business*, March 1999, 46–48.

Wild, Sarah, Gojka Roglic, Anders Green, Richard Sicree, and Hilary King. 2004. "Global Prevalence of Diabetes." *Diabetes Care* 27 (5): 1047–53.

Winson, Anthony. 2004. "Bringing Political Economy into the Debate on the Obesity Epidemic." *Agriculture and Human Values* 21 (4): 299–312.

Winson, Anthony. 2013. *The Industrial Diet: The Degradation of Food and the Struggle for Healthy Eating.* New York: New York University Press.

Winson, Anthony, and Jin Young Choi. 2017. "Dietary Regimes and the Nutrition Transition: Bridging Disciplinary Domains." *Agriculture and Human Values* 34:559–72.

WHO (World Health Organization). 2003. "Obesity and Overweight." *Global Strategy on Diet, Physical Activity and Health.* Accessed October 29, 2009. http://www.who.int/dietphysicalactivity/strategy/eb11344/en/index.html

WHO (World Health Organization). 2017. *The Top 10 Causes of Death. Fact Sheet.* Accessed April 2, 2017. http://www.who.int/mediacentre/factsheets/fs310/en/index1.html

Young, James H. 1989. *Pure Food: Securing the Federal Food and Drugs Act of 1906.* Princeton, NJ: Princeton University Press.

Yum! Brands. 2015. *Annual Report.* Accessed October 12, 2016. http://www.yum.com/annualreport

Zohary, Daniel, Maria Hopf, and Ehud Weiss. 2012. *Domestication of Plants in the Old World.* New York: Oxford University Press.

Fortified instant noodle distributed in Indonesia as food aid to the poor. (Photo by Aya H. Kimura.)

4

Food and Nutrition

Aya H. Kimura

Why do we eat what we eat? Culinary tradition, habits, convenience, price, and other factors influence our food choices, but knowledge of nutrition is increasingly powerful in shaping our relationship with food, for example, "I should not eat this piece of cake because I probably ate more than two thousand calories today" or "Maybe this chocolate is good for me because of antioxidants." Among different ways of knowing food, nutrition science powerfully defines what good/bad food is and what we should and should not be eating.

Few people would contest that the increasing nutrition literacy among the public is generally a positive development. Nutritional science has also offered a critical vantage point in critiquing big food businesses and their unhealthy foods. For instance, public health experts and food activists have critiqued saturated fat and high-calorie foods as scientific rationale for opposing the fast-food industry and its marketing, which has particularly targeted children of color. The call to improve public school lunches in the United States has also revolved around the need to make lunch offerings more nutritious and healthier.

But nutritional science has not been completely external to the logic of the corporate and global food system that is at the center of so much criticism by activists and scholars alike. This lesson examines the factors that have shaped nutrition science and how nutrition science, in turn, has influenced the way people eat and drink. Thinking about history and the social shaping of science is an exercise of the sociology of science—it looks at science as a social institution that has its own history, shaped by social and historical contexts, rather than as an ahistorical undertaking that simply uncovers truth in a linear manner (see Lesson 6). This move raises important questions: Who has the power to shape nutrition science and to push for dietary reform based on its insights? In what ways do the definitions of goodness/badness of foods reflect the social relations of power? Who gets to intervene in people's eating habits? Who is likely to be held responsible for bad food choices?

The first section of this lesson addresses these questions by focusing on how food industries have influenced nutrition science and policies by providing research funding to nutrition scientists, creating quasi-scientific groups to be spokespersons on their behalf, and influencing regulators by utilizing lobbyists.

The second section will draw on the history of nutrition science to illustrate how dietary advice has tended to develop in a way that privileged certain values of upper-middle-class whites over other social groups. What gets defined as *good food* is not simply a matter of scientific exercise but also reflects values and identities of the dominant class and race. Nutritional instructions and the call for reforming food also have a gendered history. They often targeted women, particularly mothers, to improve their knowledge and behaviors so as to enhance the health of family members.

The third section of the lesson examines the central tenets of Western nutrition science by drawing on the concept of **nutritionism**. Nutrition science has tended to depend on measures such as calories or a set of micronutrients (vitamins and minerals) as markers of good and bad food. The reliance on these measures has shaped dietary guidelines as well, constructing the ideal dietary behaviors in terms of quantifiable amounts of these parameters. Such a reductive view of food has also aligned well with the logic of capitalist food systems, creating profitable opportunities for corporations. The myopic focus on micronutrients has resulted in bourgeoning markets of processed foods that are nominally nutritionally superior, helping to expand sales opportunities for food and beverage companies.

The final section considers how nutritionism plays out in developing countries. Until the 1990s, food insecurity in the global South was typically understood to be the insufficient quantity of food, and the proposed solution tended to be modernization of agriculture with "improved" seeds and agrochemicals (see Lesson 6). However, in the 1990s nutritional framing of the issue started to highlight **hidden hunger**—micronutrient deficiencies. This section examines how nutritionism has shaped such a discursive shift. Importantly, the solutions to the global South's food insecurity now feature fortification (addition of micronutrients to processed foods) and biofortification (breeding crops themselves to be micronutrient rich, such as golden rice). The concepts of **charismatic nutrients** and **nutritional fixes** offer critical lens through which to explore their political and social consequences.

CORPORATE INFLUENCE ON NUTRITION ADVICE

To many readers of this book, the fact that nutrition advice is under immense influence from food industries might not be surprising. By now, the examination of science from a sociological vantage point has elucidated many cases of corporate influence on science. Examples such as corporate funding of scientific studies that denied the health impacts of tobacco and of research to create confusion on the existence and severity of global warming come to mind. Similar corporate influence has been documented in relation to nutrition science. For instance, Melanie DuPuis's book, *Dangerous Digestion: Politics of American Dietary Advice* (2015), points out how the US dairy industry worked closely with nutrition scientists since the late nineteenth century. These scientists popularized the view that milk was the nutritionally perfect food and their influence was powerful in formulating dietary recommendations to Americans that included milk as an indispensable component of the American diet.

The corporate influence on nutrition science and dietary advice continues today. Marion Nestle, a professor of nutrition science and the author of many books, including *Food Politics: How the Food Industry Influences Nutrition and Health* (2002), has pointed out peculiar ways dietary guidelines are translated into nutrition education tools and messages under corporate influence. The food industry has many lobbying groups to represent each commodity (e.g., sugar, salt, milk) that work to pressure politicians to circumvent any regulatory moves that might hamper their business. In addition, lobbyists might be former regulators or vice versa—the phenomenon of the **revolving door**. This results in what sociologists call **regulatory capture** where regulatory agencies are working for special interest groups rather than for the public interest.

Corporations and industry groups see dietary guidelines and nutrition education tools as one of the important factors in contracting or expanding the markets for their products; hence, they spend significant resources trying to influence the content. For instance, the US sugar industry opposed any mention of limiting sugar intake in the dietary guidelines and lobbyists worked hard to insert the words "choose a diet moderate in sugars" rather than reducing sugar intake (Nestle 2002, 83). Since 2011, MyPlate has been the nutrition education tool in the United States, replacing the older food pyramid (Figure 4.1). Although some improvement exists, Nestle has pointed out that the meat, sugar, soda, and processed food industries have successfully avoided the message of "eat less meat, soda, and processed foods," replacing it with the more euphemistic "reduce saturated fat, added sugar, and sodium."

There are various mechanisms of corporate influence on nutrition science, some of which might not be obvious. One example is direct funding of research by the private sector, and Nestle has suggested that nutrition science tends to favor the sponsoring industries. For instance, the soda industry funded research to respected scientists whose research tended to emphasize the importance of exercise as opposed to eating less and drinking less of their products; the sugar industry provided research funds to scientists so that dietary recommendations should focus on reducing saturated fat, rather than sugar, to prevent heart disease. Furthermore, industry groups often sponsor campaigns by different nutrition and health organizations such as the American Dietetic Association; they support the costs of various publications by expert organizations and sponsor individual researchers. In some cases, companies give research grants to nutrition departments at universities. For instance, Coca-Cola donates millions of dollars to university research foundations, nutrition science departments at universities, and professional nutrition organizations (you can see the list of receiving organizations and the donated amount on their website, http://transparency.coca-colacompany.com). This kind of corporate funding of academic research can be considered a positive development with the potential to quickly translate academic research to commercial opportunity. However, corporate control over the nature of research and the control of research results also raise serious questions about the public value of academic research (see Lesson 6).

In short, corporations have had powerful influence on dietary guidelines as well as the science of nutrition itself. Given that our relationship with food

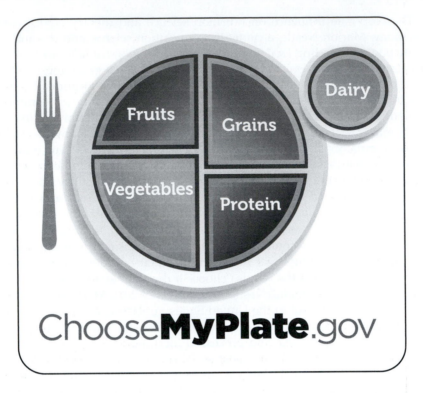

Figure 4.1 MyPlate. (US Department of Agriculture Center for Nutrition Policy and Promotion.)

is now profoundly mediated by nutrition science, this means that the societal idea of nutritious and healthy foods is increasingly under corporate influence.

CLASS, RACE, AND GENDER OF NUTRITION ADVICE

The previous section discussed corporate influence on nutrition science and dietary advice, but power relations in dietary advice are not limited to the corporate sector. This section examines how class-, race-, and gender-based hierarchies have colored nutrition science and dietary advice. The battle over what citizens should eat is not simply about food, but also about social status and morality. In her book *Dangerous Digestion*, Melanie E. DuPuis examines the history of dietary reform movements in the United States. She argues that "ideas about diet illuminate the conversation about the moral biopolitics of American reform movements" (2015, 4) and that "dietary advice, in determining how Americans should eat, also propounded a particular and fixed vision of how they should live" (5).

For instance, DuPuis shows how class interests were reflected in nutrition science's preoccupation with economical ways of cooking in the late nineteenth century and its use of the calorie as a measurement of food's worth. Explaining the political implications of nutrition research at the time, DuPuis writes, nutritionists "transformed the fight between workers and industrialists over a 'living wage' to a question of how much a worker needed to live, a conversation between workers and these professionals rather than workers and their employers" (DuPuis 2015, 68). Using the idea of the calorie, nutritional science sided with the industrialists who wanted to argue that rather than needing better wages, workers simply needed to learn to cook efficiently. Wilbur Atwater, the pioneering nutrition scientist in the United States, suggested that coal laborers could have lived better had they known that they did not have to spend their meager salary on expensive flour, meat, and butter and that cheaper foods could be as nutritious as expensive ones.

DuPuis and other scholars have shown that the history of home economics—the predecessor to nutrition science—reflected upper-class groups' emphasis on rationality, purity, and discipline that was guided by a particular sensibility of upper-middle-class whites. For instance, Ellen Richards, the first female professor at the Massachusetts Institute of Technology and a pioneer in home economics, started dietary reform programs such as the New England Kitchen, where she sought to teach scientific and economical ways of cooking particularly targeting new immigrant families. While these programs were ostensibly based in nutrition science, they were also shaped by a particular culture of home economics professionals, resulting in solidifying "Yankee Northern European culture as the definition of what good American living should be, including good American eating" (DuPuis 2015, 82). The target audience, such as Italian immigrants, did not like the foods offered and the New England Kitchen did not fit their cultural norms of communal and ceremonial meals.

Visions of dietary reformers were not only about how to reform foods per se but also about how to improve citizens and society at large. DuPuis writes, "food so easily represents ideas of free will because it is a choice: to put some things in our bodies. But it also entails control: the discipline to keep some things out, to establish boundaries. In this bifurcated world, this choice defines us as 'what we eat' and defines the world outside the protective boundary as a dangerous, unruly, disordered 'not us,' threatening to contaminate the inside, which is pure and free and orderly" (2015, 2–3). On the surface, dietary advice and campaigns by reformers were rooted in neutral scientific knowledge of nutrition, but they were shaped by a particular vision of American society and human virtues that was reflective of the background of the reformers themselves. Perhaps then it is not a surprise that dietary reforms tended to fail, since they imposed restrictions that were constructed from a particular upper-class/racial sensibility but presented as universally applicable to other groups and since the "good food" advocated by the reformers was not realistic or practical to those being preached to.

Dietary advice might no longer be patently biased against the working class, new immigrants, and certain ethnic groups, but today's dietary ideals and dietary reform movements continue to express certain values and judgments that are more congruent with upper-middle-class/white values and experiences. Popular food pundits and food documentary films tend to portray fast food, processed foods, and microwavable TV dinners in a harsh and condescending manner, while hailing the virtues of organic and local fresh fruits and vegetables and artisanal food products. They call on families to cook at home and eat together. This assumes the availability of money and time as well as certain aesthetics. Writing of contemporary dietary reformers such as the chef James Oliver, who has spearheaded the denunciation of fast/cheap foods, DuPuis writes, "romance is embedded, once again, in a troublesome politics of purity that makes romantic visions of ideal diets the solution to larger, more complex social problems. This dietary reform conversation, once again, turns larger questions of social and political inequality into a problem of self-discipline" (2015, 101). Contemporary dietary reformers might frown on cheap fast foods, but in the context of stagnant or decreasing real income for the working class, cheap foods, however disastrous their nutritious quality, are the bargain that workers need to take. Cooking from scratch and eating together might be a luxury many people cannot afford when working long hours to make ends meet (and combined with unpaid care work, as many women do).

It is also important to consider the typical target audience for dietary reform movements. Because of its cultural associations with domesticity, food and cooking are usually considered women's responsibilities. Dietary reformers at the turn of the century—who themselves tended to be women—wanted to transform how women shopped for and cooked food. Food reformers scrutinized the nutritional quality of food but usually fell short of addressing larger economic situations that made poor women cook in accordance with "scientific" guidelines. Even today, women, particularly mothers, are considered gatekeepers to the health of the family and future generations. In addition, because of women's association with reproduction, scrutiny over their dietary behaviors is particularly strenuous. Recent attention to the link between obesity and a mother's prepregnancy and pregnancy diet may exacerbate already powerful pressures mothers feel to calibrate their dietary choices to maximize benefits for their children. Contemporary criticisms by food activists about the ubiquity of fast food and the lack of home-cooked meals easily translate to social pressure on women to do more. However, the idealization of fresh and home-cooked food does not consider the everyday struggles of many women who lack both money and time as they juggle employment, household chores, and caretaking responsibilities. In the context of women's increasing employment without public policy support for child care, more equitable sharing within the household, and many poverty-wage jobs, women need quick and affordable meals that they can easily purchase. Without addressing the systemic constraints on these women's resources and time, food activists might simply accelerate feelings of stress, guilt, and inadequacy among women.

Social relations of power and status influence efforts to improve citizens' diets. Efforts to "improve" dietary behaviors and foods have often come from the dominant class, subjecting the working-class minorities to scrutiny over the correctness and morality of their diets. Furthermore, the call to improve food has historically targeted women as the responsible party to follow officially sanctioned rules for good food. While food reforms have often given (privileged) women access to public roles, such as with early twentieth-century dietary reformers, less privileged women were relegated to the position of the passive recipient of dietary advice, often set up for failure to comply by virtue of their socioeconomic positions.

NUTRITIONISM

The previous section examined who has had a strong voice in shaping nutrition science and dietary advice. Other scholars have tried to understand the core tenets of Western nutrition science itself and how they have influenced our relationship with food. The concept of **nutritionism** is important here. Originally proposed by the sociologist Gyorgy Scrinis (2013), nutritionism explains the prevailing reductive interpretation and decision-making about food based mainly on food's nutritional parameters (calorie, vitamins, minerals). Nutritionism naturalizes the view that nutritional composition is the most important characteristic of food. Under the influence of healthism, food's value is reduced to nutrients and its contribution to individuals' health status. Broccoli is "good" because it is high in vitamins A and D. Strawberries are good because of their rich vitamin C. Nutritionism assumes that a universal understanding of food's impact on the body is possible and that food's properties or values can be reduced to constitutive nutrients and calories.

Nutrition science might seem like a neutral field that provides disinterested description and guidance, but the assumptions of neutrality and objectivity are deeply political. For instance, nutritionism renders nonnutritional considerations—such as how strawberries might be produced in chemical-intensive agriculture that exploits immigrant farmworkers—marginal to the characterization of foods. The strawberries from your backyard would be considered no different than from those imported from a multinational-owned farm in a foreign country. Under nutritionism, quantifiable components expressed in terms of calories, vitamins, and minerals dominate the social understanding of food's values. For instance, when the US Department of Agriculture recommends that we eat five or more servings of fresh fruits and vegetables, they mean we need to get a certain amount of vitamins, minerals, proteins, and so on; the recommendations are not based on environmental or social considerations such as the amount of soil fumigants used for the production of strawberries or the chemicals' impact on farmworkers.

Disaggregating food into constitutive nutrients and calories is not the only way to interpret the goodness of foods. Other possibilities include bodily sensations, tastes, tradition, and communal foodways. Alternative bodies of knowledge such as Chinese, Ayurvedic, and Greco-Islamic medicines also offer different ideas of good food that might differ from modern nutrition science, which tends to look inside a particular food item. For instance, Chinese medicine not only suggests what might be good to eat, but also indicates that the combination of different foods and how they are eaten and grown matters in deciding their effects on bodies and spirits. Specifically, Chinese medicine categorizes different foods as located on the continuum between yin (dark) and yang (bright) (for instance, sugar is extremely yin and meat is yang). The yin–yang characters are not fixed, but relational, and the same vegetable might be considered stronger on the yin or yang side depending on methods of farming, storage, and cooking.

An important corollary of nutritionism is that by scientizing the social understanding of food, modern nutritional science came to be the dominant expertise of the health effects of foods, rather than other traditions or individuals themselves. Historian of science Steve Shapin observed that before the nineteenth century, the European understanding of food was influenced by Galenic traditions (nature as composed of four elements: fire, earth, water, and air) and food was understood to have qualities that were influenced by the locale where it was produced, which, in turn, influenced human nature and health. Dietary advice was individualized in that the effects of food were understood to vary in different locales and for people with different natural constitutions, dietary customs, and embodied reactions to foods. Departing from this view, modern nutrition posited that foods' values were based on their nutrients and that nutrition knowledge is more or less universally applicable. Shapin writes,

> *During the nineteenth and twentieth centuries the vocabularies of both Galenic dietetics and analogical reasoning about the qualities of aliment lost their grip on medical and physiological expertise. In their place, nutritional science supplied a new language: the constituents of foods were no longer the qualities of heat and cold, moist and dry, nor of the virtues and powers of the plants and animals eaten—they were carbohydrates, fats and protein; vitamins; minerals; and that power attached to chemical constituents, the calorie. This is what is in what you eat, and this is what makes you what you are and what powers your physiological functions. . . . Taste, and the individual experience of digestion, were powerful probes into the qualities of things . . . [but with the modern nutrition science] we are now wholly dependent upon finding reliable external expertise and then trusting it. (2014, 390)*

Modern nutritional science has tried to move away from basing its knowledge on individuals' embodied sensory experiences to quantifiable chemical components, using the concepts of calories, vitamins, and minerals. This meant that scientific experts were now needed to tell people what was good to eat. Shapin points out that the rise of nutrition science accelerated the involvement of food industries and the state. He writes, "the involvement of business and the state means, on the one hand, that modern food choices are bound up with the increasingly concentrated enterprises concerned with producing and marketing food and with the authority of national and international government in regulating the food industry and in instructing food choice" (2014, 392).

What are the implications of shifting food expertise away from individuals to experts and the industry? The following sections examine two concepts that are central to the understanding of food under the influence of nutritionism: calories and micronutrients. The stories of calories and micronutrients help clarify the dynamics that Shapin identified—that the shift of power away from individual citizens to nutrition science has tended to empower scientific experts, corporations, and government regulators as the critical mediators for good eating.

Calories

One important parameter salient under nutritionism is the concept of the calorie. We are supposed to watch the caloric intake of food; many foods are marketed based on their caloric values (e.g., one-hundred-calorie packs of snacks, zero-calorie drinks), and consumers are frequently warned of hidden calories in cocktails and mocha frappuccinos. The calorie is one parameter Americans turn to in judging the virtues of the foods they eat and dietary behaviors.

According to Jessica Mudry's *Measured Meals: Nutrition in America* (2010), the concept of a calorie of food was popularized in the late nineteenth century. Wilbur Atwater, known as the father of American nutrition, brought back an early version of a calorimeter from Europe and started measuring caloric values of various food items. Multiple social factors were behind the growing role of the calorie in nutritional conscience. Describing foods in terms of their caloric values gave the emergent field of nutritional science an authoritative voice that could speak in neutral terms about the values of foods. Calories made everything commensurable—simplicity was important in the eyes of nutrition scientists who wanted to devise easy-to-understand dietary guides for the general public. Furthermore, calories enabled scientists to design economical meals. As mentioned earlier, turn-of-the-century dietary reform movements were focused on economic efficiency as the key to social stability and welfare. Atwater was keen on suggesting that people should not waste their money on expensive cuts of meat when cheaper foods could provide a similar amount of calories. For instance, he chastised consumers for buying beef sirloin when they could get the same calories and protein at a much cheaper price by buying cabbage.

Calories became central to the social understanding of different foods' values, but also increasingly dictated social understandings of the relationship between the human body and foods. As nutrition science developed an understanding of the calorimetric values of different foods, it also tried to quantify human calorie expenditure by different activities. This framework posited that the human body was something like a combustion engine: food as fuel to be used by a human body for different physical activities. Atkins, for instance, suggested that "muscular work like that of a carpenter" would require 3,500 calories, while his wife would need eight-tenths of that caloric intake.

Mudry summarizes the social function of calories as that of quantification and how they shaped dietary guidelines issued by the experts. She writes,

> *from the first guide published in 1917, numbers defined food, standards defined eaters, and measuring replaced eating. The food guides abstracted eating from tradition, history, and location. One did not eat because he or she enjoyed food; one ate to attain standards, to gain health through various nutrients, and to reach numeric goals so that he or she might consider himself or herself a complete eater. Certain foods were "good" or "bad" based on their numbers and their ability to help the eater achieve nutritional goals. (2010, 170).*

Calories continue to play a key role in dietary guidelines. The US Department of Agriculture's dietary guideline published in 2015 recommends that individuals "consume a healthy eating pattern that accounts for all foods and beverages within an appropriate calorie level." The appropriate level of calories is set for different ages, sex, and level of physical activity, categorized as sedentary/moderately active/active (see guidelines at https://health.gov/dietaryguidelines/2015/).

What are the drawbacks of a calorie-centric evaluation of food? Reductive focus on calories has often enabled corporations to market reduced-calorie foods as healthy; examples include zero-calorie soda and an assortment of low-calorie snacks. Furthermore, the model of food as an amalgam of quantifiable parameters like the calorie to be used as fuel is scientifically inadequate. For instance, there is increasing evidence that metabolism is much more complex than what is suggested by the energy balance model, which complicates the simplistic understanding of the rise of obesity as a result of excessive caloric intake. Recent studies suggest that weight gain is not simply a matter of surplus calories. You might eat exactly the same meal in terms of calories and micronutrients, but the body's uptake of nutrients might be influenced by the timing of the meal. Food might not be simply reducible to amounts of nutrients; it is necessary to think about interactions between our bodies and food and the uniqueness of each interaction.

Mudry ultimately concludes that quantification has been ineffective as the foundation for dietary guidelines. She writes, "Clearly, a discourse of quantification, as a communicative strategy, is an unquestionable failure. In other words, communication by quantification has not been able to link scientific, dietary advice with actual eating practices" (2010, 173). By quantifying food and eating in the language of science, other ways of talking about food that are rooted in culinary traditions and one's bodily sensations, including taste, became marginalized. She calls for "an alternative rhetoric of eating" with "a broader vocabulary, a different way of figuring food, and a new system of knowing and judging what to eat" (173).

In summary, the calorie is a good example of nutritionism's heavy reliance on quantifiable components and quantification in assessing the value of food. Nutritionism has facilitated the social acceptance of calories as one of the most essential parts of food and of the dietary advice that balancing calories leads to health and well-being. As Shapin pointed out, because regular consumers do not have reliable ways to measure the caloric value of food, the idea of calories increases their reliance on experts in ascertaining food's quality. Scientists, and increasingly corporations, too, claim the authority on defining what is good for you.

Micronutrients

Mudry's book was focused on calories and their historic rise in the social discourse on good eating, but there is an increasing emphasis on micronutrients (vitamins and minerals) as the marker of goodness of foods. Micronutrients are vitamins and minerals that are vital to the proper functioning of human bodies. Food's values are increasingly tied to their micronutrient makeup and to their specific contribution to human mental and physical performance.

Micronutrients can be added to various food products in the process of fortification. The fortification of foods such as wheat flour and milk (with vitamin D) has been conducted since the early twentieth century; more recent products are often categorized as *functional foods* or nutraceuticals. Since the 1990s, functional foods have been a powerful ally for the food industry. These foods tend to be marketed on the functional merits of particular micronutrient contents (e.g., a "good source of vitamin B12 for brain health"). As one might imagine, defining functional food is tricky. Would blueberries qualify as a functional food because of their antioxidants? Would cookies made with whole wheat flour be considered a functional food because of their higher content of micronutrients in comparison with cookies made from refined flour? Any food has some nutritional value. It seems fair to say that the idea of functional foods is defined not necessarily by any scientific basis, but rather by marketing claims and market potential. Whatever the definition, the hype has been real in business, as the market potential is said to be large. The global market for functional food is estimated to be billions of dollars in sales.

There are many drivers behind the growth of functional foods. Prevailing nutritionism that sees food as a vehicle of a set of nutrients is one; health consciousness of consumers heightened by an aging population is another. It is also important to situate functional food in the broader political economy of the food industry. Functional food is important as the food industry struggles with low profit margins and intense competition. By adding micronutrients and making functional claims, companies try to differentiate their products from that of their competitors to fetch higher margins than the generic products. They can also counter the criticism of junk food and empty calories typically waged against processed foods. The primary industry strategy has been to argue that "there is no bad food, there is only bad diet," pointing the finger at consumers' dietary choices rather than at their own unhealthy products. But with functional food, manufacturers can now proudly say that their products are "healthy." For instance, Pepsi introduced a fortified soda with added vitamins and minerals and marketed it as a good source of vitamins (although after a warning from the Food and Drug Administration, they had to drop the claim). Sugar-loaded cereals could be marketed as complete nutrition in terms of satisfying micronutritional requirements. Multinational corporations can now portray themselves as contributing to, rather than undermining, the nutritional health of the public.

The growth of functional food is a telltale sign of how nutritionism creates profitable opportunities for the food industry. By singling out limited sets of micronutrients and portraying foods as their carriers, nutritionism facilitates corporate positioning as the provider of good foods.

HIDDEN HUNGER IN THE GLOBAL SOUTH: CHARISMATIC NUTRIENTS AND NUTRITIONAL FIXES

Nutritionism and functional foods are relevant not only in advanced capitalist economies like the United States, but also in developing countries. Here, it is important to think about the growing attention in international development to micronutrient deficiencies, often dubbed **hidden hunger**. Micronutrient deficiencies refer to disorders caused by a lack of key micronutrients such as vitamin A deficiency, iron deficiency anemia, and iodine deficiency disorder. These disorders are said to affect millions, particularly women and children. They differ from traditional hunger, where calories and proteins are missing from the diet, but nonetheless have significant health consequences.

Reasons for hidden hunger are complex and layered. If people are poor, they tend to spend less on foods that are micronutrient-rich (such as meat, vegetables and eggs). People might not have access to land, water, and seeds to produce micronutrient-rich foods. Because parasites obstruct the absorption of micronutrients, sanitation in living and working conditions is also important.

Therefore, micronutrient strategies could include a variety of projects such as poverty reduction, improvement in public health and health care, nutrition education, and home gardening. However, since the 1990s, a popular strategy in international development has been fortification, or the addition of micronutrients at the site of food processing. Various development organizations from the Gates Foundation to the World Bank have funded fortified food projects in the global South.

Fortified foods are typically produced by multinational corporations with the capacity for manufacturing technology, facility, and quality control. For instance, fortified cookies and instant noodles that were distributed to the poor by the World Food Program in Indonesia in the late 1990s were made by Danone, a transnational food manufacturer. In India, anthropologist Alice Street (2015) observed that various multinational corporations are collaborating with international development organizations to tackle hidden hunger through fortified foods. Fortified food products targeted at the poor are made by Coca-Cola (Vitingo, a drink that is fortified with micronutrients) and PepsiCo (Lehar Iron Chusti, fortified cookies high in iron to combat iron deficiency anemia), among others. These products are normally bought by middle- and upper-class consumers, but companies also price them at lower prices and expand supply chains to rural areas in collaboration with international development organizations. These examples from Indonesia and India reflect a global trend wherein multinational food corporations play a growing role in anti–hidden hunger campaigns. In fact, various multinational food businesses such as Nestlé, Heinz, Ajinomoto, Dannon, Unilever, and Coca-Cola formed the Business Alliance for Food Fortification to promote food fortification in developing countries. They stated that food fortification is "one of the most promising interventions for improving the nutritional status of the world's poorest and should be the first area of focus" in nutrition policy. A similar network of multinational corporations established the Scaling Up Nutrition Business Network proclaiming to help tackle global malnutrition; their commitments under the network often involve food fortification in developing countries. The network's website features corporate-sponsored nutrition projects such as the Nourishing India project by multinational agribusiness company Cargill, which fortified cooking oil with vitamins (http://sunbusinessnetwork.org).

The international development community has generally embraced these collaborations with the global food industry to tackle hidden hunger. But this strategy treads a fine line between the further facilitation of growing transnational corporate power and public health interventions (Kimura 2013). The above example of marketing by multinational companies for fortified food products in India in collaboration with development agencies can be interpreted as corporate philanthropy, a partnership that is beneficial for aid agencies because of the corporations' prowess in marketing. Alternatively, it can be understood as facilitating the extension of corporate marketing to the untapped markets of rural and poor households. Reliance on these products can also be seen as problematic for its class biases. The array of products marketed as nutritional and functionally enhancing is only available to those who have disposable cash. While fortified food products sold in developing countries with public health mandates might be repackaged in a smaller pack that is affordable even to the rural poor, the corporate intention is that these "entry-level" consumers will eventually move on to the fully priced, more profitable products. For instance, Indonesia's first fortified food aid by the government was manufactured by a multinational food conglomerate, Indofood. In its annual report in 2003, Indofood stated that "one of our main challenges is the conversion of aid-related customers into the habit of buying our commercial brands as family incomes improve." Development organizations might not think that their antihunger campaigns are helping multinational corporations, but the corporations' ultimate loyalty is to stockholders, not to the poor in the global South.

Moreover, it is important to ask, While fortified foods do provide additional micronutrients, what issues are left unaddressed? As with the problem of food insecurity in general (see Lesson 13), hidden hunger in developing countries is fundamentally linked to poverty, inequality, and a lack of social power. Malnutrition is not necessarily about food per se, but about layers of social and economic issues. For instance, we must ask why people are displaced from farmland to produce nutritious vegetables, why their work does not provide enough income to purchase nutritious foods, why social networks have disrupted people's access to foods, or why some members in a household and community suffer from malnutrition more so than others. But nutritionism makes it difficult to address these fundamental causes of food insecurity because it is highly reductive—it sees the problem simply as a lack of some nutrients.

The sociological concepts that describe these dilemmas of fortification are **charismatic nutrients** and **nutritional fix** (Kimura 2013). Charismatic nutrients refer to nutrients that capture the attention of experts and the public symbolic of the nature of the world malnutrition problem. They serve as the emblems of the food and nutrition problem and its solution. These nutrients command center stage in international politics when their suboptimal intake defines the nature of the food problem in developing countries. For instance, fortification tends to revolve around a set of charismatic nutrients, such as iron and vitamin A.

Charismatic nutrients are a product of social and cultural forces as much as scientific discovery and progress or their potency in health improvement.

One of the important mechanisms of their social and cultural power is their amenability to quantification. By delimiting the food insecurity problem to the lack of a particular nutrient (the "problem is the deficiency of vitamin A/iron/iodine"), the food problem is rendered calculable for nutrition experts and international and domestic bureaucrats. Furthermore, we should historicize the appeal of quantification; it enables number-based representations of the food and nutrition problem (the "average person in this country is only getting 30 percent of the required vitamin A"). The neoliberal era increased the stakes for quantification, given the heightened urgency of accountability politics and evidence-based programming. In other words, development agencies and bureaucrats in developed countries who receive foreign/international aid and charitable foundations are under tremendous pressure to prove concrete outcomes and achievements, oftentimes in a short time frame. Charismatic nutrients enable experts to state that they produced a tangible output, such as X milligrams of iron delivered to X children under five years old. This concreteness and calculability are invaluable in international development, where nutritional experts must satisfy increasingly quantification-oriented parameters.

The power of charismatic nutrients in mobilizing international support is that their deficiency comes with a convenient **nutritional fix**—when protein was charismatic, experts formulated superprotein cookies; vitamin A supplements were said to be a magic golden bullet that was dirt cheap, according to nutrition scientists who focused on vitamin A's health benefits; and now, we have fortified products such as wheat flour and yogurt that are to add missing nutrients to the diets of Third World people. Charismatic nutrients help embody the problem, capturing experts with a compelling tangibility and the promise of an easy nutritional fix.

Another nutritional fix that has emerged alongside fortification is biofortification. Fortification is the addition of micronutrients to food products, but biofortification alters the crops themselves to have better nutritional composition. Perhaps the most famous example of biofortification is golden rice. Golden rice is genetically modified to contain higher levels of beta-carotene, a precursor to vitamin A. Other biofortification projects include genetically engineered bananas and cassava to combat vitamin A deficiency.

Developers and proponents have heralded golden rice as a savior of children who die from vitamin A deficiencies in the developing world. However, critics point out that golden rice only works when the dietary pattern is already quite healthy. Because beta-carotene is fat soluble, the general diet must have adequate fat for golden rice to be effective. Its adoption by farmers would also be a challenge because its yield is not on par with that of conventionally adopted rice varieties. It has also raised alarms because it is a genetically modified organism (see Lesson 6).

Biofortification typically focuses on a select set of nutrients—charismatic nutrients—as the key to micronutrient deficiencies. However, as in the case of fortified products, biofortification does not address the root causes of the problem. Hunger is a complex sociocultural problem, in addition to a nutritional problem, and its cause is not simply a lack of nutrients (see Lesson 13). Furthermore, critics have pointed out that biofortification projects function as a way to push for genetically modified organisms in the global South. Global adoption of genetically modified organisms has been rather uneven and multinational seed companies see future market potential in their wider social acceptance, deregulation, and adoption in developing countries.

Similar to ways in which women tend to be the target of food reforms in the United States, anti–hidden hunger campaigns also tend to target women. The World Food Program estimates 60 percent of the world's chronically hungry people are women and girls. Micronutrient deficiencies, particularly iron deficiency anemia, is marked as a women's disease because of women's menstruation and pregnancy. Therefore, hidden hunger projects are often celebrated as women-centered projects. But is providing fortified cookies and drinks really empowering for women? The gendered nature of nutritional status is not simply rooted in biology—it is an outcome of complex interactions among socioeconomic and cultural factors, including gendered access to education, labor markets, agriculture, and other food production; participation in decision-making; and the ability to receive health care, to name a few. Addressing these fundamental and systemic inequities would be more empowering in the long term. Nutritional fixes do not address these fundamental causes of malnutrition. Moreover, nutritionism limits the scope of societal discussion to what is in food rather than what shapes one's access to high-quality food.

Conclusion

Western nutrition science is profoundly mediating the relationship between people and food. This lesson has shown that nutrition science, like any other scientific field, is embedded in society. The social influences are most obvious in corporate power over nutrition research, but it is important to understand the more subtle forces that privilege certain social groups over others along class, race/ethnicity, and gender lines. More fundamentally, the lesson introduced the concept of nutritionism to make visible assumptions in contemporary views about foods. Nutritionism reduces the value of food to its quantifiable nutritional parameters, such as calories and micronutrients, and tends toward a myopic focus on charismatic nutrients, which then narrows nutrition policies to the provision of nutritional fixes, often diverting attention away from the broader and more structural causes of lack of access to nourishing foods. Nutritionism further facilitates the already strong tendency in neoliberalism of assigning responsibility for health and well-being to individuals. Diet-related problems, from malnutrition to overnutrition, are layered problems that involve the global economic system, ecological degradation, history of colonialism, and gender relations, among others. But through the myopic lens of nutritionism, food problems are reduced to how people eat, reframing the issue as a personal behavioral problem rather than systemic and structural.

Discussion Questions

1. Think about what you ate yesterday. How did you choose the foods and why? To what extent did the parameters from nutrition science— calories, vitamins, etc.—shape your choices? Why are they so compelling to you?

2. Social valuations of foods are influenced by nutrition science, which in turn is a product of a variety of social and historical forces. Can you think of different ways of relating to foods beyond nutritionism? In other words, can you appreciate the goodness of food not in terms of its calories or vitamins, but in terms of its contribution to biodiversity and the rural economy?

Exercises

1. Find articles from nutrition science journals on specific food items (blueberries, cranberries, cacao, etc.) and look for *conflict of interest* statements at the end of the articles. What industry organizations are funding what kinds of research? How are research conclusions reported in the media?

2. Pass packages of different foods among students. Ask them to rank the foods from best to worst individually. Then ask the students to form groups and discuss a ranking for the group. Have the groups present their rankings and explain the criteria behind their ranking process. This exercise is meant to elucidate different definitions of good foods (adapted from DuPuis 2015, Chap. 8).

Additional Materials

Films

   Fed Up (2013)

Websites

   US dietary guidelines from the Department of Agriculture, https://www.cnpp.usda.gov/dietary-guidelines

References

DuPuis, E. Melanie. 2015. *Dangerous Digestion: The Politics of American Dietary Advice*. Berkeley: University of California Press.

Kimura, Aya H. 2013. *Hidden Hunger: Gender and Politics of Smarter Foods*. Ithaca, NY: Cornell University Press.

Mudry, Jessica J. 2010. *Measured Meals: Nutrition in America*. New York: State University of New York Press.

Nestle, Marion. 2002. *Food Politics: How the Food Industry Influences Nutrition and Health*. Berkeley: University of California Press.

Scrinis, Gyorgy. 2013. *Nutritionism: The Science and Politics of Dietary Advice*. New York: Columbia University Press.

Shapin, Steven. 2014. "'You Are What You Eat': Historical Changes in Ideas about Food and Identity." *Historical Research* 87 (237): 377–92.

Street, Alice. 2015. "Food as Pharma: Marketing Nutraceuticals to India's Rural Poor." *Critical Public Health* 25 (3): 361–72.

PART 2

PRODUCING FOOD

Combine harvester and monoculture. (Photo © Martin Pettitt / Flickr / CC BY 2.0.)

5

The Industrialization of Agriculture

Douglas H. Constance

There is a story in my university education that goes like this: "If we divide Earth's history into one year, humans arrive in the last ten minutes of December 31st." We are a very recent arrival. After two million years living as hunter-gatherers, around 12,000 years before the present (YBP) we domesticated a narrow genetic range of plants and animals, which created food surpluses and thereby released many of us from dependence on daily hunting and gathering. Around 6,000 YBP the first cities emerged, followed by complex, centralized agricultural dynasties about 4,000 YBP. Three hundred years ago the Industrial Revolution replaced animal power with machines, generating even more food surplus, which made possible rapid population growth and urbanization. Trade and colonialism diffused industrial agriculture around the world. The agricultural and industrial revolutions transformed human existence from a world where all of us were food gatherers to a world where, in the industrialized countries, less than 1 percent of us are farmers.

The main point of this lesson is that **agricultural industrialization** is the current manifestation of long trends in agricultural **extensification** and **intensification**. Extensification is the process of extending farming to new lands; intensification is the process of increasing yields per acre on those lands. Increased yield enabled population growth and the division of labor, which contributed to social stratification and conflict over control of the surplus. Food surplus is the original source of power by humans over other humans. Civilization has been made possible because of agricultural surplus.

Therefore, it is important to study the archeology of this phenomenon to understand the sociological dimensions of changes in the agrifood system. In the sociology of agrifood literature, the relationship between the structure of agriculture and the quality of life for rural peoples is called the agrarian question (see Buttel and Newby 1980). My paternal grandfather was a rural postman; my maternal grandparents were Ozark farmers. Growing up, I wanted to know why their lives and communities changed so much. Rural sociology in general, and the sociology of agrifood in particular, answered my questions. This lesson provides a brief history of the development of agriculture, particularly the development of industrialized agriculture that dominates the agrifood system today.

The story of how the industrial agriculture system came to be begins about two million years ago with the Stone Age and humanoids using tools, but the more important part of the story begins with the geographically dispersed agricultural revolutions around 12,000 YBP (Lenski 1970). It is at this time that agricultural societies began to displace previous societal forms. Industrialization accelerated this trend into the bifurcated global agrifood system that we have today. On the one hand, most food today comes from a small number of very large producers linked to corporations in global supply chains. On the other hand, there continue to be a large number of small farmers producing for local consumption and/or alternative markets (Howard 2016). Although industrial agriculture produces more than enough food to feed the world, it is widely critiqued for its negative ecological, economic, and social impacts (Constance, Renard, and Rivera-Ferre 2014; Ikerd 2012; Magdoff, Foster, and Buttel 2000).

This lesson provides an overview of the progressive industrialization of agriculture. While the story of this societal progression is generally known in our culture, the specific aspects are contested, fractured, and fluid due to a lack of empirical evidence and regional variations. In full disclosure, the history presented in this lesson is biased toward both Eurocentric and critical interpretations. This lesson is divided into three major sections: from Paleolithic to Neolithic, the agriculture revolution, and industrial agriculture.

FROM PALEOLITHIC TO NEOLITHIC

The Paleolithic era begins about 2 million YBP with the advent of tool making and ends about 12,000 YBP with the advent of fishing, horticultural, and pastoral societies and the Neolithic era.[1] Around 40,000 YBP, protofarmers started to manipulate their environments to encourage the growth of plants and animals beneficial to them. These nascent fishers, horticulturalists, and pastoralists steadily displaced the hunter-gatherers. These new techniques of food provisioning based on the management of beneficial plants and animals generated the first major social revolution because it freed humans from the bondage of daily provisioning.

Horticulturalism first emerged in the Fertile Crescent region of the Middle East (wheat), northeast Africa (millet and sorghum), and then China and Southeast Asia (rice) where the conducive climates supported the harvesting of large cereal seeds. With new tools such as the hoe, stone sickles for harvesting, and mortar and pestle for grinding, horticultural societies based on the domestication of plants emerged. These gardening societies spread to Europe and emerged in Meso-America with the Mayans of the Yucatan (maize) and the Incas of Peru (potatoes) about 6,000 YBP. During this Neolithic—or horticultural—revolution, societies developed into complex

---

[1] This section draws heavily on Lenski (1970), with general background provided by *New World Encyclopedia* (2016); *Encyclopedia of Food and Culture* (2013); and Bellwood (2004).

systems with organized village life, craft specialization, metal smelting, trade and markets, religious centers, state structures, and increased militarism. Food surplus was diverted to feeding armies to war against neighbors, take their land, and enslave them. Scholars note an ethical regress in these societies as the rural is exploited to serve the agenda of emerging urban elites.

While horticultural societies developed in temperate and equatorial climates, pastoralism emerged in the arid climates suited for animal grazing. **Pastoralism** is based on the domestication of animals for transport, meat, dairy, and warfare. The Fertile Crescent is also the source of many domestic animals, including goats, sheep, camels, cows, and horses. Nomadic pastoralists often came into conflict as they sourced fresh grazing and water for their animals; the losers in these conflicts often became slaves. The nomadic lifestyle led to trade and the acquisition of more possessions. Pastoralists spread the surplus food from the horticulturalists, as well as the special seeds, breeds, and technologies, along the trade routes from China to Europe and North Africa.

Horticulturalism and pastoralism generated food surplus, which supported settlements and the accumulation of possessions. Settlements generated a more complex division of labor that allowed for distinct political, economic, and religious institutions, including war, slavery, and a steady transition from matriarchal to patriarchal societies.

THE AGRICULTURAL REVOLUTION

Multiple agriculture societies emerged simultaneously from advanced horticultural societies. The agriculture revolution in Mesopotamia (Iraq) in the Fertile Crescent region about 12,000 YBP is the best documented. These Neolithic farmers selected and bred cereal crops for large seed size and persistence on the stalk. Domesticated animals provided food, traction, and manure for fertilizer. Harvests were stored in granaries and surpluses traded. About 5,500 YBP, the first fully developed Neolithic society with permanent settlements emerged in Sumeria. Agriculture soon occupied the Nile region. By 5,000 YBP the wooden plow and irrigation systems were common.

Linking cereal cropping to animal power and manure fertilizers is the key component of the agricultural revolution and permanent field cultivation. Manure provided the soil fertility amendment and the plow, a technologically advanced hoe, buried weeds and brought fresh, fertile topsoil to the surface. The use of animal traction released more people from food production and thus contributed to further increases in the division of labor.

The increased yields allowed the unification of empires over large areas. Political organization emerged to guarantee the orderly transfer of food surplus from the rural peasants to the priests and urban elites, as well as the armies. A bifurcated world emerged made up of the governors/governed, urban/rural, opulence/subsistence, and literate/illiterate. Kingdoms conquered new territories to acquire more wealth (i.e., the harvest). The state function expanded to manage larger geographies and to control the food surplus through rents, tribute, taxes, and armies. These early agricultural societies were among the most stratified in history.

During the Middle Ages the Romans spread the innovations from the Fertile Crescent across its empire. They created a sophisticated irrigation, transportation, and trading system with regions dedicated to specific commodity production for export. Cows and oxen provided diary and draft functions; sheep and goats provided hides and cheese. A practical science of manure improved soil quality and increased yield. Roman law provided protections for Roman farmers, but the vast majority of agriculture was serf based.

As the Roman Empire declined, a new agricultural system emerged in Muslim countries based on extensive irrigation and a scientific approach to farming. This system included the use of technical manuals, production incentives based on private ownership, labor rights, and harvest sharing. New varieties of plants included sugar cane, citrus fruit, cotton, almonds, figs, and bananas. These innovations diffused from the Middle East to Europe, where fertile soils facilitated rapid development and enhanced food surplus. Through the Columbian exchange, European empires imposed this model on the New World through colonialism, extracting huge amounts of wealth.

The British Case

About 1,000 YBD the agricultural revolution matured in Europe, helped by its fertile soils, favorable climate, and Roman organization. The Dutch improved the Chinese iron-tipped plow and windmills drained the wetlands. Early agriculture was based on open fields, organized in long strips radiating from the village with some fields left fallow to regain fertility. By 1400, crop rotations and legume use for soil nitrogen were common practices. In the 1600s Flanders (Belgium) farmers adopted the Norfolk four-course rotation, which introduced turnips and clover grown in the fallow field, increasing fertility and providing winter feed for animals. These innovations were diffused to Britain where large collective holdings under the crown or church were managed by nobles and populated by peasants who farmed collectively using the open field system. This system restricted the yield gains of the four-course rotation system and longer-term agricultural innovation. The key to advancing agriculture in feudal Britain and Europe was the political enclosure of public lands—the commons—to consolidate fragmented lands into intensively managed fields and pastures. The serfs were expelled and yeoman farmers bought these private lands, which they then often rented back to displaced serfs. The state developed transportation infrastructure and a nationwide private market for trade. London rationalized and coordinated the agricultural surplus, nationally and globally. In the 1800s English agriculture had the highest yields in Europe and was the model of modern agriculture. Agricultural improvement associations organized to solve the **Malthusian**

crisis of population expanding faster than food production. Extensification brought new lands into production; intensification farmed it more efficiently. By the early 1800s almost all arable land in England was farmed.

The steam-powered textile industry of the 1700s was a main driver of England's Industrial Revolution. Textiles, along with iron and coal, fueled innovations. Stronger plows; threshing, reaping, and mowing machines; and synthetic fertilizers boosted yields. Railroads linked all of Great Britain in a national market. By the 1800s Great Britain oversaw a vast empire of colonies, which were first plundered of their precious metals and then provided agricultural goods back to Great Britain through slave plantations and smallholder farming. Colonialism spread the English model of trade, private property, currency, and law around the world. In an international division of labor, the English specialized in trade and banking and outsourced less efficient functions such as agriculture. Hence, modern agriculture was diffused to the United States and other settler states where many of the displaced peasants were immigrating, ready to escape serfdom and become landowning farmers.

THE GREAT TRANSFORMATION: THE PARADIGM SHIFT

The great transformation vastly changed European society (Polanyi 1944). The political, economic, and scientific revolutions of the eighteenth and nineteenth centuries set the stage for the industrialization of agriculture as democracies replaced monarchies, capitalism replaced feudalism, and science replaced religion as the source of knowledge. The rational application of science to agriculture increased technical innovations exponentially. Democracy, capitalism, and Protestantism provided the cultural innovations to diffuse new technologies.

Modern thought based on science dispelled the traditional belief in nature as magical and reduced it to machine-like components, which could be manipulated to serve society. Utilitarian philosophies provided a rationale for self-maximizing behavior as the basis of society. Social Darwinism provided a justification for colonialism and genocide by the "civilized" over the "primitive." A laissez-faire approach guided by the invisible hand of capitalism and comparative advantage dominated political economic policy. This paradigm shift in human thought and organization transformed the planet; agricultural modernization is a central part of this process.

Historically, innovative farmers and nobles trying to stave off Malthusian famine advanced agricultural innovation. Science combined industrialization with biology, physics, and chemistry to rationalize food production. Selective breeding based on Mendelian principles increased yields. Soil was reduced to its organic parts to squeeze more yield per acre; crop rotations, fertilization, irrigation, and pesticides removed the need for fallow fields. The metabolic cycle based on a proximity of animal manures and soil fertility and human food consumption was broken, replaced by inorganic fertilizers, allowing farm and field size to increase and cities to grow distant from food production (Foster 2000). Machines replaced draft animals for traction and the four-course rotation disappeared. Economies of scale led to larger fields, specialization, monoculture, and steady rural-to-urban migration. Industrial agriculture began in Europe and then was diffused to the settler colonies and throughout the world.

INDUSTRIAL AGRICULTURE

The United States has been at the forefront of the industrialization of agriculture (Perkins and Jamison 2008). Hence, the United States will be used to illustrate the ways that agriculture has become increasingly industrialized over time.

The Civil War marks the beginning of industrialization of US agriculture (Danbom 1979). In 1862 the US government implemented several actions to purposefully modernize agriculture. First, the US Department of Agriculture (USDA) was created to develop policies and implement programs to modernize agriculture. Second, the land-grant university (LGU) system was created to educate the common man, with special focus on innovative research, teaching, and extension of agricultural innovations. The Morrill Acts of 1862 and 1890 created the agricultural universities, the Hatch Act of 1887 created the research stations, and the Smith–Lever Act of 1914 created an extension service to diffuse the innovations. Lax government immigration policies provide a steady stream of industrial workers and prospective farmers. The Homestead Act of 1862 provided incentives for recent immigrants to move west, settle the plains, and become productive, land-owning farmer citizens. At this time, the government also subsidized the transcontinental railroad system to settle the country and move the food to the cities and manufactured goods to the frontier. Last, the army subdued the Native Americans to allow ordered development of the frontier.

After the Civil War, agricultural policy focused on both extensification and intensification. The scientific management of work (Taylor 1911) was applied to agriculture through both industry and the LGUs. Irrigation technologies brought new lands into production. The government supported agricultural industrialization and agribusiness with incentives and policies. The railroads linked it all together in commodity markets. By the late 1800s oligopolies and monopolies were common in the railroad, meatpacking, and grain industries (see Lesson 7). Populist farmers argued declining rural quality of life (i.e. rural poverty) was a result of the economic power of the agribusiness trusts. They called on the government to protect them from predatory market power. The result was the Packers and Stockyards Act of 1921, which curtailed the market power of the meatpacking oligopolies, and the Capper–Volstead Act of 1922, which allowed farmers to organize in cooperatives to gain countervailing power against agribusiness (Vogeler 1981).

In 1929, the Country Life Commission was created by industrial and other elites to counter grievances and legislative success of the populist farmers

(Danbom 1979). The commission maintained that rural social problems were a result of technological backwardness and not market power. President Theodore Roosevelt supported the conclusion and the LGUs mobilized to modernize rural America, with special focus on the Cooperative Extension Service. The American Farm Bureau Federation grew out of LGU cooperative extension activities as rural counties created farmer education *bureaus* to teach and support modern farming. During this time, a major role for rural social scientists was to conduct research to enhance the adoption of innovations to remove the barriers to the adoption of industrial agriculture.

Since World War II, and especially during the Cold War, the industrial approach dominated within US government policy and LGUs (Gilbert 2015). Hence, while there have been periodic efforts to promote more agrarian and populist forms of agriculture, since the Civil War there has been a concerted effort by the government, the LGU system, and business interests to industrialized US agriculture. This includes mechanization, chemification, selective breeding, genetic modification, confined animal feeding operations, and changes in farm structure and size. The following sections briefly examine each of these developments.

Mechanization

Mechanization proceeded most quickly in the family farms in the Midwest and Northeast. In 1834 the McCormick mechanical thresher was invented, followed by the mechanical reaper, which together became the combine. In 1837 John Deere invented the self-polishing steel plow, followed in 1853 with the two-row corn planter. Adoption of these horse-drawn technologies accelerated during the Civil War because of labor shortages and were widespread by the early 1900s. The Homestead Act of 1862 settled the Midwest and Great Plains and mechanization transformed the forests and prairies into fields and pastures.

Steam-powered machines emerged in the late 1800s but were initially too cumbersome for field work. The invention of the internal combustion engine increased field-level adoption of tractors, threshers, reapers, and other farm implements. The first gas tractors were invented in 1892, but adoption was slow because of costs and lack of agility in the field. During World War I Henry Ford mass-produced modern tractors; by the 1930s tractors and combines were widely adopted and they had replaced animal traction by the 1950s. Mechanization was key to expansion of the family-farm system. It eliminated the need for hired farmworkers and thereby allowed one family using modern equipment to farm more acres. As we will discuss, this has contributed to changes in farm size.

Chemification

Mechanization was the first phase of industrialization; it was followed by chemification (Perkins and Jamieson 2008). Early forms of chemical pest control based on biological extracts existed in the mid-1800s but were expensive and degraded quickly. Pesticides based on the toxicity of metals were developed in the late 1800s. In 1917 calcium arsenate was the first widely used synthetic pesticide to control the cotton boll weevil. However, these products were expensive and too costly at large scales. World War I provided a catalyst for the development of synthetic pesticides and fertilizers when chemical warfare technologies were applied to agriculture. After World War II, the chemical pesticide industry exploded as "killing by chemicals" became the mantra of scientific pest control in industry and the LGUs. It was at this time that "better living through chemistry" became a popular culture mantra. In 2012 pesticide usage in US agriculture totaled $9 billion and 1.1 million pounds annually (Atwood and Paisely-Jones 2017).

Fertilizers are the single largest use of chemicals on the farm. In 1910 the Haber–Bosch process to manufacture synthetic ammonia was industrialized by BASF of Germany for the war effort. The other two major fertilizers, phosphorus and potassium, are synthesized from minerals. The combination of chemical pesticides and fertilizers quadrupled the productivity of agricultural land. Chemification eliminated the need for crop rotations and cultural practices to manage fertility and pests. Combined with genetic uniformity in seeds, it allows specialization, monoculture, and the rationalized use of farmland, accelerating agricultural intensification. Data from the USDA reveal the steady increase in fertilizer and pesticide use on US farms (USDA 1954, 2012; see Table 5.1) .

Selective Breeding

Scientific plant and animal breeding are the next component of the industrial agriculture system. Scientific breeding is informed by Charles Darwin's work on genetic variation and natural selection. While early plant breeders in England had some success selecting new wheat varieties, they could not control their breeding outcomes because they did not understand the scientific basis of crossbreeding. In the 1870s Gregor Mendel, an Austro-Hungarian monk, identified a systematic pattern of pea crossbreeding that is the basis of modern plant and animal agriculture today. In the 1890s Liberty Hyde Bailey of Cornell University combined Darwin's focus on genetic variation with Mendel's theory of inheritance. Bailey (1906) coined the term *plant breeding*. At the same time Rowland Biffen at Cambridge University applied Mendel's theory to improve wheat strains in England. By the 1940s plant breeders knew how to select parents for heritable traits and fix those traits in the offspring. Sir Albert Howard of Cambridge University, the imperial economic botanist of England, developed special wheat varieties for India that are still in use today.

Agricultural universities and private seed companies expanded this process to develop hybrid seeds specially bred for yield, disease resistance, and compatibility with mechanical harvesting. Professor of agriculture Henry Wallace at Iowa State University developed the hybrid crossbreeding technique on corn. He saw hybrid corn as a means of producing bountiful crops at low prices to feed masses. In 1926 he founded Pioneer Hy-Bred Corn Company, later renamed Hi-Bred Seed Company and now owned by DuPont Chemical Company. Wallace became the secretary of agriculture and vice president of the United States. In 1940, about 30 percent of the corn crop was hybrid; by 1960 that figure was 96 percent. The hybrid breeding technology was extended to other grain, forage, fruit, and vegetable crops. Contrary to open-pollinated varieties, hybrid plants do not breed true so farmers cannot save their seeds for next year's crop, but instead have to buy new seeds each year (Cummins and Ho 2005).

Genetically Modified Organisms

The development and commercialization of genetically modified organisms (GMOs) is the fastest technological revolution that has ever occurred in agriculture (Falkner 2009; Williams 2009). The GMO technology began in 1973 with the development of a recombinant DNA technique, which enables foreign genes to be inserted into organisms to enhance desired traits or suppress undesired traits. A US Supreme Court ruling in 1980 allowed intellectual property rights for living organisms, which prompted rapid investment and growth of the industry (see Lesson 6).

In agriculture, GMOs can be traced to a Rockefeller Foundation–sponsored project in the 1980s developed in response to the shortcomings of the green revolution: unsustainable water use, growing rural inequality, land degradation, pesticide resistance, and persisting hunger. The purpose was to apply transgenic molecular biology to seed package development to produce healthier and more food on less land with fewer negative environmental impacts. The first commercial GMO activity occurred in the United States with the production of canola, corn, cotton, soybeans, and tomatoes in the 1990s. The vast majority of GMO crops are of two types: BT (*Bacillus thuringiensis*; e.g., BT corn/BT cotton), with genetic coding for an insect toxin, and HR (herbicide resistant), with genetic coding for herbicide tolerance (e.g., Roundup Ready soybeans). While other crops are being developed, the high cost of research, development, and certification for each crop, combined with societal resistance, has limited the diffusion.

Despite the initial success in the United States, GMOs have encountered serious resistance in key markets and have been increasingly regulated around the world. On the one hand, proponents view GMOs as the next in a long line of beneficial and safe agricultural technologies that can sustainably feed the world through intensive monoculture. They frame GMOs as contributing to environmental sustainability through the more efficient use of resources such as reduced pesticide use, reduced water use, and increased yields. These ecoefficiencies lead to increased food security—feeding the world. On the other hand, opponents point out the environmental, health, and community risks, while supporters emphasize economic efficiency, environmental sustainability, and food security (Shiva 1997).

Industrial Animal Production: Confined Animal Feeding Operations

The industrialization of animal agriculture followed a similar pattern as crop agriculture. Selective breeding specialized different species according to traction, meat, dairy, and/or fiber textile breeds to serve different functions. In the 1930s vitamin D was synthesized, allowing animals to be grown indoors. Starting with the poultry industry, confinement housing and specialized feeds were developed by industry and the LGUs. Livestock farming transformed from small to moderate-sized, family-owned, diversified operations to large confined animal feeding operations (CAFOs), often directly owned by or contractually linked to major agribusiness integrators. Such CAFOs are now the preferred model of intensive, industrialized animal production, including dairy, veal, beef, eggs, broiler chickens, turkeys, and hogs. The model has now also extended into aquaculture for shrimp and various fish species.

The CAFOs are the physical manifestation of animal intensification based on the principles of scientific management. Scientific management rationalizes the production system to achieve maximum efficiency. They are also a prime example of the **McDonaldization** of society based on efficiency, calculability, predictability, and nonhuman forms of control (Ritzer 2014). Confinement inside a specially designed enclosure minimizes environmental uncertainty and allows maximum control of the factors of production. Specialized genetics is matched to specialized feed rations with constant phytosanitary and animal health oversight. Today, most meat is produced intensively in CAFOs, as part of agribusiness vertical integration systems. This model is diffused around the world (extensification) as part of the globalization of the agrifood system (Heffernan 2000). Although CAFOs are very efficient regarding production, they are problematic regarding the environmental, community, public health, and animal welfare impacts (Imhoff 2010).

Farm Structure

The industrialization of agriculture has greatly affected the structure of the farming sector in the United States. There have been significant changes in both farm size and ownership over time. In the United States, there has been a decline in the number of farmers and an increase in the size of farms over time (see Table 5.1). The number of farms has declined from a high of about 6.5 million in 1920 (farm numbers peaked at 6.8 million in 1935) to about 2.1 million in the 2000s. Over time we also see a change in farm size. The number of small and very large farms continues to expand while the medium-sized farms decline in numbers. Ninety-seven percent of US farms are family farms, with 88 percent of those farms classified as small, with agricultural sales of less than $350,000 (see Table 5.2). These small family farms cover about 50 percent of the farmland. However, they only account for 20 percent of agricultural sales and generate about 3 percent of net farm income. In contrast, while large family farms ($1 million or more in sales) make up only 3 percent of farms and 20 percent of farmland, they account for 45 percent of sales and 56 percent of farm income. Non–family farms make up 3 percent of farms, 16 percent of sales, and

Table 5.1 Census Data on Farm Structure: 1850 to 2012

All farms	2012	2002	1992	1982	1969	1954	1920	1850
Farms (no.)	2,109,303	2,128,982	1,925,300	2,240,976	2,730,250	4,782,416	6,448,343	1,449,073
Land in farms (acres)	915,527,657	938,279,056	945,531,506	986,796,579	1,062,892,501	1,158,191,511	955,883,715	293,560,614
Average farm size (acres)	434	441	491	440	389	242	148	202
Farms by size								
1 to 9 acres	223,634	179,346	166,496	187,665	161,111	484,291		
10 to 49 acres	589,549	563,772	387,711	449,252	473,465	1,212,831		
50 to 179 acres	634,047	658,705	584,146	711,652	1,001,706	1,817,172		
180 to 499 acres	346,038	388,617	427,648	526,510	726,363	945,944		
500 to 999 acres	142,555	161,552	186,387	203,925	215,659	191,697		
1,000 to 1,999 acres	91,273	99,020	101,923	97,395	91,039	130,481Com-		
2,000 acres or more	82,207	77,970	70,989	64,577	59,907	bined		
Market value of agricultural product ($1,000)	394,644,481	200,646,355	162,608,334	131,900,223	45,563,891	24,644,727		
Average per farm ($1,000)	187,097	94,245	84,459	58,858	16,689	5,153		
Farms by value of sales								
Less than $10,000	1,188,977	1,263,052	806,517	1,096,337	1,778,985	4,197,380		
$10,000 to $49,999	397,872	414,063	496,158	589,082	896,159	582,948		
$50,000 to $99,999	129,366	140,479	187,760	251,501	Combined	Combined		
$100,000 to $499,999	232,955	240,746	286,951	274,580	47,916	N/A		
$500,000 or more	155,178	70,652	46,914	27,800	4,079	N/A		
Farms by legal status								
Family or individual	1,828,946	1,909,598	1,653,491	1,945,639	N/A	N/A		
Partnership	137,987	129,593	186,806	223,274				
Corporation	106,716	73,752	72,567	59,792				
Other (coop/estate/trust and institutional, etc.)	35,654	16,039	12,436	12,271				
Selected farm production expenses ($1,000)								
Total	328,939,354	173,199,216	130,779,261	N/A	37,559,615	N/A		
Purchased feed	75,706,467	31,694,850	24,084,507	18,592,984	7,082,272	3,906,048		
Fertilizers/soil amendments	28,532,713	9,751,460	8,204,324	7,689,365	2,209,185	N/A		
Fuels	16,573,188	6,675,419	6,120,452	7,888,052	1,906,579	1,366,244		
Hired labor	26,986,669	18,588,446	12,961,639	8,441,180	3,375,203	2,279,247		
Interest expense	12,123,573	9,571,577	8,111,337	11,668,942	N/A	N/A		
Chemicals	16,459,840	7,608,921	6,133,705	4,282,213	908,036	N/A		

Source: USDA 1954; 2012.

Table 5.2 Profile of US Farm by Type, 2012

	US total	Family farms, small	Family farms, medium	Family farms, large	Non–family farms
		Percentage Total of United States			
No. of farms	2.1 million	88	6	3	3
Farmland acres	915 million	48	20	20	11
Value of land and buildings	$2.3 trillion	47	20	25	8
Agricultural sales	$396.6 billion	20	19	45	16
Net farm income	$78.6 million	5	26	56	13

Source: USDA/NASS 2012.

12 percent of income. As the data indicate, there is a trend toward a bi-furcated system of a large number of small farms accounting for a small percentage of production and a small percentage of large farms accounting for a large percentage of production.

The USDA data also show that there has been significant intensification of US farming over time. Although the number of acres of farmland has slowly decreased, the market value of agricultural products has increased signifi-cantly, almost doubling between the 2002 and 2012 censuses. We also see major increases in chemical, fertilizer, and fuel expenses from 1969 to 2012. Notice that fertilizer expenses tripled, while chemical and fuel expenses more than doubled between 2002 and 2012 (see Table 5.1).

Conclusion

Agriculture in the United States has been characterized by a tension be-tween two competing visions (Thompson 2010). One path is informed by agrarian ethics and the other by industrial ethics. The agrarian ethic views agriculture as a special social structure with associated norms that creates virtuous citizens with substantive values resulting in enhanced quality of life (see Berry 1978). Jeffersonian agrarianism creates a culture of agriculture based on middle-class people who know the value of hard work and community service. These diversified family-farm operations provide ecosystem services to planetary sustainability. The industrial ethic views agriculture as just another commodity sector whose role is to efficiently produce food inputs for the industrial world. From the industrial view, any negative externalities can be corrected with science and technology. Nature and agriculture should be reduced to their com-ponent parts and managed scientifically to maximize production for the public good.

As this lesson illustrates, much of agriculture in the United States has become industrialized. Industrial agriculture technologies and practices have also been exported to much of the world via the green revolution, a set of initiatives aimed at modernizing agriculture in the global South beginning in the 1950s (see Lesson 6). The result is a global food and agriculture system that is increasingly industrialized. Industrialized agriculture is highly productive, and today there is more food than ever before. This has benefited consumers in many parts of the world in that food is often cheaper. However, industrial agriculture has also had many negative impacts and faces significant criticism as a result. These criticisms of industrial agriculture can be organized around four key questions: the environmental question, the agrarian question, the food question, and the emancipatory question (Constance 2008; Constance, Renard, and Rivera-Ferre 2014).

The environmental question asks, What is the relationship between industrial agriculture and the quality of the environment? The answer is that large-scale, chemical-intensive, productivist, monoculture agriculture has a negative relationship with the environment, which it extracts wealth from and externalizes costs to in the forms of soil, water, air, and species degradation (see Lesson 12; see Carson 1962). Environmental sociology and political ecology emerged as critical alternative analytical frameworks to the dominant natural resource management perspectives (Buttel 1987), rekindling an old debate between the conservationists and the preservationists. This research documented how industrial agriculture was unsustainable ecologically. The state responded to social movement pressure with soil conservation programs (Soil Conservation Service/Natural Resources Conservation Service), chemical regulation of agriculture by the government (US Environmental Protection Agency), and the organic and sustainable agriculture programs (US National Organic Program, US Department of Agriculture/Sustainable Agriculture Research & Education). The previously contested but now generally accepted realization that the industrial agrifood system is a primary contributor to greenhouse gas emissions, and global warming is damning evidence of this relationship.

The agrarian question asks, What is the relationship between industrial agriculture and the quality of life for farmers and rural communities? The answer is that as industrial agriculture increases, the quality of life in rural areas decreases (Lobao and Stofferahn 2008; Magdoff, Foster, and Buttel 2000). Studies on the relationship between farm structure and rural quality of life conducted by anthropologist Walter Goldschmidt (1947) concluded that middle-class, family-farm systems of agriculture contributed to a higher community quality of life than industrial systems based on large-scale, absentee-ownership, and hired labor. Specifically, family-farm systems of agriculture create a more vibrant community system that generates social capital, community attachment, and socioeconomic development. As agriculture becomes more industrialized, there is a weakening of community attachment and a transfer of wealth from the producer to the corporate shareholder, decreasing the quality of life in rural areas.

The Goldschmidt findings are supported by more recent research (Lobao and Stofferahn 2008; Lyson 2004).

The next question is the food question, which asks, What is the relationship between the industrial food and agriculture system and the quality of food we eat? The answer is that the dominant food system is characterized by an industrial diet of unhealthy *pseudofood* commodity chains centered on fats, sugars, starches, salt, and empty calories (Winson 2013; see Lesson 3). This system leads to heart disease, diabetes, obesity, *Escherichia coli* contamination, mad cow disease, *Salmonella* outbreaks, and burgeoning public health crises. It also includes moral economy concerns about the quality of life of food animals produced in confinement facilities. Similarly, this question deals with the quality of life of agricultural workers on the farms and in the processing plants. Importantly, as part of the *food from somewhere* movement, the food question brings consumers into the discourse who are demanding a healthier agrifood system with quality control mechanisms to certify the health and safety of the food we eat (Wright and Middendorf 2008; see Lesson 1).

Finally, the emancipatory question asks, What is the relationship between the industrial agrifood system and civil rights and social justice for all actors in the system? The answer is that the industrial agriculture privileges the market over civil society, which marginalizes the rights of the majority of the people, cultures, and animals on the planet (Allen 2008; see Lesson 20). There are disturbing race, class, and gender dimensions to the agrifood precariat, especially related to migrant farmworkers (Gertel and Sippel 2014). More recently, the ascending corporate rights framework of neoliberal free trade coordinated by global governance organizations, such as the World Trade Organization, is further exacerbating inequalities associated with food and agriculture.

Discussion Questions

1. The industrialization of agriculture has largely focused on increasing productivity (i.e., intensification). Can industrial technologies and practices be used for other purposes, such as increasing the nutritional content of food or lessening environmental impacts? Is industrialization a good approach for meeting these other objectives?
2. Do the benefits of the industrialization of agriculture outweigh the costs? Why or why not?
3. Can we feed the world's population through nonindustrialized forms of agriculture?

Exercise

Pick a crop or form of livestock and research the ways that its production has been industrialized. This may include the ways that it has been mechanized, selectively bred, genetically modified, treated with chemicals, etc. Answer the following questions: (1) What are the benefits of such industrialization? (2) What have been the costs of such industrialization? (3) In your opinion, do the benefits outweigh the costs? Why or why not?

Additional Materials

Readings

Elwell, F. 1999. "The Industrialization of Agriculture." http://www.faculty. rsu.edu/users/f/felwell/www/Theorists/Essays/Berry1.html

McKenzie, S. 2007. *A Brief History of Agriculture and Food Production: The Rise of Industrial Agriculture.* Baltimore: Johns Hopkins University. https:// www.saylor.org/site/wp-content/uploads/2015/07/ENVS203-7.3.1-ShawnMackenzie-ABriefHistoryOfAgricultureandFoodProduction-CCBYNCSA.pdf

Films

Food Inc.
Supersize Me

Websites

The Meatrix, http://www.themeatrix.com/
National Farmers Union, https://nfu.org/
Rural Foundation Advancement International, http://rafiusa.org/
National Center for Appropriate Technology, https://www.ncat.org/

References

Allen, P. 2008. "Mining for Justice in the Food System: Perceptions, Practices, and Possibilities." *Agriculture and Human Values* 25:157–61.

Atwood, D., and Paisely-Jones, C. 2017. *Pesticides Industry Sales and Usage: 2008–2012 Market Estimates.* Washington, DC: US Environmental Protection Agency.

Bailey, L. H. 1906. *Plant Breeding: Six Lectures upon the Amelioration of Domestic Plants.* New York: Macmillan.

Bellwood, Peter. 2004. *First Farmers: The Origins of Agricultural Societies.* Malden, MA: Blackwell.

Berry, W. 1978. *The Unsettling of America: Culture and Agriculture.* San Francisco: Sierra Club Books.

Buttel, F. H. 1987. "New Directions in Environmental Sociology." *Annual Review of Sociology* 13:465–88.

Buttel, F. H., and Newby, H. 1980. *The Rural Sociology of Advanced Societies: Critical Perspectives.* Montclair, NJ: Allenheld, Osmun.

Carson, R. 1962. *Silent Spring.* Boston: Houghton Mifflin.

Constance, D. H. 2008. "The Emancipatory Question: The Next Step in the Sociology of Agrifood Studies." *Agriculture and Human Values* 25:151–55.

Constance, D. H., Renard, M. C., and Rivera-Ferre, M., eds. 2014. *Alternative Agrifood Movements: Patterns of Convergence and Divergence.* Bingley, UK: Emerald Group.

Cummins, J., and Ho, M. W. 2005. "Hybrid Seed." *Science in Society Archive.* February 9, 2005. http://www.i-sis.org.uk/hybridSeed.php

Danbom, D. B. 1979. *The Resisted Revolution: Urban America and the Industrialization of Agriculture, 1900–1930.* Ames: Iowa State University Press.

Encyclopedia of Food and Culture. 2013. "Agriculture since the Industrial Revolution." Accessed November 12, 2016. http://www.encyclopedia.com/plants-and-animals/agriculture-and-horticulture/agriculture-general/agriculture-industry

Falkner, R. 2009. "The Troubled Birth of the 'Biotech Century': Global Corporate Power and Its Limits." In *Corporate Power and Global Agrifood Governance*, edited by J. Clapp and D. Fuchs, 226–51. Cambridge, MA: MIT Press.

Foster, John Bellamy. 2000. *Marx's Ecology: Materialism and Nature*. New York: Monthly Review Press.

Gertel, J., and Sippel, S. R., eds. 2014. *Seasonal Workers in Mediterranean Agriculture: The Social Costs of Eating Fresh*. London: Earthscan, Routledge.

Gilbert, J. 2015. *Planning Democracy: Agrarian Intellectualism and the Intended New Deal*. New Haven, CT: Yale University Press.

Goldschmidt, W. 1947. *As You Sow*. Glencoe, IL: Free Press.

Heffernan, W. D. 2000. "Concentration of Ownership in Agriculture." In *Hungry for Profit: The Agribusiness Threat to Farmers, Food, and the Environment*, edited by F. Magdoff, J. B. Foster, and F. H. Buttel, 61–76. New York: Monthly Review Press.

Howard, P. H. 2016. *Concentration and Power in the Food System: Who Controls What We Eat?* New York: Bloomsbury.

Ikerd, J. 2012. *The Essentials of Economic Sustainability*. Sterling, VA: Kumarian Press.

Imhoff, D., ed. 2010. *The CAFO Reader: The Tragedy of Industrial Animal Factories*. Berkeley: Foundation for Deep Ecology.

Lenski, G. 1970. *Human Societies: A Macrolevel Introduction to Sociology*. New York: McGraw–Hill.

Lobao, L., and Stofferahn, C. 2008. "The Community Effects of Industrialized Farming: Social Science Research and Challenges to Corporate Farming Laws." *Agriculture and Human Values* 25 (2): 219–40.

Lyson, T. 2004. *Civic Agriculture: Reconnecting Farm, Food, and Community*. Medford, MA: Tufts University Press.

Magdoff, F., Foster, J. B., and Buttel, F. H., eds. 2000. *Hungry for Profit: The Agribusiness Threat to Farmers, Food, and the Environment*. New York: Monthly Review Press.

New World Encyclopedia. 2016. "History of Agriculture." Accessed November 21, 2016. http://www.newworldencyclopedia.org/entry/History_of_agriculture

Perkins, J., and Jamieson, R. 2008. "History, Ethics, and Intensification in Agriculture." In *The Ethics of Intensification*, edited by P. Thompson, 59–83. Dordrecht, the Netherlands: Springer.

Polanyi, K. 1944. *The Great Transformation: The Political and Economic Origins of Our Time*. Boston: Beacon Press.

Ritzer, D. 2014. *The McDonaldization of Society*. Thousand Oaks, CA: Sage.

Shiva, Vandana. 1997. *Biopiracy: The Plunder of Nature and Knowledge*. Cambridge, MA: South End Press.

Taylor, F. W. 1911. *The Principles of Scientific Management*. New York: Harper & Brothers.

Thompson, P., ed. 2010. *The Ethics of Intensification: Agricultural Development and Social Change*. New York: Springer.

USDA (US Department of Agriculture). 1954. "Chapter 1: Farms and Land in Farms." Accessed November 21, 2016. https://www2.census.gov/prod2/decennial/documents/21895591v2ch02.pdf

USDA (US Department of Agriculture). 2012. "Historical Highlights: 1987 and Earlier Years." Accessed November 21, 2016. https://www.agcensus.usda.gov/Publications/2012/

USDA/NASS (US Department of Agriculture, National Agriculture Statistics Service). 2012. "Small Farms." ACH12-34. September 2016. https://www.agcensus.usda.gov/Publications/2012/Online_Resources/Highlights/SmallFamilyFarms.pdf

Vogeler, I. 1981. *The Myth of the Family Farm: Agribusiness Dominance in U.S. Agriculture.* Boulder, CO: Westview Press.

Williams, M. 2009. Feeding the World: Transnational Corporations and the Promotion of Genetically Modified Food. In *Corporate Power and Global Agrifood Governance*, edited by J. Clapp and D. Fuchs, 155–86. Cambridge, MA: MIT Press.

Winson, A. 2013. *The Industrial Diet: The Degradation of Food and the Struggle for Healthy Eating.* New York: New York University Press.

Wright, W., and Middendorf, G., eds. 2008. *The Fight over Food: Producers, Consumers, and Activists Challenge the Global Food System.* University Park: Pennsylvania State University Press.

Engineers from the US Department of Agriculture adjusting wireless infrared thermometers. (Photo: US Department of Agriculture / Flickr / CC BY 2.0)

6

Science, Technology, and Agriculture

Leland L. Glenna and Daniel Tobin

S cientists, politicians, and development specialists have long promoted agricultural science and technology as the solution to food shortages around the world. Over the past few decades, many of these commentators have expanded the problem-solving promises of science and technology to include social and economic problems, such as poverty. For example, a 2005 Consultative Group for International Agricultural Research Consortium report stated that for small farmers, the "chances of rising out of poverty depend directly on their ability to increase the productivity of their crop and livestock husbandry activities" (Harris and Orr 2014, 84). And the Bill and Melinda Gates Foundation (2008)—a prominent funder of agricultural science and technology research and outreach—claims that improving science and technology will "boost the yields and incomes of small farmers in Africa and other parts of the developing world so that they can lift themselves and their families out of hunger and poverty."

Embedded in many of the promises to increase food security and end poverty through science and technology is the use of markets and private firms to generate and diffuse agricultural science and technological outputs. Efforts to commercialize agricultural science and technology through public–private partnerships or even through the outright privatizing of government or university laboratories, according to this rationale, will reduce public expenditures while yielding greater efficiencies and, hence, greater social welfare.

The emphasis on agricultural science and technology as a way to solve problems is seductive because there are historical examples of advanced scientific research and technologies leading to higher productivity and increased wealth. Applications of improved crop seeds and animal breeds, the introduction of synthetic crop inputs, and advancements in agricultural machinery in the United States, Japan, and western Europe during the middle decades of the twentieth century led to dramatic increases in farm productivity, which were part of the industrialization in agriculture and manufacturing in those countries. Furthermore, these countries experienced substantial economic growth as they industrialized. The same scientific research that fueled **agricultural industrialization** in those advanced nations was later extended to developing nations beginning in the 1960s in what came to be known as the green revolution, which is often credited with saving a billion people from starvation.

Although these examples could lead one to conclude that agricultural science and technology are driving social and economic improvements, a closer examination reveals that this perspective is too simplistic. Portraying science and technology as offering the means to overcome obstacles to social progress is an example of **technological determinism**, the idea that culture and society develop around technological advancements. An alternative, sociological perspective is that scientific research and new technologies emerge in particular social contexts. As new technologies are adopted into society, they often have both negative and positive impacts on different social groups, and their impacts tend to be mediated by a range of social factors, such as access to roads and other infrastructure, markets, and adequate information, as well as the development of favorable government policies.

In this lesson, we will review the varied social impacts of some prominent applications of agricultural science and technology. We will pay close attention to the social contexts that affect and are affected by these prominent applications. These highlighted lessons will then be used to point to some ways that agricultural science and technology could be used to improve societal well-being.

TOMATO HARVESTER

Through much of the twentieth century, the US government and private firms sought to maximize agricultural production through the application of new machinery and improved crop varieties with the goal of lowering food prices for the urban workers in manufacturing sectors. However, many farmers resisted these efforts to industrialize agriculture because they recognized that higher yields would likely lead to lower agricultural commodity prices. Cochrane (1993) refers to this phenomenon as the **technology treadmill** because producers must always strive to produce more just to keep up, but they never quite move forward. That is, implementing new technologies to increase efficiency is critical to remaining competitive, but the required investments can make farmers vulnerable to debt. As a result, one consequence of pursuing maximum efficiency through the application of new science and technology to enhance production has been a decline in farm numbers. After farm numbers peaked at 6.8 million in 1935 in the United States, the number of farmers dropped as productivity increased. Just 2.1 million farms remain as of 2013. However, even that number overstates the relevance of many farmers. According to a recent analysis of the US Census of Agriculture, approximately 10 percent of farmers, mostly mid-sized and large farms (farms with revenues of $350,000 or more), account for about 74 percent of the value of agricultural production (Hoppe 2014).

Because these new technologies and techniques often lead to a decline in labor needs, they are typically referred to as labor-saving technologies. Perhaps the most controversial of these labor-saving technologies was the tomato harvester in California. The adoption of the technology corresponded with the termination of the *bracero* program, a program that brought an influx of Mexican laborers into California and consistently undermined farmworker efforts to organize. The new tomato technologies, created by professors at the University of California, Davis (UCD), had dramatic effects on farmworkers. In 1962, there were fifty thousand farmworkers in California. By 1964, they had been replaced by 1,152 machines and only eighteen thousand laborers ran the machines, a net loss of thirty-two thousand jobs (Rogers 2003).

This case is relevant for this lesson, not just because a labor-saving technology reduced the need for labor, but also because a coalition of students and professors at UCD and a public-interest law firm filed a lawsuit against UCD, arguing that this case represented the application of scientific research that undermined the public good. The claim was that a land-grant university was obligated to contribute to the public good when, in fact, it had done the opposite. Land-grant universities were created in the United States through the 1862 and 1890 Morrill Acts, which granted land to states to establish and to endow higher-education institutions with the expressed purpose of promoting scientific and technological advancements in agricultural and manufacturing to enhance social welfare. Each state in the United States has at least one land-grant university today. Subsequent legislation to the Morrill Acts has also included several historically African American and Native American colleges and universities in the list of land-grant universities. Although the plaintiffs won the initial case against UCD, the decision was later overturned on appeal (Friedland 1991). Despite the ultimate demise of the effort to hold universities accountable for the social impacts of their research and extension efforts, the case indicates that the application of science and technology in agriculture can be contentious.

Our goal is not to take sides in the debate, but rather to highlight how evaluating the social and economic impacts of agricultural science and technologies is complex and open to debate. United States citizens tend to pay a low share of their income for food as a result of an agricultural system that is productively efficient. However, these consumer benefits have not come without social and economic costs and disruptions. The costs are further exacerbated after considering that the US government has invested in many farm subsidization policies to slow the dramatic decline in farm numbers. The point, however, is not to say that the drive to maximize production is inherently bad, but rather to clarify that agricultural science and technology applications may bring some benefits, as well as social, financial, and environmental costs.

GREEN REVOLUTION

Even more widespread have been the impacts of the scientific innovations and technologies associated with the green revolution. Concerns that food production could not meet the demand of a growing global population prompted scientists to breed new, high-yielding crop varieties of staple cereals (e.g., wheat, rice, and maize). Originally led by Norman Borlaug, a plant breeder from the United States, the green revolution started with wheat production in Mexico in the 1940s. A plant breeder is a scientist who selects for or crosses two related varieties to produce a new variety that contains desirable traits. Through these techniques, plant breeders developed semidwarf varieties of wheat and rice (i.e., varieties with short stems so that they do not fall over under the weight of their grain) that were subsequently planted by farmers throughout Latin America and Asia. The impact on productivity was impressive: estimates indicate that yields in developing countries between 1960 and 2000 increased by 208 percent for wheat, 109 percent for rice, and 157 percent for maize (Pingali 2012). These yield increases helped stave off food shortages for millions in countries like Mexico, India, and Pakistan. Borlaug was awarded the Nobel Peace Prize in 1970 for his role in initiating and promoting the green revolution.

Although the new varieties developed for the green revolution constituted an important technological innovation, their success was tied to additional inputs necessary to maximize production, including fertilizer, pesticides, mechanization, and irrigation. As farmers adopted green revolution seeds, they increased their use of these inputs substantially. For example, across Asia, rates of fertilizer use rose more than 10 percent between 1967 and 1982 in Bangladesh, China, India, Indonesia, Myanmar, Nepal, and Pakistan (Rosegrant and Hazell 2000). Herbicide and pesticide use also expanded dramatically, often because those inputs were subsidized (Pingali 2012). In the 1970s, Mexico experienced a more than 8 percent increase in pesticide usage (Paalberg 2010). Environmental consequences accompanied the use of these inputs. As Evenson and Gollin (2003) assert, the green revolution exacerbated soil degradation, water pollution, declining water tables, and soil salinity. The yield benefits of green revolution seed varieties also encouraged monoculture (i.e., planting only one or a few varieties), thereby eroding biodiversity and ecosystem health (Zeigler and Mohanty 2010).

The unintended consequences of the green revolution also included social problems. Regions with ideal ecological, agronomic, and economic conditions were more likely to benefit from the new crop varieties than those regions without. For example, the benefits of the green revolution largely bypassed sub-Saharan Africa due to a poorly developed market infrastructure and a mismatch between the green revolution varieties and the crops commonly grown there. Even in countries where the green revolution technologies were appropriate, poorer farmers who did not enjoy the same access to credit, inputs, and government support as wealthier farmers struggled to take advantage of these new technologies (Pingali 2012; Zeigler and Mohanty 2010). Evidence also indicates that the green revolution technologies, which favored intensive agricultural production systems, contributed to the diminished viability of smallholder farmers. This often led unviable smallholders to migrate in search of other job opportunities and, thus, contributed to **depeasantization** in many developing nations. This is problematic because, when migration occurs without a corresponding surge in employment opportunities, which is often the case in developing countries, poverty is transferred but not reduced (Pingali 2012). This could explain the rise of slums around major cities in developing countries as the green revolution unfolded. Furthermore, even those farmers who were able to access green revolution technologies were susceptible to unintended consequences. For example, agricultural laborers who applied pesticide were susceptible to adverse health effects (Zeigler and Mohanty 2010).

Debates about the green revolution are often reduced to whether the technologies developed by scientists and applied by farmers were either good or bad. This analytical approach is misguided because it oversimplifies the consequences of the green revolution. In many ways, the green revolution accomplished what it set out to do: increase production, enhance food security, and perhaps even reduce the expansion of agricultural production onto marginal lands, thus limiting some environmental degradation (Evenson and Gollin 2003).

At the same time, however, a host of unanticipated environmental and social consequences arose that now must be addressed. Future efforts to apply science and technology to solving agricultural production problems would benefit from hard thinking about how to deal with unintended consequences. For example, Conway (2012) proposes that, to confront continued global food insecurity, a second green revolution needs to be pursued. This time, though, he argues it cannot only focus on intensifying production; it also needs to be environmentally responsible, to pursue equity, and to promote resilience in the face of unpredictable markets and long-term climate change. To accomplish this type of second green revolution, Conway promotes the use of new technologies but also argues that they alone cannot solve all the problems. Rather, **appropriate technologies** (i.e., technologies that make sense to implement and are accepted by local populations in a particular context) must be coupled with appropriate policies and opportunities to ensure that producing more food does not lead to further inequality and environmental damage. This recognition demonstrates the problem with viewing the green revolution as good or bad. Implementing technologies, like those of the green revolution, always has a range of effects beyond their primary intention, and the consequences that are potentially negative will best be minimized through well-developed policies and institutions, not by relying on science and technology alone.

The varying impacts of the green revolution, both positive and negative, have provided lessons for the scientists, development professionals, and policymakers regarding how to assess the development and implementation of scientific innovations and technologies. Among the key theoretical frameworks guiding the green revolution was **modernization theory**, which established a set of assumptions about how societies become more developed. In brief, those assumptions are that industrialization, urbanization, and increasingly complex divisions of labor are signs of social progress. Utilizing modernization theory, one might deem the green revolution a success because the intensification of agricultural production led to productive efficiency, higher yields, and a reduced rural population.

It is important to note that modernization theory was not the only theoretical framework in existence at the time of the green revolution. Although modernization theory viewed development as a linear process appropriate across different contexts, other scholars, such as those using **dependency theory** and **world systems theory**, argued that countries with strong economies (referred to as the core) were only able to achieve their impressive economic growth through exploiting the labor and materials of less powerful countries (known as the periphery). Others focused their criticism of the green revolution on its top-down, one-size-fits-all approach. For example, Robert Chambers, a development scholar and practitioner, was instrumental in developing participatory methods for crop improvements, which are strategies designed to incorporate the perspectives and priorities of local people so that they can be the drivers of the development of research and development projects.

Despite these alternative approaches, modernization theory was the perspective that drove the green revolution. Science and technology play an important role in the modernization perspective, since research and technological advancements are typically behind new mechanical, biological, and chemical applications to agricultural production and food processing. A 1959 article in *Time* magazine explained that agricultural production was on the cusp of becoming a "pushbutton cornucopia," as the new scientific and technological breakthroughs behind the industrialization of the agricultural and food system would help to overcome obstacles to meeting national and global food needs (Ramey 2010). The implication was that agricultural science and technology are inevitably and essentially driven toward progress and that this version of progress is beneficial to all people.

SCIENCE OF REPAIR

Modernization theory has given way to less sanguine perspectives on how agricultural science and technology are developed and applied. With the concept of the **science of repair**, Henke (2008) describes how agricultural science and technology are typically employed to fix the problems created by an agricultural system designed to exploit resources and overproduce agricultural commodities. For example, large-scale agricultural production faces several problems, including water pollution, pest problems, and labor exploitation. Rather than address these issues with systemic changes, scientific research and technological changes tend to be implemented to enable this system to survive until the next crisis. When that next crisis emerges, the science of repair kicks in again. As a result, much of agricultural science and technology is developed less for achieving some goal of social progress than to fix the social and environmental problems created by a flawed system and problems generated by previous innovations. So, for example, when considering the unintended consequences of the green revolution, those who apply a science of repair perspective often advocate for new scientific innovations and technologies such as genetic modification as the panacea for environmental problems like pesticide use and pest resistance without considering how these new scientific discoveries and technologies might very well create new environmental and social problems.

Furthermore, the benefits from the introduction of science and technology are often mediated by a range of social, political, and economic contexts. These include the establishment of extension and social services, government programs to support farmers in lean years, and infrastructure to facilitate the creation of markets. Although these initiatives may offer some general social benefits, they are seldom equally accessible to everyone in the population. Often, marginalized populations, like those who are poor, have less access to these services and infrastructure than those populations with more financial resources, which risks creating further social inequality. Some claim that this was the case with the green revolution (Pingali 2012).

Rather than accepting agricultural science and technology as inevitably contributing to social progress and the public good, a sociological approach encourages people to question whose interests are being advanced and how agricultural science and technology might be distracting people from underlying systemic problems.

NANOTECHNOLOGY AND GENETIC ENGINEERING

Proponents of high-technology approaches to improving agricultural production and food provisioning often point to demographic projections that the global population will reach nine billion people by 2050. To meet the growing food demand that will likely accompany the population growth, they claim that the newest technologies, like nanotechnology or genetic engineering (GE), are necessary.

Scientists have been working on nanotechnologies for decades, but they have only recently sought to apply them to agriculture and food. Nanotechnologies refer to the use of materials between approximately one and one hundred nanometers, which basically spans the size of atoms and molecules. In a review of the current and potential applications of nanotechnology to agriculture and food, Sekhon (2014) claims that this new technology enables scientists to develop new chemicals that will improve the applications of crop pesticides and fertilizers, helps to detect crop diseases and chemical residues, improves the capacity to genetically engineer plants, enhances the ability to diagnose crop diseases, improves animal health and breeding techniques, and helps to improve the nutritional content and shelf life of foods. Although the food industry is investing substantial resources in some of these efforts, Sekhon claims that the level of investment is still insufficient to fully capitalize on the potential for these technologies to solve so many problems related to the challenges of a growing global population.

The use of GE in crop and animal agriculture began in the early 1980s, and the first crop was approved for commercialization in 1992, a tomato modified to delay ripening. Genetic engineering refers to a direct human intervention to change an organism's genome or epigenome by editing or introducing new proteins. This differs from conventional breeding, since it usually involves sexual crossing of plants and animals or using chemicals or radiation to alter the genetic makeup so that desirable traits are expressed in those plants and animals. Genetic engineering techniques are considered more precise and faster (NAS 2016).

Many new crops have been commercialized since the mid-1990s. Wheat, maize, cotton, and soybeans are the most commonly planted. Alfalfa, apples, papaya, and squash are others. A fairly up-to-date list of GE crops is available in the National Academy of Sciences report (NAS 2016), *Genetically Engineered Crops: Experiences and Prospects*. Since GE manipulates plants and animals at the molecular level, it has generated controversy among the public and some scientists, especially in the European Union, where nearly all GE crops are banned. Some raise concerns about the human health and environmental safety, as well as the harmful social and economic impacts. By contrast, others claim that GE technologies bring human health, environmental, and social and economic benefits.

Although proponents of this technology have made bold claims about the benefits that GE can deliver to the world, the reality has been more modest. The most common application of this technology has been to modify major row crops, such as maize, cotton, and soybeans, to tolerate the application of herbicides that would otherwise kill the crops. This herbicide tolerance technology improves weed management capacities, but it has also been linked to more herbicide usage. And that heavy usage has led weeds to evolve resistance to the herbicides. Agribusiness firms have responded by engineering crops to withstand additional herbicides that many scientists warn will have negative human health and environmental impacts.

One of the more promising developments has been with GE crops that produce their own pesticides, which has helped to reduce insect crop losses in maize and cotton while also reducing the spraying of dangerous pesticides on those crops. However, as was the case with herbicide tolerance, insects have evolved to become resistant to the pesticides.

There are many other GE developments that bring environmental and consumer benefits, such as the development of virus resistance in papaya, potatoes, squash, and plums. Nonbrowning and low-acrylamide potatoes are other examples. However, these technologies represent a very small portion of all GE crops. The vast majority of GE crops that have hit the market are either herbicide tolerant or pest resistant. The potential to develop varieties and breeds that exhibit other beneficial traits such as stress tolerance (drought, floods, or salinity) or contain higher densities of micronutrients are still mostly unrealized. Although some claim that government regulations are inhibiting the development of these new technologies, there is little evidence to support that claim (NAS 2016). The more likely explanation is that the institutional context favors the development of technologies that benefit the private sector while providing few public benefits, an issue we turn to in the next section.

INSTITUTIONAL CONTEXTS OF AGRICULTURAL RESEARCH AND TECHNOLOGY

To critically assess whose interests are being advanced by a particular research agenda or technology, one could ask where the research is being conducted and also where the research funding comes from. Scientific research is typically conducted in either private (industry) or public (government or university) laboratories. In the case of agricultural research in the United States, private research is mostly done by large agricultural firms. For example, much of the research on crop seeds is conducted by Monsanto, Dupont Pioneer, and Syngenta. Most public agricultural research is done at land-grant universities, and some is done in government and non–land grant university laboratories. Scientists in other nations also do public research in universities, but some rely more on government laboratories. Research funding can also be divided into public and private sources. The federal government is the primary sponsor of public research in the United States, and agricultural firms are the primary sponsors of private research.

The main goal of agricultural science and technology over the past century in industrialized and developing nations has been directed at increasing crop yields. When crop yields began to stagnate during the latter decades of the twentieth century and the beginning of the twenty-first century, many scholars expressed alarm. Furthermore, those scholars noted that the leveling off of crop yield increases has coincided with a shift in the proportion of public and private research funding (Fuglie et al. 2012).

These changes have also coincided with a shift in the ways policymakers think about the need for public investments in agricultural research. Traditionally, policymakers and scholars expected governments to fund agricultural research because having a stable food supply was deemed a public necessity. Furthermore, because the opportunities for profiting from agricultural research were minimal, agricultural firms lacked an incentive to invest in that research. However, by the late 1970s in some industrialized countries, policymakers began promoting a greater reliance on the private sector to provide research funding and for markets to diffuse knowledge and technologies. In 1981, approximately 44 percent of food and agricultural scientific research funding came from the private sector in industrial nations. By 2000, that had shifted to 54 percent (Glenna, Shortall, and Brandl 2015).

The reasoning behind the promotion of private investments in agricultural research is that agricultural firms often have substantial resources that can be directed at developing useful innovations and because they often have access to marketing and distribution channels that university scientists do not have. However, there are also shortcomings to this approach. Although private firms have an incentive to cut costs and to promote efficiencies, that same incentive often leads them to focus on short-term profits at the expense of basic research that is needed to make profound advancements in scientific knowledge, which, in turn, is often necessary to provide substantial impacts in things like crop yields (Galushko and Gray 2014).

The shift to a reliance on private funding across countries masks even more radical changes within countries. For example, in the United Kingdom, the proportion of private investment in research shifted from 56 percent in 1981 to 72 percent in 2000 (Glenna, Shortall, and Brandl 2015). Moreover, the United Kingdom began privatizing its public wheat breeding program in 1987. Although it was seen as a way to promote private investments in agricultural research, it has ultimately had negative impacts on wheat breeding and wheat production in the United Kingdom. In the process of breeding wheat, the most important breakthroughs that lead to genetic improvements that enhance wheat yield tend to occur in university and government laboratories that are funded by the public sector. In other words, basic research is necessary for long-term improvements in crop yields. By privatizing the wheat breeding sector, the United Kingdom disrupted the links between basic and applied research and undermined funding for the basic research necessary for improving the genetic quality of the wheat. Many factors may help to explain the flat wheat yields in the United Kingdom after privatization, including climate change, environmental regulations that led to fewer crop input applications, and changes in tillage practices. However, the reliance on the private sector at the expense of the public sector is the primary cause of stagnant wheat yields (Galushko and Gray 2014).

Other countries have not privatized their agricultural research to the extent that the United Kingdom has, but they have still made efforts to privilege the private sector. For example, in the United States research partnerships between agricultural science corporations and universities are increasingly common. Examples include South Dakota State University and the University of Nebraska establishing research collaborations with Bayer Crop Science and Kansas State University, North Dakota State University, and Virginia Tech University establishing research collaborations with Monsanto (Galushko and Gray 2014).

As a result, universities that were traditionally responsible for publicly funded agricultural research are becoming more dependent on agricultural firms to fund their research and to drive their research agendas. Although the research is still being conducted in university laboratories by university scientists, the goals of the research often shift because of the funding source and collaborations. Scientists whose research is funded by the private sector tend to have different research goals and different research outputs than those funded by the public sector. For example, scientists receiving private funding are more likely to seek patent protections on their research outputs (Glenna et al. 2011).

Patents are a way for inventors to secure ownership rights. There is nothing inherently wrong with doing this. Nearly all nations strive to develop patent rights so that inventors will have an incentive to invest their time and energy into research and development while also promoting the sharing of new ideas and innovations. The debate is whether the private–public distribution in patent law can become unbalanced so that knowledge sharing and innovations become hindered. There is some evidence to suggest that, in the United States, the balance has been tilted in favor of the private sector, since patents are being used to prevent university scientists from doing research. For example, in one study, approximately one-third of entomologists who responded to a survey stated that their research had been blocked by a company that had an interest in the research outcomes, and approximately two-thirds of entomologists stated that they are not able to pursue some research avenues because of intellectual property obstacles (Glenna et al. 2015).

Variations in crop yield may be an indicator of the prominence of private research funding in agricultural and food research and the possible lack of balance in patent law. Glenna et al. (2015) find that crop yields vary by nation and by crop. Globally, nations that are most aggressively pursuing private funding and market approaches to agricultural research tend to have the poorest results in crop yield. However, even within these nations, some crop yields are better than others. Specifically, agricultural firms are more interested in some crops than others, mostly because they are hybrids, have patent protection, or are more widely grown (and thus have bigger markets). One of the challenges with agricultural production, from the perspective of an agricultural firm, is that farmers can save part of the harvest to replant the next year. That means that farmers do not have to purchase new seeds each year. However, hybrid crops are not conducive to seed saving. And some crops, especially genetically engineered crops, have patent protections that prohibit seed saving. As a result, private firms are more willing to invest in those hybrid and patented crops, such as maize and soybeans, than other open-pollinated crops, such as wheat. Glenna et al. (2015) find that, in countries pursuing more privatization in crop research, the hybrid and patented crops have higher yields than the open-pollinated crops. This raises concerns because many open-pollinated crops, like wheat, are staple food crops.

It is important to clarify that the pursuit of yield increases is not the only goal of agricultural research. Understanding relationships between agriculture and ecosystem well-being and enhancing crop biodiversity are two other worthy goals. And there are strong arguments for why improving crop yields should not even be a primary goal. We highlighted earlier how the pursuit of productivity has led to declines in farm numbers, an outcome that some deem undesirable and that has had a number of unintended consequences. Furthermore, there is no direct relationship between higher production and lower levels of hunger. And, as we noted earlier, there are many social factors that mediate the availability of food (see Lesson 13). Thus, there are many agricultural and food production challenges that can be addressed through scientific research. Yield measures are only one important indicator of a nation's willingness to invest in addressing those challenges.

There are good reasons to promote private investments in agricultural research and to promote patenting to enhance innovation. However, policymakers need to be aware of the limitations of these efforts. In addition to potentially limiting public-interest research, a greater reliance on the private sector can limit access for farmers who are economically or geographically marginalized. In other words, private solutions to agricultural challenges are not a substitute for long-term, basic research that is needed to solve problems that are important to society, including food insecurity, poverty, and environmental degradation.

ENDING POVERTY BY EXPANDING AGRICULTURAL PRODUCTIVITY AND MARKETS

The emphasis on privatization of public research to solve problems tends to be accompanied by a faith in privatization and markets to solve nearly any public problem. This has been prominent in industrialized nations since the early 1980s (Glenna, Shortall, and Brandl 2015). Many also assume that the private sector and the flow of its goods and services through markets will enhance farmer prosperity and food security in developing nations. And that rationale is appealing at first glance. Introducing new technologies in the form of improved crop seeds and livestock breeds can enhance agricultural productivity. And farmers with more produce will be able to sell more of it for more money if they have access to markets. Therefore, enhancing access to technologies through input markets and access to output markets to sell commodities at competitive prices would seem to be an effective strategy to end poverty. Although there is some evidence that increased productivity and market access leads to benefits for farmers and consumers (Pingali 2012), such studies focus on all farmers and overlook nuanced challenges facing smallholder farmers.

Harris and Orr (2014) evaluated whether it is possible for agricultural productivity to lead to both improved food security and higher incomes for smallholder farmers. They analyzed household surveys from nine sub-Saharan African nations and India to answer several research questions, including, How much can technology raise income per household? and What impact will this gain in income have on poverty? They find that the adoption of new technology may enable farmers from average-sized households to gain, on average, $372 per hectare each growing season. This is not insubstantial, but it is important to remember that most small farmers have very few hectares of land. Therefore, the impact of income gain on poverty would be minimal unless there was substantial land consolidation, which would lead to departures from farming. Therefore, Harris and Orr (2014) conclude that higher yields through improved technology could enhance food security for smallholder farmers by increasing the amount of staple crops used for subsistence. However, this is not likely to lift them out of poverty. Furthermore, although producing higher yields of staple crops can enhance food security from a caloric perspective, the impact on micronutrient deficiencies is likely very limited without other complementary scientifically informed endeavors, such as biofortification programs (i.e., enhancing nutritional quality of crops through conventional breeding, biotechnology approaches, and/or crop management practices).

The potential for the private sector and markets to solve social problems is also limited by the assumption that small farmers will have access to markets that will provide a fair price for their higher-yielding crops. Because this is not always the case, various development efforts have sought to enhance market access for small farmers. One of the more popular efforts to do this is by expanding farmer opportunities to connect to value chains. Value chains can be conceptualized as all the various activities connecting production to consumption. Theoretically, value chain analyses build on the insights of commodity chain analyses (see Lesson 8), but the shift in terminology represents an effort to add nuance in distinguishing among different kinds of products and to shift focus from the commodity itself to the human activity required to produce, distribute, consume, and dispose of a commodity (Sturgeon 2008). Given that the terminology of value chains has become widely accepted among development scholars and practitioners, we use it here instead of commodity chains.

Increasingly, value chains have shifted from an analytical strategy to a development one. Value chain development has been seized on by organizations like the World Bank, the US Agency for International Development, and the Consultative Group for International Agricultural Research Consortium as an approach to providing access to markets. These efforts are often driven by agricultural and food firms that pay competitive and stable prices to small farmers for their products. The idea is that by linking farmers who typically sell their commodities in unstable local and regional markets to value chains, incomes will increase and, in turn, other development goals will be achieved, such as poverty alleviation and enhanced food security.

Several examples of successful value chain development have been documented where farmers have been able to benefit from tapping into new market opportunities. For example, Minten, Randrianarison, and Swinnen (2009) describe a case in Madagascar, where thousands of farmers signed contracts with an export company to deliver hand-picked French beans to European supermarkets. One-year contracts are signed with producers stipulating production methods, quantity, price, time of delivery, and payment dates and guaranteeing the supply of the most advanced seeds, fertilizers, and pesticides on credit to be paid back in kind. Company representatives serving as technical support have extensive contact with producers, and the company sets competitive prices and offers premiums for beans that are of high quality. Analysis of these contracts has shown that participants earn higher incomes than nonparticipants and that participants also enjoy better food security.

Although there are such documented successes, some have raised concerns about the full range of impacts of value chains. Increasing evidence exists that the most prosperous farmers in developing countries are most likely to access value chain opportunities. This means that value chains may intensify social inequality, rather than minimize it. Furthermore, even those farmers who do access value chain opportunities may become more vulnerable to risk, since the requirements to produce for agricultural and food firms can require high investments and, depending on the contract, farmers may have to bear the brunt of loss if the products they harvest do not adhere to quality standards (Tobin, Glenna, and Devaux 2016). The point is, as with the other issues addressed above, these development strategies that ostensibly address social problems like poverty are not straightforward and produce a range of intended and unintended consequences. Impacts sometimes generate desirable results, like increased incomes, but unanticipated consequences like intensified social inequality can also emerge.

AGRICULTURAL SCIENCE AND TECHNOLOGY AND GENDER

One way to explore the uneven social impacts of agricultural science and technology is to investigate differences between farmers of various social and economic statuses. As discussed previously, evidence indicates that farmers with more resources are those who typically benefitted from green revolution technologies and those who have an easier time capitalizing on value chain development. However, other farmer characteristics are also important in explaining differential impacts. Increasingly, development organizations, scholars, and practitioners are emphasizing the importance of gender. For example, the Food and Agriculture Organization (FAO) of the United Nations focused on women in agriculture in their annual report of global food insecurity in 2011, and gender equality and women's empowerment figure prominently in US Agency for International Development funding opportunities. As the following discussion demonstrates, agricultural technologies often impact women differently than men and have both marginalized and empowered women.

Though gender has recently been receiving needed attention in the development sector, it is important to recognize that these issues have been on the radar for several decades. In the 1970s, feminist scholars began to highlight the absence of women in development programs, which gave rise to the women in development approach. Women in development focused on integrating women into development projects to ensure that they, too, were presented with opportunities. Despite women receiving increasing attention among the development community, women in development was critiqued for not pursuing broader structural changes that would better guarantee equality. As a result, a new strand of thought influenced by critical perspectives like dependency theory, women and development, emerged and focused primarily on transforming structures and institutions to become more equitable so that participation in development was less exploitative and more advantageous to both women and men. In the 1980s, proponents of the gender and agriculture approach built on the women in development and women and development insights by noting that both overlooked the way that patriarchy affects women's opportunities. Gender and agriculture, therefore, promoted a vision of development that focused not on women themselves, but on the relations between men and women as an important strategy to pursue more equitable opportunity across gender categories.

Although the spotlight on gender equality in food and agriculture has recently become brighter, it is important to recognize that scholars have been making observations regarding gender dynamics for several decades. Over twenty years ago, Carney (1993) depicted how investments in Gambia from foreign donors and the government in irrigation for rice production diminished women's access to land, increased their labor burden, and created tensions within communities and households between men and women. As men increasingly staked claims on the land that women had traditionally cultivated, women were forced to adapt and sought strategies to maintain some independent production or ensure that they were compensated for their labor. Through this case study, Carney illustrated the disproportionate power dynamics that exists between men and women and shows how the marginalization of women is reinforced by the pursuit of specific development strategies and the implementation of particular technologies.

In the case of genetically modified maize in South Africa, although both male and female farmers tended to favor the new technology, they valued it for different reasons. Since women do much of the weeding in this farming system, they tend to favor the herbicide-tolerant maize for reducing weed pressures. Men tended to favor it because of the higher yields. Female farmers also tended to place a higher importance on other characteristics, such as taste and quality (Gouse et al. 2016). These insights are important because they reveal that men and women often have different perspectives based on the division of labor within the household and on the farm. In this case, both men and women seemed to gain benefits. However, gendered divisions of labor can vary by farming system and by country. A new technology that might increase yield but create more labor needs for one gender might lead to household conflict and exacerbate inequities.

Unfortunately, the divisions between male and female access to employment opportunities, land, and technologies, often referred to as the **gender gap**, persist. The FAO (2011, 4) reports that "female farmers are just as efficient as their male counterparts, but they have less land and use fewer inputs, so they produce less." Across the globe, men enjoy more access to land, inputs, and credit than women. According to the FAO (2011), closing the gender gap in agriculture would not only increase global production but also reduce global **food insecurity** by 12 to 17 percent. Therefore, focusing solely on scientific and technological solutions to agricultural problems would have minimal impacts without also addressing these additional sociological challenges.

Furthermore, female farmers are not a homogenous social category (Quisumbing et al. 2014). Important differences exist among female farmers, just as variance exists among male farmers, small farmers, and other demographic categories. Therefore, it is important to undertake multilayered analyses to better understand how gender relations play out in specific contexts and in relation to technological innovations. Intersectionality, a term that encapsulates the idea of conducting multilayered analyses, refers to the way that different social categories, such as gender, age, education, ethnicity, and religion, may be embodied by a single individual and combine to create unique experiences. Quisumbing et al. (2014) describe an example in Guatemala where older women in rural areas possess more resources and decision-making power than either younger males or females, thus indicating the shortcomings of assuming that relationships among and between men and women are invariably consistent across all other characteristics that constitute the identities of individuals.

Despite these caveats, there is convincing evidence that men generally reap more benefits from advances in science and technology than women. Continuing to disseminate new innovations using the same strategies will continue to reproduce gender inequalities. As indicated previously, the pursuits and implementation of science and technology are mediated by the social world. Because men typically have better access to credit and information, they are more likely to benefit from new technologies or production practices. Without addressing the basic inequities that exist in accessing resources among men and women, the diffusion of technology is likely to intensify these differences. In other words, to assume that social problems can be fixed by advances in science and technology alone ignores the ways that social institutions, like gender, affect who benefits and who does not.

Conclusion

Scientific research and technological advancements in food and agriculture have been used to improve material well-being for many people. However, the distribution of those benefits has not always been equitable. Furthermore, there are often negative unintended consequences, which are also seldom distributed fairly or equally. We have highlighted some prominent examples of how agricultural science and technology have generated controversies to emphasize how social contexts affect the generation of scientific research and technologies, as well as the diffusion of the outputs.

The relatively recent emphasis on the ability of markets and the private sector to generate and diffuse agricultural science and technology as a strategy to improve human well-being is especially problematic. Specifically, the idea that agricultural science and technology could solve problems of poverty and inequality is backward. Making the inequitable social institutions more equitable is needed before scientific research and new technologies are likely to be generated and diffused to solve the problems that poor people face.

Although access to appropriate technologies could be useful tools, they alone cannot fix the social and environmental problems that the world currently faces. In fact, as we explained in the section on the science of repair, science and technology may even play a role in distracting society from addressing underlying systemic problems.

As technologies are implemented, they produce unintended consequences, both positive and negative. Increasingly, scholars are taking a more comprehensive view of the importance of science and technology, claiming that relevant and appropriate policies and institutions that simultaneously promote production, stability, resilience, and equity must be pursued (Conway 2012). Amartya Sen, the Nobel Prize–winning development economist, has articulated a worthwhile way to conceptualize these types of policies and institutional contexts. According to Sen (1999), development occurs when people are able to successfully construct lives that they themselves find meaningful. To accomplish this, a series of freedoms must be guaranteed, including political freedoms, economic opportunities, and social supports. Without these institutional contexts to promote equity, opportunity, and justice, agricultural science and technology are not likely to contribute to societal well-being.

Discussion Questions

1. What are the positive and negative impacts of the tomato harvester and green revolution examples discussed in this lesson?
2. Why have the private sector and markets been promoted as a strategy to diffuse agricultural science and technology for societal well-being? Is this an effective strategy or one that is problematic?
3. How do gender dynamics provide evidence that technological determinism is problematic in its approach to address social issues?
4. How do the science of repair and Sen's perspective on freedoms differ?
5. Do you agree that institutional contexts must change for science and technology to most effectively contribute to social problems? Why or why not?

Exercise

You are in charge of distributing Foundation X funds to support food security and rural livelihoods in less developed countries. Company Y has just submitted a proposal to develop and disseminate a genetically modified maize variety that both has higher yields and is more nutritious. However, initial research indicates that the maize variety is also more susceptible to pests and drought. The seeds are also patented, meaning that the farmers would need to purchase new seeds every growing cycle. Break the class into small groups. Each group will be asked to evaluate the proposal. Discuss the benefits and drawbacks (including potential unintended consequences) and decide whether to fund it.

Additional Materials

Readings

Committee on Genetically Engineered Crops, Board on Agriculture and Natural Resources, Division on Earth and Life Sciences. 2016. *Genetically Engineered Crops: Experiences and Prospects*. Washington, DC: National Academies Press.

Folger, Tim. 2014. "The Next Green Revolution." *National Geographic*, October 2014. http://www.nationalgeographic.com/foodfeatures/green-revolution/

Royal Society. 2017. "Genetically Modified (GM) Plants: Questions and Answers." https://royalsociety.org/topics-policy/projects/gm-plants/

Video Clips

FAO (Food and Agriculture Organization). 2016. "FAO Policy Series: Sustainable Agribusiness and Food Value Chains." August 4, 2016. Video file. https://www.youtube.com/watch?v=DChZsUDZ-s4

References

Bill and Melinda Gates Foundation. 2008. "$306 Million Commitment to Agricultural Development." January 25, 2008. http://www.gatesfoundation.org/Media-Center/Press-Releases/2008/01/$306-Million-Commitment-to-Agricultural-Development

Carney, Judith. 1993. "Converting the Wetlands, Engendering the Environment: The Intersection of Gender with Agrarian Change in the Gambia." *Economic Geography* 69 (4): 329–48.

Cochrane, Willard W. 1993. *The Development of American Agriculture: A Historical Analysis*. 2d ed. St. Paul: University of Minnesota Press.

Conway, Gordon. 2012. *One Billion Hungry: Can We Feed the World?* Ithaca, NY: Cornell University Press.

Evenson, Robert E., and Douglas Gollin. 2003. "Assessing the Impact of the Green Revolution, 1960 to 2000." *Science* 300 (5620): 758–62.

FAO (Food and Agriculture Organization). 2011. *2010–11: The State of Food and Agriculture. Women in Agriculture: Closing the Gender Gap for Development*. Rome: FAO. http://www.fao.org/docrep/013/i2050e/i2050e.pdf

Friedland, William H. 1991. "Engineering Social Change in Agriculture." *University of Dayton Review* 21 (1): 25–42.

Fuglie, Keith, Paul Heisey, John King, Carl E. Pray, and David Schimmelpfennig. 2012. "The Contribution of Private Industry to Agricultural Innovation." *Science* 338 (6110): 1031–32.

Galushko, Victoriya, and Richard Gray. 2014. "Twenty Five Years of Private Wheat Breeding in the UK: Lessons for Other Countries." *Science and Public Policy* 41 (6): 765–79.

Glenna, Leland, Sally Shortall, and Barbara Brandl. 2015. "The University, Public Goods, and Food & Agricultural Innovation." *Sociologia Ruralis* 55 (4): 438–59.

Glenna, Leland L., John Tooker, J. Rick Welsh, and David Ervin. 2015. "Intellectual Property, Scientific Independence, and the Efficacy and Environmental Impacts of Genetically Engineered Crops." *Rural Sociology* 80 (2): 147–72.

Glenna, Leland L., Rick Welsh, David Ervin, William B. Lacy, and Dina Biscotti. 2011. "Commercial Science, Scientists' Values, and University Biotechnology Research Agenda." *Research Policy* 40 (7): 957–68.

Gouse, Marnus, Debdatta Sengupta, Patricia Zambrano, and Jose Falck Zepeda. 2016. "Genetically Modified Maize: Less Drudgery for Her, More Maize for Him? Evidence from Smallholder Maize Farmers in South Africa." World Development 83: 27-38.

Harris, David, and Alastair Orr. 2014. "Is Rainfed Agriculture Really a Pathway from Poverty?" *Agricultural Systems* 123:84–96.

Henke, Christopher R. 2008. *Cultivating Science, Harvesting Power: Science and Industrial Agriculture in California*. Cambridge, MA: MIT Press.

Hoppe, Robert A. 2014. *Structure and Finances of U.S. Farms: Family Farm Report, 2014 Edition*. Washington, DC: US Department of Agriculture, Economic Research Service.

Minten, Bart, Lalaina Randrianarison, and Johan F. Swinnen. 2009. "Global Retail Chains and Poor Farmers: Evidence from Madagascar." *World Development* 37 (11): 1728–41.

Paalberg, Robert. 2010. *Food Politics: What Everyone Needs to Know*. Oxford: Oxford University Press.

Pingali, Prabhu L. 2012. "Green Revolution: Impacts, Limits, and the Path Ahead." *Proceedings of the National Academy of Sciences of the United States of America* 109 (31): 12302–8.

Quisumbing, Agnes R., Ruth Meinzen-Dick, Terri L. Raney, André Croppenstedt, Julia A. Behrman, and Amber Peterman. 2014. "Closing the Knowledge Gap on Gender in Agriculture." In *Gender in Agriculture: Closing the Knowledge Gap*, edited by A. R. Quisumbing, R. Meinzen-Dick, T. L. Raney, A. Croppenstedt, J. A. Berhman, and A. Peterman, 3–30. Dordrecht, Holland: Springer.

Ramey, Elizabeth A. 2010. "Seeds of Change: Hybrid Corn, Monopoly, and the Hunt for Superprofits." *Review of Radical Political Economics* 42 (3): 381–86.

Rogers, Everett M. 2003. *Diffusion of Innovations*. 5th Edition. New York, NY: Free Press.

Rosegrant, Mark W., and Peter B. R. Hazell. 2000. *Transforming the Rural Asian Economy: The Unfinished Revolution*. Hong Kong: Oxford University Press.

Sekhon, Bhupinder Singh. 2014. "Nanotechnology in Agri-Food Production: An Overview." *Nanotechnology, Science and Applications* 7:31–53.

Sen, Amartya. 1999. *Development as Freedom*. New York: Random House.

Sturgeon, Timothy J. 2008. "From Commodity Chains to Value Chains: Interdisciplinary Theory Building in the Age of Globalization." In *Frontiers of Commodity Chain Research*, edited by Jennifer Bair, 110–35. Stanford, CA: Stanford University Press.

Tobin, Daniel, Leland L. Glenna, and Andre Devaux. 2016. "Pro-poor? Inclusion and Exclusion in Native Potato Value Chain in the Central Highlands of Peru." *Journal of Rural Studies* 46:71–80.

Zeigler, Robert S., and Samarendu Mohanty. 2010. "Support for International Agricultural Research: Current Status and Future Challenges." *New Biotechnology* 27 (5): 565–72.

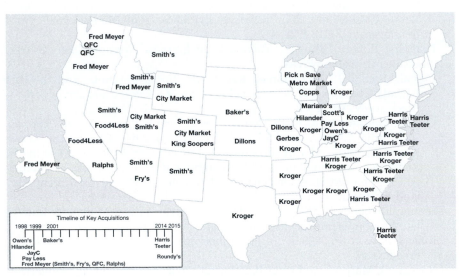

Map and timeline of Kroger's acquisitions, 1998 to 2016. (Adapted from Howard 2016, 25.)

7

Increasing Corporate Control: From Supermarkets to Seeds

Philip H. Howard

I f you go into any grocery store, you will likely find at least half an entire aisle devoted to breakfast cereal. Although it may appear that there are many choices, if you look very closely at the packaging, you can determine that most of the brands are owned by just four corporations: General Mills, Kellogg Company, Post Consumer Brands and Quaker Oats (a division of Pepsi). The task is somewhat complicated by hidden or stealth ownership, such as General Mills' ties to Cascadian Farm and Kellogg's ties to Kashi and Bear Naked. The top four firms, however, are reported to control more than 85 percent of US sales.

Cereal is not a unique case: nearly every part of the food system is increasingly dominated by just a few corporations, such as Coke and Pepsi's control of soft drinks and Monsanto and DuPont's control of commercial seeds. Why is this a problem? Institutional economists suggest that when four firms control 40 to 50 percent of sales, that market is no longer competitive. This means that the dominant firms have much more power to raise prices in comparison to less concentrated markets. Control by a few firms is typically described as an **oligopoly**, but some analysts use the less technical term *shared monopoly*. In 1995, for example, a leading cereal maker, Post, admitted that its prices were too high after being criticized in a congressional report. The corporation reduced their prices by 20 percent, and other leading firms followed with their own price reductions (Cotterill 1999).

Many other negative impacts may result from high levels of **market concentration**, including reduced innovation, lower prices paid to suppliers, lower wages for workers, fewer consumer choices, and environmental impacts (such as pollution and higher energy consumption). Frequently, these consequences disproportionately affect certain populations, such as recent immigrants, ethnic minorities, people of lower socioeconomic status, women, and children. An argument frequently made by firms that are pursuing acquisitions, however, is the potential to reduce both costs and prices through economies of scale, which may benefit society as a whole. Although price reductions do occur in some in cases, critics suggest that a full accounting of hidden costs (such as government subsidies, or impacts on communities and the environment) would undermine these claims (Adams and Brock 2004).

The US food system can be compared to an hourglass, with approximately two million farmers at the top and over three hundred million people who eat at the bottom, but a much smaller number of corporations controlling the stages that connect farmers to everyone else (Figure 7.1). The middle of the hourglass gets smaller as markets become more concentrated. Why do these trends continue, despite their negative impacts? One key reason is that the US government has changed the way corporations are regulated, particularly in response to the efforts of the largest firms to further increase their power. This lesson explores how such changes have affected key links in the food chain, including retailing, distribution, packaged food manufacturing, and commodity processing, as well as farming and farm inputs. It concludes with a discussion of efforts to oppose these trends.

THE REINTERPRETATION OF ANTITRUST LAWS

Current levels of economic concentration in most food and agricultural markets are significantly higher than they were in the mid-twentieth century. At that time, most markets were composed of numerous firms, each with a very small share of total sales. The more typical situation today is that a few firms control a very large percentage of the market. This trend is not new, however—in the late 1800s and the early 1900s corporations were successful in increasing their control over a number of industries, such as railroads, banking, and meat processing. Concerns about these trusts, or powerful combinations of firms, and the costs they imposed on the public led to social

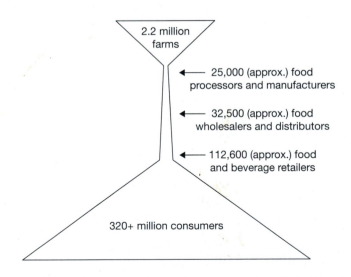

Figure 7.1 The hourglass shape of the US food system. (Adapted from Carolan 2016, 38)

movements advocating **antitrust** actions. These included the Populist movement of the late 1800s and the Progressive movement of the early 1900s. Such efforts contributed to regulations that were supposed to prevent markets from becoming less competitive. Some significant laws included the Sherman Antitrust Act of 1890, the Clayton Antitrust Act of 1914, and the Federal Trade Commission Act of 1914, which helped to break up some trusts and hindered concentration in others for decades following their implementation.

The interpretation and enforcement of these laws has been weakened over time, however. One important change in more recent decades involved reshaping the views of federal judges. A group of economists and law professors, primarily from the University of Chicago, suggested that consumers typically benefited from the increased market share by dominant firms, purportedly through increased efficiency. These *Chicago school* or **neoliberal** views were heavily promoted by corporations through funding think tanks based at other universities, beginning in the late 1970s. George Mason University and Northwestern University, for example, frequently hold all-expenses-paid seminars at golf resorts in warm-weather states to "educate" judges on procorporate legal perspectives. Nearly two-thirds of federal judges were estimated to have participated in just one of these programs (George Mason's) by the early 1990s (Aron et al. 1994).

In the decades since, antitrust cases have achieved some victories in lower courts, but nearly all were overturned on appeal. One example was the $1.28 billion judgment a jury awarded cattle ranchers in their lawsuit against the meat processor IBP (which was acquired by Tyson before the case went to trial in 2004). The corporation was accused of violating antitrust laws by manipulating markets to drive down the prices they paid for cattle. The judge in the case, however, made the rare move to overturn the jury's verdict on a set of technicalities. After an appeal, the judge's decision was upheld by a higher federal court, and the Supreme Court refused to hear the case.

Another key event was the election of Ronald Reagan as the US president in 1980. He had campaigned on a platform of more limited government intervention, which followed decades of pressure from industries to allow more mergers and acquisitions. Reagan appointed heads of federal agencies who shared these views and directed them specifically to reduce antitrust enforcement. Subsequent administrations did not substantially change this approach. In addition, the federal government stopped collecting data that would more accurately characterize the degree of competition in markets.

More recently, in 2009, the Obama administration employed the rhetoric of reinvigorating antitrust actions in food and agriculture and even took the appearance of actions to achieve these goals, but ultimately accomplished very little over the following eight years. For example, high-level administrators sympathetic to antitrust enforcement were appointed to the Department of Justice and US Department of Agriculture. These two agencies subsequently held a series of joint hearings to investigate reported abuses of power in food and agriculture in 2010. The Department of Justice report acknowledged a number of these abuses, such as bid rigging, price manipulation, and one-sided contracts. The agency concluded, however, that many potential enforcement actions would be unsuccessful because of the way judges now interpret antitrust laws. In addition, within just a few years, all of the reformers had left the federal agencies after being frustrated by the power of lobbyists from food and agricultural firms.

SUPERMARKETS

As recently as the 1990s, chain supermarkets typically had very large market shares in regions (such as metropolitan areas), but not at the national level. This was in part a result of the Robinson–Patman Act of 1936, which was passed in reaction to the rise of the Great Atlantic & Pacific Tea Company (A&P) at that time. The Great Atlantic & Pacific Tea Company was the first supermarket, and its rapidly increasing share of retail food sales led to concerns that smaller grocers would be driven out of business. One practice of particular concern was the price breaks that A&P negotiated from its suppliers in exchange for their large volume of orders, which allowed the retailer to sell food at prices impossible for competitors to match. The Robinson–Patman Act prohibited these price breaks and contributed to slowing the growth of A&P (Lynn 2006).

Walmart took advantage of the relaxing of antitrust enforcement when it moved into food sales in the 1990s. The retail chain began as a general merchandise store in Arkansas in 1962. Its business model was based on a strategy similar to A&P's, offering lower prices made possible by discounts from suppliers. By 2011, Walmart controlled an estimated 33 percent of supermarket sales in the United States. Many competing supermarket chains have acquired other competitors and expanded nationally as a defensive strategy.

Currently, the second-largest supermarket is Kroger, with a 9 percent market share. Its dominance is not as visible as Walmart's because the corporation has retained the names of many of the regional supermarket chains it has acquired (see the chapter opening figure). Kroger has also adopted many of the innovations of Walmart, such as putting more pressure on suppliers to reduce the prices the firm pays. Safeway controlled 5 percent of the market in 2011 and has since acquired Albertsons, while Supervalu controlled 4 percent. As a result, the top four firms currently control well over half of sales.

Many supermarkets often charge slotting fees, or payments to ensure that a given supplier's products are placed on the retailer's shelves. The practice is very secretive, but it is estimated that it costs tens of thousands of dollars for a single product placement in stores owned by a regional retail chain and as much as millions of dollars to be carried by a national chain. Total estimates suggest that food manufacturers spend $9 billion annually on these fees, which limits the availability of foods from smaller-scale producers that cannot afford to pay them.

Supermarkets remain the most common source of groceries for people in the United States, but these retailers are beginning to lose sales to other formats, such as warehouse stores and convenience stores. Not surprisingly, the leading supermarket chains are also involved in these industries. Walmart, for example, owns Sam's Club, which has a 38 percent share of warehouse club sales, and both Walmart and Kroger are increasing their presence in the convenience store sector.

DISTRIBUTORS

The segment of the food system that connects food manufacturers to retailers is distribution. Although it is much less concentrated than the two segments it connects, the market share of leading firms has increased significantly in recent decades. This has occurred primarily through the largest firms acquiring their competitors, rather than increasing sales in existing divisions.

National supermarket chains have also expanded their own role in this segment to reduce costs and become less reliant on *middlemen*. Walmart, for example, innovated a strategy called cross-docking, which involves carefully coordinating direct deliveries from suppliers on one side of their regional warehouses and quickly moving the products to trucks destined for individual stores on the other (Baines 2014).

Most restaurants, even large chains, do not yet employ cross-docking and must rely on middlemen for the very wide range of supplies that they carry. The most dominant *broadline* distributor is Sysco, which is a result of the combination of more than 150 firms or divisions of firms since it was founded (Figure 7.2). The Wall Street firm Goldman Sachs played a key role in these combinations, first funding the initial merger of nine distributors to form the company in 1969, as well as providing most of the funding for an attempt to acquire its largest competitor, US Foods, in 2013.

At the time, US Foods was the only other distributor with a fully national scope. Unusually, the Federal Trade Commission opposed the $8.2 billion deal, estimating that it would result in one firm controlling 75 percent of the national broadline distribution market. The Federal Trade Commission also noted that many customers encouraged the two firms to outbid each other in service and price and that this competition would be eliminated for numerous customers without alternative suppliers. The agency's injunction to halt the acquisition was upheld by a US district court in 2015, and Sysco then terminated the deal. Both firms have continued to acquire smaller competitors since this time, however.

United Natural Foods, Inc., and KeHE are distributors that are more specialized than Sysco and US Foods, but just as dominant in the category of natural and organic foods. These are the only two national distributors in this niche, and United Natural Foods is much larger than KeHE. This gives United Natural Foods enormous power over suppliers because natural and organic food producers that want to distribute nationally have no choice but to channel their products through this firm.

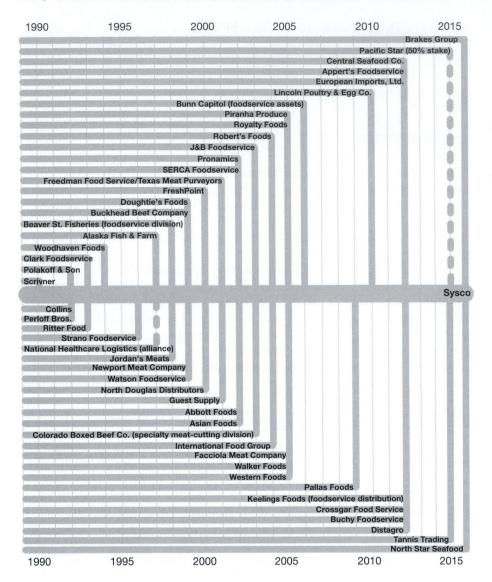

Figure 7.2 Sysco: selected acquisitions and alliances, 1990 to 2016. (Adapted from Howard 2016, 41)

One exception is for products that have high values relative to their weight, such as coffee, spices, and teas. This is the reason Frontier has survived as the only remaining cooperatively owned natural food distributor in the United States, a decline from twenty-eight in the 1980s (Howard 2009). Frontier specializes in spices and teas and is able to ship these products using Federal Express, rather than creating its own infrastructure for national distribution.

PACKAGED FOOD MANUFACTURERS

The top ten firms controlled nearly 32 percent of food and beverage sales by 2011, but for more specific categories levels of concentration are usually much higher. Some packaged food categories, such as breakfast cereal, soft drinks, snacks, and canned soup, have been dominated by a very small number of firms for many decades. Other product categories have consolidated into fewer hands more recently. Because packaged food categories are so diverse, in this section I focus on milk and a milk substitute made from soybeans, usually called soy milk. Similar trends apply to most others, however. Wine, for example, offers more choices than perhaps any other product category, but more than half of sales in the United States are controlled by just three firms.

Milk

Packaged milk firms were not very concentrated nationally until the 1990s. At that time, Gregg Engles, who had successfully combined several packaged ice firms, had the idea to employ this strategy in the dairy industry. By 2002, what were once sixty separate firms were combined into Dean Foods. Like the retailer Kroger, many of the regional brand names were retained. The national share of the market held by the top four firms was 43 percent by this time, twice the percentage of just five years earlier. By 2010 it was estimated that just one firm, Dean Foods, controlled 40 percent of the market.

One result of this industry consolidation was a decline in prices paid to dairy farmers. Dean developed a close relationship with the farmer cooperative Dairy Farmers of America and convinced its executives to make the cooperative the exclusive supplier to Dean in 2001, even though it reduced the prices received by its farmers to record lows. This may have contributed to one-third of all US dairy farmers going out of business in the following decade. Business partners of these firms, however, turned investments of $5 to $7 million into payouts of $80 to $100 million in just two years (Martin 2012). Dean and Dairy Farmers of America have each paid more than $100 million to settle antitrust suits brought by dairy farmers in subsequent years.

Although milk is a highly visible product, with strong consumer awareness of price increases, allegations of price-fixing are common in the industry. Dean has been accused of bid rigging with competitors to drive up the prices paid by public schools for their products, for example. Retailers in areas dominated by just a few firms have also been accused of keeping milk prices artificially high, such as two Chicago-area supermarkets that kept the price approximately one dollar higher per gallon in comparison to other regions in the late 1990s.

Soy Milk

Soy milk was once a relatively obscure product category—it was limited primarily to natural food stores before the 1990s. At that time Steve Demos had the idea to move soy milk from shelf-stable cartons to the refrigerator case, right next to cow's milk. Demos was an idealist who had been less successful with other ideas to increase consumption of soy products, such as soy ice cream. Placing soy milk in the refrigerator case, however, required the payment of slotting fees to supermarket chains. Demos approached several food manufacturers, such as Kraft and Coca-Cola, to finance slotting fees, but the firm that eventually agreed to a partnership was Dean Foods.

Refrigerated soy milk was very successful, and sales increased rapidly. Dean Foods exercised an option to convert partial ownership in Demos's soy company, WhiteWave, to full ownership. Demos was forced out after a few years, and some of his ideals followed as a result of the firm's efforts to increase its power. One example was a significant reduction in the commitment to organic ingredients and another was a shift to sourcing globally, such as importing soybeans from China and Brazil, rather than North American farmers. The firm's share of the soy milk market remained dominant, however, even as sales increased dramatically—at one point rising 3 to 5 percent per week. The firm currently claims a 74 percent share of the soy milk market.

Dean Foods was also acquiring organic dairy milk companies in the late 1990s and early 2000s. Engles eventually came under pressure from investors for his very large compensation package, relative to poor performance of the firm—one year he received $65 million. His solution was to spin off the natural and organic brands into a separately traded company in 2012, which took the WhiteWave name, and to become its chief executive officer. He then continued to acquire other natural and organic food firms—these included the firm that dominated organic bagged salads, Earthbound Farm, as well as a major soy milk competitor, So Delicious. In 2016 the French yogurt giant, Danone, proposed to acquire WhiteWave for $12.5 billion, which includes the debt WhiteWave took on to purchase so many other firms. Several consumer advocacy organizations expressed concern that the deal would reduce competition and lead to increased prices for consumers in organic yogurt, milk, and milk alternatives. The acquisition was subsequently approved by government regulators, however, with the concession that one of WhiteWave's yogurt brands, Stonyfield, be sold to another French dairy giant, Lactalis.

COMMODITY PROCESSORS

The processing segment connects farmers to food manufacturers when there is not a direct link between them. This is particularly true for commodities, which are products that are not easily distinguishable from those sourced from any other supplier. One example is meat processing, an industry that provides poultry, beef, and/or pork to most supermarkets and fast-food chains. Meat processing has become much more concentrated since the 1980s, with market shares of 53 to 82 percent held by the top four firms (Constance et al. 2014). It has also become much more global—the leading US pork processor Smithfield was acquired by a Chinese firm (Shuanghui, renamed the WH Group), and several other dominant US beef and poultry processors were acquired by a Brazilian firm (JBS). This section focuses more specifically on milk and grain processors, to follow the connections to milk and soy milk manufacturers described previously.

Milk Processors

The firms that connect farmers to milk buyers are often organized as **cooperatives**. In the early 1900s there were approximately 2,700 dairy cooperatives, which formed to fight the power of the *milk trust*. Their numbers have declined substantially since then, with some of the largest continuing to merge and combine with each other (Shields 2010). Dairy Farmers of America, for example, is a result of the merger of four farmer cooperatives in 1998. Its executives have behaved more like their corporate counterparts, however, such as lowering prices paid to farmers, as mentioned previously.

In addition, executives have reportedly manipulated markets to increase the prices paid by Dairy Farmers of America customers. The former chief executive officer, Gary Hanman, bragged that he increased the price of cheese, resulting in an extra $1 billion in revenue, when he headed the firm. He was able to manipulate one of the few open markets, which was influential in determining national prices, because it had so few buyers and sellers. This led to federal charges and eventually tens of millions of dollars in fines and lawsuit settlements. More recently, Dairy Farmers of America and other dairy cooperatives were accused of encouraging farmers to kill dairy cows at young ages to reduce the milk supply and inflate prices. These cooperatives agreed to pay $52 million to settle a resulting class action lawsuit.

Grain Processors

Grain processing continues to be controlled by many of the same firms that have dominated this industry since the late 1800s. The four largest firms globally are sometimes called the ABCD firms, after the first letter of their name: Archer Daniels Midland, Bunge, Cargill, and (Louis) Dreyfus. The first three, along with one farmer cooperative, currently control approximately 85 percent of the processing capacity in the United States. As with dairy, thousands of cooperatives formed in the early 1900s to transport and store these commodities and to counteract the power of corporations. In the decades since, the number of cooperatives has declined, and many of the remaining firms have increased in scale through both mergers and joint ventures with corporations.

These corporations have reduced the number of open markets in the industry by contracting with individual farmers. Such contracts specify in advance what the farmers will grow and the price they will receive for the harvest. The strategy can be appealing for farmers because it reduces uncertainty, but it also allows corporations to bypass spot markets and exert more control over prices. Over time, the number of open markets tends to decline, and contracts tend to have terms that are even more favorable for the processors.

Farmer and consumer advocates have expressed concern that contracts, in combination with acquisitions and alliances that help corporations extend their influence through numerous links in the food chain, will result in a *seamless system*. This means that stages in the food system that were previously separated in ownership, and characterized by competitive markets, could be replaced. Corporate control could extend from the seed to the supermarket shelf, with no opportunities to publicly discover the prices they pay—this is more like the former Soviet Union's centralized and planned economy than a competitive market. Cargill, for example, has joint ventures with seed/chemical firms, contracts with grain and livestock farmers, and processes grains and meats. Because it is a privately held corporation, even less information about its operations is disclosed when compared to publicly traded corporations.

FARMERS

Farming is one segment of the food chain that has yet to be dominated by the large, multinational corporations in terms of ownership, although processors and retailers may exert significant control through contracts. The number of farms in the United States is getting smaller, however, and average farm sizes are increasing. This segment is still made up of millions of operations, but fewer than one hundred thousand account for more than two-thirds of sales.

Growing crops or livestock requires a large amount of land and is highly risky compared to other segments of the food system. Risks of damage to crops or livestock include pests, disease, and weather (e.g., drought, frost, storms). In addition, farming requires more extensive amounts of time in comparison to producing goods in a factory. Some corporations have developed ways to avoid these risks by focusing on providing inputs and encouraging farmers to purchase more each year.

Farmers are sometimes described as being on a **treadmill**, because for many commodities increasing the supply results in lower prices. Farmers therefore have little choice but to increase production and reinforce this trend to make the same amount of money as the previous harvest. To accomplish this goal they must frequently rent more land or buy more seeds, chemicals, fertilizers, tractors, etc. As a result, they pay increasing amounts of money to input firms to obtain the same revenues. They also face the choice of getting bigger, often at the expense of their neighbors, or leaving the business of farming.

The number of dairy farmers in the United States has declined from approximately 135,000 in 1992 to less than 50,000 by 2012. In this same period the median number of cows increased from 101 to 900. Soybean farmers have experienced similar trends, with the median farm size doubling from 1997 to 2007, to five hundred acres. By this time there were approximately ninety thousand farms harvesting soybeans. Many rely on off-farm incomes, as well as government subsidies, which allow them to continue farming even when commodity prices are less than their costs of production.

FARM INPUT FIRMS

Perhaps no part of the food system has consolidated as fast as the inputs that farmers purchase to raise crops and livestock. The previous section described the treadmill that encourages farmers to continually spend more on these products, such as fertilizers and farm machinery. This section focuses more specifically on this process for seeds and animal genetics.

Seeds

Just a few decades ago the seed industry was made up of thousands of small firms, and no firm had even a 1 percent share of the market. Today, nearly half of the global proprietary seed market is controlled by just two firms, Monsanto and DuPont. Notably, these are not just seed firms; they are also agricultural chemical firms. Beginning in the 1970s, several corporations dominant in other industries (e.g., oil companies, grain processors) began acquiring seed firms. By the 1990s the agricultural chemical companies focused their efforts on concentrating the seed industry. One motivation was to tie monopolies on their patented herbicides to emerging monopolies for patented, genetically engineered seeds that were resistant to herbicides (Howard 2009).

These firms were also consolidating the chemical industry, and thirty firms were combined into the *Big Six* by the late 1990s. They have made hundreds of acquisitions of seed companies since that time, and the number of independent seed companies that sell soybeans in the United States is now under one hundred. At this writing, the Big Six firms are in the process of consolidating into a Big Four. Dow is merging with DuPont, and Bayer is acquiring Monsanto. In addition, Syngenta is being acquired by the agrichemical firm ChemChina.

The seed industry has experienced much higher prices as firms consolidated. The price of corn and cotton seeds, for example, increased fivefold in less than twenty years, which is much faster than other agricultural inputs. This led to a Department of Justice antitrust investigation of Monsanto in 2010, but it ended two years later without any enforcement action. In addition, the diversity of seeds has narrowed as seed firms have dropped varieties that are less profitable. This trend increases the risk of disease and threatens food supplies. The genetic uniformity of potatoes in Ireland in the 1800s and corn in North America in the 1960s, for example, led to blight epidemics that substantially reduced harvests for these crops.

The right to save and replant seeds is also being eroded though increasing **intellectual property** protections, which take the common resource of seeds that have been developed over millennia and privatize them (Howard 2015). This has reduced the rate of seed saving for many commodities, particularly soybeans, and steered more farmers into purchasing these inputs every year. The US Supreme Court has made many rulings that have strengthened corporate intellectual property protections in recent decades. Governments enforce these laws, subjecting farmers to fines and even prison terms for saving patented seeds. Seed firms are trying to strengthen intellectual property laws in several countries in the global South through multilateral trade agreement negotiations. Executives from these firms are allowed to serve as "advisors" and have access to the draft texts of these agreements, although they may be kept secret even from members of Congress.

Animal Genetics

Animal genetics is a much smaller industry than seeds, but it has become even more concentrated as large-scale animal agriculture has increased. Globally, the genetics for more than 99 percent of turkeys and 94 percent of egg-laying chickens are controlled by just two European firms, EW Group and Hendrix Genetics. These firms, with the addition of Tyson, also control 95 percent of the genetics for chickens raised for meat. Pork is quite concentrated as well, with four firms controlling approximately two-thirds of research and development.

As a result of this concentration, the number of breeds used in animal agriculture has declined, and the genetics of these breeds have narrowed. More than 85 percent of dairy cows in the United States, for example, are Holsteins. This breed has been selected for high milk production, but is more fragile than most of the other one thousand breeds of cattle. The effective population size for Holsteins has been reduced to just thirty-nine, well below the threshold of one hundred that is considered a minimum for maintaining genetic diversity. Other commercial livestock breeds for key species are also likely to have effective population sizes below one hundred, although this is difficult to confirm because genetic diversity is considered a trade secret.

One of the consequences of this trend is greater susceptibility to disease. Genetic selection has focused on efficiency of converting feed to animal products, rather than disease resistance, and large-scale operations frequently use antibiotics to prevent disease and promote faster growth. Despite this, epidemics of avian influenza and porcine epidemic diarrhea virus have significantly impacted livestock operations in North America and Asia in recent years (IPES-Food 2016). Epidemics have also affected animal genetics firms, such as an outbreak of avian influenza that devastated Groupe Grimaud in France in 2006. This corporation had consolidated its operations into one location, but subsequently decentralized its operations (but not its ownership) to include several other countries in the Northern Hemisphere.

WILL CORPORATIONS CONTINUE TO INCREASE CONTROL?

Most food industries have become more concentrated in recent decades, with fewer and larger firms gaining the power to increase prices in many cases or reduce prices (at least temporarily) to drive competitors out of business in others. This power has also resulted in many other negative impacts, such as less diversity, the loss of smaller-scale farms, and fewer choices for consumers. Can we expect these trends to continue? In the short term the answer is probably yes, because some of the largest combinations on record have occurred in 2016. In the longer term, however, the ability of corporations to expand their influence will face an increasing number of challenges.

The sizes of recent mergers and acquisitions have increased public awareness, as well as the potential negative impacts of these trends. As the Sysco–US Foods example illustrates, US and EU governments have been more willing to take some antitrust actions as a result. Most, however, have addressed near-monopoly situations, and regulators seem quite willing to allow industries to be dominated by as few as two firms, as with the Coke and Pepsi model. In the beer industry, the world's largest firm, AB InBev recently acquired the second largest firm, SABMiller. In many countries in the global South, this will result in a monopoly. In the United States, however, SABMiller's brands are being sold to Molson Coors to preserve the current duopoly.

Even without strong antitrust action by governments, large firms are finding it difficult to increase their power at rates that satisfy investors. Acquiring their largest competitors is a short-term solution, especially when there are fewer companies left to acquire and fewer other avenues for increasing sales and/or cutting costs. Merging with firms in other industries remains an option—analysts speculate that the beer giant AB InBev may acquire Coca-Cola or Pepsi, for example—but the efficiency argument for mergers is exaggerated. It is estimated that one-third of these combinations are eventually undone because they are so unwieldy and fail to achieve their expected advantages.

Many corporations involved in the food system are losing sales to new alternatives that circumvent this highly concentrated system or bypass the hourglass to make more direct connections between producers and consumers. Some of these alternatives include farmers' markets, specialty distributors, artisanal food manufacturers (e.g., craft brewers), food hubs, and smaller-scale input firms (e.g., heirloom seed companies) (see Part 4). One response from dominant firms has been to buy out the most successful of these firms or to imitate them. AB InBev, for example, first introduced "crafty" beers that were similar in appearance to craft brewers' offerings, but has also acquired ten formerly independent craft brewers in the past few years (Howard 2018). These strategies may help them continue to grow, but depend on consumers' lack of awareness or their acceptance of corporate control over new alternatives.

The movements involved in opposing corporate power over the food system are quite diverse and motivated by many different goals. They are increasingly finding commonalities, however, and forming larger coalitions. If these networks continue to become more connected, demands to reduce the negative impacts of greater corporate control will become even more effective and may threaten to reduce the control of more dominant firms. This would require tremendous effort on the part of these resistance movements, however, as well as the participation of significantly more people than we see at present.

Discussion Questions

1. Should food and agriculture-related industries be regulated differently than other industries? Why or why not?
2. If increasing market concentration resulted in lower prices paid to suppliers (such as farmers), but also lower prices for consumers, would you be in favor of this change? Why or why not?
3. Imagine you own a small food business and a large corporation offers to purchase it. What are some reasons for and against making such a deal?
4. Should corporations headquartered in foreign countries be able to acquire US food and agricultural firms as easily as domestic corporations? Why or why not?

Exercises

1. Go to a grocery store and make your way to the refrigerated margarine section. How many brand names are there? Look closely and see whether you can find an indicator of corporate ownership. How many firms account for all the brands of margarine on the shelves? How obvious is this pattern to a typical consumer? Choose another food product and determine whether its ownership patterns are similar or different.
2. Search a news archive such as LexisNexis or Google News (or a single major newspaper like the *New York Times*) using the keywords "price-fixing." What headlines referencing food or agricultural industries do you find? Read several of these articles to learn who was involved in the alleged or admitted price-fixing and how it occurred. Discuss how price-fixing in this industry might be prevented in the future.

Additional Materials

Readings

Leonard, Christopher. 2014. *The Meat Racket: The Secret Takeover of America's Food Business*. New York: Simon & Schuster.

Films

Under Contract: Farmers and the Fine Print. 2017. Sixty-three-minute documentary film. https://vimeo.com/ondemand/undercontract

Websites

Food & Power, http://www.foodandpower.net
Food & Water Watch, http://www.foodandwaterwatch.org
SEEDcontrol. 2016. "A Consolidated Market." Multimedia presentation. http://seedcontrol.eu/en/market.php

References

Adams, Walter, and James W. Brock. 2004. *The Bigness Complex: Industry, Labor, and Government in the American Economy.* 2nd ed. Redwood City, CA: Stanford University Press.

Aron, Nan, Barbara Moulton, and Chris Owens. 1994. "Judicial Seminars: Economics, Academia, and Corporate Money in America." *Antitrust Law & Economics Review* 25 (2): 1–33.

Baines, Joseph. 2014. "Wal-Mart's Power Trajectory: A Contribution to the Political Economy of the Firm." *Review of Capital as Power* 1 (1): 79–109.

Carolan, Michael. 2016. *The Sociology of Food and Agriculture.* 2nd ed. New York: Routledge.

Constance, Douglas H., Mary Hendrickson, Philip H. Howard, and William D. Heffernan. 2014. "Economic Concentration in the Agrifood System: Impacts on Rural Communities and Emerging Responses." In *Rural America in a Changing World: Problems and Prospects for the 2010s,* edited by C. Bailey, L. Jensen, and E. Ransom, 16–35. Morgantown: West Virginia University Press.

Cotterill, Ronald W. 1999. "Jawboning Cereal: The Campaign to Lower Cereal Prices." *Agribusiness* 15 (2): 197–205.

Howard, Philip H. 2009. Visualizing Food System Concentration and Consolidation. *Southern Rural Sociology* 24 (2): 87–110.

Howard, Philip H. 2015. "Intellectual Property and Consolidation in the Seed Industry." *Crop Science* 55 (6): 2489–95.

Howard, Philip H. 2016. *Concentration and Power in the Food System: Who Controls What We Eat?* London: Bloomsbury Academic.

Howard, Philip H. 2018. "Craftwashing in the U.S. Beer Industry." *Beverages* 4 (1).

IPES-Food. 2016. *From Uniformity to Diversity: A Paradigm Shift from Industrial Agriculture to Diversified Agroecological Systems.* Brussels, Belgium: International Panel of Experts on Sustainable Food Systems.

Lynn, Barry C. 2006. "Breaking the Chain." *Harper's Magazine,* July, 29–36.

Martin, Andrew. 2012. "In Dairy Industry Consolidation, Lush Paydays." *The New York Times,* October 28, 2012, BU1.

Shields, Dennis A. 2010. *Consolidation and Concentration in the U.S. Dairy Industry.* R41224. Washington, DC: Congressional Research Service.

Small-scale producer in Honduras who works with local nongovernmental organizations and sells to Walmart. (Photo by Dara Bloom.)

8

Globalization of Food: The World as a Supermarket

J. Dara Bloom

G lobalization is not a new phenomenon; global trade in food and agriculture has existed for centuries. We can see the legacy of global trade in some of the most "traditional" foods that we eat today. Take, for example, a typical Italian meal of spaghetti and tomato sauce. Noodles were originally an Asian dish, and legend has it that it was Marco Polo who brought them back to Europe on one of his expeditions in the 1200s, along with a wide array of spices and other foods that influenced the development of culinary tastes in many European countries. The tomatoes in your marinara sauce once only grew in Central America and were introduced to Europe in the 1500s as part of the Colombian exchange (the introduction of plants and animals from the Americas to Europe; Kipple 2007).

Despite the long history of global trade in food and agriculture, the term *globalization* refers to a more recent phenomenon of intensified global relations that really took off after World War II. What characterizes the current system of global trade in food and agriculture? What factors facilitated globalization in agriculture and the food system? We will explore these questions in this lesson, looking first at the history of globalization and then at the current state of global trade in food and agriculture, and finally we will examine the implications of these trends.

In general, globalization is often thought of in terms of how the introduction of new technologies—from advanced shipping methods to the internet—has brought us all closer together. Globalization is seen as reducing cultural differences while introducing an overarching global culture that is epitomized by the presence of McDonalds and Coca-Cola in even the most remote rural villages. However, sociologists of food and agriculture remind us that globalization is not static or predetermined; rather, globalization is a process, one that includes adaptations to local contexts and one that has frequently been contested by those whom it affects. There are many theories that help to elucidate the phenomenon of globalization, particularly in the field of the sociology of food and agriculture. We are going to start with **food regime theory** to trace the history of globalization and then move to **theories of governance** and **global commodity chain analysis** to understand the current state of globalization and its implications. While each theory takes a slightly different approach, they all share a focus on identifying the organizations that have the power to make decisions and rules that determine the relationships between people, countries, the land, and markets. We can use these theories as a lens that magnifies the power dynamics that are embedded in the rules and relationships that make up the current food system and that determine the trajectory of the process of globalization.

HISTORY OF GLOBALIZATION

As mentioned above, there is a rich history of global trade in the food system, from the Colombian exchange to trade in tea, sugar, and rum, all products that relied on relationships between European colonizers and the agricultural systems in the countries they colonized. These colonizer/colonized relationships in many ways form the basis of the relationships we see today in the global food system between developed countries in the global North and developing countries in the global South.

Food regime theory can help us trace backward to understand the origins of the most recent globalizing trends in the food system; this theory was first developed by Harriet Friedmann and Phil McMichael in 1989. Food regime theory highlights relationships and power dynamics in the global food system and suggests that there are three stages in the recent development of the global food system, which they call **regimes**.

According to Friedmann and McMichael (1989), the first food regime lasted from approximately 1870 through the 1930s and was dominated by the British. In this regime, the British had relationships with settler colonies, such as the United States. Family farmers in the United States produced wheat and exported it to European markets. This wheat was used to feed a growing population of workers, who increasingly left their own farms to migrate to cities and work in factories. Urbanization (migration to cities) and industrialization (a shift to factory work) was happening in the United States during the same period. This system of relationships between family farms in the United States and markets in Europe eventually led to overproduction in the United States, partially starting with the Great Depression. It might seem odd to think of there being too much food during one of the worst financial crises in the United States, but during that time farmers kept farming, although consumers could not afford to buy their products. As a result, the US government stepped in with policies to support farmers during this difficult time. These policies remained in place even as the economy improved, leading farmers to produce more than could be sold on US or European markets.

This is when we see the beginnings of the shift to the second food regime in the 1950s to 1970s. During this regime, developing countries in the global South were brought into the globalized food system. This happened in a couple of new ways that differed from previous relationships between colonizer and colonized countries. First, agricultural surpluses from the United States were distributed internationally as *food aid* to developing countries. Food aid is a concept that might seem very straightforward: the United States was producing too much food, so it sent the surplus to countries where many people were hungry. However, many people felt that food aid had negative consequences, since it flooded markets in developing countries with cheap food, which drove down domestic prices and made it more difficult for farmers in those countries to sell their products. Because of this, instead of calling it food aid, many people refer to this practice as *dumping*. The result of food aid/dumping was that many smaller-scale farmers in developing countries could not compete and left their farms to work in factories or as migrant labor on larger-scale farms. The loss of small-scale farmers across the global South because of the pressures of globalization has led to a disintegration of rural communities and increased urbanization. Many developing countries across the world struggle to provide basic services to rapidly growing urban populations, leading to unsanitary living conditions and issues with organized crime.

Those farmers who stayed on their land in developing countries during the second food regime were introduced to new production technologies designed to increase their yields. This is known as the green revolution, which meant that farmers in developing countries purchased packages of seeds, pesticides, and fertilizers from large, international corporations (see Lesson 6). In addition to the green revolution, farmers in developing countries were encouraged to start producing crops for export rather than for local markets. These crops included the types of fresh fruits and vegetables that you see in a typical US supermarket today. In addition to bringing farmers in developing countries into the globalized food system, this regime also saw changes in consumption in the United States by allowing supermarkets to offer a wider assortment of products, such as tropical fruits, year round. Before this time, buying a tomato in the United States in December was unheard of!

This second food regime began to shift toward a third regime in the 1970s, sparked by rising food and fuel prices. This is where food regime theory gets interesting. Have you ever wondered about how theories are formed and who decides what they look like? Within food regime theory, there is debate among scholars about how we should define the third food regime, the one that characterizes the current global food system. Should we call it the *corporate–environmental food regime* to highlight how corporations are responding to consumers' environmental concerns and integrating sustainability into their operations and marketing (Friedmann 2005)? Or should we call it the *food from somewhere regime* to reflect the need to incorporate social and ecological feedback loops into food systems that recognize that food is produced in specific ecological and social contexts and to counter the invisible repercussions of many global supply chains (Campbell 2009)? Maybe it should just be called the *corporate food regime* to illustrate how corporations, specifically supermarkets, increasingly have more power in the food system than national governments (McMichael 2005, 2009).

We will talk about the themes identified in these potential third food regimes in the following sections. For now, it is important to note that just as what we call the third food regime is up for debate, so is the future of the food system itself. As you become more aware of issues in the global food system, you may want to ask yourself, What do *you* want the third food regime to look like?

GLOBALIZATION IN THE CURRENT FOOD SYSTEM

To better understand the relationships and power dynamics that constitute the emerging third food regime, we can turn to **theories of governance**. Governance focuses on the distribution of power between social spheres and how different configurations of relationships between spheres affect who benefits and who does not. Social spheres consist of (1) the **nation-state**, (2) the **market**, and (3) **civil society**. Who are the actors in each of these spheres? The nation-state refers to *national governments*; historically, governments played a large role in creating the regulations that determined how food was grown and traded, including laws that protected consumers. The market consists primarily of *corporations*, whose primary goal is to increase profits. Civil society can be understood as the large *network of nonprofit and nongovernmental organizations and social movements* that represent the interests of people who may not always be well represented by the other two spheres, including women and indigenous groups. Theories of governance examine how the relationship between these spheres has changed over time, which can help us to understand the trend of globalization in food and agriculture (see Lesson 9 for further elaboration of governance; Higgins and Lawrence 2005).

Let's look at an example to illustrate how theories of governance can help explain globalization in the current food system. Food safety laws traditionally came from national governments. In a democratic society, the national government's role is to ensure that food is produced, traded, and consumed in a safe manner that protects consumers, as well as to ensure that environmental damage is minimized. However, over the years many food safety outbreaks, such as mad cow disease in Europe, reduced consumer confidence in the ability of state-based regulations to protect them. In addition, globalization means that food is often produced in one country and consumed in another, making it hard for any single national government to monitor the product along the whole supply chain. As a result, a group of supermarkets came together in 1997 to create their own food safety standards, known as Global GAP.[1] Global GAP standards (Good Agricultural

---

[1] These standards were called EurepGAP when they were created in 1997 and were renamed Global GAP in 2007.

Practices) are designed to reduce the risk of microbial contamination, including safe pesticide usage and some regulations involving fair labor practices, and are the most influential food safety standards in the marketplace today.

The rise in importance of Global GAP over national food safety standards is an illustration of the shift in governance from the *nation-state* (government-based regulations) to the *market* (corporate-based regulations). The rise in power of corporations in a global economy (and the corresponding decline in the power of the nation-state) to determine regulations that affect who can participate in markets, who benefits, who bears risk, and who loses out is referred to as **neoliberalism** (McCarthy and Prudham 2004). Neoliberalism is an economic theory that became popular in the 1980s that references the earlier work of Adam Smith (1925), which assumes that the "invisible hand of the market," or a **free market** that has fewer regulations and allows corporations to operate freely, will naturally create the most optimum results (see Lesson 9 for greater discussion of neoliberalism).

What are the implications of this shift in governance in the case of food safety standards, and where does *civil society* come into play? Let's take the Walmart corporation as an example to understand how food safety standards work in the global market. You are probably aware that Walmart is the largest supermarket in the United States, but did you realize that Walmart is also the largest supermarket in many other countries? Walmart operates in twenty-three countries around the world, with over eleven thousand stores, making it the largest supermarket in the world. Some of the produce that Walmart stores buy is imported from one country to another (often from developing countries into developed countries). However, some produce is sourced locally within the countries where Walmart operates and sold within its stores in those countries. Therefore, the regulations that Walmart requires of farmers who want to sell to their stores in the United States or developing countries are very influential. Walmart requires that the farmers it buys from are Global GAP certified, meaning that US Department of Agriculture GAP certification (the state-based national standard that was developed by the US Department of Agriculture) will not help farmers who want to sell to Walmart. Why does this matter? Getting Global GAP certified is an expensive process, both for the certification itself and for the changes that farmers must make to their farms to be able to qualify. In addition, the standards were made in consideration of agricultural environmental conditions for farmers in developed countries in the global North, and therefore they often are not applicable for small-scale farmers in developing countries in the global South (Campbell 2005).

Obtaining Global GAP certification is something that large-scale farms in the United States and developing countries who want to sell to Walmart can afford; they often hire food safety specialists to organize their operations and meet the standards. Smaller-scale farmers in the United States often find it prohibitive to obtain Global GAP certification and are therefore excluded from selling to Walmart. For smaller-scale farmers in developing countries, where Walmart buys produce for its local stores, GAP regulations can be overwhelming. This is where *civil society* organizations come into the picture. Walmart has formed public/private partnerships with the US Agency for International Development in many developing countries, such as Guatemala, Honduras, Nicaragua, El Salvador, Zambia, Kenya, Ghana, and Bangladesh. The US Agency for International Development works with local nongovernmental organizations to provide technical assistance to small-scale farmers to help them change their practices (including implementing food safety practices) so that they can sell to Walmart (Bloom 2014, 2015). This is typical of the role of *civil society* under *neoliberalism*. While the theory of neoliberalism assumes that the free market will operate fairly, what we often see is the exclusion of small-scale farmers from being able to participate in (and profit from) markets. It is civil society's role under neoliberalism to help buffer small-scale farmers from the negative consequences of the free market, in this case, to help them to be able to sell to Walmart. Walmart's relationship with the US Agency for International Development also fits with the corporation's sustainability initiative, which includes helping small-scale farmers in developing countries increase their profits (Bloom 2014, 2015). Remember the corporate environmental food regime? Walmart's sustainability initiative, which also includes reducing waste, sourcing sustainable products, and monitoring its suppliers' labor practices, is a prime example of what the food system looks like under the corporate environmental food regime.

The example of food safety regulations and how they are implemented by Walmart illustrates the shifting relationships in neoliberalism. This leads us to the next section, where we can look more closely at the implications of globalization for the North and South.

IMPLICATIONS OF GLOBALIZATION FOR NORTH AND SOUTH

To understand the impacts of globalization in food and agriculture in both the global North and South, let's follow one product from production to consumption. This approach is called **global commodity chain analysis** (Gereffi, Korzeniewicz, and Korzeniewicz 1994). Global commodity chain analysis has been used to show how supply chains, or the path that our food takes to get from farm to fork, have become transnational and increasingly complex with globalization. For this example, let's return to the plate of spaghetti and tomato sauce that began this lesson. Where were the tomatoes in the sauce grown, and how did they make it to your plate?

If you live in the United States, the tomatoes in your sauce probably came from either California or Mexico. Deborah Barndt, in her book *Tangled Routes: Women, Work, and Globalization on the Tomato Trail*, follows the tomato commodity chain from Mexico, through the United States, and to a Canadian supermarket. She highlights the impacts and influences of globalization at each step of the supply chain, reminding us that globalization is not just about the fact that tomatoes are crossing national boundaries; it is also about the history of how the conditions of production and consumption have changed and the role of corporations and state/international policies that affect people at both ends of the chain. Barndt focuses specifically on how globalization affects workers along the commodity chain. Her analysis starts with the Colombian exchange that we mentioned earlier and then moves into the history of tomato production in Mexico, which was industrialized to mimic US production models in the 1920s. This included standardization and assembly line work in the pack house and an increased reliance on women in the workforce. Barndt also points out that these industrialized tomato farms, which in 1994 accounted for 22.5 percent of all the fruits and vegetables produced in Mexico, were monocultures. Monocultures mean that they only produced one variety of tomato, compared to diversified farms, which grow many crops all together. As standardized seeds were developed by corporations to support industrialized farming, as well as to create produce that could withstand the long-distance shipping that is characteristic of the global food system, we have lost 80 percent of the different tomato varieties that were once grown (Barndt 2002).

The year 1994 was pivotal for the relationship between the United States and Mexico, which affected how tomatoes were grown and traded. This was the year that the North American Trade Agreement (NAFTA) went into effect. An example of a free trade agreement that illustrates how the free market works under neoliberalism, NAFTA reduces the ability of national governments to enact regulations to protect domestic markets. The agreement affected the trade in tomatoes in a couple of ways: NAFTA increased foreign investment in large-scale agriculture in Mexico and reduced trade barriers (such as taxes on imports of fruits and vegetables) that led to direct competition between US and Mexican farmers. Some farmers benefitted, while others were negatively affected. For example, US corn is very inexpensive, in part because it has historically been subsidized by the US government. When NAFTA went through, Mexico could no longer tax imports of US corn; as a result, the Mexican market was flooded with cheap corn, which made it impossible for many small-scale Mexican farmers to compete. Many of these small-scale farmers were indigenous and ended up losing their farms and becoming migrant laborers. Tomato farms, however, benefitted from NAFTA. This is because they had a comparative advantage in growing cheap tomatoes. This advantage is in part natural, in terms of a warmer climate, and in part social, since labor in Mexico is cheaper than in the United States and since there was an influx of migrant workers who had lost their land and were looking for work. These smaller-scale farmers who became migrant workers were often exposed to pesticides and other dangerous chemicals and struggled to survive on low wages. In addition, many of these migrants risked their lives to cross the border into the United States in search of higher-paying jobs so that they could support their families (see Lesson 11).

So where does the tomato in your sauce come from? If it was grown in Mexico, it was most likely on a large-scale farm, where it was picked by an indigenous migrant laborer. It was then sorted in a pack house, most likely by a female worker, since the delicate job of packing tomatoes is considered women's work. If you made your own sauce from fresh tomatoes, then your tomato was packed in a crate and shipped by tractor trailer. If you prefer to make sauce from canned tomatoes or tomato paste, then it was most likely shipped to a processor, still within Mexico, before making its way to your local supermarket. Barndt's (2002) commodity chain analysis also highlights the role of transportation and consumption in the globalized food system and the effect on workers. Your tomato must make it to the US/Mexico border, where it is inspected to ensure that it is being transported at the right temperature and meets standards related to the quality of the fruit (such as the color). The tomato then passes through a series of brokers and wholesalers, including large-scale terminal markets, where multiple produce buyers sell to the final buyer. In Barndt's analysis, the tomato makes its way to Canada, a three-day journey by truck across the United States, before entering the Ontario Food Terminal (and crossing yet another border). When the tomato is finally put on a shelf in a supermarket, Barndt points out how technology enables supermarkets to monitor their inventory, pricing, and the productivity of its workers. In this way, work in supermarkets for employees such as cashiers has also changed under the context of globalization. This workforce is now much more flexible, meaning that most employees work part time. This means that they are often not paid benefits and very often are not allowed to be in unions that could advocate on their behalf for better pay and work conditions (see Lesson 11).

Finally, Barndt (2002) looks at changes in consumption and consumer expectations. In addition to wanting year-round availability of fresh fruits and vegetables, consumers increasingly expect that the fruits and vegetables they purchase in supermarkets will be uniform in size, shape, and color (see Lesson 1). These expectations have led to a large amount of food waste, since produce that does not meet these standards may never make it to the supermarket shelf, despite being completely safe and healthy to eat. By some estimates, 40 percent of food is wasted in the US food system, representing an estimated $165.6 billion (Buzby and Hyman 2012; Gunders 2017).

Pritchard and Burch (2003) also look at how the tomato industry has changed because of the processes of globalization. However, rather than looking at one specific commodity chain, as Barndt did, they analyze how the economics and geography of the production, processing, and consumption of tomatoes have changed across the globe. They look specifically at processing tomatoes (the ones that end up in tomato paste and sauces), showing how increased consumption of products such as ketchup and pizza have led to an increase in processing tomato production. Like Barndt (2002), they mention the consolidation in the seed industry, spurred by the need to breed tomatoes that can withstand mechanized harvesting and shipping. Pritchard and Burch explain that one-third of processing tomatoes come from California, and 10 percent of these are destined to be used in pizza sauce in the United States. Unlike Mexico, California tomato farms use machines to harvest their tomatoes. Pritchard and Burch also look at production and processing across the globe; for example, they look at one instance where tomato paste is processed in China, sent to Italy, where it is cooked with beans from Mexico, and then canned and shipped to Great Britain, where it is sold and consumed.

Clearly, the globalized food system is complex. It is a network of producers, workers, processors, distributors, and consumers who are all influenced by international policies and changes in consumption patterns. However, as mentioned earlier, globalization is not predetermined or unilinear; rather, it is a process that is influenced by local contexts and is often contested. We have seen many social movements develop over the years to resist some of the negative consequences of globalization, opening up spaces for resistance (Hendrickson and Heffernan 2002). For example, in 1994, the same year that NAFTA went into effect, indigenous groups in Mexico staged an uprising to protest their loss of land. Known as the Zapatistas, this movement drew attention to the uneven process of globalization, reminding us that not everyone has benefited (Barndt 2002).

Another example of a social movement that developed as a reaction to the globalization of the food system is Via Campesina. The Via Campesina movement brings together small-scale and medium-sized farmers across the world, including women and indigenous farmers, as well as landless people, migrants, and agricultural workers. The main emphasis of this social movement is the promotion of food sovereignty, which it defines as "the right of peoples to healthy and culturally appropriate food produced through sustainable methods and their right to define their own food and agriculture systems" (https://viacampesina.org; see also Lesson 18). Via Campesina began as a grassroots movement in 1993 and now is one of the most influential organizations representing civil society on the global scale. One of the interesting things about Via Campesina is their global approach; this social movement recognizes that small-scale farmers around the world are negatively affected by the corporate dominance of agriculture and the food system that has occurred as part of neoliberalism and globalization. Via Campesina promotes solidarity between farmers and farmworkers in the global North and South, resisting neoliberal trends by asserting that those who produce food have the right to make decisions about how agriculture and the food system are governed. In a sense, you could say that this is a different vision of what *globalization* can look like.

Much of the resistance to the globalization of the food system is grounded in the idea that food production and consumption are inherently *embedded* in local places, including those places' natural environments and social systems. This is the idea behind the "food from somewhere" food regime (Campbell 2009). In the United States, this has led to a movement that prioritizes developing *local* food systems (see Lesson 17). Researchers have reminded us that localized production is not free from local power structures, nor does it guarantee that sustainable agricultural or labor practices are used (DuPuis and Goodman 2005; Hinrichs 2003). However, the local food movement in the United States is often related to promoting economic development and supporting small-scale agriculture, echoing themes identified by Via Campesina and other social movements that seek to reassert control over an increasingly globalized food system.

Conclusion

This lesson has introduced us to the concept of globalization in agriculture and the food system. We started with the idea that global trade is not new; rather, it intensified as a result of relationships between colonizer/colonized countries and the emerging power of corporations. We turned to **food regime theory** to highlight these changes and to illustrate how something that might seem positive in the global food system, like food aid, looks different depending on your perspective. Some of the major themes that we can identify across the three major food regimes include those of urbanization and industrialization, the movement of small-scale farmers from owning their own land to becoming migrant workers on larger-scale farms or in factories in urban areas. In this way, many small-scale farmers have been negatively affected by globalization, since they have lost their land in exchange for potential exposure to unsafe working environments and low wages. In this lesson, we also demonstrated how theories themselves are emerging and contested.

Next, we turned to **theories of governance** to understand how globalization functions in the current system. We saw how globalization often relates to neoliberalization, or the rise in power of corporations compared to nation-states. We took the example of food safety standards and saw how standards that were developed by governments have largely been replaced by corporate standards and how organizations representing civil society often bear the responsibility for working with small-scale farmers to make sure that they are integrated into new markets.

Finally, we turned to the implications of globalization, starting first with a **global commodity chain analysis** that traced the history and multiple paths of the tomato. This example once again highlighted common themes of industrialization and the shift of small-scale farmers to migrant farmworkers. This led us to examine how small-scale farmers and farmworkers have resisted globalization, including by forming the social movement of Via Campesina. Once again, this example reminded us that globalization is not a predetermined track, leaving us to wonder what the future of the food system holds.

Discussion Questions

1. What name would you give to the third food regime? What are the primary relationships and trends that you observe in the current food system?
2. Do you care where your food comes from? Why or why not?
3. In your opinion, which social sphere should have ultimate control over decision-making and regulations in the food system, the nation-state, the market, or civil society? Why?

Exercise

How globalized is your dinner? Look at your dinner and try to identify what country each of the components of your dinner originated from and where it was processed. How much came from the country in which you live and how much came from other countries? Next, choose one food item and analyze why the food item was grown where it was and what the implications are for that country.

Additional Materials

Readings

> Estabrook, Barry. 2011. *Tomatoland: How Modern Industrial Agriculture Destroyed Our Most Alluring Fruit*. Kansas City, MO: Andrews McMeel.
> NPR story about the green revolution, http://www.npr.org/2009/04/14/102944731/green-revolution-trapping-indias-farmers-in-debt

Websites

> Food Waste, https://www.epa.gov/sustainable-management-food
> Global GAP, https://www.google.com/search?q=global+gap&ie=utf-8&oe=utf-8
> Green revolution, http://geography.about.com/od/globalproblemsandissues/a/greenrevolution.htm, http://www.nationalgeographic.com/foodfeatures/green-revolution/
> US Department of Agriculture GAP, https://www.ams.usda.gov/services/auditing/gap-ghp
> US Agency for International Development, https://www.usaid.gov/sites/default/files/documents/15396/usaid_partnership report_FINAL3.pdf
> Via Campesina, https://viacampesina.org/en/
> Walmart Sustainability Report, http://corporate.walmart.com/2016grr
> Zapatistas, http://www.bbc.com/news/world-latin-america-25550654

Video Clips

> Food Aid video, https://www.youtube.com/watch?v=PUYAjoZCc9w
> John Oliver clip about food waste, https://www.youtube.com/watch?v=i8xwLWb0lLY
> Zapatistas video, https://www.youtube.com/watch?v=lDNuzFQW3uI

References

Barndt, Deborah. 2002. *Tangled Routes: Women, Work, and Globalization on the Tomato Trail*. Lanham, MD: Rowman & Littlefield.

Bloom, J. Dara. 2014. "Civil Society in Hybrid Governance: Non-Governmental Organization (NGO) Legitimacy in Mediating Wal-Mart's Local Produce Supply Chains in Honduras." *Sustainability* 6:7388–411.

Bloom, J. Dara. 2015. "Standards for Development: Food Safety and Sustainability in Wal-Mart's Honduran Produce Supply Chains." *Rural Sociology* 80 (2): 198–227.

Buzby, Jean C., and Jeffrey Hyman. 2012. "Total and Per Capita Value of Food Loss in the United States." *Food Policy* 37 (5): 561–70.

Campbell, Hugh. 2005. "The Rise and Rise of EurepGAP: European (Re)Invention of Colonial Food Relations?" *International Journal of Sociology of Agriculture and Food* 13 (2): 1–19.

Campbell, Hugh. 2009. "Breaking New Ground in Food Regime Theory: Corporate Environmentalism, Ecological Feedbacks and the 'Food from Somewhere' Regime?" *Agriculture and Human Values* 26 (4): 309–19.

DuPuis, E. Melanie, and David Goodman. 2005. "Should We Go "Home" to Eat?: Toward a Reflexive Politics of Localism." *Journal of Rural Studies* 21 (3): 359–71.

Friedmann, Harriet. 2005. "From Colonialism to Green Capitalism: Social Movements and Emergence of Food Regimes," in Frederick H. Buttel, Philip McMichael (ed.) *New Directions in the Sociology of Global Development (Research in Rural Sociology and Development, Volume 11)* Emerald Group Publishing Limited, pp.227–264

Friedmann, Harriet, and Philip McMichael. 1989. "Agriculture and the State System: The Rise and Decline of National Agricultures, 1870 to the Present." *Sociologia Ruralis* 29 (2): 93–117.

Gereffi, Gary, Miguel Korzeniewicz, and Roberto P. Korzeniewicz. 1994. "Introduction: Global Commodity Chains." In *Commodity Chains and Global Capitalism*, edited by G. Gereffi and M. Korzeniewicz, 1–14. Westport, CT: Praeger.

Gunders, Dana. 2012. *Wasted: How America Is Losing up to 40 Percent of Its Food from Farm to Fork to Landfill*. Natural Resources Defense Council Issue Paper 17-05-A. August 2017. https://www.nrdc.org/resources/wasted-how-america-losing-40-percent-its-food-farm-fork-landfill

Hendrickson, Mary K., and William D. Heffernan. 2002. "Opening Spaces through Relocalization: Locating Potential Resistance in the Weaknesses of the Global Food System." *Sociologia Ruralis* 42 (4): 347–69.

Higgins, Vaughan, and Geoffrey Lawrence. 2005. "Introduction: Globalization and Agricultural Governance." In *Agricultural Governance: Globalization and the New Politics of Regulation*, edited by V. Higgins and G. Lawrence, 1–15. Abingdon, Oxon: Routledge.

Hinrichs, C. Clare. 2003. "The Practice and Politics of Food System Localization." *Journal of Rural Studies* 19 (1): 33–45.

Kipple, Kenneth F. 2007. *A Movable Feast: Ten Millennia of Food Globalization*. Cambridge: Cambridge University Press.

McCarthy, James, and Scott Prudham. 2004. "Neoliberal Nature and the Nature of Neoliberalism." *Geoforum* 35 (3): 275–83.

McMichael, P., 2005. "Global development and the corporate food regime," in Frederick H. Buttel, Philip McMichael (ed.) *New Directions in the Sociology of Global Development (Research in Rural Sociology and Development, Volume 11)* Emerald Group Publishing Limited. (pp. 265-299).

McMichael, Philip. 2009. "A Food Regime Genealogy." *The Journal of Peasant Studies* 36:139–69.

Pritchard, Bill, and David Burch. 2003. *Agri-Food Globalization in Perspective: International Restructuring in the Processing Tomato Industry.* Burlington, VT: Ashgate.

Smith, Adam. 1925. *An Inquiry into the Nature and Causes of the Wealth of Nations.* Edited by E. Cannan. Vols. 1 and 2. London: Methuen.

Misshapen or "ugly" carrots and tomatoes. (Photos: carrots, © Mohammad Jangda / Flickr / CC BY-SA 2.0; tomatoes, Stephanie Cobb.)

9

Governing Agriculture: Public Policy and Private Governance

Elizabeth Ransom

I f you have ever spent any time growing your own fruits or vegetables, you quickly discover that your produce comes in all sorts of shapes, with your carrots not being perfectly straight or your tomatoes appearing perfectly round. Yet, walk into most supermarkets in North America or Europe and all those misshapen fruits and vegetables are nowhere to be found. Why? In the United States, retailers have historically refused to purchase so-called ugly fruit from farmers or wholesalers (who buy from the farmers), while in Europe the European Union (EU) has regulations that prohibit oddly shaped fruits and vegetables from being sold. To be clear, a crooked carrot offers the same nutritional benefit as a straight carrot; this is simply about aesthetics, which are controlled in the United States by private retailers and in Europe by the EU. Should you want to eat more misshapen fruit, there is good news! Both the United States and the EU have seen some changes to the ban on ugly fruit in recent years as a result of increasing concerns expressed by individuals and activist groups over the amount of food waste caused by misshapen fruit and vegetables being thrown away instead of consumed. The EU announced a loosening of their rules in the midst of the global economic downturn in 2008, when many people found themselves food insecure and some leaders saw it as morally repugnant to throw away produce that instead could be sold at cheaper prices (Castle 2008). In 2016 in the United States, the largest retailer, Walmart, announced plans to start selling ugly fruits and vegetables on a trial basis in select stores (Godoy 2016). There is even a Twitter handle created by someone in California dedicated to raising awareness about ugly fruit in an effort to reduce food waste (https://twitter .com/UglyFruitAndVeg)!

This lesson focuses our attention on governance of our food system, whether it relates to misshapen fruits and vegetables or ensuring the safety of the foods we eat. Focusing on governance reveals how governance regulates both humans and nonhumans and, in doing so, demonstrates that governance has political and moral significance. In this lesson, I present four areas of governance in our food system, including multinational (quasi-public) governance, private retailers governance, nongovernmental organization (NGO)–led sustainability governance, and alternative agrifood governance. Understanding governance will challenge readers to consider why the governance of our food system should be of great interest to anyone interested in power, inequality, and creating a more just and sustainable food system.

OVERVIEW OF GOVERNANCE

Governance refers to the institutions, both formal and informal, that promulgate the rules that govern society and support human economic activities and social interactions (North 1990; Nelson 2010). Laws, policies, and constitutions fall under formal institutions, which distribute and delimit the powers of the state and citizens, whereas norms, customs, and ethical beliefs make up informal institutions that govern human behavior through social interactions (Nelson 2010, 7). Food safety laws are an example of formal governance that identifies whether foods are fit for human consumption. Food safety laws exist at the local, state, national, and international levels. Despite **formal governance** through laws, it is noteworthy that **informal governance** can support or contradict formal governance. Raw milk consumption in the United States (Paxson 2008) is an example of an activity that takes place in contradiction to authorities having deemed the product illegal. Thus, in the realm of the governance of our agriculture and food system, informal governance should be understood as situated alongside formal governance. Much of the discussion in this lesson will focus on formal governance, but there will be instances where informal governance clearly plays a role in shaping our agrifood system. Toward the end of this lesson, we will consider examples in which formal governance emerges in response to informal governance practices, for example, the creation of formal animal welfare policies and standards or retailers agreeing to sell ugly produce in the context of increasing demand by consumers and activist groups.

Governance of our food system has experienced considerable change in the past half century because of economic policies and technological innovations. The most recent set of changes in our food system occurred under the banner of neoliberal globalization. According to social scientists, **neoliberalism** is both an economic theory and a political project (Harvey 2005). The premise of neoliberalism is an emphasis on reducing the role of governments, creating strong private property rights, and increasing free markets and trade (Harvey 2005). The private sector or public–private partnerships have more responsibility for governing under neoliberalism.[1] An example of public–private partnerships is the transformation of the inspection process for food-processing facilities. Whereas previous inspections were carried out

---

[1] The degree to which this occurs differs by nations, with some nations having ironically expanded the role of the state in certain sectors, while implementing neoliberal policies in other sectors (see Ferguson 2015, analysis of African nations).

entirely by government officials, private facilities now conduct the majority of their inspections, usually contracting the work to a third-party private company. Records of the inspections are documented and kept on file for government inspectors who visit the plants, but with less frequency. These records are also now required by supermarkets, who set specific standards that processors must comply with if they wish to sell to supermarkets, a topic discussed later.

While governments and lawmakers began putting neoliberal policies in place in the 1980s, scholars see the founding of the World Trade Organization (WTO) in 1995 as the full realization of neoliberal policies. In concrete terms, neoliberal policies allow companies to now import and export products or portions of products across multiple countries. Historically, national governments heavily regulated and protected agriculture, and when international agricultural trade occurred, it took a rather linear path. What this means is that raw commodities, like sugar, were harvested in developing countries, shipped to industrializing countries for processing, and then shipped to industrialized countries for consumers to purchase. In contrast, today's commodity chains are much more complex and sometimes follow circular routes. For example, farmers in developing countries still grow sugar. However, the sugar may be sent for processing to multiple different countries, which then may ship the processed sugar to several other countries where it is integrated into additional products (e.g., cereal, soda, chocolate), which are then shipped out to multiple countries for consumers to purchase, including consumers in the countries that produced the sugar as a raw commodity. Neoliberal globalization facilitates the flow of goods around the globe, although not everyone benefits equally from this, as smallholder producers often find themselves unable to compete in this new trading environment (see Jayne, Mather, and Mghenyi 2010; Lee, Gereffi, and Beauvais 2012).[2] With the rise of neoliberal globalization, there are two important features of governance in today's food system.

First, governance of our food system, while designed by humans, aims to control the actions not only of humans, but also of nonhumans. It is estimated that more than two hundred known diseases are transmitted through food by a variety of agents that include bacteria, fungi, viruses, and parasites (Oliver, Jayarao, and Almeida 2005). The emphasis on governing nonhumans (e.g., animals, seed, diseases, pathogens, pests) has increased under neoliberal globalization, as more humans and nonhumans traverse the globe. Take, for example, the spread of diseases that originate from farm animals. I traveled to southern Africa in the midst of the global pandemic of *swine flu* in 2009. Swine flu (officially known as H1N1 influenza virus) can be contracted from close contact with infected humans or pigs. Officially, in 2009 swine flu

---

[2] Smallholders generally refer to farmers who farm on a limited amount of land and who often have limited access to resources, such as capital, labor, and skills. Despite this broad categorization, smallholders as a category are diverse in composition and exist throughout the world, although the majority are located in Africa, Asia, and the Pacific (see Birner and Resnick 2010; Van der Ploeg 2008).

was identified as having begun in Mexico, but it quickly spread around the globe, in the end killing an estimated 285,000 people with almost all countries eventually confirming the presence of the virus (CDC 2012; WHO 2010).

In 2009, as I arrived at the airport in Namibia, a country located in southwest Africa, approximately seventy-four countries and territories had reported confirmed infections. I was greeted, as were all the other airline passengers, by two women wearing surgical masks handing out a flyer that said, "the patient who gave this to you likely had swine flu." Despite the possible negative tourist implications, the goal was to raise awareness about swine flu and how to prevent the spread of the virus, with the flyer providing warning signs (e.g., high fever) and ways to prevent the spread of the disease (e.g., wash your hands, wear a mask over your nose and mouth). The women handing out the flyers in the airport were government employees. In this instance, the Namibian government was trying to control the spread of a disease through educating humans because infected humans can spread the disease to other humans and pigs. The Namibian government's efforts were important, although perhaps not particularly effective, because the goal was to stem the tide of people (and pigs) infected on the continent of Africa, which likely experienced a higher proportion of human deaths as a result of limited health-care facilities and poorer nutritional status, among other reasons.

Returning to the example of raw milk, the US government bans the interstate sale or distribution of raw milk (US Federal Regulation 21 CFR § 1240.61) because of concerns that raw milk can contain pathogens like *Salmonella*, *Listeria monocytogenes*, *Staphylococcus aureus*, and *Escherichia coli*, all of which can contribute to human illnesses and, in some cases, death. The degree to which raw milk sales are allowed within states varies (because the federal government only regulates sales across state lines) and has shifted in recent years as a result of pressure from citizens who want to be able to consume raw milk. Citizens lobbying for raw milk accessibility believe there are many "good" microorganisms—bacteria, yeast, and mold found in raw milk that are lost in the pasteurization process (see Paxson 2008).[3] Thus, federal law allows only for the interstate sale of pasteurized milk, which not only impacts the actions of humans, but also impacts the presence of microbes found in milk, which raw milk advocates see as impacting good microbes, in addition to the bad microbes. As of 2016, eleven states allow the sale of raw cow's milk in retail stores, while twenty states have a complete ban prohibiting the sale of raw milk, with the remaining states falling along a continuum of permissibility.

Both examples provided above, controlling the spread of swine flu in Namibia and the case of good versus bad microbes in raw milk in the United States, point to the need to control humans and nonhumans in our food system. These examples also highlight a tension in governing our global

---

[3] Pasteurization involves heating foods (e.g., milk, cheese, wine) to an elevated temperature to kill potentially harmful microorganisms.

food system today. In the words of a famous anthropologist, Sidney Mintz (2002, 27, quoted in Paxson 2008), the tension is "how to provide protection to the citizenry on one hand, yet maintain freedom of choice on [the] other." Governance of our food system has historically focused on keeping a safe food supply and these efforts were historically the domain of national governments, including the United States, nations within western Europe, and, by extension, the former European colonies (King 2002). However, who oversees the regulation of safe food has shifted under neoliberalism. What used to be the sole domain of the nation-state now includes international and quasi-public organizations (e.g., WTO, World Organisation for Animal Health), private organizations (e.g., supermarkets), NGOs, and even private citizens. This **shift from governments to governance** is the second important feature of food governance today.

Governance of food and agriculture was historically the domain of governments, but very recently, we have seen an increase in private actors regulating our food system. Private actors refer to NGOs, private food processors and retailers, and multinational (quasi-public) entities, alongside national governments. Ugly fruits are an example of this shift in our food system as EU regulations, North American supermarkets, and even one citizen in California are all active in determining whether ugly produce is regularly available to consumers. Thus, we have seen a shift from government to governance in our food system, and this has important implications for thinking about our food system moving forward, especially if you are interested in creating a more sustainable and just food system. Let us turn to a discussion of the four areas of governance in our food system today, multinational (quasi-public) governance, private retailer governance, nongovernmental-led sustainability governance, and alternative agrifood governance, to better understand the consequences of the shift from governments to governance.

MULTINATIONAL (QUASI-PUBLIC) GOVERNANCE

As previously mentioned, a key change to governance of our food system occurred in 1995 with the founding of the WTO, which today has 164 member countries. Whereas previously agriculture had been largely protected by nation-states from negotiations in trade agreements, the founding of the WTO and subsequent growth of regional trade agreements (RTAs) brought agriculture squarely into global trade negotiations and governance. The WTO is the only international organization that deals with rules of trade between nations, with the goal of ensuring trade flows as smoothly, predictably, and freely as possible (WTO 2016). In the realm of agriculture, prior to the founding of the WTO, there were many barriers to trade. The WTO attempted to confront barriers to trade by dealing directly with some of the most common barriers, which included: (i) tariffs (e.g., when countries applied an extra fee on imported foods); (ii) rules of origin (e.g., when countries required that a product, like fruit, be labeled with the country of origin); and (iii) nontariff measures, such as food safety regulations (e.g., when a country blocked a product from entry on the grounds that the pesticide residue on the fruit or vegetable was too high; these are known as sanitary and phytosanitary and technical barriers to trade regulations in the WTO).

One consequence of the WTO has been the growth of RTAs. Figure 9.1 provides an overview of the growth of these agreements, which, not coincidentally, began to increase in the lead-up to and subsequent founding of the WTO. One of the earliest RTAs impacting agricultural systems in North America is the North American Free Trade Agreement (NAFTA), which was implemented in 1994. One well-documented consequence of NAFTA on agriculture is the case of Mexican corn farmers. With the passage of NAFTA, cheap US agricultural products, particularly corn (a crop that is subsidized by the US government), flooded the Mexican markets, which contributed to declines in the prices that Mexican farmers received for their corn. As testimony to the US Senate Subcommittee on International Trade of the Committee on Finance summarized in 2006, "Mexican agriculture has been a net loser in trade with the United States, and employment in the sector has declined sharply. U.S. exports of subsidized crops such as corn have depressed agricultural prices in Mexico" (Polaski 2006, 1; see also Zanhiser and Coyle

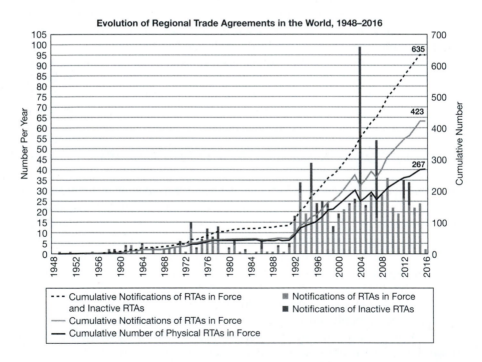

Figure 9.1 World Trade Organization Database of Regional Trade Agreements. (World Trade Organization 2016, https://www.wto.org/english/tratop_e/region_e/regfac_e.htm.)

2004). As Lesson 8 in this book noted, not all Mexican farmers lost out, because tomato production in Mexico benefited from NAFTA, but that does not help the primarily indigenous, small-scale corn farmers who joined a steady stream of other small-scale farmers leaving farming because it was no longer a viable occupation.

Despite the efforts of the WTO to increase trade flows, trade talks for the WTO effectively stalled in 1999 at the Ministerial Conference in Seattle, with agriculture being one of the key issues around which significant disagreement existed. Figure 9.1 shows that after 1999, most trade negotiations now happen via RTAs, as opposed to working through the WTO. In 1999, there were approximately 150 RTAs in force, and since that time an additional 273 agreements have come into force. To put this into perspective, over a fifty-one-year period (1948–99) there were a total of 150 RTAs, whereas in a sixteen-year period (2000–16) there were 273 RTAs according to the WTO graph (Figure 9.1). While these RTAs cover a wide range of topics, agriculture features prominently in many RTAs, because agriculture has been one of the thornier topics covered within the WTO. For example, one of the biggest roadblocks as it relates to agriculture has been between the United States, Europe, and developing countries, as developing countries have appropriately noted they cannot compete with the massive amount of farmer subsidies the United States and the EU continue to provide to farmers (McBride 2016).

Because of the growing importance of RTAs in global governance of agriculture and food, the WTO keeps a database of RTAs, with many interested parties studying their impacts. An analysis of fifty-three RTAs as they relate specifically to agriculture found that these agreements do have significant effects on agricultural trade flows (OECD 2015). Not having a free trade agreement with a specific market is considered a disadvantage in the current world trading system (OECD 2015). For example, the US RTAs include NAFTA, along with thirteen other free trade agreements that are in force with twenty countries. One of the more recent RTAs entered into by the United States allowed US exports of corn, soybeans, and soybean meal to Columbia to more than double within three years of the beginning of the free trade agreement in 2012 (USDA 2016).

Thus, while the WTO was created with the goal of reducing barriers to trade, in part through increasing transparency in trade rules, the new terrain of RTAs presents countries with a "spaghetti bowl of trade rules and commitments," with the average WTO member having thirteen RTAs and some members having over twenty RTAs (OECD 2015, 8). To be clear, each RTA represents a combination of economic and political objectives. For example, it is argued that consumers benefit from RTAs like NAFTA, with, for instance, increased availability of grape tomatoes and avocadoes at a reasonable price in the United States (USDA 2016). At the same time, RTAs are seen as a mechanism to increase institutional and policy cooperation and coordination between national governments (USDA 2016). Less discussed but obviously both an economic and a political concern is the impact that these policies have on workers and availability of jobs; for example, in the case of NAFTA, Mexico saw a dramatic decline of farmers, without an equal increase in other job opportunities (Zanhiser and Coyle 2004). More recently, US president Donald Trump pulled out of a recently negotiated RTA, known as the Trans-Pacific Partnership, as part of his campaign promise to help American workers, because there was a perception that lower-paid workers in Vietnam and Malaysia, two signatory countries to the Trans-Pacific Partnership, would be in competition for the jobs of higher-wage workers in the United States (Baker 2017). In this way, RTAs are similar to other governance initiatives in that they have not only economic, but also political implications.

While much of the discussion in this section has focused on the WTO, it is important to note there are many other quasi-public governance groups that are shaping the food system. There are official groups that are reference bodies to the WTO, such as the World Organization for Animal Health and intergovernmental groups that have observer status. There are also so-called for-profit standards developers like the International Organization for Standardization and the Food Marketing Institute. Public citizens rarely recognize these quasi-public entities in the role they play in governance, with these entities increasingly setting standards or certifications that governments then adopt or accept as their own. To be clear, some of these organizations are actually private organizations, but we refer to them as quasi-public because these groups take a variety of forms, including trade associations, professional societies, and not-for-profit organizations, with national governments accepting to varying degrees the standards and certifications promulgated by these groups (Busch 2011; Rudder, Fritschler, and Choi 2016).

PRIVATE RETAILERS/SUPERMARKET GOVERNANCE

The rise of private retailers and their power within our agriculture and food system is another profound shift that we have seen in the past thirty years. There has been a real shift in the concentration and therefore the power of food retailers around the globe (see Lesson 7). With massive retailers like Walmart, headquartered in the United States, and Tesco, headquartered in the United Kingdom, they use their "oligarchic position in the marketplace, together with their ability to source products from around the globe, to establish themselves as the primary gatekeeper to consumer markets" (Bain, Ransom, and Higgins 2013, 3). What this means is, because of their size and the amount of the market that they control, retailers have increasingly dictated the terms of exchange with suppliers and farmers. The US food retail market remains less concentrated than that of many European nations, but Figure 9.2 demonstrates the growing concentration, with the top four retailers, Walmart Stores, Inc., Kroger, Safeway, and Publix Super Markets, controlling close to 40 percent of the US retail market by 2013.

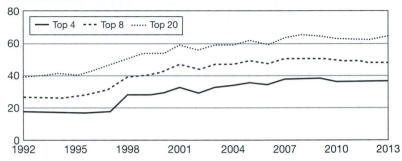

Top 4, 8, and 20 firms' share of U.S. grocery store sales, 1992–2013

In 2013, the share of sales in the top 20 U.S. grocery retailers rose for the first time since the 2007–09 recession

Percent of sales

Figure 9.2 Concentration in the US Food Retail Sector. (Economic Research Service, US Department of Agriculture 2016; https://www.ers.usda.gov/topics/food-markets-prices/retailing-wholesaling/retail-trends.aspx.)

Retailers have increasingly gotten in the business of implementing so-called private standards that act as a form of governance in our food system. The types of standards run the gamut from food safety standards that go above and beyond those required by governments to so-called product standards, which can include a wide range of specifications including the color and size of fruits and vegetables or ensuring producers conform to organic production practices. Oftentimes, retail standards are put in place because the company sees an opportunity to create a competitive advantage with consumers. As attractive as some of these retailer standards may seem to you as a consumer, the problem is that retailers rarely bear the brunt of the increased costs of production. Indeed, with concentration, retailers like Walmart are able to set the price they are willing to pay for a product, which means that suppliers and farmers often shoulder the costs of retail standards (see Lesson 8). For example, Walmart is famous for pushing costs on to suppliers, all the while demanding lower prices (Gereffi and Christian 2009). Walmart also changes strategies as it relates to supply chain management and labor, depending on the country of operation. For example, in Mexico and Honduras Walmart attempted to bypass middlemen and work directly with farmers (Gereffi and Christian 2009).

There are also instances where consumers are willing to pay more for particular products because of guaranteed higher retail standards. For example, specialty stores like Whole Foods in the United States has been nicknamed *whole paycheck* because of the retailer's high prices. Yet, consumers clearly are willing to pay more for Whole Foods' commitment to providing the "finest natural and organic foods available," while they also "maintain the strictest quality standards in the industry, and have an unshakeable commitment to sustainable agriculture" (Whole Foods 2017). Despite these high food standards, Whole Foods has also been accused of being antiunion for those who labor in their stores, similar to Walmart's labor practices in North America (Harris 2006, cited in Gereffi and Christian 2009). To be clear, retailers are not only changing the governance of our food system, but also responding to the broader global neoliberal economic policies, which reveals how these various forms of governance in our food system are interwoven (see Davis 2005; Gereffi and Christian 2009).

NONGOVERNMENTAL ORGANIZATION–LED SUSTAINABILITY GOVERNANCE

Alongside the growth of retail governance, we have seen the rise of NGOs exerting pressure on the governance system, especially on private-sector actors. Most labels you find in the grocery store today that make some type of non–health related claim are actually the domain of NGOs. For example, fair trade bananas, dolphin-friendly tuna, and sustainably produced palm oil are all created (along with the accompanying practices that allow for use of the label) by NGOs. The rise of NGO certification has largely been in response to what many people perceive as the destructive environmental, social, and consumption practices within the modern agriculture and food system (Bain et al. 2013). These NGOs seek to develop alternative governance in the food system, which for many includes prioritizing nonmonetary values, like the environment and the equitable treatment of agricultural workers, farmers, and/or animals (see Part 4).

A good example of NGO activity to pressure retailers is the case of sustainable beef initiatives. Cattle ranching in Brazil was identified to be one of the largest causes of deforestation worldwide by Greenpeace, an environmental activists group, in 2009 (see Figure 9.3). The Greenpeace report made the connection that this was a global problem because the bulk of beef produced in Brazil was being consumed by US and European consumers and they put pressure on the largest retailers, Walmart in the United States and Tesco in the United Kingdom, as well as meat processors in Brazil (see Cameron 2016).

Since that time several initiatives have been put in place in Brazil and across the globe to push for more sustainable beef production. Beyond deforestation for grazing land, cattle are seen as problematic for the environment in relation to water (e.g., fecal contamination of water) and air pollution (e.g., methane from flatulence), among other reasons. Each initiative has met with varying degrees of success. For example, in Brazil, some farmers now qualify to have their beef labeled with the Rainforest Alliance's little green frog seal and this beef is sold in gourmet supermarkets in Brazil. However, the bulk of beef farmers in Brazil do not subscribe to a program that would allow them to label their beef in this way, in part because consumer demand for sustainable beef, both in Brazil and throughout the world, is simply not there, which means there are not enough price incentives for farmers to invest in

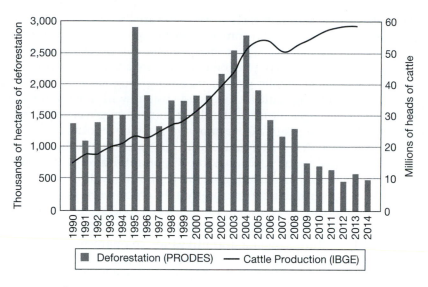

Figure 9.3 Deforestation and Cattle Production in Brazilian Amazon. (Cameron 2016.)

the shift to environmentally sustainable production practices. In addition, if all Brazilian farmers switched to strictly sustainable beef production, the outcome would be contradictory. The price of beef would increase, which would effectively prevent poorer consumers from being able to purchase more sustainable beef.

Because of the sheer number of NGO-led sustainability governance initiatives, it is tempting to consider these forms of governance as equally viable as multinational and private retailer governance. While NGOs have an important role to play in our food system, there are many reasons to doubt that their power rivals that of private retailers in our current governance system. Nongovernmental organizations often rely on consumer campaigns, whereby they make claims about harmful or negative aspects of the agrifood system or, more often, about how a specific company operates in our agrifood system. If enough consumers accept these claims, they put pressure on companies to change their policies.

However, NGOs are up against massive retailers that have immense amounts of discursive power through advertising campaigns, and these companies also make claims on behalf of consumer interests, particularly in terms of price, quality, and safety (Clapp and Fuchs 2009). Of course, consumers are not endlessly malleable to accepting claims made on behalf of companies, but in the new landscape of governance in our food system, the sources of and motivations for claims making can be difficult to disentangle. Consumers may not always be aware who sponsors various claims being made and consumers may also be confused by multiple claims (see Abrams, Meyers, and Irani 2010).

At issue in this discussion of claims making are the ways in which public goods, such as long-term environmental sustainability or the well-being of animals, are incorporated into governance systems. Generally, public goods will only coincide with corporate interests if there are economic incentives. The vast majority of public goods, including long-term environmental sustainability of our agriculture and food system, will remain outside the scope of corporate agriculture without pressure from government regulation and/or NGO campaigns. Government regulation at local, national, and international levels has historically been the space that recognizes long-term public goods, with NGOs making important, but only periodic, interventions. However, as eluded to at the beginning of this lesson, under neoliberalism, governments increasingly rely on or work in partnerships with private actors to govern our agriculture and food system. This public–private governance system does not bode well for sustainability initiatives that do not fit within economic incentives for companies and individual actors in the supply chain or for consumers who may not know, may not care, or cannot afford to pay more to ensure sustainable food systems.

ALTERNATIVE AGRIFOOD GOVERNANCE

The final section engages with a burgeoning landscape of people and organizations that are seeking alternatives in our food system, many of which can be considered local or more informal types of governance, as opposed to formalized governance that dominates the global agrifood system. Alternative food movements represent a wide range of issues, with several focused on individual shopping habits, such as farmers' markets, community-supported agriculture, and buying organic. There are many reasons alternative food movements have gained so much traction in the United States and beyond. The benefits include the opportunity to build community, to support artisan production practices (as opposed to industrial production), and to support regional cuisines, as well as to protect oneself or one's family from perceived harmful production practices (e.g., pesticides, genetically modified crops) (see Hinrichs 2003; see also Part 4).

The degree to which each of these movements affects the governance of our food system is debatable, and at times their impact may seem elusive. Take, for example, consumers who are concerned with animal welfare in industrial meat production. Consumers, both in the United States and in Europe, alongside NGO campaigns, contributed to major US companies, such as McDonald's, adopting animal welfare policies out of concern for public perception and, ultimately, the companies' profitability. The animal welfare standards adopted by companies like McDonald's represent a real change in our food system, but it is not necessarily the type of change that many animal welfare activists conceptualized, in that McDonald's still uses feedlot production for cattle, which animal welfare activists see as the source of the problem.

To be sure, alternative food movements, like consuming most of one's food locally, have become popular because they "represent modest socio-economic, cultural and environmental shifts in encouraging directions" (Hinrichs 2003, 43), but these modest gains are not guaranteed and this reveals that there is still a role for other forms of governance in our food system. In other words, for local actions to affect the broader governance structure, the actions must eventually align with other forms of governance, including local, state, or national governance policy, NGOs, or private retailers. Take, for example, a multidimensional governance approach to solving the environmental degradation of the Chesapeake Bay (situated on the East Coast of the United States, it is the largest estuary in the contiguous forty-eight states). If you have ever eaten blue crab, oysters, or rockfish (a type of striped bass) while visiting Maryland or Virginia, these likely originated from the Chesapeake Bay. Yet, all three of these have been under threat of extinction as a result of overharvesting and polluted waters (and disease for oysters) in the bay. The primary environmental threat to the bay is excessive nutrient runoff into the Chesapeake waterways, with the majority of nutrient runoff coming from agriculture, urban/suburban runoff, vehicle emissions, and numerous other sources (DEQ n.d.). This runoff ultimately contributes to the killing of marine species caused by oxygen deprivation in the water. Only through concerted efforts of nonprofit organizations, especially the Chesapeake Bay Foundation, multistakeholder initiatives, like the Chesapeake Bay Program, and government regulations have the bay and the species in the bay begun to recover. Local and informal governance in many ways can be a source of new ideas for creating change in our food system, but local governance must eventually connect to the other forms of governance discussed in this lesson to create change on a broader scale.

Conclusion

As should be obvious from this lesson, the shift from government to governance of our food system brings many more actors into the realm of governance, and this affects the entire supply chain. In closing, let us return to the point at which we started. Governance regulates both humans and nonhumans and, in doing so, governance has political and moral significance. The techniques used to enforce governance of our food system do not simply describe the landscape of our agriculture and food system; the governing techniques actually reorganize relationships between people by "defining their rights and their exposure to the rights of others" (Bain, Ransom, and Higgins 2013, 5) and nonhumans (e.g., industrial poultry production has moved to keeping birds completely inside large, enclosed buildings to prevent their coming into contact with wild aquatic birds who carry avian influenza). This is why, despite techniques of governance appearing to be seemingly quite technical (e.g., Rainforest Alliance–certified sustainable beef), they are deeply political (Konefal and Hatanaka 2010).

The Rainforest Alliance–certified sustainable beef at its inception did not simply describe the landscape of beef production in Brazil; it actually delimited which farmers count as producing beef sustainably and who benefits financially from growing sustainable beef. It also creates new opportunities for farmers to get into the business of growing sustainable beef. Yet, only a small percentage of smallholder farmers in Brazil qualify as sustainable producers and benefit financially from that production, despite the importance of saving the rainforests. This means that the bulk of beef reared in Brazil is harmful for the environment and that the bulk of consumers in the United States and Europe seemingly do not care, since they are not insisting on only consuming beef made from rainforest-certified production systems. If you do not eat burgers, we can follow a similar logic as it relates to coffee or ugly produce. The bulk of coffee consumed around the globe is not environmentally sustainable or representative of fair labor practices. The majority of ugly produce grown for European and North American markets goes unused and is wasted; this is suboptimal for both the environment and the issues surrounding food insecurity. Despite the seemingly technical nature of governance in our food system, I hope this lesson has impressed on you that what appears technical can also be highly political. Agriculture and food governance can reproduce or change existing social structures and impact a society's shared ethics and values. For these reasons, we should care about the seemingly mundane topic of governance in our agriculture and food system.

Discussion Questions
1. In what way have neoliberal economic policies changed agricultural trade and governance?
2. Why do we now refer to governance in our food system today, as opposed to government?
3. In the future, what will be the role for NGOs in promoting environmental sustainability?
4. In each of the four areas of governance discussed, how can informal governance play a role in shaping our agriculture and food systems?

Exercises
Go online and view this slideshow featuring deforestation in Brazil: http://apps.npr.org/lookatthis/posts/brazil/. After watching the slide show and based on your new understanding of governance within global food systems, discuss the following:
1. What types of local, national and international governance could assist in reducing deforestation?
2. What is the role of governments, NGOs, private businesses, and consumers in solving the problem of deforestation?
3. Do you think any one of the actors (e.g., governments, NGOs, private businesses, consumers) has a more important role to play and why?

Additional Materials
Websites

To learn more about governance and the Chesapeake Bay, visit http://www.cbf.org/ and https://www.chesapeakebay.net/.

To learn more about the role of NAFTA in promoting agricultural trade between the United States and Canada, see https://www.marketplace.org/2017/05/03/economy/texas-cattle-ranchers-dependent-mexican-trade-keep-eye-nafta.

References

Abrams, K. M., C. A. Meyers, and T. A. Irani. 2010. "Naturally Confused: Consumers' Perceptions of All-Natural and Organic Pork Products." *Agriculture and Human Values* 27:365–74.

Bain, Carmen, Elizabeth Ransom, and Vaughn Higgins. 2013. "Private Agri-food Standards: Contestation, Hybridity and the Politics of Standards." *International Journal of Sociology of Agriculture and Food* 20 (1): 1–10.

Baker, Peter. 2017. "Trump Abandons Trans-Pacific Partnership, Obama's Signature Trade Deal." *New York Times*, January 23, 2017. https://www.nytimes.com/2017/01/23/us/politics/tpp-trump-trade-nafta.html?_r=0

Birner, R., and D. Resnick. 2010. "The Political Economy of Policies for Smallholder Agriculture." *World Development* 38 (10): 1442–52.

Busch, L. 2011. "Food Standards: The Cacophony of Governance." *Journal of Experimental Botany* 62 (10): 3247–50.

Cameron, B. 2016. "A Drive to Protect Forests: Introducing Sustainable Cattle Certification in Brazil, 2009–2016." Innovations for Successful Societies, Princeton University. https://successfulsocieties.princeton.edu/sites/successfulsocieties/files/BC_Certification_Brazil_FINAL_0.pdf

Castle, Stephen. 2008. "Europe Relaxes Rules on Sale of Ugly Fruits and Vegetables." *New York Times*, November 12, 2008. http://www.nytimes.com/2008/11/13/world/europe/13food.html.

CDC (Centers for Disease Control and Prevention). 2012. *First Global Estimates of 2009 H1N1 Pandemic Mortality Released by CDC-Led Collaboration*. June 25, 2012. https://www.cdc.gov/flu/spotlights/pandemic-global-estimates.htm

Clapp, Jennifer, and Doris Fuchs, eds. 2009. *Corporate Power in Global Agrifood Governance*. Cambridge, MA: MIT Press.

Davis, Gerald F. 2005. "New Directions in Corporate Governance." *Annual Review of Sociology* 31:143–62.

DEQ (Department of Environmental Quality). n.d. "Nonpoint Source Pollution." Accessed May 1, 2017. http://www.deq.virginia.gov/Programs/Water/WaterQualityInformationTMDLs/NonpointSourcePollutionManagement/NonpointSourcePollution.aspx

Ferguson, James. 2015. *Give a Man a Fish: Reflections on the New Politics of Distribution*. Durham, NC: Duke University Press.

Gereffi, Gary, and Michelle Christian. 2009. "The Impacts of Wal-Mart: The Rise and Consequences of the World's Dominant Retailer." *Annual Review of Sociology* 35:573–91.

Godoy, Maria. 2016. "Wal-Mart, America's Largest Grocer, Is Now Selling Ugly Fruit and Vegetables." *The Salt*, NPR. July 20, 2016.

http://www.npr.org/sections/thesalt/2016/07/20/486664266/walmart-world-s-largest-grocer-is-now-selling-ugly-fruit-and-veg

Harris, M. T. 2006. "Welcome to 'Whole-Mart': Rotten Apples in the Social Responsibility Industry." *Dissent* 53 (1): 61–66.

Harvey, David. 2005. *A Brief History of Neoliberalism*. New York: Oxford University Press.

Hinrichs, Clare C. 2003. "The Practice and Politics of Food System Localization." *Journal of Rural Studies* 19:33–45.

Jayne, T. S., D. Mather, and E. Mghenyi. 2010. "Principal Challenges Confronting Smallholder Agriculture in Sub-Saharan Africa." *World Development* 38 (10): 1384–98.

King, Nicolas B. 2002. "Security, Disease, Commerce: Ideologies of Postcolonial Global Health." *Social Studies of Science* 32 (5/6): 763–89.

Konefal, Jason, and Maki Hatanaka. 2010. "The Michigan State University School of Agrifood Governance and Technoscience: Democracy, Justice, and Sustainability in an Age of Scientism, Marketism, and Statism." *Journal of Rural Social Sciences* 25 (3): 1–17.

Lee, J., G. Gereffi, and J. Beauvais. 2012. "Global Value Chains and Agrifood Standards: Challenges and Possibilities for Smallholders in Developing Countries." *Proceedings of the National Academy of Sciences of the United States of America* 109 (31): 12326–31.

McBride, James. 2016. "The World Trade Organization (WTO)." CFR Backgrounders. Council on Foreign Relations. September 12, 2016. http://www.cfr.org/international-organizations-and-alliances/world-trade-organization-wto/p9386

Mintz, Sidney. 2002. "Food and Eating: Some Persisting Questions." In *Food Nations: Selling Taste in Consumer Society*, edited by Warren Belasco and Philip Scranton, 24–32. New York: Routledge.

Nelson, Fred. 2010. "Introduction: The Politics of Natural Resource Governance in Africa." Chap. 1 in *Community Rights, Conservation & Contested Land: The Politics of Natural Resource Governance in Africa*, edited by Fred Nelson. London: Earthscan.

North, Douglas. 1990. *Institutions, Institutional Change and Economic Performance*. Cambridge: Cambridge University Press.

Oliver, S. P. B. M. Jayarao, and R. A. Almeida. 2005. "Foodborne Pathogens, Mastitis, Milk Quality, and Dairy Food Safety." *Foodborne Pathogens and Disease* 2(2): 115–129. https://www.ncbi.nlm.nih.gov/pubmed/15992306

OECD (Organisation for Economic Co-operation and Development). 2015. "Regional Trade Agreements and Agriculture." OECD Food, Agriculture and Fisheries Papers No. 79. Paris: OECD.

Paxson, Heather. 2008. "Post-Pasteurian Cultures: The Microbiopolitics of Raw-Milk Cheese in the United States." *Cultural Anthropology* 23 (1): 15–47.

Polaski, S. 2006. *The Employment Consequences of NAFTA Before the Senate Subcommittee on International Trade of the Committee on Finance*. September 11, 2006. http://carnegieendowment.org/files/naftawrittentestimony.pdf

Rudder, Catherine E., A. Lee Fritschler, and Yon Jung Choi. 2016. *Public Policy Making by Private Organizations: Challenges to Democratic Governance*. Washington, DC: Brookings Institution.

USDA (US Department of Agriculture). 2016. *Free Trade Agreement and U.S. Agriculture.* International Agriculture Trade Report. June 2016. https://www.fas.usda.gov/sites/default/files/2016-06/2016-06_iatr_ftas.pdf.

Van der Ploeg, J. D. 2008. *The New Peasantries Struggles for Autonomy and Sustainability in an Era of Empire and Globalization.* London: Earthscan.

WHO (World Health Organization). 2010. *What Is the Pandemic (H1N1) 2009 Virus?* February 24, 2010. http://www.who.int/csr/disease/swineflu/frequently_asked_questions/about_disease/en/

Whole Foods. 2017. Accessed May 2, 2017. http://www.wholefoodsmarket.com/company-info

WTO (World Trade Organization). 2016. "About the World Trade Organization." Accessed December 10, 2016. https://www.wto.org/english/thewto_e/thewto_e.htm

Zanhiser, Steven, and William Coyle. 2004. *U.S.–Mexico Corn Trade during the NAFTA Era: New Twists to an Old Story.* Electronic Outlook Report from the Economic Research Service. Washington, DC: USDA.

Planet Ocean Sphere, pen and ink on paper with acrylic paint overlay, 12 × 12 inches, 1991. (Artwork © Ray Troll, 2018.)

10

From Ocean to Plate: Catching, Farming, and Eating Seafood

Rebecca Clausen, Stefano B. Longo, and Brett Clark

After twenty years of controversy, in 2015 the US Food and Drug Administration approved the nation's first genetically altered animal for human consumption—a salmon that grows twice as fast as its natural counterpart. This new genetically engineered species was created, or some might say invented, and legally patented accordingly. It is an Atlantic salmon that contains genetic material from two other species of fish, allowing it to be harvested in eighteen months, rather than three years. Food safety activists, environmentalists, and the salmon fishing industry have long opposed this animal, sometimes calling it the Frankenfish. Opponents have argued that the approval would open the floodgates, allowing other genetically engineered animals to end up on our plates. They worry that the inclusion of transgenic animals in the food system and the environment could result in unpredictable outcomes that negatively influence both ecosystems and human health.

In contrast, the supporters of genetically engineered salmon believe that the production of this fish will potentially reduce the overfishing of wild salmon stocks and create a nutritional source of protein to help feed the world's population. They propose that the genetically engineered fish is more environmentally sustainable, since less feed is required for it to reach full size. Additionally, they suggest that there is little to no chance that transgenic salmon will harm the environment as safeguards have been put into place, such as raising only sterile salmon in closed, inland tanks.

This controversial food issue has raised many questions and concerns. Is genetically engineered salmon a solution to hunger and overfishing? Is it more environmentally sustainable? Are transgenic foods a slippery slope with unintended consequences? To develop an informed understanding of this issue, it is important to first consider the social and historical context of seafood production in general. This context helps situate the changing nature of seafood production and the latest controversial questions associated with the genetic engineering of food.

In this lesson, we discuss the capture of wild-caught seafood, including how fishing practices have changed over time. Next, we examine fish farming (also known as *aquaculture*) and its growth as a significant source of seafood globally. Throughout these discussions, we outline the **political economy** of both wild and farmed seafood in regard to global trade, labor issues, and environmental concerns. In the last part of the lesson, we consider how and why people's seafood consumption habits are changing. With this broader sociological understanding of how humans capture and farm seafood, it is clear that the questions regarding genetically engineered seafood do not have simple answers. Rather, decisions about seafood and the sustainability of marine systems must address issues related to who controls production, knowledge, and information, what is the larger ecological context, and who it will benefit and who may be harmed. In short, we contend that discussions regarding global seafood must include considerations of global justice.

SEA CHANGE: THE HISTORY OF CATCHING WILD SEAFOOD

The world's oceans are under increasing ecological stress from the consequences of human activities, including pollution, offshore oil drilling, and acidification resulting from climate change. One of the long-standing human impacts on marine systems is the harvesting of fish and shellfish for human consumption. The methods used to harvest seafood have not been constant over time; rather, they have varied based on a society's economic processes, cultural practices, and technological development. Fishing can be done in a sustainable manner or it can lead to the collapse of a species, depending on the way in which it is carried out.

Humans have captured and consumed seafood for thousands of years. Coastal communities often harvested large numbers of mollusks—such as abalone, clams, or oysters—along with accessible near-shore fish. For example, modern archeologists have uncovered deposited mounds of shells and fish remains that date back over 10,000 years on the West Coast of the United States. These Neolithic communities sometimes captured such large numbers of organisms that they likely had some local impacts on the populations of these species. However, it was not until very recently in human history that captures began to have significant consequences on the global marine systems. Approximately 150 years ago, there was a major increase in fisheries captures. By the mid- to late twentieth century, fisheries collapse, or the overexploitation and decline of a fishery, began to occur at an extraordinary rate (Jackson et al. 2001).

The onset of the **Industrial Revolution** marked a significant change in the ways in which human communities harvested and consumed marine species. New technologies, including systems of transportation such as railways and the steam engine, affected the production and consumption of seafood. For example, steam engines in boats allowed fishers to venture farther out at sea to catch a broader range of species, and the growth of railways extended the geographic range of the fish market. New refrigeration systems helped reduce fish losses resulting from spoilage, allowed boats to stay out at sea longer, and improved people's accessibility to seafood. These conditions and developments helped create a time of intensified and industrialized fishing.

Following the Second World War, the scale of fish production expanded to such a degree that it began to have global impacts and threatened the biodiversity of marine systems. According to the Food and Agriculture Organization of the United Nations (UNFAO), between 1950 and 2000, global fish captures increased from twenty million tons to over eighty million tons (UNFAO 2016a). This astonishing growth in captures was strongly associated with the employment of new fishing techniques, cutting-edge industrial operations, and enormous ships outfitted with advanced technologies, such as sonar and radar.

Many modern industrial fishing operations make use of three types of fishing systems: trawlers, longlines, and purse seines. Factory trawlers pull giant nets through the sea capturing hundreds of tons of fish per day. Some trawlers, called bottom trawlers, drag gear along the ocean floor to capture valuable species of ground fish (e.g., halibut) or crustaceans (e.g., shrimp). Industrial trawling operations have been criticized for the high-level of **by-catch**, or the capture of unwanted or untargeted species, associated with the practice. Many of these unwanted captures are simply dumped overboard at sea, already dead but unable to be sold to fish markets. Some estimates suggest that fishing operations from the United States, usually considered one of the better managed fishing fleets, can have levels of by-catch that reach one-third of the total capture. That means that about one-third of all fish that are caught are dumped overboard. Further, bottom trawlers have been known to cause damage to the ocean floor as the gear clears much of what is in its path, causing serious disruption and degradation to marine ecosystems.

Industrial longlines have hundreds or thousands of baited hooks that can stretch for miles. This practice is used to harvest species like tuna or swordfish that tend to inhabit the open ocean near the surface. Purse seine fishing uses giant nets to encircle species, like tuna. With nets that can have a perimeter of over a mile in length, purse seines can capture many tons of fish in a single haul. Like industrial trawlers, longline and purse seine fishing systems are notorious for the large amount of by-catch. Further, accidental captures also include sea turtles, sea birds, and marine mammals, such as dolphins. These fishing systems also make use of technology to locate fish, thus making it much easier to secure very large harvests. Together, the high-tech navigation and location devices result in highly effective systems of capture (see Figure 10.1).

While there are many debates related to fisheries management, the scale of fishing is overshooting limits and has reached a point that is global in its reach. The UNFAO (2016a) finds that approximately one-third of all fisheries are overfished. More alarming is that over 90 percent of the world's fisheries are categorized as either overfished or fished to capacity. This heavy fishing pressure on the world's oceans has resulted in what has been referred to as **peak fish**. Peak fish refers to a trend in which global fish captures peaked in the mid-1990s, then leveled off, and now may be in decline. Recent studies

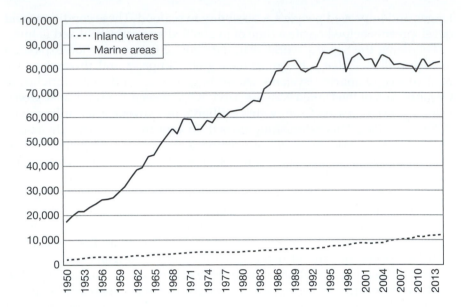

Figure 10.1 Inland and marine fisheries captures in thousands of tons (1950–2014). (UNFAO 2016b.)

by fisheries scientists show high levels of depletion of large predatory fish (e.g., cod, sharks, halibut, swordfish, marlin) throughout the world, sometimes as high as a 90 percent decline since the preindustrial level (Pitcher and Cheung 2013). Others predict serious consequences if trends of increasing fishing pressure continue unchanged, including massive fisheries collapse by the middle of the twenty-first century (Myers and Worm 2003).

Keeping good records on the total fish captured everywhere in the world is a difficult task. There is disagreement on what constitutes peak harvest and by how much a species has declined. For example, it is officially documented that marine fish captures grew to a peak of close to ninety million tons in 1996, but have since been in slight decline. However, some fisheries scientists argue that these numbers do not capture the total amount of wild marine fish harvested because of the presence of **illegal, unregulated, and unreported (IUU) fishing**. Because of the prevalence of IUU fishing, the world's marine fisheries have been exploited on a scale much higher than previously predicted.

Illegal, unregulated, and unreported fishing is a serious problem in many fisheries. Most countries and localities have laws and rules that regulate the amount, type, timing, and location of fishing practices. Any IUU fishing occurs when fishers violate conservation and management policies by using gear that has been banned, catching fish out of season, or surpassing limits on captures, among other activities. Catching more fish than allowed is considered an international environmental crime. Unlicensed or illegal fishing boats often target high-value species such as cod, salmon, lobster, and shrimp because they can be traded in small quantities and demand high prices. Dynamite fishing is another example of IUU, in which illegal explosives are used to stun or kill large schools of fish, damaging the surrounding ecosystem and habitat. Illegal, unregulated, and unreported fishing may account for up to twenty-six million tons of fish a year, or more than 15 percent of the world's total annual harvest (UNFAO 2016a). Since much seafood harvest happens out of sight and out of mind of the average person, there is often little direct observation of these IUU practices. Fisheries management agencies are continually making efforts to gain better knowledge about fishing practices and captures, such as requiring management observers on fishing boats. However, to date, this problem has been difficult to resolve.

It was once thought that the bounty of the oceans was infinite and that fish could be captured without concerns about depletion of stocks. This view was sadly proven wrong when some of the most abundant and historically active fisheries, like the Peruvian anchoveta and the Atlantic cod fisheries, collapsed in the late twentieth century. That is, the populations of fish fell to such low numbers that an active fishing sector could no longer be sustained, and the species and ecosystems were under stress. The loss of these fisheries caused a great deal of anguish in communities that had relied on fishing for many generations, even centuries. These concerns were not only economic, but also cultural. For example, when the Atlantic cod fishery collapsed in Canada, fishers lost a way of life that had been passed down through generations. Thousands of people left the cod fishery for work in other industries and regions, leaving behind their home and heritage. Similarly, in many African and South Asian coastal communities, fish accounts for as much as 50 percent of the protein in an individual's diet. When a fishery collapses, so, too, does the cultural context around that food source. Because of the ecological, economic, and cultural implications of overfishing, scholars began increasingly talking about the onset of a crisis in fishing communities.

Many people are not aware of the severe depletion of ocean fisheries because they continue to see seafood being offered at restaurants and supermarkets. The depletion of top predators sometimes leads fishers to target species lower on the food chain. Marine biologist Daniel Pauly and Maria Lourdes Palomares (2005) refer to this as **fishing down marine food webs** and explain how this process has masked the true ecological consequences of overfishing in regard to the oceans' ecosystems. Fishing down the food web occurs when one species is overfished or depleted and fishers capture a different species that is lower in the food web. In other words, fishers simply move to the next fish in line, capturing a smaller fish. For example, since the abundance of cod, swordfish, and tuna has declined, fishers now increasingly pursue the smaller forage fish such as herring, sardine, and anchovy that are lower within the food web. If we follow this trend, Pauly explains, "we are eating bait and moving on to jellyfish and plankton" (quoted in Weiss 2006). Fishing down the food web has continued to provide fish for markets, and therefore individuals may not realize the extent of ocean degradation that is happening as a result of overfishing. There always appears to be another choice of seafood on the menu, accompanied with an advertising campaign promoting the new target fish. As fishers begin to exploit species lower and lower within the food web, the resiliency of the entire marine ecosystem is undermined. Exacerbating these problems are the growing concerns associated with climate change, ocean acidification, and pollution.

Although the modern, industrial fishing system described above captures the bulk of global seafood, it is important to recognize that fishing practices can take a variety of forms. Small-scale and **artisanal fishing** systems are still practiced in many parts of the world, particularly the global South. Like all fishing practices, artisanal fishing does impact the stocks of fish that it targets. Nevertheless, small-scale fisheries contribute to food security and support rural livelihoods by providing food, income, and employment to millions of people. Additionally, women account for about 50 percent of the workforce in small-scale fisheries (UNFAO 2016a). These fishing systems tend to be less energy intensive and include very little to no by-catch. For example, Alaskan salmon fishers use very specific mesh sizes for their nets that only allow a certain size of salmon to be caught, thereby significantly minimizing the accidental catch of other species. As another example, small-scale fishers in the global South often use hand- or wind-powered boats, travel close to shore, and provide their harvest to local markets. Their small-scale operations use comparatively little fossil fuels and therefore have less impact on the environment. Small-scale fishers are facing challenges, however, such as declining fish stocks (largely resulting from the practices of large-scale fishing operations), lack of access to resources, and limited opportunity for local fishers to participate in decision-making regarding national and international fishery policies. Thus, beyond food security, some fishing people are at the forefront of the efforts toward food sovereignty (see Lesson 18), which includes components of local control, human rights to food, and sustainability.

The World Forum of Fisher Peoples is an international activist organization representing the rights and voices of small-scale fishing families from twenty-three different countries. The organization was formed in India in 1997 to confront the pressures being put on small-scale fisheries such as habitat destruction, pollution, encroachment by industrial fishing fleets, illegal fishing, overfishing, and climate change. The organization advocates for the rights of fisher people to access and manage fisheries resources, for human rights, and for the protection of biodiversity. The advocacy efforts of the World Forum of Fisher Peoples and partner organizations were directly responsible for the 2014 UNFAO decision to adopt the first set of international guidelines to defend and promote small-scale fisheries. The guidelines outline how the practices associated with small-scale fisheries can address food security and sustainable livelihoods, including gender equity, decent work, and risks of climate change and overfishing (UNFAO 2015). Thus, there is the potential that people who have the longest traditions with catching and eating seafood can have a seat at the table to ensure that small-scale fisheries can continue to thrive.

Overfishing of marine species is one of the main justifications for introducing new seafood production technologies, such as industrial fish farms and genetic engineering. Oftentimes, those who support these approaches argue that human greed will always lead to the overharvest of a species, often invoking the well-known **tragedy of the commons** thesis (Hardin 1968). The tragedy of the commons hypothesis suggests that humans have a tendency to overexploit any natural resource that is held in common, meaning that the resource is not privately owned or tightly regulated by state laws and policies. The overexploitation occurs, it is argued, because humans are essentially selfish and will tend to use up the collective resources for personal gain.

However, although it highlights an important issue, the tragedy of the commons argument is sociologically naive. From a sociological perspective, the idea that overfishing is largely a result of innate human characteristics is simplistic and one-sided. Rather, the collapse of marine fisheries is linked to social and historical changes in the ways we interact with marine ecosystems (Longo, Clausen, and Clark 2015). For example, under a capitalist system of producing seafood as commodities, specific species of fish are targeted and deemed more profitable than others, regardless of their nutritional value. For example, Atlantic bluefin tuna has been severely overharvested because it is being sold for a high price to elite sushi markets. The significant profit potential for Atlantic bluefin tuna influences the fishery, rather than its potential to feed people who are hungry or malnourished (Longo 2011). By focusing primarily on the market value of fish, policymakers fail to recognize the many other ways that fish species are valued—such as cultural, ecological, or intrinsic values (e.g., their use in ceremonies, their ecological services, and/or the inherent right of a species to exist).

NOT ALL FISH FARMS ARE THE SAME

Fish farming, also known as fish **aquaculture**, is the raising and harvesting of fish under controlled conditions using some form of containment like pens, tanks, or cages. Fish farming has been practiced for centuries as a way to supplement protein for human populations. For example, the Chinese raised carp in inland ponds as early as 2500 BCE. In modern industrial aquaculture production, the farmed species are privately owned for their entire life cycle. Individual or corporate owners provide management techniques to increase the efficiency of producing seafood, such as feeding the fish pelleted food and protecting the fish from predators and harsh weather. As worldwide marine fish populations decline because of overharvest and other environmental impacts, aquaculture is witnessing a rapid expansion. In fact, seafood production through aquaculture is the fastest growing animal production sector, surpassing the rate of growth of land-based livestock rearing (Little, Newton, and Beveridge 2016). Advocates for fish farming argue that the increasing human population requires more food, so it is necessary to supplement wild capture with farmed fish. While this argument sounds logical, it is important to ask sociological questions regarding the types of seafood being raised, the conditions under which fish are being produced, and for whom the food is being produced. As the debate and research on these issues continues, industrial fish farming is quickly gaining momentum.

While farmed fish provided only 7 percent of fish for human consumption in 1974, this share increased to 39 percent in 2004. Aquaculture reached a new milestone in 2014 when farmed fish's contribution to human consumption surpassed that of wild-caught fish for the first time (UNFAO 2016b). In 2017, more than half of all fish consumed were produced in aquaculture facilities. The most common type of fish farming is carried out in inland ponds, raising freshwater fish such as tilapia, carp, and catfish. Inland finfish aquaculture greatly contributes to food security and nutrition in the global South. Marine aquaculture is the farming of seafood in the ocean environment in cages and specially designed pens, accounting for 36 percent of total fish farming in the world. The top-producing countries in marine and coastal aquaculture are Norway, China, Chile, and Indonesia (UNFAO 2016a).

Hailed as the **blue revolution**, fish farming is frequently compared to agriculture's green revolution as a way to achieve food security and economic growth to help the world's poor. However, this claim depends largely on which fish species is being raised. Further, aquaculture production can take on many forms and practices, from intensive industrial methods to small-scale subsistence systems. Some forms of marine fish farms raise species lower within the food web, called low trophic-level species, like mollusks or carp, and others rear high-trophic-level species, like salmon or tuna. High-trophic-level species must be fed pellets containing fish meal and fish oil to grow to the desired market size. Fish meal and fish oil are products made from the flesh of other fish, usually derived from wild fish stocks. Growth in fish farming has been faster for these species that need to be regularly fed high-protein pellets. An important part of the aquaculture industry raises high-value fish that are exported to other countries to be eaten by wealthy consumers. The cultivation of high-value, carnivorous species for markets in wealthy nations has emerged as one of the more profitable (and controversial) endeavors in fish-farming production.

For example, during the early 1980s, the global market for salmon greatly expanded as a result of fish farms. This is because the ocean farms produced salmon year round and could sell them for a cheaper price to grocery stores and restaurants. These changes are significant as salmon has become the most profitable and abundant form of fish farming (see Figure 10.2). From 1985 to 2010, the amount of farmed salmon produced increased from approximately 500,000 tons to 2.5 million tons, valued at almost $9 billion (UNFAO 2016b). Salmon aquaculture practices emphasize conformity, control, and predictability of the fish that are being produced. In short, it is organized to obtain the most profit for the least amount of investment. It aims for faster growth rates of production and higher profits based on the sale of salmon as commodities in year-round, global markets. The ability to produce salmon of

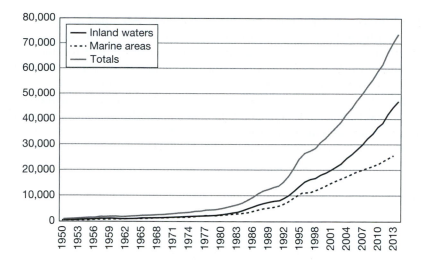

Figure 10.2 Inland and marine aquaculture production in thousands of tons (1950–2014), excluding plants. (UNFAO 2016b.)

uniform size, quality, and flesh color requires control of biological and reproductive cycles. For example, salmon that are raised in ocean pens no longer migrate to freshwater streams to reproduce. Rather, artificial reproduction occurs in controlled environments. This intense management represents a significant change in the way humans produce seafood, which also results in significant changes in the ecological and social conditions of fisheries.

Farming high-trophic-level species like salmon has ecological consequences for the marine environment. Raising tens of thousands of fish in a small contained area results in excessive waste (e.g., fish feces) being introduced into the local ecosystem and onto the ocean floor. The waste is a significant source of nutrient pollution and changes the ecosystem dynamics in the area. Given the high number of fish living in a small pen, antibiotics are often required to try to control disease within farmed salmon populations. As discussed above, high-trophic-level fish must be fed pelleted food that is made in part from processing smaller fish like sardines and anchovies from other parts of the world. These smaller fish could be used as a direct source of protein for people for whom fish have historically been an important part of their diet. Instead of being eaten by local people, these fish are turned into feed for salmon destined for expensive markets. Finally, there is concern that the nonnative salmon being produced in fish farms may escape captivity and enter into the habitat of wild fish species, negatively affecting biodiversity. Each of these ecological considerations must be taken into account while also addressing the external costs of modern intensive fish farming.

Recognizing the ecological consequences inherent in some forms of fish farming, especially those that involve high-trophic-level fish, does not mean that all options for fish farming create problems. All aquaculture is not de-signed for the same purposes. For example, some ocean farms are not relying on monoculture (raising only one, high-value species of fish). Rather, they are experimenting with **polyculture**, a model of raising multiple, low-trophic-level species that complement one another. One such model raises oysters, mussels, and scallops for local food and fertilizer, as well as seaweed. Filter-feeding shellfish have the potential to clean up polluted waters. In addition, the rapid pace of seaweed growth can sequester large amounts of carbon dioxide and aid in climate change mitigation. This model of combining low-trophic-level species and plants has the potential to grow environmentally restorative species that can enhance, rather than degrade, ocean ecosystems (Eckberg 2016).

SEAFOOD JUSTICE IN GLOBAL MARKETS

To understand the political economy of seafood, we must ask questions about how it is produced and distributed, who does the work, and who con-sumes the meal. By analyzing the politics, economics, and cultural relations of seafood production, we can continue to explore important issues associ-ated with social justice and ecological sustainability.

Trading Seafood around the World

Seafood represents one of the most-traded products of the world food sector, with about 78 percent of seafood products contributing to international trade. Fish can be caught in the waters of one country, filleted and processed in a second country, and show up on the menu in a third country. Related to changes in the operation and organization of fishing systems, as discussed above, there has been a large shift in seafood consumption from local to international markets. Local consumption is still very important in many costal communities throughout the world, but international trade has ex-panded considerably over the past century and particularly over the past few decades. In 1976, almost eight million tons of seafood were exported worldwide with a value of approximately $8 billion. By 2013, over thirty-six million tons of seafood were exported throughout the global market, and the value of those commodities reached over $139 billion (UNFAO 2016b). Trade in seafood is largely driven by demand from wealthy countries. For example, the top exporters of seafood are China, Norway, Vietnam, and Thailand. The top importers of fish are the United States, Japan, China, and Spain (UNFAO 2016a). As a whole, the European Union is the largest importer of seafood products in the world.

An important share of seafood trade consists of high-value species such as salmon, shrimp, tuna, and groundfish (e.g., flounder, sole, and halibut). This raises important questions about the production and distribution of the world's food. Food that could be staying within a nation to feed the general population is often being exported to wealthy individuals in distant lands. Developing economies represented just 37 percent of world fisheries trade in 1976, but by 2014 they saw their share of total fishery export value rise to 54 percent (UNFAO 2016a). Some scholars argue that a root cause of fishery depletion is the transition from seafood providing local community subsistence to it being focused on generating profits by being exported to a global market.

As discussed above, global fish supplies from both wild capture and fish farms have increased dramatically since the end of the Second World War. Interestingly, the rate of wild fish capture has been faster than the rate of human population growth. One may wonder, What political and economic factors have contributed to the increasing seafood production, beyond increased numbers of people to feed? An important issue to consider is that much of the global seafood production is not just being used to feed people; rather, it is also going to feed other animals. This expanded use of seafood has been a major source of growth in the livestock feed sector. Beyond its use in fish farms as pelleted food, **fish meal** provides a source of protein that is incorporated into poultry and swine production and used in pet foods. Is this the best way we can use protein from the world's oceans? Further, fish meal is used as a fertilizer in agriculture production. Although fish oil represents the richest source of fatty acids important for human diets for a wide range of biological functions, most fish oil goes to feeding other animals. Twenty-one million tons of world fish production was destined for nonfood products, of which 76 percent was reduced to fish meal and fish oil (UNFAO 2016a).

Fishermen, Fisherwomen, and the Global Fishery Workforce

Who are the people catching, farming, and processing all of this seafood? The most recent estimates indicate that 12 percent of the world's population relies on fisheries and aquaculture for their livelihood (UNFAO 2016a). This number encompasses all aspects of the seafood industry, including processing, packing, transporting, and selling seafood. Most of the word's fishers and fish farmers have entered the fishing industry as an occupation to provide a source of income and livelihood, whether that is on large-scale factory trawlers or small, independently owned boats. Fishing has always been a dangerous and labor-intensive occupation. There is no doubt that many fishers, particularly small- to medium-scale fishers, have strong ties to the sea and the craft. Nevertheless, the global seafood sector is much broader than the romantic images we may have of the independent, rugged fisherman on the high seas that we see on television programs like *Wicked Tuna* or *The Deadliest Catch*. First, contrary to the conventional gendered view of seafood production, women make up an important part of the fishing industry. While it is true that men comprise a large majority of fishing activities, women also engage in 15 to 20 percent of these activities globally. Further, in fish processing sectors, women are the vast majority of workers. Second, as we discussed above, it is important to emphasize that the greatest contributor to seafood production worldwide is large-scale industrial capture and aquaculture operations, not independent fishing boats. The character of the fishing labor changes dramatically once workers enter into the factory-style production process, either on boats or in the processing plants. For example, fish processing plants are often referred to as the *slime line*, where workers are organized in assembly-line fashion to head and gut fish in a repetitive motion (Jeebhay, Robins, and Lopata 2004). This **deskilled labor** often requires long working hours with sharp knives and wet/cold conditions.

In the contemporary period, there is growing concern for a sector of workers who are being forced onto commercial fishing boats against their will. These workers are called *sea slaves*. They remain on fishing ships year round, receive meager meals, and experience extreme hardships. The actual number of sea slaves is unknown; however, it has been estimated that 145,000 to 200,000 people are enslaved under such conditions in Thailand alone (Irvine, Mohsin, and Olarn 2015). Away from land and governmental oversight, this forced labor is largely invisible and is difficult to regulate. Many of the people who end up on fishing boats as sea slaves migrated from other nations and were seeking employment opportunities. Individuals from Cambodia, Myanmar, Laos, and Indonesia were promised work abroad in factories. When they arrived in Thailand, their documents were confiscated and they ended up on a fishing boat as forced labor. In some cases, individuals made arrangements with brokers for employment, only to end up in debt bondage, trying to pay off fees associated with recruitment (International Labor Organization 2015; UNIAP 2009; Urbina 2015). While slavery at sea is not the norm, it is a horrific side of the global seafood fishery of which many people are unaware.

Seafood Buffet: Who Is First in Line?

Fish are a significant protein source for billions of people. In 2013, fish accounted for about 17 percent of the global population's intake of animal protein (UNFAO 2016a). It is important to note that seafood consumption is not equally distributed. Although the annual consumption of fish has grown steadily in the global South, it is still considerably lower than in the North. These disparities are a product of the global trade relationships described above, as domestic fisheries in the global South have been replaced by export-oriented fisheries bound for nations of the North.

Consumer habits in the global North are changing because of capitalist marketing, urbanization, and global trade, as well as modern issues such as convenience, health, ethics, and sustainability. Health and well-being are increasingly influencing consumption patterns; however, debates continue as to whether all seafood is healthy. Seafood is seen as a rich source of easily digestibly proteins containing amino acids, fats, vitamins, and minerals. It is also noted that pollutants such as mercury and polychlorinated biphenyl from the marine environment can bioaccumulate within fish species. Additionally, many types of industrially farmed fish require pesticides and antibiotics similar to livestock feedlots on land. As with many of these debates around health and sustainability, social and histori-cal context matters.

The rise in seafood consumption in the global North can also be attributed to the new infrastructure for selling fish. Modern retail outlets such as large supermarkets are now shaping seafood sales, whereas historically people relied on fishmongers in local markets. Frozen seafood is now transported around the world, and in some countries sales at supermarkets account for 70 to 80 percent of retail purchases. Transnational supermarkets are driving consumption patterns, offering consumers year-round choices that ignore the seasonal fluctuations associated with fish migrations.

Some individuals are beginning to understand that global seafood is in decline and they are changing their consumption practices. Nonprofit organ-izations have offered certification and labeling mechanisms to try to inform customers about which fish are harvested sustainably and which contribute to overall ocean degradation, either through direct overharvest of the species or through consequences of the fishing technique (i.e., by-catch, habitat loss). The Marine Stewardship Council is one such organization that provides stan-dards to assess the sustainability of wild-capture fisheries, and many retail-ers are committing to selling sustainably certified seafood. Important debates exist regarding the effectiveness of relying on consumer labeling to produce social change, with some scholars contending that the label is not telling the whole story. The sustainable certification label allows specific fish to be sold at a higher market price, but this program might only have a superficial analysis of sustainability (Konefal 2013). Labeling and market-based approaches alone are not able to reduce the overall exploitation of seafood and do not change the primary economic drivers of unsustainable fishing and fish farming practices. It is important to include regulatory oversight by governments as well as de-mands from social movements to influence change in the seafood production process itself.

Conclusion

This lesson has reviewed the social and historical context of fishery decline, the ecological impacts of marine fish farms, the inequities of global seafood trade, the promise/perils of fishery labor on the open seas, and the current trends of seafood consumption. Let us now return, briefly, to the current seafood controversy surrounding the approval of the first genetically engi-neered fish for human consumption.

At the beginning of the lesson, we briefly outlined the debate regard-ing whether genetically engineered fish could serve as a solution to world hunger, alleviate overfishing, and enhance environmental sustainability. At this point, you may not have entirely formed your personal opinion on this issue. But after reading this lesson, you will hopefully have a better idea of the kinds of social and historical questions that must be asked to evaluate this hotly debated topic. Here we offer a set of questions that are related to producing genetically engineered salmon that we think can be helpful in developing your position on this controversial food concern:

- Why were the wild salmon fisheries depleted in the first place?
- How has technology been used to increase the pace and scale of wild salmon harvest?
- How might the wild salmon fishery be affected by the introduction of genetically engineered salmon?
- What are the ecological characteristics of genetically engineered salmon that will be farmed? Is it a high- or low-trophic-level species? What kind of feed inputs will be required to grow this fish to market size?
- Who are the people who will be working to feed, grow, and harvest the genetically engineered salmon? What are the conditions of their workplace?
- Where will the genetically engineered salmon be produced, and where will it be sold? Is the market geared toward food security/food sovereignty?
- Should the genetically engineered salmon be labeled so individuals are aware what they are eating?
- How might unintended consequences of genetically engineered salmon affect the ecological integrity of the ocean, the social well-being of fishing communities, and the health of people who eat it?

We believe that all questions regarding the catching, farming, and eating of seafood must be held up to the same level of scrutiny as the questions outlined above. To act in the best interest of the world's population and the oceans on which they depend, we must always consider the ecological integrity and social well-being of all involved. At its core, it is important to consider how humanity's relationship to the marine environment is socially and historically organized.

Discussion Questions

1. What do you believe are the most important factors affecting global seafood issues?
2. What might be potential ecological and social impacts if global seafood fisheries collapsed in the future?
3. How can we raise awareness about issues facing the world ocean?
4. Do you feel that genetically engineered salmon should be labeled? Why or why not?

Exercises

1. Go to your local grocery store and visit the seafood counter. Can you determine by the labels which fish were farmed and which were wild caught? Ask whether the grocery staff knows in which country the seafood was harvested. Draw a map to visualize how far the seafood has traveled to get to your store. Consider the range of other resources used in the production of the fish as a commodity.

2. Ask your friends and family members whether they have heard about the recent approval of genetically engineered salmon. Would they eat the genetically engineered fish? Why or why not? Do their answers raise any concerns about the production process, environmental impacts, or consumer health and safety?

Additional Materials

Readings

Bavington, D. 2010. *Managed Annihilation: An Unnatural History of the Newfoundland Cod Collapse.* Vancouver: University of British Columbia Press.

Clover, C. 2006. *End of the Line: How Overfishing Is Changing the World and What We Eat.* Berkeley: University of California Press.

Greenberg, P. 2011. *Four Fish: The Future of the Last Wild Food.* New York: Penguin Books.

Longo, S. B., R. Clausen, and B. Clark. 2015. *The Tragedy of the Commodity: Oceans, Fisheries and Aquaculture.* New Brunswick, NJ: Rutgers University Press.

Films

The End of the Line: Imagine a World without Fish, 2009 (1:30:00). Rupert Murray, http://endoftheline.com/about-the-film

Salmon Wars: Aquaculture, Wild Fish and the Future of Communities, 2013 (1:14:51). Ecology Action Centre, https://www.youtube.com/watch?v=5qsERAosVyw

Video Clips

Slavery at Sea: Thai Fishing Industry turns to Trafficking, 2015 (14:14). Guardian Investigations, https://www.youtube.com/watch?v=qNwoqLB_wKs

References

Eckberg, Hannah. 2016. "3-D Ocean Farming." *Permaculture* 2:9–12.

Hardin, Garrett. 1968. "The Tragedy of the Commons." *Science* 162:1243–48.

International Labor Organization. 2015. *International Expert Meeting on Labour Exploitation in the Fishing Sector in the Atlantic Region.* Geneva, Switzerland: Fundamental Principles and Rights at Work Branch.

Irvine, Dean, Saima Mohsin, and Kocha Olarn. 2015. "Seafood from Slavery: Can Thailand Tackle the Crisis in Its Fishing Industry?" CNN. May 17, 2015. http://www.cnn.com/2015/05/11/asia/freedom-project-thailand-fishing-slave-ships/

Jackson, Jeremy B. C., Michael X. Kirby, Wolfgang H. Berger, Karen A. Bjornda, Louis W. Botsford, Bruce J. Bourque, et al. 2001. "Historical Overfishing and the Recent Collapse of Coastal Ecosystems." *Science* 293:629–38.

Jeebhay, M. F., T. G. Robbins, and A. L. Lopata. 2004. "World at Work: Fish Processing Workers." *Occupational and Environmental Medicine* 61:471–74.

Konefal, Jason. 2013. "Environmental Movements, Market-Based Approaches, and Neoliberalization: A Case Study of the Sustainable Seafood Movement." *Organization and Environment* 26:336–52.

Little, David C, Richard W. Newton, and Malcolm C. Beveridge. 2016. "Aquaculture: A Rapidly Growing and Significant Source of Sustainable Food?

Status, Transitions and Potential." *Proceedings of the Nutrition Society* 75:274–86.

Longo, Stefano B. 2011. "Global Sushi: A Political Economic Analysis of the Mediterranean Bluefin Tuna Fishery in the Modern Era." *Journal of World-Systems Research* 17 (2): 403–27.

Longo, Stefano B., Rebecca Clausen, and Brett Clark. 2015. *The Tragedy of the Commodity: Oceans, Fisheries, and Aquaculture*. New Brunswick, NJ: Rutgers University Press.

Myers, Ransom, and Boris Worm. 2003. "Rapid Worldwide Depletion of Predatory Fish Communities." *Nature* 423 (6937): 280–83.

Pauly, Daniel, and M. L. Palomares. 2005. "Fishing down Marine Food Web: It Is Far More Pervasive Than We Thought." *Bulletin of Marine Science* 76:197–211.

Pitcher, Tony, and William Cheung. 2013. "Fisheries Hope or Despair?" *Marine Pollution Bulletin* 74 (2): 506–16.

UNFAO (Food and Agriculture Organization of the United Nations). 2015. *Voluntary Guidelines for Securing Sustainable Small Scale Fisheries in the Context of Food Security and Poverty Alleviation*. Rome: UNFAO.

UNFAO (Food and Agriculture Organization of the United Nations). 2016a. *State of the World Fisheries and Aquaculture*. Rome: UNFAO.

UNFAO (Food and Agriculture Organization of the United Nations). 2016b. *Fishery and Aquaculture Statistics (FishStatJ)*. Rome: UNFAO.

UNIAP (United Nations Inter-Agency Project on Human Trafficking). 2009. *SIREN Case Analysis Exploitation of Cambodian Men at Sea*. Bangkok, Thailand: United Nations.

Urbina, Ian. 2015. "Tricked and Indebted on Land, Abused or Abandoned at Sea." *New York Times*, November 9, 2015. http://www.nytimes.com/2015/11/09/world/asia/philippines-fishing-ships-illegal-manning-agencies.html?_r=0

Weiss, Kenneth R. 2006. "A Primeval Tide of Toxins." *Los Angeles Times*, July 30, 2006. http://www.latimes.com/news/local/oceans/la-me-ocean30jul30,0,952130.story?page=8

PART 3

FOOD, EQUITY, AND ENVIRONMENT

Rural & Migrant Ministry's March for Farmworker Justice.
(Photo by Javier E. Gomez.)

11

Food and Labor

Margaret Gray

W hen I was a junior in college I met an advocate for New York farmworkers. My reaction: New York has farmworkers? I grew up in
suburbia and my food came from the supermarket; having no exposure to farming, it never occurred to me to think about where my food
came from or the labor behind my meals. I was born too late to be influenced
by the United Farmworkers Union grape boycotts of the 1960s and 1970s and
too early to be raised in the environmental movement. Both were influential
in shaping the public understanding about food.

In contrast to my experience, today's youth is immersed in food culture
and has been reared in an era of environmental activism. The environmental
movement and the food movement are, at their cores, education campaigns
that have successfully taught us about food, largely through the media. Both
have been concerned with pesticides, genetically modified organisms, eating
seasonally, supporting open space and diverse farming, animal welfare, and
how globalization has impacted the food industry (among other issues). The
food movement, specifically, educates us about where our food comes from,
how it is grown and raised, the supply chain that brings those lentils and
tomatoes to your lunch plate, the benefits of Greek yogurt, and the ills associated with a McDonald's hamburger.

Owing to the food movement, consumers have been primed to inquire
about how our food choices sustain the environment, promote animal welfare, and help smaller farms survive. Yet when it comes to questions about
food labor, much of the food movement has been silent. The food movement
promotes itself as focused on sustainability. If we follow this logic, then we
should be concerned about the livelihoods of those who labor in the fields,
milk the cows, and process our food. To truly promote a food system that
supports equality and public health, we must ask whether food workers
have sustainable livelihoods, analyze workplace power dynamics, and question the relationship between their jobs and inequality.

This lesson focuses on two of the most hidden groups of food workers in
the United States, farmworkers and food processing workers. It explores how
the structure of food jobs reproduces inequality, constrains workers' abilities
to improve their situations, and creates work environments ripe for labor
abuses. I also address government regulation and inaction in protecting food
workers as well as movements to improve workers' conditions. Along the

183

way, I will introduce concepts to help analyze the situation of these workers. The concepts include structures, exploitation, ethic succession, power hierarchies, precarious work, paternalism, labor abuse, government regulation, worker centers, collective action, consumer campaigns, and code of conduct.

FOOD CHAIN WORKERS IN THE UNITED STATES

The food industry is the largest employer in the United States, accounting for 14 percent of all US jobs, yet the jobs offered are not well paid, as described in "No Piece of the Pie," a report published by the Food Chain Workers Alliance (Food Chain Workers Alliance and Solidarity Research Cooperative 2016). Compared to other industries, food workers earn the lowest median hourly wages ($10 an hour versus $17.53 in all industries), rely more on food stamps (2.2 times the use of all other industries), and are more food insecure (20 percent compared to 13 percent of the US population). In addition, the report reveals that over time, food jobs provide little opportunity for advancement, an increase in injuries and illnesses, a decline of labor union representation, and rampant racism and sexism (Food Chain Workers Alliance and Solidarity Research Cooperative 2016).

The Food Chain Workers Alliance describes five food employment sectors: production, processing, distribution, retail, and service. Production and processing workers are the focus of this lesson, but it is worth mentioning the whole food chain. (1) Production workers are the farm hands who plant, cultivate, and harvest fruits, vegetables, and grains and tend to animals. (2) Processing workers take farm products and prepare them, whether they butcher and package meat or turn milk into yogurt. (3) The distribution sector includes transportation workers, such as those who transport food from farms, to and from food processors, and to restaurants and supermarkets. This sector also includes the warehouse workers who package food for delivery. (4) In regard to the retail sector, workers are found in grocery stores and other outlets and include not only cashiers, but also those who prepare food, such as in the bakery section of the grocery store, and those on the janitorial staff. (5) Finally, the service sector, by far the largest employer of food workers, is where food is served—restaurants, fast-food locations, and even food trucks.

FARMWORKERS IN THE UNITED STATES AND THE STRUCTURES OF FOOD WORK

The structures of farm jobs affect workers' livelihoods. By **structures**, I mean the patterns and arrangements that have had an effect on the job, as opposed to an individual worker's experience. For example, hiring marginalized workers, ethnic succession, power hierarchies, labor laws, and paternalistic management practices are all structures that have led to farm jobs being unstable and on the bottom rung compared to other US jobs. Although I focus on farmworkers here, many of these structures affect other food workers, including food processing workers (who are examined in the next section). The structures that shape the jobs create the circumstances under which the labor abuses occur, so understanding the structures allows for a fuller comprehension of workers' situations.

Misfortune Home and Abroad

Agriculture in the United States has long depended on marginalized workers, those living on the sidelines of society with little economic, political, or social clout. A US government report from 1951 describes this scenario and is as relevant today: "We depend on misfortune to build up our force of migratory workers and when the supply is low because there is not enough misfortune at home, we rely on misfortune abroad to replenish the supply" (Long 1951, 249–51). During the country's founding period, the largest farming sector was the Southern plantation system, based on the labor of African slaves. That racist system led to modern-day farming's hiring practices, which rely on workers' race, place of birth, citizenship status, ethnic succession, and other power hierarchies that involve dominance and subordination, all structures that have produced the nature of farm jobs.

Today's US farmers are highly reliant on, if not addicted to, cheap labor. Because most US citizens are reluctant to do hard manual labor for low wages, farmers have sought out vulnerable workers who are willing to take these jobs. Present-day farmworkers are mostly immigrants; 72 percent of US crop workers are foreign born and 46 percent are undocumented (Hernandez, Gabbard, and Carroll 2016). Workers who are not citizens are easier to control than citizen workers. New immigrants are not immersed in US culture. They do not understand the norms, are often ignorant of protective labor laws, and are likely coming from countries with limited opportunities and so they tend to have a high level of desperation. These factors discourage workers from questioning their circumstances (Gray 2014).

Immigrants, in particular recent arrivals in the United States, tend to evaluate their economic and social reality in comparison to those in their home countries and not in relation to other US workers. This helps them rationalize their poverty-level wages and poor working conditions, even when they realize the same would not be accepted by US citizens. For the farmworkers I interviewed, a day's pay at home was often less than the US minimum hourly wage. In a sense this makes immigrants a party to their own exploitation. **Exploitation** involves someone benefiting by unfairly taking advantage of the resources of someone else, in this case taking advantage of someone's labor.

The demographics of today's farm workforce is a consequence of the history of US farms hiring workers who are already marginalized and then offering jobs that reproduce employee inequality. While Southern agriculture was first staffed by slaves and later by free blacks, California—the largest farming state in the country—entered the union as a free state and therefore could not rely on slaves. Instead, Japanese, South Asian Hindus, Armenians, Mexicans, and Filipinos all toiled in California's fields. Each group started as highly exploitable, but, over time, some began to organize; at that point they were replaced by a new group that was more easily exploited. This cycle of worker replacement is called **ethnic succession**, when employers move from hiring a group of workers with a shared demographic (race, for example) who have some power in the workplace to a more vulnerable group of workers.

The East Coast has its own history of ethnic succession. The region's farmers relied on successive groups of mostly European immigrants until the midtwentieth century when the largest group of nonlocal farm hands became African American migrants. Extremely disempowered politically, socially, and economically, African Americans embodied the misfortune that the US government report described. While technically US citizens, because of the long history of US racism, black workers' disenfranchisement greatly resembled the experience of undocumented workers today. Some towns even had vagrancy laws that required workers to move on after the season; those who did not could be arrested. A vagrant is someone who is homeless, transient, or even traveling. The laws made sure farmworkers who had finished their seasonal stint left town; they were not allowed to hang around local villages with their coworkers.

In the 1980s, as the number of African American farmworkers started to decline, they secured more power in the workplace. In other words, when fewer workers are available to be hired, those employed tend to have increased negotiating power. As a result, black workers were replaced. Today, Latin Americans are the primary agricultural workforce on East Coast farms, which is a late twentieth-century story of ethnic succession. In contrast, California has had much longer dependence on Latin American workers, primarily Mexicans. That does not mean that California has run out of those with misfortune; the seemingly endless supply of undocumented workers means a steady stream of vulnerable workers. Furthermore, today you can find non–Spanish speaking indigenous workers from Latin America on West Coast farms—they have more significant language and cultural barriers in the workplace and tend to earn less.

Power hierarchies are differences in status that lead to an expectation of one party having dominance. For example, citizens have a higher status than the undocumented population and those who speak, read, and write English are considered to have an edge over those who cannot. Power hierarchies shape the employer–employee relationship. This hierarchy or status is socially constructed; in other words, it is not a natural or organic occurrence. The farmworkers I interviewed in New York's Hudson Valley were almost all immigrants (99 percent), were mostly noncitizen (97 percent), had a low level of literacy in their native language (a self-reported average of 1.2 on a scale from 0 to 5), had limited formal education (sixth grade on average), and had few job skills, and many did not feel welcome in local towns. Compare this to the profile of the Hudson Valley farmers I met who were mostly white, college-educated citizens, often born in the area, who were not only welcome in local towns, but also celebrated as businesspeople and preservers of open space. Those on the lower end of the hierarchy, the workers, were acutely aware of their position and told me that they felt greatly constrained in their ability to push for better wages and working conditions.

A primary example of this was in farmworkers' reluctance to ask for improvements in employer-owned housing. I visited workers in housing where windows were replaced with cardboard, outdoor lights were broken, floor tiles were peeling or missing, and roofs were leaky. (I also saw farmworker housing that was well maintained.) In one case, where eight workers shared a room and slept on thin, bare, filthy mattresses, not one saw fit to complain. In another instance, workers did not even report that they lacked mattresses to sleep on; they were so afraid to ask their employer for beds that they opted to sleep on the floor. Reluctance to demand basic necessities displayed the psychology of extreme compliance and sacrifice that is molded by their situation.

Excluded from Labor Laws

Federal law and the vast majority of state laws deny farmworkers important labor rights including the right to overtime pay and the right to a day of rest. This lack of legal rights and protections further contributes to the exploitive conditions of farm work. One fruit and vegetable worker I met, Oscar from Guatemala, logged eighty to ninety hours a week, six and a half days a week, for many months in a row, at minimum wage. (I doubted that he often worked six o'clock in the morning until eleven o'clock or midnight, so I drove by the farm at those times on several occasions and it was true.) This is perfectly legal. If Oscar worked in another industry, his boss would have to pay him time and a half after the first forty hours or, in some states, after eight hours a day. Oscar's family told me they barely saw him and his teenaged daughter reported earning a higher hourly rate as a babysitter.

While the link from slavery to hiring vulnerable workers described above might be clear, what is the connection between nineteenth-century slavery and the labor rights of twenty-first-century farmworkers? In the 1930s when Franklin Delano Roosevelt was pushing for strong New Deal labor legislation, Southern Democrats did not want "their" workers to be included. Thereby, two groups of workers were excluded from New Deal labor legislation, farmworkers and domestic workers, jobs that were previously held by field slaves and house slaves. In one telling comment from the floor of the House of Representatives, Congressman J. Mark Wilcox of Florida argued that if the Fair Labor Standards Act (1938) included farmworkers, then the Negro and the white man would be on the same basis. This would then result in "grave social and racial conflicts" and force black workers out of their jobs since whites would be attracted to farm jobs if they paid better wages. This twisted logic pretended to protect black workers' jobs and, in turn, taxpayers, since out-of-work farmworkers might become dependent on the state (US House of Representatives 1937). The reality was that the success of Southern farming was based on the cheap wages paid to farmhands and the future of that success was dependent on making sure farmers had access to the misfortune of workers who could legally earn a lower minimum wage than white workers.

Another significant New Deal labor law that excluded farmworkers and domestic workers was the National Labor Relations Act (1935), which would guarantee them collective bargaining protections. We think of collective bargaining protections as the right to form unions. At a more basic level, collective bargaining protections mean that coworkers can join together to approach their employer and ask for a change in wages, benefits, or workplace conditions without fear of being fired. Furthermore, most employees cannot be fired for organizing other workers or meeting with organizers to discuss improving working conditions. However, if a group of apple pickers approached their employer and asked for an increase of fifteen cents per hour, they could all be fired. That is illegal in other industries.

In 2015, Crispin Hernandez and Saul Pinto, who worked at an upstate New York dairy farm, were fired for meeting with organizer Rebecca Fuentes from the nonprofit Workers Center of Central New York (WCCNY). Fuentes was visiting workers in their homes, which were located on farm property, and the farmer called the police. The authorities could not remove Fuentes because no law was being broken; workers in farm housing have the same rights as tenants to receive visitors. But this did not stop the police from interrogating the organizer and separating and questioning the workers. Being questioned by the police is very intimidating, especially because the workers were undocumented. A week later, Hernandez, Pinto, and Fuentes went door to door to assure the other workers they were allowed to host guests of their choosing. The next day Hernandez and Pinto were fired.

In sum, agricultural workers are excluded from important labor legislation, which means they have fewer protections on the job. This results not only in lower wages and workers' difficultly in addressing their concerns, but also in a path to labor abuses.

Poor Working Conditions

Precarious work describes temporary or contingent jobs that offer few benefits or promotion opportunities. For example, "No Piece of the Pie," the 2016 report by the Food Chain Workers Alliance, details the precarious characteristics of food jobs: unstable, temporary, low paid, with unpredictable schedules and difficult hours. Jobs in the United States used to offer more security, but have changed since the 1970s because of the increase in global trade, neoliberal policies, and countries' *race to the bottom* with deregulation and the weakening of labor protections. We know the United States has the largest gap between the wealthy and the poor of any developed nation. While precarious work now abounds in jobs from the tech industry to the service sector, farm jobs have long typified precarious work and indeed are the prototype (Keller, Gray, and Harrison 2017).

The public at large seems to have a sense that farmworker conditions on monocrop factory farms are poor. Yet, when it comes to local, smaller farms, my research was one of the first to detail that the working conditions are remarkably similar to those on factory farms. In addition, working conditions on organic farms can also be exploitive (Guthman 2003). Some of the conditions farmworkers face (on farms large and small) are related to power hierarchies. Workers fear being fired or deported, have no job mobility, and feel trapped on farms.

Long hours can compromise decision-making and be physically exhausting, and both conditions make it easier for workers to be injured or become ill. Since they usually do not have paid sick or vacation days, workers tend not to take time off to recuperate and thus risk worsening their conditions. Workers must deal with pesticide exposure, dangerous equipment, and repetitive tasks. Thus, not surprisingly, the agriculture sector has the highest rate of fatalities, injuries, and illnesses, and the rates are even higher among the industry's immigrant workers (Bureau of Labor Statistics 2017).

It is easy to romanticize local or small farms, particularly when media stories emphasize the hard work and dedication of the farmers. While the same labor conditions can be found on farms whether they are small or large, monocrop or diverse, corporate or family run, I did find something unique to smaller farms in terms of their labor management practices. What I found was **paternalism**, an extremely hierarchical relationship in which the employer's control extends into workers' everyday lives, affecting even their personal and recreational habits. Paternalism is a form of labor control in which employers offer workers a series of rewards for good behavior. The key is the inequality in the relationship, because workers can never pay back what they received, leading them to always feel indebted to their boss. They often feel the best way to make up for this is to be compliant and docile.

Paternalistic benefits revolve around individuated relationships that address workers' material and psychological needs. On the small family farms I surveyed, the system of paternalism in place was relatively complex: there were varying degrees of benefits, implicating different levels of involvement in and control over worker habits and behavior, depending on what was being offered from the employer. The simplest form of benefits was farm related, such as letting workers take home farm produce or use a farm vehicle. A second degree I call *help* is when the farmer goes out of his or her way to assist a worker. Examples would be letting nonworking family members stay in farm-owned housing or extending a loan to a worker. Another help situation I learned about was when a farmer gets a call from the local police, whom they often know, to pick up a worker who was driving without a driver's license or who has caused a disturbance. Finally, a third, more extreme degree of benefits might be a farmer's promise to help secure a green card. The paternalism I uncovered was extremely complex and allowed farmers to manipulate their workers. At the same time, however, many farmers I interviewed seemed to have genuine concern for their workers. The trouble is that farmer generosity cannot be disentangled from the benefits reaped through paternalistic labor control.

As this discussion illustrated, many structures are in place in farm work that create an exploitable workforce. Ethnic succession is a good example. Some structures are rooted in workers' vulnerabilities, in power hierarchies, and in the fact that farming does not offer the same labor rights as industry. Working conditions are precarious and on smaller farms paternalism can be used as an effective form of labor control.

PROCESSING WORKERS IN THE UNITED STATES AND LABOR ABUSES IN THE FOOD INDUSTRY

In this section, I will examine challenges facing food processing workers and describe some of the more common labor abuses they experience. Some of these abuses also occur in agricultural work, even though working in a field and working in a processing factory are very different experiences. Again, the last section honed in on the way structures create vulnerable workers who have difficulty addressing the problems they face on the job. Now we turn to a further exploration of how employers take advantage of power hierarchies to extract labor and reduce costs.

In 1906 Upton Sinclair published *The Jungle* about immigrant workers in Chicago's slaughterhouses and their deplorable working conditions. The novel's impact was profound and led to the passage of some of the country's first consumer safety regulations, including the Pure Food and Drug Act (1906) and the Meat Inspection Act (1906), but policymakers did not address labor conditions. Today, we may be repeating the past by focusing on food safety at the expense of working conditions. For example, in chicken processing, speed is the key to profits. In 2014 the US Department of Agriculture proposed increasing the number of chickens that could be processed per minute from 140 to 175. There was advocacy on behalf of workers to limit line speeds; however, the major outcry addressed whether the meat could be properly inspected. Keep in mind there has been an increase in foodborne illnesses across the globe. In the end, twenty companies were allowed to apply for the 175-bird-per-minute line speed. When consumers care about food safety, it can positively influence workers, but workers note they are often sidelined when they are not the priority.

Even though he was writing one hundred years earlier, Sinclair would find much that is familiar in a report published in 2004 by Human Rights Watch about conditions in meat and poultry processing (Compa 2004). The report addresses changes in the industry, including higher expectations for numbers of animals slaughtered and butchered, a significant shift to immigrant workers, hazardous conditions, and high rates of injuries. The author describes how fear drives workers to comply and outlines the risks they face, particularly the difficulty workers have securing compensation when they are hurt on the job.

Since the early 2000s there has been an increase in immigrant workers in food processing. In poultry processing alone, more than half the workforce is immigrant and employers have actively recruited them to take the place of local workers in an attempt to find cheaper, more docile workers—this is another case of ethnic succession (Stuesse 2016). Other research mirrors the claims of the Human Rights Watch report and describes the denial of bathroom breaks (in response, some workers wear diapers) (Oxfam America 2015), discrimination in hiring and job assignments, and probably the most common labor abuse in the food industry: wage theft.

Wage theft occurs when an employer does not pay the employee for his or her hours worked. The most basic element of the wage–labor relationship is that the employer agrees to pay the worker for every hour worked; yet wage theft, when workers are not paid fully, is quite common. Wage theft is an example of a **labor abuse**, which is when the law is broken and workers are harmed. (When an apple picker works an eighty-hour workweek at straight minimum wage, that is not a labor abuse because it is legal.) What exacerbates wage theft is that when workers first get a paycheck with missing hours, they assume it was an innocent mistake. The second time it happens they start to wonder whether it was intentional, and by the third time it becomes a significant problem, making it more difficult for workers to address. It might not happen three paychecks in a row, so one could be employed for many weeks or even months before a pattern emerges. Some workers are owed thousands of dollars before they secure legal representation and they often agree to accept less than what they earned because it is faster and workers can be desperate for money. Wage theft is one of the most common labor abuses in farm work as well.

Another significant problem in food processing is workers being denied medical care, being fired after an injury, or not receiving workers' compensation. (Workers' compensation is insurance that pays for medical care related to on-the-job issues and some wages while a worker is out because of the health issue.) By exploiting workers' existing vulnerabilities, processing plants direct injured workers to company doctors, who prioritize company profits over worker health. For instance, anthropologist Angela Stuesse, in a book about chicken processing, documents the case of a Mexican worker from Chiapas whose hand was mutilated by a machine. The company's preferred doctor improperly set the bones and a month later a second doctor had to break and reset the worker's hand, leading to additional surgery. In another example, a teenager who lost half his hand on the job was repeatedly visited by a company representative who tried to convince the teenager to drop his lawyer (Stuesse 2016). Similarly, I met a New York dairy worker, Lazaro, who was attacked by a bull and badly needed medical care. His boss was there, but told him to wait until the cows could be milked. Lazaro was deeply upset that the cows came first and that his employer did not try to find someone else to drive him to the emergency room. A week later he was fired and was not told about workers' compensation.

Blocking unionization efforts is another tool that companies use to keep workers from improving their conditions. Remember, agricultural workers in most states do not form unions because they are denied collective bargaining protections. Food processing workers do have collective bargaining rights and historically meat processing workers had strong unions that greatly improved working conditions from the 1930s to the 1980s. That changed with consolidation of the industry (see Lesson 7) as smaller unionized factories were forced to close and the large processors moved their facilities to states that had antiunion sentiment and laws. As the Human Rights Watch report, "Blood, Sweat, and Fear", documents, companies engage in spying on workers, harassing them, putting pressure on them to stop organizing, threatening them, and, when all else fails, suspending or firing them (Compa 2004).

Stuesse's (2016) book also discusses the mass firing of unionized workers at Tyson Foods plants.

Another set of workplace abuses concerns sexual harassment and sexual assault, which affect female employees in particular. Sexual harassment can be a tool of labor control; it works by intimidating workers and, as the Food Chain Workers Alliance report, "No Piece of the Pie," points out, can make them feel afraid and fear losing their jobs (Food Chain Workers Alliance and Solidarity Research Cooperative 2016). Sexual harassment is endemic in farm work and one study found 80 percent of California's female farmworkers experienced it, compared to 25 percent of the US female workforce (Waugh 2010). One former New York female farmworker, Librada Paz, recipient of the Robert F. Kennedy Human Rights Award, once testified that she never met a female farmworker who had not experienced sexual harassment. More serious is sexual assault, and farm fields can offer cover for predatory managers and contractors. Human Rights Watch also documented this phenomenon in a report that opens with the story of Patricia, a farmworker who was raped by her manager; she told no one because she was alone in the United States and felt she had no choice but to continue working on the farm. Multiple rapes by the manager eventually lead to pregnancy and Patricia pressed charges. Instead of being prosecuted, the manager was deported. Not only was the manager not punished, but also he could potentially cross the border and return to the area where Patricia lived; indeed, she heard through the grapevine that he was planning to do so to see the child (Meng 2012).

One of the major employers of meat processing workers is Tyson Foods; it is the world's largest processor of chicken, beef, and pork, with more than $40 billion in revenue in 2015. Some of its products are sold under different labels such as Jimmy Dean, Hillshire Farm, and Ball Park. It is the face of corporate food and has a record of felony environmental violations, price-fixing, lying about antibiotic use in chickens, and animal abuse. Tyson managers were also indicted for colluding with immigration officials to smuggle workers into the United States to work at their factories; the company itself escaped charges. Reports do not often detail how corporations are actively recruiting undocumented workers; more often the story is about how undocumented workers take American jobs.

Some may expect a company like Tyson Foods to offer poor labor conditions and be involved in labor abuses, but it is not only the corporate giants that participate in poor labor practices. Ideal Snacks, a New York–based food processor, bills itself as producing healthier snacks using a holistic approach and claims that its employees are its most important resource. Yet the company fired two hundred workers with no notice in May 2015. It also paid fines for safety and health violations and workers complained about a lack of bathroom breaks, intimidation by company attorneys, and being forced to lie about injuries. Hence, smaller and local processors and farmers do not necessarily have better labor conditions than the corporations that run very large operations. Both are part of a food system that relies on cheap labor and marginalized workers and are structured in a way that makes labor abuses common. Whether the revenue is $40 billion or $400,000, cutting labor costs are an effective, although unethical, way to increase profits. Some of the ways this is accomplished include speeding up the work (which risks injuries), underpaying workers, replacing empowered workers with vulnerable ones, preventing unionization, firing injured workers, and delaying or blocking workers' compensation claims. It should be apparent at this point that these food jobs are structured in such a way as to allow for, if not promote, labor abuses.

GOVERNMENT OVERSIGHT

Government regulation is a frequent news topic, in particular, how it can be bad for business since it is costly and time-consuming. But it can be difficult to understand what government regulation is since it is a catch-all phrase. **Government regulation** is a set of rules enforced by regulatory agencies that oversee business activities to protect the public interest, for example, in regard to environmental and consumer protections. One aspect of government regulation includes monitoring wages and labor conditions. Employers must keep records to demonstrate they are following the law, and the government can request these records. The government also responds to complaints about labor issues and sometimes government officials perform surprise inspections.

The main role of government regulators is to ensure that businesses are following the law. In the case of federal labor law, the Fair Labor Standards Act (1938) details wages, hours, and child labor laws. In addition, the Occupational Safety and Health Act (OSH Act) of 1970 governs issues relating to worker health and safety, including research, training, rules about the design of workplaces, what sort of protective and emergency equipment must be available, and how employers must respond to worker illness or injury. For agriculture, the Migrant and Seasonal Agricultural Workers Protection Act (1983) covers certain farmworkers in regard to wages, housing, transportation, and the registration of farm labor contractors. Federal government employees implement the federal laws and all those mentioned above are overseen by the US Department of Labor. In addition to the federal government, states have their own labor laws and most have their own state departments of labor to oversee them. Other government agencies may play a role at the state level. For example, the New York State Department of Health inspects some farmworker housing.

While there are laws that protect workers, ensuring those laws are followed can be a challenge. For instance, on the federal and state levels there are twenty-two hundred Occupational Health and Safety Administration (OSHA) inspectors for eight million workplaces—one inspector per fifty-nine thousand workers. As a result, health and safety inspectors tend to be reactive and respond when there is a worker complaint, injury, or fatality. They are reliant on hearing from workers who can call a hotline to make a compliant. Even though government workers and nonprofits do outreach to workers about their rights and offer them resources, food workers are often afraid to make the phone call. One worker I met, Jose, told me he was not afraid to talk about the poor conditions on the farm where he worked, but his coworkers put pressure on him to stay quiet and told him if he did speak, just to speak for himself.

Some workers are even afraid to meet with outreach workers, worried about risking their livelihoods. One nonprofit employee told me, "They stay quiet even though they are suffering." In general, I heard from those who work with undocumented workers that they have little expectation of their circumstances changing, and they have no reason to believe that they have the power to effect change. Lawyers and paralegals both spoke to me about farm laborers' pressure from coworkers to ostracize anyone who broke ranks to lodge a complaint. In addition, organizers regularly heard from workers that farmers explicitly warned them not to associate in any way with organizers. In general, I had the impression that most workers, fearful of employer repercussions, did not want their concerns raised until the end of the season, after they had left the farm, and legal service providers and a Department of Labor representative expressed similar understandings to me.

Workers' unwillingness to complain is an obstacle for the work of OSHA, but the agency has a more significant obstacle. Representatives of OSHA are not allowed to regulate on farms with fewer than eleven nonfamily employees. This restriction was put in place to help smaller farmers since regulations can be expensive to follow and there is the risk of being fined by the government if the regulations are not met, but it results in dangerous workplaces not being inspected. For example, of the thirty-four deaths on dairy farms between 2007 and 2012 in New York State, OSHA was only able to inspect four because the rest were on farms with fewer than eleven hired workers.

Despite the difficulties implementing the law, worker organizations often make policy recommendations. For meat processing workers there is a consensus that slowing down line speeds would reduce injuries. There is also advocacy for more specific and enforceable safety and health guidelines for both food processing and agriculture. A proposal that is unpopular with employers is for the government to increase fines against employers who break the law or who allow safety violations; this could act as a deterrent. In the case of fatalities, there is a proposal for criminal investigations whenever they occur, not just administrative remedies. Among worker advocates and legal service providers there is a great awareness that workers' legal status creates worker vulnerability and so there is a call for immigration authorities to not seek out workers who do not have a criminal record.

MOVEMENTS FOR CHANGE

Despite the challenges workers face, there have been successful movements to improve workers' conditions. Some have been based on the collective action of workers and others on consumer campaigns. Organizations such as the United Farm Workers of America and the Farm Labor Organizing Committee have played important roles in farmworker struggles for several decades; new organizations have also developed to represent agricultural workers. And while unions such as the United Food & Commercial Workers and the United Packinghouse Workers still organize food processing workers, other organizations have stepped in to develop worker power and push for workplace improvements. Many of the organizations that have developed in the past few decades are referred to as **worker centers**; these nonprofits are focused on improving workers' conditions, although they do not have the negotiating power of unions. In addition, worker centers are not solely focused on organizing in a single workplace or even only in workplaces, since many also do community organizing.

One example is the WCCNY, which is affiliated with Interfaith Worker Justice, a national coalition of worker centers. Located in Syracuse, the WCCNY not only caters to urban workers including restaurant and hotel workers, but also has a dairy worker campaign. Like many worker centers, this organization empowers workers to take initiative to combat labor abuses, develops worker leaders, and trains workers on their rights and health and safety issues. Their community organizing includes taking part in a campaign to push for the undocumented to have access to drivers' licenses in New York State and a poli-migra effort to convince law enforcement not to share information with federal immigration authorities. One of WCCNY's efforts led to a significant policy change. When dairy workers explained their concerns about the injuries and fatalities they were experiencing and witnessing, they engaged in **collective action**, the process of coming together as a group to push for a common goal. The WCCNY, along with the Worker Justice Center of New York, facilitated a meeting between dairy workers and OSHA officials. The result was a local emphasis program on New York dairies, whereby OSHA would act in a proactive way (compared to the usual reactive way) to train farm owners and managers about how to improve health and safety on the farms and then conduct surprise inspections. Some workers reported significant changes in trainings, protective gear, and overall safety (Workers Center of Central New York n.d.).

If you remember the previous discussion, two New York dairy workers were fired after meeting with an organizer from the WCCNY. That is now the basis for a lawsuit against New York State and the governor of New York, Andrew Cuomo, on behalf of Crispin Hernandez, the WCCNY, and the Worker Justice Center of New York. The case is challenging the exclusion of agricultural workers from collective bargaining protections because the New York State constitution guarantees every worker in the state the right to organize. This is a lawsuit, not collective action, but it is another way to try to improve worker conditions.

The Coalition of Immokalee Workers has engaged in collective action with Florida tomato pickers since the early 1990s and then developed a

consumer campaign. Consumer campaigns rely on consumers to put pressure on companies to make a change, sometimes with boycotts (see Lesson 1). The coalition's first successful effort was against Taco Bell in 2005 and since then it has won agreements with more than a dozen corporate giants to improve working conditions through the Fair Food Program. The program targets large corporate buyers of Florida's fresh tomatoes and presses them to pay one penny per pound more and only do business with growers who committed to a code of conduct.

A **code of conduct** is a set of ethical practices related to the way business is conducted; it may or may not have enforcement mechanisms. In this case, the Fair Food Program's code of conduct requires worker-to-worker education, health and safety councils on each farm, break times, appropriate housing, and zero tolerance for forced labor (the Florida tomato industry had repeated problems with human trafficking), violence, or sexual assault (among other requirements). In addition, each participating farm is audited twice a year (Coalition of Immokalee Workers, Fair Food Program). I asked representatives of the program about wage theft and they said with the complaint hotline that operates twenty-four hours a day, seven days a week, it had all but disappeared because workers call the first time wage theft occurs and the situation is remedied—that system is dependent on workers knowing their rights and feeling empowered. In 2017 Ben & Jerry's signed an agreement with the Vermont nonprofit Migrant Justice to promote better conditions for the state's dairy farm workers, including improved wages, schedules, housing, and safety. The Milk with Dignity consumer campaign was integral to the effort.

Many other initiatives are under way. In food processing, the Northwest Arkansas Workers Justice Center was able to pressure Tyson to create safer worker conditions and has pushed the state legislature to consider lowering line speeds. Wage theft ordinances have been passed in sixteen states, including New York, as well as in some counties and municipalities. Because of worker center pressure, the Environmental Protection Agency has established stricter pesticide application guidelines. In addition, the City of Los Angeles adopted the Good Food Purchasing Program, which includes a commitment to the environment, workers, and nutrition standards (Food Chain Workers Alliance and Solidarity Research Cooperative 2016).

Conclusion

Studying food offers innumerable entry points for social, economic, and political analysis and it helps us make decisions about what we eat and how we think about what we eat. Much of food studies intersect with food ethics—taking care of our planet, being responsible in how we produce and consume food, and aiming toward sustainable practices, including how animals and workers are treated.

This lesson aimed to instigate a conversation about the relationship between food ethics, sustainable food systems, and food workers. If we are striving for an equitable food system, we must include food workers in our priorities. One significant barrier to improving conditions for food workers is the price we pay for food. The United States has the least expensive food of all the industrialized countries and one-quarter of what we purchase is thrown away. If we are going to improve worker conditions, we need to develop a pricing system that allows smaller farmers and processors to pay their workers well. Tyson is quite unusual with its billion-dollar profits. Many small farmers and food producers are struggling to stay afloat, yet they are competing with the corporate giants who dictate food prices and can still benefit with slim profit margins. At the same time, Philip Martin, an agricultural labor economist, demonstrates that raising farmworker wages to fifteen dollars an hour would cost the average consumer twenty dollars a year if that money went directly to workers.

Restructuring food jobs so that they will be sustainable and offer a way out of poverty will not be easy and there are many opponents to such efforts, but the social movements highlighted here show that even with structural challenges, power hierarchies, a lack of labor rights, labor abuses, and management practices that put profit over people, changes can be made to uplift workers.

Discussion Questions

1. Have you ever not been paid for the hours you worked? What did you do? What would you do if this happened? Can you imagine letting it go on for months without saying anything? For those who do not complain, but wish they could, what do you think their internal conversation is like? Do you think factors like legal status or other power hierarchies play a role?

2. Did you ever get a group of people together to ask for change? Maybe you asked your professor to change an exam date? Perhaps you got together with colleagues and asked to get paid for training or to be able to use your phones during break time? Why did you work collectively? Why do you think working collectively makes a difference?

3. Can you try to trace your last meal? Consider the five food employment sectors: production, processing, distribution, retail, and service. Who do you think the workers were? How do you think they were paid and treated?

4. Are you willing to pay more for the food you eat so that farm and food workers would earn more? Why or why not? If yes, how much more?

Exercise

Similar to many campuses, your campus likely has a large food services operation. Have you ever paused to consider who prepares your food on campus? For this exercise, explore who the food service workers are on your campus and how they are treated. Engage in observation: Who are the workers? Are they students, off-campus workers, or a combination? What are their demographic characteristics? Who are the employers—the university, or does the university contract out food services? Ask workers questions: What are worker wages and benefits? Are they unionized? If you have fast-food chains on your campus, are those workers treated the same as other food service workers? Do the food service workers on your campus think they are fairly compensated? Why or why not?

Additional Materials
Readings

Barlow, Zenobia. 2009. "Raising Chickens Student Handout," 29; and "Chapter 5: In the Grass." In *Food Inc. Discussion Guide*, 55–60. Los Angeles: Participant Media and the Center for Ecoliteracy.

Estabrook, Barry. 2011. *Tomatoland: How Modern Industrial Agriculture Destroyed Our Most Alluring Fruit*. Kansas City, MO: Andrews McMeel.

Food Chain Workers Alliance. 2012. *The Hands That Feed Us: Challenges and Opportunities for Workers Along the Food Chain*. Berkeley; University of California Press.

Fox, Carly, Rebecca Fuentes, Fabiola Ortiz Valdez, Gretchen Purser, and Kathleen Sexsmith. 2017. *Milked: Immigrant Dairy Farmworkers in New York State*. Syracuse, NY: Workers Center of Central New York and the Worker Justice Center of New York.

Holmes, Seth. 2013. *Fresh Fruit, Broken Bodies: Migrant Farmworkers in the United States*. Berkeley: University of California Press.

Horton, Sarah Bronwen. 2016. *They Leave Their Kidneys in the Fields: Illness, Injury, and Illegality among U.S. Farmworkers*. Oakland: University of California Press.

Jayaraman, Saru. 2014. *Behind the Kitchen Door*. Ithaca, NY: Cornell University Press.

Lo, Joann. 2014. "Social Justice for Food Workers in a Foodie World." *Journal of Critical Thought and Praxis* 3 (1): 7.

Marosi, Richard. 2014. "Product of Mexico." *Los Angeles Times*, December 7, 2014. Four news stories with interactive features. http://graphics.latimes.com/product-of-mexico-camps/

Oxfam America. n.d. "Lives on the Line: The High Human Cost of Chicken." https://www.oxfamamerica.org/livesontheline/

Ribas, Vanesa. 2015. *Slaughterhouses and the Making of the New South*. Oakland: University of California Press.

Striffler, Steve. 2002. "Inside a Poultry Processing Plant: An Ethnographic Portrait." *Labor History* 43 (3): 305–13. Reprinted in *Utne Reader*, January/February 2004. http://www.utne.com/community/undercover-in-a-chicken-factory

Films

Bergman, Lowell, and Andres Cediel. 2013. *Rape in the Fields*. WGBH Educational Foundation. June 25, 2013. http://www.pbs.org/wgbh/frontline/film/rape-in-the-fields/

Rawal, Sanjay. 2014. *Food Chains*. New York: Screen Media Films. http://www.foodchainsfilm.com/

Websites

Food Chain Workers Alliance. http://foodchainworkers.org/

Video Clips

Colbert, Stephen. 2010. *Statement to the Subcommittee on Immigration, Citizenship and Border Security.* September 24, 2010. Washington DC: C-SPAN. https://www.youtube.com/watch?v=k1T75jBYeCs.

Jayaraman, Saru. 2014. *Behind the Kitchen Door: Saru Jayaraman at TEDxManhattan.* https://www.youtube.com/watch?v=Gc8uOWAiKmw

References

Bureau of Labor Statistics. 2017. "Census of Fatal Occupational Injuries Charts, 1992-2016 (final data)." Accessed April 20, 2018. https://www.bls.gov/iif/oshwc/cfoi/cfch0015.pdf

Coalition of Immokalee Workers. n.d. Accessed February 10, 2017. http://www.ciw-online.org/

Compa, Lance A. 2004. *Blood, Sweat, and Fear: Workers' Rights in U.S. Meat and Poultry Plants.* New York: Human Rights Watch.

Fair Food Program. n.d. Accessed February 10, 2017. http://www.fairfoodprogram.org/.

Food Chain Workers Alliance and Solidarity Research Cooperative. 2016. *No Piece of the Pie: U.S. Food Workers in 2016.* Los Angeles: Food Chain Workers Alliance.

Gray, Margaret. 2014. *Labor and the Locavore: The Making of a Comprehensive Food Ethic.* Oakland: University of California Press.

Guthman, Julie. 2003. "Fast Food/Organic Food: Reflexive Tastes and the Making of 'Yuppie Chow.'" *Social & Cultural Geography* 4 (1): 45–58.

Hernandez, Trish, Susan Gabbard, and Daniel Carroll. 2016. *Findings from the National Agricultural Workers Survey (NAWS) 2013–2014: A Demographic and Employment Profile of United States Farmworkers.* Research Report No. 12. Washington, DC: US Department of Labor.

Keller, Julie C., Margaret Gray, and Jill Lindsey Harrison. 2017. "Milking Workers, Breaking Bodies." *New Labor Forum* 26 (1): 36–44.

Long, Erven J. 1951. "The President's Commission on Migratory Labor in American Agriculture." *Land Economics* 27 (3): 249–51.

Meng, Grace. 2012. *Cultivating Fear: The Vulnerability of Immigrant Farmworkers in the US to Sexual Violence and Sexual Harassment.* New York: Human Rights Watch.

Oxfam America. 2015. *Lives on the Line: The Human Cost of Cheap Chicken.* Boston: Oxfam America.

Stuesse, Angela. 2016. *Scratching out a Living: Latinos, Race, and Work in the Deep South.* Oakland: University of California Press.

US House of Representatives. 1937. 82 Cong. Rec. 1404. https://www.gpo.gov/fdsys/pkg/GPO-CRECB-1937-pt2-v82/content-detail.html

Waugh, Irma M. 2010, "Examining the Sexual Harassment Experiences of Mexican Immigrant Farmworking Women." *Violence against Women* 16 (3): 237–61.

Workers Center of Central New York. n.d. Accessed March 1, 2017. https://workerscny.org/

Cattle feedlot, Bovina, Texas. (Photo © CGP Grey / Flickr /CC BY 2.0.)

12

Food and the Environment

Sean Gillon

F ood systems are inseparable from the global environments in which food is produced, processed, transported, sold, consumed, and wasted. Food systems are shaped by and shape biological, ecological, and other environmental processes. Food serves as a lens into a wide range of environmental issues, as resources are organized to constitute a meal along its way to your table. These issues include climate change, water quality and availability, biodiversity, toxic environments, and land degradation and stewardship. This lesson explores the environments that food systems produce and pathways for positive change. Questions considered include: What are key environmental issues associated with the contemporary, industrialized food system? How are they related to industrialized agriculture and food systems' basis in nature? How are food systems' environmental problems related to society and social decisions and priorities? And, given what we know, what might be done?

This lesson is organized to provide a broad overview of the intersections between food and the environment at various points in the food system—from agricultural production to food processing, distribution, consumption, and waste. The lesson first considers the importance of understanding environmental questions as fundamentally social ones. Subsequent sections consider agriculture's biological and ecological foundations, agricultural industrialization, and the environments produced by the modern food system. Key environmental outcomes explored include problems with soil erosion, land degradation, habitat and biodiversity loss, water quality and availability decline, pesticide and fertilizer pollution, and intensive energy use that is a significant contributor to climate change. Throughout, the lesson points to social dynamics that underpin our food systems' environmental consequences and result in both hunger and waste at tremendous social and environmental cost. The lesson concludes by noting how people are working to improve the sustainability and equity of food systems.

THE SOCIAL NATURE OF ENVIRONMENTAL QUESTIONS

This lesson begins by explaining how *the environment* in food systems is as fundamentally social as it is ecological so that we might better understand and improve food systems' environmental outcomes. To say that the environment is social is to say that (1) environmental conditions are influenced by social decisions (e.g., policies, individuals' context-dependent behaviors that contribute to outcomes) and that (2) the environment and understandings of environmental questions influence how society is organized and how decisions are made. For example, policies can incentivize agricultural production practices that steward the environmental resources on which food systems depend; drive decisions about food supply, use, and waste; affect how food systems' benefits and burdens are distributed; structure the organization of food processing and distribution; and influence eating practices through guidelines and standards.

While environments and societies are always inextricably intertwined, food systems illustrate this point particularly well. Agrifood system scholars Margaret FitzSimmons and David Goodman (1998, 209–10) offer a brief history of corn that illustrates how difficult it is to separate the social and environmental aspects of food systems; the authors demonstrate what we can learn by thinking about social and environmental categories together:

> *A history [of corn] might encompass, selectively, the agricultural origin story of the corn mother told by Indians in eastern North America . . . the place of corn in meso-American cultures, the Columbian exchange . . . and the expansion of corn as a commercial crop, supported in the USA by an extensive institutional infrastructure.*
>
> *. . . [Corn] is also metabolized industrially and in human stomachs as, for example, corn flour, tortillas, bread, cornstarch, and as an ingredient of many thousands of food products. Corn as animal feed similarly is metabolized in the double gut of feedlot cattle and dairy cows, and by factory-farmed chickens and hogs, before its secondary metabolism as animal protein for human consumption.*

We could further, for example, tie corn through high-fructose corn syrup to the soft drinks served in fast-food restaurants around the globe; and corn ethanol production means corn kernels end up mixed with gasoline and combusted in automobile engines to be released into the atmosphere, connecting the story to climate change, energy policy, the automobile industry, and food insecurity. Thus, social–environmental arrangements produce different and consequential environments and outcomes, relying on resources and social decisions, priorities, and policies to do so.

This straightforward point, that food–environment relations are as fundamentally social as they are ecological or biological, can have profound implications for how we define and address environmental problems. There is no environmental issue that is just an environmental issue; they always involve social decisions, political positions, and policy negotiations and unevenly affect human well-being. Paying close attention to the social causes and consequences of environmental change moves us away from thinking about the environment as a thing out there to act on or use as a raw material. It moves us toward thinking about how we participate in creating the environment and how we can work with (and from within) environments that help us to produce food. From this perspective, we can more fully consider how to interact with food systems' lively biological and ecological components that we depend on for plant pollination and growth and soil fertility, for example. Likewise, this perspective leads us to consider how to interact with disease, bacteria, pests, and other ecological change as we organize our food system to meet basic human needs.

How society organizes itself relative to environmental questions is not predetermined, natural, or unchangeable. Even the environmental dimensions of food systems that seem to be unbending and absolute should be examined closely for their social underpinnings. To illustrate this point, consider the question of the ecological limits on producing adequate food or other resources to provide for a growing population. Whether and how we can provide for the planet's people is a centuries-old debate. The kind of agricultural production we have, how many people are considered too many by whom, and the distribution and use of global resources all have major implications for food systems' organization and outcomes. We will consider these questions in general terms here and then return to the question of global food production, insecurity, and waste later in the lesson.

Discussions of food scarcity, or resource scarcity in general, often focus on the environmental limits of adequate resource provision, but without questioning underlying assumptions about how resources are used, for whom scarcity is a problem, or how society is organized to meet (only some) human needs. Asking these questions is critical if we are to accurately define and effectively address persistent global social and environmental problems. Geographer David Harvey (1974, 273) illustrates this point in a foundational essay on resource scarcity and population. He explains how once a resource is thought of as having an absolute limit on its availability, then an absolute line is drawn between a population that available resources can support and overpopulation that the resources cannot sustain. He spells out the implications:

> And what are the political implications ... of saying there is "overpopulation" or a "scarcity of resources"? The meaning can all too quickly be established. Somebody, somewhere, is redundant, and there is not enough to go round. Am I redundant? Of course not. Are you redundant? Of course not. So who is redundant? Of course, it must be them. And if there is not enough to go round, then it is only right and proper that they, who contribute so little to society, ought to bear the brunt of the burden.

One of Harvey's points here is that arguments about ecological limits and overpopulation cast some people (*they*, an undefined other) as an unwelcome burden on planetary resources. Those with political power and social standing determine who those people are, even while avoiding questions about the inequitable use and distribution of resources. Consider Garrett Hardin's statement (quoted in Castree 2005, emphasis added):

> We *should go lightly in encouraging rising expectations among the poor . . . for if everyone in the world had the same standard of living as we do, we would increase pollution by a factor of 20. . . . Therefore it is questionable morality to increase the food supply.* We *should hesitate to make sacrifices locally for the betterment of the* rest *of the world. (113)*

Implying *they* should starve may seem shocking, but it is an all too common symptom of focusing on environmental impacts and limits without taking seriously social questions of inequitable resource distribution and use. Elsewhere, Harvey (1996, 145) warns about understanding scarcity as something entirely environmental and not social, indicating that we might think differently to create positive change:

> *What exists in "nature" is in a constant state of transformation. To declare a state of ecoscarcity is in effect to say that we have not the will, wit, or capacity to change our state of knowledge, our social goals, cultural modes, and technological mixes, or our form of economy, and that we are powerless to modify either our material practices or "nature" according to human requirements. To say that scarcity resides in nature and that natural limits exist is to ignore how scarcity is socially produced and how "limits" are a social relation within nature (including human society) rather than some externally imposed necessity.*

Such an understanding of the environment helps us to avoid extreme interpretations of it as either an absolute limit or a passive stage on which a separate, human trajectory unfolds. This understanding helps us to think about social and environmental problems together and about the environment as a fundamental and lively element in food systems to be worked with and not in spite of or against. If we are unable to engage social and environmental problems together, we risk creating social problems from environmental ones and vice versa. This lesson focuses on the environments that industrial agriculture produces, but these outcomes, as products of social decisions, are not inevitable. Industrial agriculture is currently dominant, but engagement with the social and ecological organization of the food system can change its trajectory. The next section discusses the linked social and environmental origins and consequences of industrialized agriculture. The section that follows considers processing, consuming, and wasting food.

ENVIRONMENTS OF INDUSTRIALIZED AGRICULTURE

It is commonplace today to say that where your food comes from matters. Eaters are increasingly concerned about the social and environmental costs of putting food on their plate. That food is a universal human need and that its environmental origins are more easily visible than those of, say, a microchip, make food a likely recipient of greater scrutiny for its environmental costs. But, what precisely makes food and agriculture unique within a mainly industrial and financial global economy? How can we characterize food's basis in the environment and the difference it makes? How are we to understand what is at stake when we consider the environmental costs of food production? This section addresses these questions, examining the development and consequences of industrial agriculture as a foundation of contemporary food–environment relations.

All industrial, productive, or extractive processes rely on environmental resources to create products; and they typically depend on the environment as a place to lodge waste. Agriculture and food production, somewhat uniquely, also depend on the environment for its biological and ecological attributes and processes, such as plant genetics and evolution, pollination, and photosynthesis. Agriculture also relies on very particular, place-based resources like water and expansive, high-quality soil. Unlike a factory in the industrial sector that uses machines indoors year round, and sometimes around the clock, agricultural production requires waiting for sunlight and for plants to grow, suitable climatic conditions within seasonal cycles, and that all of this happens in relatively large, carefully prepared spaces.

Scholars of agricultural political economy have discussed environmental factors as key barriers to making agriculture profitable. **Agriculture's basis in nature** (the biological process, seasonal cycles, and land-based requirements noted previously) makes surplus revenue generation challenging and requires large up-front investments. Land is often expensive and needed in large quantities to profit from the production of relatively cheap goods. Agricultural machinery and infrastructure necessary for large-scale production are also costly. To make matters worse, in many climates and for many crops, agricultural land is only productive for part of the year, offering just one crop cycle and opportunity for farm income (see Mann and Dickinson [1978] and Goodman, Sorj, and Wilkinson [1987] for foundational explanations). These characteristics of agriculture have influenced patterns of food systems development and their environmental effects, especially through agricultural industrialization.

Agricultural industrialization can be described as a set of technologies and practices that aim to maximize agricultural productivity and profitability and minimize the challenges that nature or the environment poses, typically by substituting industrial processes for biological processes and human labor (see Lesson 1). Understanding exactly how agriculture was industrialized is essential for understanding the environment in food systems and for defining and addressing related environmental problems. David Goodman and colleagues (Goodman, Sorj, and Wilkinson 1987) described how industrialization occurred both in agricultural production and further downstream in the food system. In agricultural production, mechanization minimized the challenge of growing cheap products on large swaths of land, while chemical and biological technologies have intervened in biological production cycles to make them more profitable. Postproduction, agricultural products of the industrialized food system have become more like industrial inputs than food. Standardized agricultural products can be variously assembled via more predictable, efficient, and profitable industrial processes. Global food system infrastructure facilitates the processing, packaging, transportation, distribution, and waste of continually reimagined food products.

The sections that follow consider how food systems' basis in nature has influenced, indeed defined, agricultural industrialization and the organization of the food system. Each section examines environmental issues and the social arrangements that create and maintain environmental problems, particularly around agricultural practices and decision-making power. Considering social context helps to identify causes of and solutions to environmental problems and to understand how and why most food is produced the way it is, especially when more equitable and ecologically sustainable production models are possible. Examples are primarily drawn from the United States, which has had a considerable role in agriculture's industrialization, but also from global contexts. Agriculture's expanding basis in land and key land use change issues in the contemporary food system are discussed next as extensification. The following section explores agricultural industrialization through intensification, defined as increasing agricultural productivity per unit of land.

Food System Environments of Extensification

Initial stages of agricultural industrialization depended on **extensification**, defined as increasing agricultural productivity or output by expanding the land base in agricultural production. Extensification was facilitated by mechanization and crop specialization, or growing one crop instead of several on the same farm. Farmers were able to plow more ground and farm increasingly large areas in less time with the aid of steam-driven and then fossil fuel–powered tractors, which substituted for animal power. Crop specialization and mechanization minimized the constraints of agricultural production associated with its basis in land and the requirements of animal husbandry. The new environments produced by extensification resulted in some of agriculture's most persistent environmental issues: soil erosion, land use change and degradation, and water issues, which are discussed here.

As the agricultural land base expanded and crop production specialized, the number of tractors used on US farms rose from approximately

246,000 to 4.5 million between 1920 and 1959. The number of horses and mules used on US farms declined from 25.1 to 2.1 million over the same period, indicating the magnitude and rapid pace of this transition. The Dust Bowl disaster of the 1930s illustrated the environmental consequences of extensification as portions of several Great Plains states were engulfed by dust storms from soil blowing off eroding land, recently brought into mechanized agricultural production, encouraged by agricultural policy and markets. Yields declined with soil quality in the absence of sufficient nutrients or the nitrogen fertilizer that would soon become widely available. Illustrating social–environmental connections, Holleman's (2017) history of the Dust Bowl makes clear the ecological disaster's roots in rapidly expanding settler colonialism, imperialism, and a racialized global division of labor. Concerns about soil quality in agriculture reach further back in history, particularly when agricultural expansion onto new lands that still retained soil nutrients accumulated over millennia was difficult without the aid of mechanization. Foster and Magdoff (2000) detail how global soil quality emerged as a major concern in mid-nineteenth-century European and US societies. The United States, for example, seized dozens of islands around the globe in search of nitrogen- and phosphate-rich guano under the Guano Island Act passed in 1856.

The social and ecological disaster of the Dust Bowl and Great Depression in the United States also led to the creation of policies and practices intended to better steward agricultural land. Subsequent policy established institutional infrastructure and resources to support US farmers in implementing conservation practices to reduce soil erosion and eventually improve water quality and wildlife habitat availability. Gilbert and colleagues (Gilbert, Sharp, and Felin 2002) describe, however, how some were excluded based on race from conservation and other farm programs; it was not until the civil rights movement that African American farmer participation improved. Like white farmers, farmers owning large land areas dominated in terms of participation rates and decision-making power, marginalizing poorer rural residents' access to conservation and other support (see West 1994). Conservation programs that pay farmers who voluntarily implement specific conservation practices are more widespread in the United States and elsewhere today, although they are vulnerable to shifts in policy and competitive agricultural markets that incentivize increased production over dedicating land to resources stewardship. In the United States, soil erosion from cropland has decreased with a rise in the use of grassed waterways, cropland buffer strips that reduce runoff, and no-till agriculture, which reduces erosion caused by tilling fields for weed control but can increase herbicide use. According to the US Natural Resources Conservation Service, which administers conservation programs, soil erosion from rainfall declined from 1.59 to 0.96 billion tons per year between 1982 and 2012; erosion from wind decreased from 1.38 to 0.71 billion tons. This, however, means that US agriculture still results in the loss of over 1.6 billion tons of soil annually or 4.5 million tons of soil each day.

Well beyond the United States, food production has a massive global land use footprint, which expanded rapidly in the nineteenth century as cheap food was sought to feed increasingly urban, industrializing societies. Without the forthcoming agricultural technologies associated with intensification discussed in the next section (e.g., fertilizers, pesticides, and hybrid seeds), farming more land was necessary to increase food production and keep food prices (and wages) low. More recently, according to the UN Food and Agriculture Organization (FAO), over 38 percent of the world's land is agricultural, with pasture accounting for 26 percent of the total and cropland accounting for the remainder. Agricultural land increased from around 4.5 billion hectares in 1960 to near 5 billion today. While total land in agriculture seems to be stabilizing at this level, significant regional changes are occurring, such as the conversion of forest to agricultural land. Latin America, for example, accounted for 35 percent of the 5 million hectares of annual agricultural expansion over the past thirty years. Further, the FAO estimates that approximately 25 percent of agricultural land is highly degraded and 8 percent is moderately degraded. Continued degradation of soil through, for example, excessive tilling, uncontrolled grazing, and monoculture production without cover cropping or crop rotation undermines future food production.

Because of this footprint, the FAO places agriculture among the top five global threats to biodiversity, especially because of habitat conversion, but also for its contributions to climate change and water pollution. Conversely, the organization finds that stewarding agribiodiversity in terms of landscapes, ecosystems, species, and genetics will be critical for improving food security and adapting to climate change. Water security is also critical; agriculture uses 70 percent of the world's supply and this use will likely increase in the near term. The global area of irrigated land doubled to 240 million hectares between 1960 and 2003 and is expected to increase to 350 million hectares by 2025. Overdrawing groundwater aquifers to irrigate agriculture is a major concern throughout the world and especially in China, India, Mexico, Pakistan, North Africa, and the Middle East. Water shortages increasingly afflict the world's poorest people; an estimated 40 percent of the world's rural population lives in river basins classified as *water scarce* by the FAO.

The kind of agricultural production pursued as land use has changed matters a great deal for environmental outcomes. Agricultural practices hinge on prevailing policies, markets, environmental conditions, and the social situation in which producers find themselves. Consider, for example, the land ownership in the context of extensification. Over the past several years, food systems scholars and advocates have drawn public attention to **land grabs**. A land grab, Ben White and colleagues (White et al. 2012, 619) explain, is "the large-scale acquisition of land or land-related rights and resources by corporate (business, non-profit or public) entities." Global land grabs over the past several years are estimated to have occurred on fifty to sixty-seven million acres. Given the scale of these changes, the potential for lasting negative environmental change and food insecurity under new patterns of ownership is significant. The degree to which, for example, corporate farm operators seeking short-term profit in agricultural and land markets will steward the resources on which the food system depends is not clear; and whether these agricultural lands will produce food or biofuels is a critical, ongoing issue. Land grabs may also exacerbate existing gender inequity in the food system (see Behrmen and colleagues' [Behrmen, Meinzen-Dick, and Quisumbing 2013] review). Understanding the connections between land ownership, decisions about agricultural practices, and environmental outcomes is critical for addressing environmental change in the food system. The next section considers the environments that the food system produces through agricultural industrialization based on intensification.

Environments of Intensification

After agricultural extensification and mechanization, agricultural industrialization continued though intensification. **Intensification** describes the process of increasing agricultural productivity per unit of land, without necessarily expanding the area under agricultural production. This is one of the most consequential organizing forces in the food system and has had tremendous environmental implications. In this section, we discuss the use of fertilizer, pesticides, and seed technologies that made it possible for global agricultural production to increase dramatically over the past century with significant environmental consequences.

Industrially-produced nitrogen fertilizer has been a key driver of productivity increases in agriculture and a hallmark of the industrial food system. Produced since the end of the First World War as the military–industrial infrastructure was transitioned to civilian use, nitrogen fertilizer use increased globally from 11.5 to 84.6 million tons between 1961 and 2001. Global use increases have continued, particularly in Asia. Total global mineral fertilizer use rose from 30 to 154 million tons between 1950 and 2005 and an increase to 188 million tons is expected by 2030. Consequently, nitrogen flows to terrestrial ecosystems have doubled since 1960 and phosphorus influxes have tripled. That crop production often only utilizes 30 to 40 percent of nitrogen fertilizers applied makes clear the reason for widespread nitrogen pollution. Researchers are quick to point to marine *dead zones*, areas where aquatic life is impossible because of nutrient pollution and the dissolved oxygen depletion that results. The FAO indicates that the number of dead zones increased from less than fifty in 1950 to over five hundred by 2010, covering well over 245,000 square kilometers. Groundwater contamination is also a serious issue, particularly in areas of intensive corn production in the US Midwest.

The increased availability and use of nitrogen fertilizer under intensification also facilitated the spatial separation of livestock from crop production, further compounding nutrient pollution problems. First, tractors replaced animal power and nitrogen fertilizer made their manure less essential. Second, the availability of a nitrogen-based, external nutrient source reduced the need for rotating or cover-cropping with nitrogen-fixing (legume) crops after grain harvests to restore soil fertility. Since cover crops were often fed to animals, the reduction in the feed source made having livestock on farms less desirable. Animals also moved off the farm as live-stock processing industries were concentrated in particular regions by a consolidating industry that prefers to purchase from a few large rather than many small farms (e.g., chicken production in the US South, beef produc-tion in the US Great Plains). Concentrated livestock production creates its own nutrient pollution problems because of the large quantities of animal manure amassed, disconnected from crop farms that need those nutrients. In short, two nutrient problems (concentrated manure production and ni-trogen fertilizer pollution) have resulted from the spatial separation of crop and livestock production.

Pesticides also aim to increase food systems' productivity by dealing with the ecological consequences of large-scale monocrop production, which is more susceptible to pest and disease pressure than more diversified farm-ing systems. The rise, expansion, and intensification of industrial agricul-ture brought with it massive pesticide use; global pesticide sales grew from US $8.1 billion to nearly $35 billion between 1990 and 2014. In 2007, for ex-ample, the United States used over two hundred thousand tons of herbi-cides, seventy-eight thousand tons of insecticides, and nineteen thousand tons of fungicides and bactericides. Globally, pesticides poison millions of people and kill over two hundred thousand annually. Human health effects range from cancer and birth defects to disruption of the endocrine system. Those working in and living around agricultural fields on which pesticides are regularly applied are most vulnerable (see Lesson 11). Jill Harrison (2011), for example, documents the serious effects of pesticide use in California on farmworkers and others living near agricultural lands, detailing efforts to regulate pesticides. This example serves as an important illustration of the dynamics of many environmental problems and food system externalities, or costs not reflected in the price of food: they are disproportionately visited on the marginalized and impoverished.

Seed technologies have been developed to complement fertilizer and pes-ticide use to increase global agricultural productivity; each is now a defining feature of the global food system. Hybrid seeds, for example, are inbred seed lines that provide higher yields, but produce grain that cannot be replanted. These seeds respond well to nitrogen fertilizer, are more efficient in photo-synthesis, and have uniform growth that aids in mechanical harvesting. The environmental effects of hybrid seed use did not come so much from the seed itself, but from the role it played in solidifying a package of technologies—that is, mechanization, nitrogen fertilizers, and irrigation where necessary. These technologies were developed through public and private agricultural research partnerships in the United States and then exported around the world during the green revolution (see Lessons 5 and 6).

Patel (2013) examines green revolution policy and practice, explaining that while food production increased, changes favored larger farmers with access to the capital necessary to participate and did not get food into the hands of those without access to land or income. It also undermined women's roles in agricultural economies and increased pest pressure, pesticide use, and the other environmental problems under consideration here. Patel further suggests that we are entering a second green revolution, marked by continued focus on capital-intensive agricultural technology (i.e., genetically modified crops), the expansion of land acquisitions and agricultural markets, and new partnerships between governments, philanthropic foundations, and the private sector. Here, new agricultural technologies make for a more productive agriculture without disturbing its fundamental and oppositional relationship to the environments on which food production depends. Further, these technologies are developed and mobilized by corporate, industrial entities whose interest in market power, growth, and short-term productivity gains may undermine our ability to correct the social and ecological course of the food system (see Lesson 7). Genetically modified crops have indeed become a touchstone for debate as their use has massively increased over the past decades. According to the US Department of Agriculture, between 1996 and 2015 the percent of genetically modified corn and soy plants in the United States increased from less than 20 percent to 92 and 94 percent, respectively. Genetically modified seeds are often altered to include pest-resistant traits that make the plants inedible to particular pests. Other varieties embed herbicide resistance, which means that weeds die but crops do not when fields are sprayed. Each of these technologies has raised concerns about unintended ecological consequences, as well as technology and seed ownership and livelihood implications. Productivity increases have been minimal and concerns raised about the simplification of agricultural systems to just a few crop varieties when abundant genetic diversity could instead be drawn on to adapt crops to varied environmental conditions.

Returning to the broader question of agricultural industrialization and the environments it draws on and produces, we now see how mechanization maneuvered around agriculture's challenge of an extensive land base and how chemical and biological technologies targeted biological production cycles for efficiency and productivity gains. Each of these agricultural technologies and their environmental effects are born out of agriculture's basis in nature and reflect and reproduce the social and ecological organization of the food system. To change the environments that we produce in today's industrialized food system, it is necessary to confront the social relations of industrialized agricultural production. It is also critical to understand that agricultural producers' decisions to implement practices with high environmental costs are highly constrained. Competition in agriculture, compromised environments, and volatile crop prices compel farmers to maximize production in the face of environmental degradation. Not using fertilizer or pesticides, for example, would compromise productivity, profits, and farm viability, as long as other farms' productivity rose with the supply of a particular agricultural product and put downward pressure on prices. Consequently, these environmental problems have more to do with the social context of decision-making and agricultural policy than they do with bad management, inadequate technology, or a result of the pressure of global population on resources.

Global trade, for example, is an important element of social policy to consider in this context. Food systems scholar Ryan Galt (2013, 643) explains:

> By increasingly sourcing food from new areas, trade liberalization subjects more farmers to cost-price squeezes through increased competition, forcing farmers to neglect conservation, use agrochemicals, and use shorter rotations and cultivate fewer crops or livestock breeds. Downward price pressure from liberalization is made worse by farmers increasing production to make up for lower prices, further decoupling the costs of production from market prices because of increased overproduction.

Prepared with this understanding of the social and environmental organization of the food system through industrial agriculture, we consider in the next section the environmental dimensions of food system elements that are further "downstream," or what we do with all of this industrially produced food.

PROCESSING, CONSUMING, AND WASTING FOOD

The development of the food system through industrialized agriculture has been accompanied by significant change in the processing, packaging, distribution, consumption, and waste of food. Each of these food systems components effects significant environmental change. Picking up where we left off, in an industrialized food system, farms produce simplified, standardized agricultural products selected for their use in further processing and under the conditions described previously. As Goodman, Sorj, and Wilkinson (1987, 60) put it,

> with this foundation . . . the food industry subsequently could turn its attention to effecting qualitative changes in the organic composition of food and in the general perception of what constitutes food. . . . Industrial capital thus embarked on the path that was to transform consumption patterns, distribution systems and the domestic routines of daily life.

From this quote (see also Goodman and Redclift 1991), we see how food system industrialization based on agriculture's basis in the environment connects to everyday life patterns and relationships with food. In this light, the environment is clearly not out there, separate from society.

Changes in agricultural production maximized output with great environmental cost and facilitated the movement of agricultural produce from food to standardized, industrial inputs that could be recombined and assembled via more predictable, efficient, and profitable industrial processes (see Lesson 3). A product like corn, for example, is incredibly useful for making processed food and sweeteners, as livestock feed, and even as fuel for cars. Soy can be processed into meat substitutes, milk, or ink. So how does this industrial "food" come to be, where does it all go, and what are the consequences? In this section, the lesson considers the environmental implications of food processing and distribution, the conversion of agricultural products into animal protein, and food consumption and waste.

With regionally specialized agriculture organized to produce industrial inputs, elaborate processing, packaging, storing, transport, and preparation infrastructures become required to produce food and distribute and serve it globally. The environmental questions and costs that accompany this change are significant. The US Department of Agriculture (Canning et al. 2010) estimates food-related energy use constituted 15.7 percent of the national energy budget in 2007. The energy used to produce food purchased by US households increased at a rate six times larger than the rate of overall US energy use between 1997 and 2002, representing over 80 percent of energy use increases for the period. Eighty-five percent of the energy used in the food system came from fossil fuels.

Some of this increased energy use in the US food system can be attributed to the growth of the sector, but the US Department of Agriculture found that on a per capita basis food-related energy use went up 16.4 percent, even while total per capita energy use declined 1.8 percent. The study found that half of the growth in energy use is attributable to energy-intensive technologies in food processing (e.g., freezing, baking, and cleaning food) and the conversion of food preparation labor from human to automated processes (e.g., the trend toward processed, packaged convenience foods that require less household preparation time). Consequently, food processing surpassed the wholesale and retail sector to become the food system sector that uses the most energy after households. Kitchen appliances have also substituted energy for human labor. Given the energy-intensive practices of industrialized agriculture discussed above, it is notable that it ranks third, after food processing industries. Packaging and transportation rank last, but each category grew over the study period.

Energy use in the food system translates into climate-change–inducing greenhouse gas (GHG) emissions. Agriculture accounts for most of food systems' total GHG emissions, even if it ranks lower in energy use than other food system sectors; livestock manure (methane) and nitrogen fertilizer use are significant contributors. As expected, the food system's contributions to climate change are closely associated with the type and intensity of agricultural production that replaces prior land uses. The FAO estimates that global GHG emissions from agriculture nearly doubled from 2.7 to

5.2 million tons of carbon dioxide equivalents between 1961 and 2014. The largest contributors are methane production by livestock (39 percent of the total) and emissions generated by the use of synthetic fertilizers (13 percent of the total). Globally, Asia (44 percent) and the Americas (25 percent) are the largest contributors. In short, the industrialized model has very high energy and climate change costs.

Even while the industrial food system is responsible for a high percentage of global GHG emissions, it has been called on to reduce them via the production of biofuels. Although not ultimately food, biofuels constitute another key destination for the produce of industrial agriculture. The European Union, the United States, and Brazil, among others, all hope to simultaneously bolster agricultural and industrial sectors, reduce GHGs, and increase energy security through biofuels. Scholars, however, have pointed out biofuels' limits for reducing GHGs and strengthening rural economies, as well as their tendency to create food insecurity. Biofuel production has also been directly responsible for driving agricultural production expansion, as described previously. Researchers have demonstrated that the production of biofuels, particularly corn ethanol and soy-based biodiesel, release more GHGs than they save relative to their fossil fuel counterparts, largely because of the energy-intensive production processes and the land use change that increasing crop demand and prices inspire.

In addition to processed foods and biofuels, agricultural products' use as feed for livestock represents another downstream component of food systems with significant environmental consequences. With the spatial separation of crop and livestock production described earlier, increasingly productive grain farms feed larger and denser populations of livestock. Feeding grain and oilseeds to livestock bolsters crop prices by reducing supply, but creates significant environmental problems in its attempt to find outlets for an increasingly productive agricultural sector. Average per person meat consumption has doubled since 1961; affluent countries and populations consume the vast majority. Tony Weis (2013) describes the "ecological hoofprint" of increasing meat production and consumption, detailing its consequences for expansion of agricultural land, fossil fuel use and GHG emissions, soil erosion, nutrient pollution, and toxic runoff from livestock confinements and industrial agriculture (see also Foster and Magdoff 2000). This issue is made more urgent for its contributions to climate change, which threatens to exacerbate pest and disease pressure, reduce freshwater availability, and facilitate the spread of invasive species and land degradation. In the context of climate change and persistent food insecurity, Weis (2013, 80) suggests that "rather than ratcheting up insufficient yields and production [to increase food security], a much more compelling priority is to urgently ratchet down meat consumption and confront the social and ecological disaster that is industrial livestock production."

So, what have all of these industrial innovations in the food system and their environmental costs meant for fulfilling food systems' key purpose of feeding people? While there are certainly enough calories produced, many are hungry. The FAO estimates that 795 million, or approximately 13 percent of all people, are undernourished (see Lesson 13). This number has been declining, although food insecurity spiked in the mid and late 2000s as global food prices rose and put food out of reach of the poorest people. Lang and Barling (2012) argue that we need a fundamental change in how we conceptualize food security and its connections to agriculture, the environment, and policy. They suggest that focusing on increased production is insufficient and that our core task is to create a sustainable food system. The authors indicate key areas for future work at the environment–food insecurity nexus: focusing on the whole food system instead of just farms; reconsidering the value and ecological efficiency of labor on small farms, long considered inefficient relative to industrial agriculture; monitoring possibilities for big business' alignment with social and environmental sustainability goals; thinking about regional differences in sustainable diets and about how to encourage them; and acknowledging and questioning power relations in food systems that condition policy opportunities.

Despite widespread and recently exacerbated conditions of food insecurity, the FAO suggests that the world produces more than one and a half times the quantity of food needed to feed its seven billion inhabitants. Further, **food waste** is increasingly recognized as a social and environmental problem. The FAO finds that 1.3 billion tons of food, or one-third of the food intended for human consumption, is discarded. The environmental consequences of food waste are significant in terms of growing global trash heaps, but more so in the wasted resources used to produce it. The GHG emissions embodied in food wasted each year are estimated to be equivalent to the combined annual emissions of Japan and the Russian Federation. Food waste clearly represents a pressing environmental problem because of the resources necessary for its production. It is also a glaring social problem that demands serious attention: how can it be that we have a food system that produces and wastes plenty of food without feeding everyone?

In his analysis of food waste and recovery, Alex Barnard (2016) notes that the United States wastes enough calories of food to account for the entire world's nutritional deficit. He suggests that this problem is a result of food's status as a commodity, an item intended for sale for profit. This means that it may be more profitable to expunge excess food from the food system than to direct resources toward its repurpose. Indeed, doing the latter might undermine the full-price sale of goods for a food business, even if it improved food security or reduced food's environmental burden. Connecting to our exploration of industrialized food systems' drive for productivity at high environmental costs, those who produce, process, and distribute food depend on large quantities of cheap food moving through the system to maintain their industry's profitability, independent of food's use or destination, whether it be a human stomach, a cow, a car, or a landfill.

Again, understanding the social origins of environmental problems in the food system is critical for making progress. Scarcity, as discussed, is often a key rationale used in arguments that the expansion of industrial agricultural production is an absolute necessity. Remembering Harvey's points, however, we recognize scarcity as something that is socially produced, or created through social decisions and circumstances (e.g., converting grain into fuel; food access limited by global inequality; food waste). Food scarcity indicates a social dysfunction, not necessarily a demand for new production to be met through greater environmental costs. The need may not be for more industrial agricultural production, but for equitable policies and poverty reduction that would enable the hungry to access food that already exists. The environment can indeed accommodate the production of food for all; in fact, it already does. What is more challenging is getting that food to people. Addressing this need sustainably and equitably will require engagement with the social organization of the food system, including consolidated economic power in the food system with interests in increasing productivity above all else. In the next section, we conclude by briefly considering alternative options for the social and environmental organization of the food system.

Conclusion

The production of massive quantities of cheap food comes at a high environmental cost and the environments produced by the industrialized food system are unsustainable and inequitable. Industrial agriculture's attempts to minimize or evade the role of biological and ecological components of food production have resulted in environmental problems in the same categories. Extensification's circumvention of the barrier that agriculture's basis in land poses instead creates problems with soil erosion, land degradation, habitat and biodiversity loss, and water quality and availability. Efforts to increase production through intensive monocrop agriculture exacerbate pest pressure and declining soil fertility, resulting in environmental contamination from pesticides and fertilizers. Excess agricultural nutrients contaminate groundwater and make large areas of the world's waterways uninhabitable for marine life. Pesticide use is poisoning people and wildlife, in addition to creating *superweeds* (i.e., weeds that are resistance to pesticides) that illustrate the temporary nature of this fix. Increasing productivity by substituting machinery for animals and industrial processes for human labor makes for a highly energy-intensive food system that is a significant contributor to climate change, which may, in turn, undermine our food system.

Given the state of things, what is to be done? What opportunities are there for reforming, challenging, or building different food systems? The environments the industrial food system produces are not the only ones possible. Assuming humanity should succumb to ecological disaster and social, political, and economic systems that undermine our ability to feed ourselves and steward the resources on which our lives depend is to say that "we have not the will, wit or capacity to change," to return to Harvey's (1996, 145) statement. Indeed, we already are doing things differently in some places and have been doing so for quite a while and in quite a varied set of ways. This last section briefly explores how food system participants have worked to address the environmental consequences of the food system that many of them have inherited, noting agroecology and food sovereignty movements in particular.

Agricultural industrialization sees the environment as a barrier to productivity and profitability. But what if we saw the environment as an essential companion for sustainable agriculture? How might things change? In many ways, agroecology answers these questions. **Agroecology** can be defined as "the science of applying ecological concepts and principles to the design and management of sustainable agroecosystems" (Gliessman 1998, 339). Miguel Altieri (2002) suggests that agriculture be directed toward the maximization of agroecosystem attributes and functions, not just productivity. He describes how agroecological production systems can enhance organic matter accumulation and nutrient cycling; soil biological activity; natural control mechanisms (disease suppression, biocontrol of insects, weed interference); resource conservation and regeneration (e.g., soil, water, germplasm); and general enhancement of agrobiodiversity and synergisms between components. Agroecological engagements and applications have grown to increasingly consider social relations. Francis et al. (2003, 100) suggest agroecology is "the integrative study of the ecology of the entire food system, encompassing ecological, economic and social dimensions." Keith Warner's (2007) work describes how social relations that emphasize place-based experimentation and knowledge-sharing are essential for the development of agroecological practices, challenging more common top-down, productivity-driven, technological intervention. The International Assessment of Agricultural Knowledge, Science and Technology for Development (IAASTD 2009) Global Report makes a clear case that pro-poor agroecological practices are critical for more effectively addressing hunger, poverty, and the environmental degradation that industrial agriculture causes.

The **food sovereignty** movement also offers potential for addressing the social and ecological components of the food system that require change. Briefly, food sovereignty is the right of peoples to define their own food and agricultural systems. In support of food sovereignty, La Via Campesina (2009, 71) suggests, true solutions must "emerge from organized social actors that are developing modes of production, trade and consumption based on justice, solidarity and healthy communities. No technological fix will solve the current global environmental and social disaster." They suggest broader changes including agrarian reform prioritizing food production to meet human needs; small-scale, energy-saving, labor-intensive sustainable farming to reduce contributions to climate change; and changes in production and consumption patterns to reduce waste and hunger (71–72; see Lesson 18).

We have not yet realized food sovereignty or widespread agroecological practice, but the principles can provide direction. In any alternative formulation of food–environment relations, it is necessary to engage both sustainability and equity in the food system, focusing on food systems' race, class, and gender dimensions (see Lesson 20). In concluding, this lesson focused on two primary efforts that directly engage both the social and the ecological dimensions of food systems in radical ways, arguing for a different way of doing things in both categories. These movements suggest that both opposition to inequitable industrialized food systems and experimentation with new systems are necessary. Likewise, they suggest that to fundamentally transform food systems, making the "right" decisions about consumption in the supermarket, or looking for marginal conservation or efficiency gains in industrial agriculture without altering its fundamentals will not suffice. Instead, it will be necessary to develop social policies that prioritize meeting basic human needs and working with nature through food systems to produce more equitable and sustainable environments.

Discussion Questions

1. How are the environment and scarcity social concepts?
2. Global agricultural systems have focused on maximizing productivity. What problem does this approach address and what alternative problem definitions might one offer?
3. How is it possible that food is wasted while people go hungry?
4. What principles and practices of efforts to improve food system sustainability and equity do you find most compelling?

Exercises

1. *Develop an environmental history of your food system.* Develop an environmental history of food produced near you. Investigate using your library, news media, and conversations with those who have experienced longer-term change in your regional food system. As you develop your history, consider the following questions:
   - What foods are produced nearest you and how?
   - How has this changed over time?
   - How does the production of food work with, around, or against its biological and ecological components?
   - How do resources, policies, technologies, and labor support the food system?
   - How are the benefits and burdens of this food system configured?
   - What social–environmental connections do you see?
2. *Consider your ecological hoofprint.* Consulting Weis's (2013) explanation of ecological hoofprint, consider the ecological hoofprint or footprint of your diet. First, record your diet for a day or a week and consider its most resource-intensive elements. Then, briefly document and explain

the environmental costs of your diet or portions of it; you may wish to use one of the many ecological footprint calculators available online.

Reviewing the results, consider:

- how your diet might compare to others in different social circumstances economic, cultural, and geographical situations;
- what impact changes in your diet may have;
- how your food choices are constrained (or not);
- and what you see as the most effective approaches to improving food system sustainability and equity—whether through diet or other means.

Additional Materials
Readings

Cochrane, W. 1979. *The Development of American Agriculture: A Historical Analysis.* Minneapolis: University of Minnesota Press.

Constance, D. H. 2009. "Sustainable Agriculture in the United States: A Critical Examination of a Contested Process." *Sustainability* 2 (1): 48–72.

FAO. 2017. *The Future of Food and Agriculture—Trends and Challenges.* Rome: FAO. http://www.fao.org/publications/fofa/en/

IAASTD (International Assessment of Agricultural Knowledge, Science and Technology for Development). 2009. *Global Report: Agriculture at a Crossroads.* http://www.fao.org/fileadmin/templates/est/Investment/Agriculture_at_a_Crossroads_Global_Report_IAASTD.pdf

Kloppenburg, Jack Jr. 2004 [1988]. *First the Seed: The Political Economy of Plant Biotechnology.* Madison: University of Wisconsin Press.

Websites

Center for Agroecology and Sustainable Food Systems. University of California, Santa Cruz. https://casfs.ucsc.edu/

FAO Agroecology Knowledge Hub. http://www.fao.org/agroecology/en/.

FAOStat. "Food and Agriculture Data." United Nations Food and Agriculture Organization. http://www.fao.org/faostat/en/#home

Food First. "Agroecology." https://foodfirst.org/issue-area/agroecology/

US Department of Agriculture, Economic Research Service. "Data." https://www.usda.gov/topics/data

US Department of Agriculture, Natural Resources Conservation Service. https://www.nrcs.usda.gov/wps/portal/nrcs/site/national/home/

References
Altieri, Miguel. 2002. "Agroecology: The Science of Natural Resource Management for Poor Farmers in Marginal Environments." *Agriculture, Ecosystems & Environment* 93 (1): 1–24.

Barnard, Alex V. 2016. *Freegans: Diving into the Wealth of Food Waste in America.* Minneapolis: University of Minnesota Press.

Behrmen, J., R. Meinzen-Dick, and A. Quisumbing. 2012. "The Gender Implications of Large-Scale Land Deals." *Journal of Peasant Studies* 39:49–79.

Canning, Patrick, Ainsley Charles, Sonya Huang, Karen R. Polenske, and
Arnold Waters. 2010. *Energy Use in the U.S. Food System.* Economic Research
Report No. ERR-94. Economic Research Service. Washington, DC: US
Department of Agriculture.

Castree, N. 2005. *Nature.* London: Routledge.

Foster, John Bellamy, and Fred Magdoff. 2000. "Liebig, Marx, and the Depletion
of Soil Fertility: Relevance for Today's Agriculture." In *Hungry for Profit: The
Agribusiness Threat to Farmers, Food, and the Environment,* edited by F. Magdoff,
J. B. Foster, and F. H. Buttel, 43–60. New York: Monthly Review Press.

Francis, C., G. Lieblein, S. Gliessman, T. A. Breland, N. Creamer, R. Harwood,
L. Salomonsson, et al. 2003. "Agroecology: The Ecology of Food Systems."
Journal of Sustainable Agriculture 22:99–118.

Galt, Ryan. 2013. "Placing Food Systems in First World Political Ecology:
A Review and Research Agenda." *Geography Compass* 7 (9): 637–58.

Gilbert, Jess, G. Sharp, and S. Felin. 2002. "The Loss and Persistence of Black-
Owned Farms and Farmland: A Review of the Research Literature and Its
Implications." *Southern Rural Sociology* 18 (2): 1–30.

Gliessman, S. R. 1998. *Agroecology: Ecological Processes in Sustainable Agriculture.* Chelsea, MI: Ann Arbor Press.

FitzSimmons, Margaret, and David Goodman. 1998. "Incorporating Nature:
Environmental Narratives and Reproduction of Food." In *Remaking Real-
ity: Nature at the Millennium,* edited by B. Braun and N. Castree, 194–220.
London: Routledge.

Goodman, David, and Michael Redclift. 1991. *Refashioning Nature: Food,
Ecology & Culture.* London: Routledge.

Goodman, D., B. Sorj, and J. Wilkinson. 1987. *From Farming to Biotechnology.*
Oxford: Basil Blackwell.

Harrison, J. 2011. *Pesticide Drift and the Pursuit of Environmental Justice.*
Cambridge, MA: MIT Press.

Harvey, David. 1974. "Population, Resources, and the Ideology of Science."
Economic Geography 50:256–77.

Harvey, David. 1996. *Justice, Nature, and the Geography of Difference.* Oxford:
Blackwell.

Holleman, H. 2017. "De-naturalizing Ecological Disaster: Colonialism, Racism
and the Global Dust Bowl of the 1930s." *The Journal of Peasant Studies* 44 (1):
234–60.

IAASTD (International Assessment of Agricultural Knowledge, Science and
Technology for Development). 2009. *Global Report: Agriculture at a Crossroads.* http://www.fao.org/fileadmin/templates/est/Investment/Agricul-
ture_at_a_Crossroads_Global_Report_IAASTD.pdf

La Via Campesina. 2009. *La Via Campesina Policy Documents.* Accessed April 26,
2018. https://viacampesina.org/en/wp-content/uploads/sites/2/2010/03/
BOOKLET-EN-FINAL-min.pdf

Lang, Tim, and David Barling. 2012. "Food Security and Food Sustainability:
Reformulating the Debate." *The Geographical Journal* 178 (4): 313–26.

Mann, S. A., and J. M. Dickinson. 1978. "Obstacles to the Development of a
Capitalist Agriculture." *The Journal of Peasant Studies* 5 (4): 466–81.

Patel, Raj. 2013. "The Long Green Revolution." *The Journal of Peasant Studies* 40 (1): 1–63.

Warner, Keith. 2007. *Agroecology in Action: Extending Alternative Agriculture through Social Networks.* Cambridge, MA: MIT Press.

Weis, Tony. 2013. "The Meat of the Global Food Crisis." *The Journal of Peasant Studies* 40 (1): 65–85.

West, P. C. 1994. "Natural Resources and the Persistence of Rural Poverty in America: A Weberian Perspective on the Role of Power, Domination, and Natural Resource Bureaucracy." *Society and Natural Resources* 7:415–27.

White, Ben, Saturnino M. Borras Jr., Ruth Hall, Ian Scoones, and Wendy Wolford. 2012. "The New Enclosures: Critical Perspectives on Corporate Land Deals." *The Journal of Peasant Studies* 39 (3–4): 619–47.

Volunteers at a local food bank. (Photo by Chief Petty Officer Leeanna Shipps, Naval Station Norfolk Public Affairs Office.)

13

Food and Hunger

Justin Sean Myers

Mitchell County, Iowa, is flyover country for most Americans, but almost eleven thousand people call it home. The area is quintessential rural Midwest, a flat landscape of corn and soybean fields as far as the eye can see. Yet, even here, in a landscape of massive food surpluses, hunger abounds (McMillian 2014). Meet the Dreiers. Christina is a stay-at-home mom for her two children, both under the age of four. Her husband, Jim, works as a pesticide sprayer on local farms for fourteen dollars an hour. Both labor very hard to put food on the table for their family but they are often forced to choose between buying groceries or paying their bills because Jim's income is not enough to cover expenses. This economic squeeze pushes the Dreiers to rely on local food pantries and the Supplemental Nutrition Assistance Program (SNAP), more commonly known as food stamps, to feed themselves. However, the local food pantries often have empty shelves and their monthly SNAP allotment has been cut by a Republican-dominated Congress and does not go very far. In the end, the Dreiers often bounce one bill against the other; what other option do they have? In Christina's words, "We have to eat, you know . . . We can't starve" (McMillian 2014).

Hunger is not just a domestic problem though; it is also a global issue. Welcome to El Carmen Tequexquitla, a rural farming community in the Mexican state of Tlaxcala, nearly two thousand miles south of the Dreier family (Althaus 2013). At close to eight thousand feet above sea level, the beauty of the sweeping vistas in the Mexican highlands offers a stark contrast to the omnipresent and chronic poverty of its residents, many of whom live in thatched-roof or tin-roof homes with dirt floors and no running water. As in numerous rural farming communities across the globe, hunger is pervasive here because of the lack of well-paying manufacturing jobs, minimal state supports for smallholder agriculture, and weak social programs to combat poverty. This poverty is why Juana Alvarez is standing in line at a grocery store with numerous other women, largely indigenous, to receive food aid to prevent her family from starving. A single mother of three whose husband abandoned her, she tries to put food on the table but can only find part-time work as a maid, so she stands in line waiting to receive rice, beans, corn flour, and cooking oil, because in her own words, "Without it I wouldn't be able to feed my children. This is all that we have" (Althaus 2103).

Despite the great geographical distance between Christina and Juana and the fact that they are of different races and nationalities, both women struggle to feed their children because of the absence of well-paid work and weak social safety nets. In this aspect, they are not alone but just two of hundreds of millions of people, principally women and children, who face hunger every day around the world. This occurs even though enough food is produced to feed everyone on the planet, so why are people going hungry? In the United States one dominant explanation is that the hungry, who are generally also poor, are lazy. Such a belief reflects the dominant logic of individualism, which attributes social outcomes principally to the actions of individuals and moralizes their success or failure as a result of the work ethic, or lack thereof, in this case. Through this lens, one's food choices are seen solely as the province of the individual. Yet, if one looks at the statistics, the majority of people who are hungry, struggling with food insecurity, and recipients of food assistance programs are either too young or too old to work, medically unable to work, or working (Coleman-Jensen et al. 2015; Gray and Kochlar 2015). Such a juxtaposition between facts and beliefs begs for an alternative way of understanding and explaining hunger.

This lesson offers such a way through shifting from an individualistic mode of thinking toward a structural and relational analysis that locates the actions of people within their social and physical environments. As C. Wright Mills (1959) emphasized in his book, *The Sociological Imagination*, people's personal problems are often not personal troubles, but public issues rooted in the structure of society. People struggling with hunger may blame themselves, and others often do, but they generally are in situations that are shaped and molded by much broader social forces and institutions that they have little control over. Through utilizing the sociological imagination, this lesson will focus on both explicit hunger (i.e., lack of access to sufficient food) and implicit hunger (i.e., a lack of access to healthy food), domestically and globally, and link these conditions to the social processes producing poverty and the social structures shaping the production and distribution of food. In particular, the lesson will emphasize how the political economy of work (the vast number of low-wage jobs), the political economy of food (the privileging of corporate, industrial, and capitalist food actors), and the political economy of welfare (the limited social safety net) intersect in several important ways to create hunger as a normal outcome of how society is organized. At the same time, strategies for reducing the existence of hunger, both domestically and globally, will be discussed.

THE STATE OF HUNGER TODAY

Has someone in your life experienced hunger? It could be you, a friend, a neighbor, an aunt or uncle. Did they have to skip meals because they could not afford to buy food? Did they depend on SNAP, food pantries, or soup kitchens to ward off hunger? Were they often worried about where their next meal was going to come from? It not, then count yourself and the people you know as privileged. If so, have you given any thought to how that person's chances of experiencing hunger may have been connected to larger social groups, institutions, and structures? When it comes to hunger, your class matters, your race matters, your gender matters, your age matters, and your geographic location matters.

When people say someone is hungry, they generally mean that person does not have enough food to support the physiological needs of the body, that the person is malnourished. This malnourishment can come in two forms: individuals can be deficient in macronutrients (protein, fat, and carbohydrates) or in micronutrients (vitamins, minerals, and antioxidants), and both are important (see Lesson 4). While people use the word hunger to describe lack of access to food, the US Department of Agriculture (USDA), nongovernmental agencies, and antihunger activists often employ the language of **food insecurity** to conceptualize hunger and malnutrition, with food security being defined as "access by all people at all times to enough food for an active, healthy life" (USDA 2016; see Table 13.1). I will use the terms hunger and food insecurity interchangeably.

Based on the USDA's definition, 42.2 million Americans lived in food-insecure households in 2015, and close to one-third of this number, about 13.1 million, were children (Coleman-Jensen et al. 2015). In all, about 13 percent of US households are food insecure and the majority of them struggle with low food security. However, 6.3 million households, about 5 percent of all households, experience very low food security. Hunger does not affect everyone equally though; race plays a large role in shaping an individual's odds of being one of these 42.2 million Americans. Black and Latino/a households are more than twice as likely to be food insecure as white non-Latino/a households. As a result, more than one in four black children and nearly one in four Latino/a children live in food-insecure households compared to one in seven white non-Latino/a children. (Coleman-Jensen et al. 2015). Gender also plays a role in one's odds of experiencing hunger, with female-headed households

Table 13.1 US Department of Agriculture's Definitions of Food Security and Food Insecurity

Food security	Food insecurity
High food security: no reported indications of food-access problems or limitations	Low food security: reports of reduced quality, variety, or desirability of diet; little or no indication of reduced food intake
Marginal food security: one or two reported indications—typically of anxiety over food sufficiency or shortage of food in the house; little or no indication of changes in diets or food intake	Very low food security: reports of multiple indications of disrupted eating patterns and reduced food intake

Note: USDA 2016.

being more than twice as likely to be food insecure compared to other US households, 30.3 versus 13 percent (Coleman-Jensen et al. 2015). Such findings reveal the intersectionality of race, class, and gender when it comes to hunger because the higher odds for black, Latino/a, and female-headed households, compared to white, male-headed, and dual-parent households, are a direct outcome of the disproportionate concentration of people of color and women at the bottom of the US class structure.

THE INTERSECTIONALITY OF GEOGRAPHY, RACE, AND CLASS: PLACE MATTERS

I asked you to think about whether someone in your life has experienced hunger and how this might be connected to that individual's class, race, or gender. Now I want you to think about your food environment growing up, how it might have been shaped by these social group characteristics, and how these social factors subsequently shaped your food choices. Was your community full of grocery stores and farm-to-table restaurants or corner stores and fast-food restaurants? Was it easy or difficult to get to and from the grocery store? Were the primary food choices fresh local produce or processed foods?

While you probably did not have much of a say as to where you grew up, odds are high that it played a large role in shaping your food choices. For instance, twelve states have higher household food insecurity rates than the US average of around 13 percent, with the top five being Mississippi, 20.8 percent; Arkansas, 19.2 percent; Louisiana, 18.4 percent; Alabama, 17.6 percent; and Kentucky, 17.6 percent (Coleman-Jensen et al. 2015). On the other hand, if you grew up in North Dakota, Minnesota, and New Hampshire you would have had a much lower chance of experiencing food insecurity because their rates are 8, 10.4, and 10.5 percent, respectively (Coleman-Jensen et al. 2015). These statistics underscore that explicit and implicit hunger are not equally distributed geographically across the country; they often map over persistent poverty areas and, with respect to the aforementioned states, the South. For instance, high-food-insecurity counties are more likely to be rural, and the South contains 90 percent of all high-food-insecurity counties, such as Jefferson County, Mississippi, which has a food insecurity rate of 37.5 percent (Feeding America 2015).

If you lived in a community full of quality grocery stores and could afford to shop there, count yourself privileged. But if you grew up in a community with little to no access to grocery stores, you grew up in what is called a **food desert**. Food deserts are low-income areas with limited access to fresh vegetables and fruits because grocery stores or supermarkets are out of reach (more than one mile in an urban area and more than ten miles in rural areas). According to the USDA, 29.7 million people in 2010, 9.7 percent of the US population, lived in food deserts and the majority of these people were located in urban areas and were disproportionately black and

Latino/a (Ver Ploeg et al. 2012). While the food desert concept is in vogue today, it only partially reflects the food environment of many low-income communities, which has led to the creation of a new term that spatializes implicit hunger, a food swamp. While the food desert concept reflects a lack of absolute access to a grocery store, the term **food swamp** refers to the lack of relative access to a grocery store, with a food swamp defined as an "area in which large relative amounts of energy-dense snack foods inundate healthy food options" (Rose et al. 2009). These urban communities are often stocked full of bodegas, liquor stores, and fast-food restaurants that provide cheap foods low in vitamins and minerals yet high in fats, sugars, and salts. Additionally, if a grocery store is to be found in these communities, the produce sold may be of low quality; it is often damaged, spoiled, or past the sell-by date. Once you combine the limited access to fresh produce with easy access to cheap processed foods, constant junk food advertising, and limited incomes, what emerges is a path of least resistance toward the over-consumption of foods that should be eaten in moderation. Consequently, these communities suffer from the **hunger–obesity paradox**, having higher than average rates of chronic malnutrition as well as chronic diet-related diseases, including obesity, diabetes, heart disease, and high blood pressure (see Lessons 3 and 14).

Overall, a large body of research has found that race and class play a significant role in shaping geographical disparities in food access (Treuhaft and Karpyn 2010; Walker et al. 2010). Affluent and predominantly white communities tend to have higher rates of grocery stores and lower rates of fast-food restaurants while low-income communities of color tend to have the opposite, higher rates of fast-food restaurants and lower rates of grocery stores. The logic of individualism would explain these findings by saying that affluent communities know how to eat healthy and low-income communities have a preference for unhealthy foods. However, food environments emerge not from the aggregation of individual food choices but rather from structural and historical processes that are created out of the economic and political practices of public and private institutions. In this case, the federal government and private banking industry have played a prominent role in the creation of food deserts and food swamps. Since the 1930s these two actors have disinvested from and outright demolished low-income black and Latino/a communities while shifting federal and private investment dollars via mortgage, transportation, and infrastructure development to affluent white communities in the suburbs. This process has taken many names, redlining, urban renewal, benign neglect, and planned shrinkage, to name a few, but the outcomes have generally been negative for black and Latino/a communities. This shift in funding facilitated white flight and coincided with growing opposition to the civil rights movement and efforts to racially integrate education, housing, and employment. As investment shifted to suburban communities, so did disposable income, and grocery stores followed. Grocery retailing is a very competitive industry with low profit margins and an economic model that relies on volume sales. In this environment, stores left cities for the suburbs to take advantage of cheaper land, lower tax rates, price premiums on upscale products, and the larger volume sales that can come from having a bigger store. The outcome was food access barriers for low-income urban communities. Given this history of racial inequity, people in the food justice movement may utilize the term **food apartheid**, rather than food desert or food swamp, to underscore that food inequities are the outcomes of racialized social processes that privilege whiteness and are not naturally occurring phenomena or rooted in the individual choices of residents (see Lessons 19 and 20).

COMBATING HUNGER IN THE UNITED STATES OF AMERICA

Have you ever volunteered at a soup kitchen, food pantry, or food bank? Have you ever donated a can of food or a box of dried food to a food drive during the holidays? Maybe you even helped glean produce on a farm for donation to a local food bank? Odds are you have. Millions of people donate food, time, and money every year to organizations that are part of this **emergency food network** (EFN) that works to put food in empty bellies every day. Think about your act of charity. Did it make you feel good that something was being done to provide food to those going hungry? Or maybe the experience pushed you to question whether such food donations could end hunger. If you had such conflicted thoughts, then you are not alone. A tension exists in the US between addressing hunger through short-term, charity-oriented stop gaps (food banks, soup kitchens, volunteer-run meal programs) or long-term, rights-oriented structural solutions (higher wages, full employment, better income redistribution programs, state-funded food assistance programs). This tension is reflective of differing framings of what causes and what can reduce hunger in the United States.

Almost nonexistent in the 1970s, today the EFN consists of over forty-six thousand agencies and close to sixty thousand food assistance programs that rely on the free labor of volunteers and large-scale donations in kind and money from wealthy individuals, philanthropic foundations, and corporations to stave off hunger. And the need is great. Every year the EFN feeds over 46.5 million people, about one in seven people in the United States. Janet Poppendieck (1998) investigated the EFN and their ability to combat long-term hunger in her book, *Sweet Charity?: Emergency Food and the End of Entitlement*, and her findings were not rosy. She found that the growth of the EFN is in direct relationship to the federal cutbacks on food entitlement programs and the ascendancy of conservative claims that charity and volunteer efforts can replace government programs and demand-side policies in the fight against hunger. Moreover, Poppendieck found that the EFN serves as a "moral safety valve" that makes people feel good about doing their small part, but the EFN is not intended to, nor can it, address the broader forces producing hunger.

While the EFN is an example of a short-term, charity-oriented model to address hunger, SNAP is an example of long-term, rights-oriented solution. The Supplemental Nutrition Assistance Program is a governmental response to hunger that frames it not as a personal failing but as a structural outcome of how a capitalist economy unequally distributes access to work and therefore income. It is a food assistance program that provides cash assistance to families to help them put food on the table, as we saw with the Dreier family at the beginning of the lesson. However, in recent decades, conservatives and the Republican Party have sought to enforce cuts to SNAP, if not outright eliminate the program, under the claim that it creates a culture of dependency that skirts work ethic. This claim does not match up with the body of scholarship on the food assistance program, however. In Fiscal Year 2014, the federal government allotted $74 billion for the program, which covered about 46.5 million people living in nearly 22.7 million US households (Coleman-Jensen et al. 2015; Gray and Kochlar 2015). This represents about 14 percent of the US population and means that more than one in seven US residents obtains food stamps, with the average SNAP participant receiving about $126 per month, or $1.40 per meal. Of this population, nearly two-thirds were children (44 percent), elderly (10 percent), or disabled nonelderly adults (10 percent). Additionally, nearly 43 percent of all SNAP participants lived in a household with work-related earnings. These numbers underscore that SNAP participants are those who are unable to work, those marginalized from work, and those who are the working poor. Moreover, SNAP is a countercyclical program rather than a dependency-creating program (Tiehen et al. 2012). When the economy is going strong and growing, people are able to find jobs and leave SNAP. When the economy contracts and businesses stop hiring and start firing, SNAP participation expands. These economic fluctuations of growth and contraction are the primary reason why SNAP roles grew during the Great Recession and have declined as the economy has slowly improved. Research on SNAP has also found that it decreases poverty, in depth and severity, among both households and children (Joliffe 2003; Tiehen et al. 2012). Therefore, SNAP is effective at combating hunger by allowing people to buy food when they otherwise could not afford it.

HUNGER: AN OUTCOME OF POLICY

Let us think about the numbers on hunger again. Thirteen percent of US households are food insecure. One in seven people uses the EFN. One in seven uses SNAP. If we look at other developed countries, principally in Europe, we see that the United States stands apart with a very high rate of food insecurity. While in many European countries one in fifteen people face food insecurity, in the United States the rate is more than one in eight, almost double that of its European counterparts (Taylor and Loopstra 2016). To understand the prevalence and perseverance of hunger in the United States, particularly when compared to Europe, we must understand its structural roots, which is an outcome of the lack of labor market policies that push for high wages and full employment, as well as the absence of wage support policies emblematic of a robust welfare state where people's basic needs are met regardless of their capacity to work.

Compared to other wealthy nations, the United States has the highest proportion of workers in low-wage jobs, defined as those where employees earn less than two-thirds of the median wage (OECD 2014). For example, in 2014, 1.3 million people earned the federal minimum wage of $7.25 and over 25 million workers earned less than $11.50 per hour, which left many of them in or near poverty (Oxfam America 2014). If you earn $7.25 an hour and work forty hours a week all year round with no time off, your take-home pay before taxes is $15,080. If you earned $11.50 an hour under the same conditions your income would be $23,920. These jobs are emblematic of the growing ranks of the working poor in the United States, where having a job does not keep you out of poverty or provide you and your family with a decent quality of life. This has not always been the case for minimum wage jobs or near minimum wage jobs, however (Desilver 2017). In 1968 the real value of the minimum wage stood at 99 percent of the poverty level for a family of two adults and two children. Since then, the real value of the minimum wage has declined significantly and hovered around 60 percent of the poverty level.

Therefore, it is difficult to address the roots of hunger in the United States today without focusing on the inability of minimum wage employment and near minimum wage employment to feed a person, let alone a family. This is most apparent for food chain workers, where the irony of hunger is profound. Those who grow, process, prepare, and serve the food we eat have higher rates of marginal food security, low food security, and very low food security than the general population (FCWA 2012, 2014). Overall, 30 percent of the twenty million food chain workers in the United States are food insecure, double the rate of food insecurity in the US workforce (FCWA 2012, 2014). In fact, farmworkers have rates of food insecurity over three times greater than that of the general US population because they are excluded from the basic labor protections and worker rights that many Americans take for granted, such as collective bargaining rights, the right to join a union, and overtime pay (FCWA 2012) (see Lesson 11). The low pay of food chain workers also pushes them to utilize food stamps at one and a half to two times the rate of the rest of the US workforce (FCWA 2012). The restaurant industry in particular, which has over ten million workers, alone accounts for almost half of workers earning at or below the federal minimum wage (USBOL 2017). As a result, 16.7 percent of restaurant workers live below the poverty line compared to 6.3 percent for workers outside the restaurant industry (Shierhloz 2014). This is a direct outcome not only of a poverty-level minimum wage, but also of the fact that millions of restaurant workers do not even legally qualify for the regular nontipped minimum wage because they are servers who receive the tipped minimum wage (Jamieson 2012). The federal tipped minimum wage came into existence in 1966 to ensure that servers were not living solely off tips and was pegged at 50 percent of the federal nontipped minimum wage. However, since 1966 the nontipped minimum wage has not kept up with inflation and in 2010 was worth only

29 percent of the nontipped minimum wage. Tipped minimum wage workers receive less than the nontipped minimum wage in forty-three states and in seventeen states they are only paid the federal minimum tipped wage of $2.13 per hour. All these employment and wage policies matter because these jobs are disproportionately held by women and people of color and the extensive gender and racial segregation in food industries confines both groups to the bottom of the labor market in low-paying positions, thereby increasing their, and their children's, chances of facing hunger (FCWA 2012; Liu and Apollon 2011).

Looking at the restaurant industry, we can tell that hunger and poverty are outcomes of specific political and economic policies. They are choices we collectively make about how society is to be organized and who is to bear the burden of these choices. While the US has chosen a low-wage model, other countries, such as Denmark, have chosen a high-wage model. The base wage for fast-food workers in Denmark is twenty dollars an hour, about two and half times what fast-food workers earn in the United States (Alderman and Greenhouse 2014). This high wage exists because there are strong unions, durable collective bargaining arrangements, and a culture of cooperation between unions and companies. In addition to the higher hourly wage, workers receive five weeks of paid vacation, a pension, and paid parental leave, benefits that their US counterparts do not receive. Between this wage structure, employment-related benefits, and the strong social supports of the Danish welfare state, working in the food industry does not create a poverty-level existence; in fact, it provides a decent quality of life. Moreover, such policies are integral to Denmark having a food insecurity rate of only 4.9 percent (Taylor and Loopstra 2016).

GLOBAL HUNGER: THE POLITICAL ECONOMY OF FOOD AND DEVELOPMENT

According to the United Nations Food and Agriculture Organization (FAO), there are around 795 million people globally, one in nine of whom suffer from chronic undernourishment (FAO 2015). This population is generally the poorest of the poor, principally women and children, who tend to live in rural areas of developing countries and are often marginally employed in agriculture. Akin to their US counterparts, a major factor creating this problem is marginalization from high-wage jobs and the lack of a social safety net, issues compounded by inequitable trade policies that make it nearly impossible for small farmers to remain agricultural producers.

Meet Griselda Mendoza, twenty-three, who was born and raised in Santa Ana Zegache, a small rural community in the southern Mexican state of Oaxaca (Burnett 2016; Darlington and Gillespie 2017). Located at 5,587 feet, the town lies in a beautiful mountain valley, is full of hand-built adobe houses and unobtrusive dirt-lined streets, and is fairly well known for its restored seventeenth-century painted church. The community of three thousand also has a large indigenous Zapotec population with a history that traces back thousands of years in the area. Griselda's father, Benancio, was a corn farmer and comes from a long line of corn farmers, like many of their neighbors, who cultivate indigenous maize in hues of yellow, white, and burgundy on small plots of land. They primarily grew corn to feed their family but would sell whatever surplus they had for income. It was not a wealthy life, but people got by. This all changed with the passage of the North American Free Trade Agreement (NAFTA). Cheap corn from the United States flooded over the border at prices that Mexican farmers could not compete with. Many gave up farming and migrated north to the US to look for work. This was the case for Benancio as well: "He went north looking for a job and I didn't see him again for 18 years," states Griselda (Darlington and Gillespie 2017). He ended up getting a job in a restaurant in Tennessee and sends money home to help the family. If you talk to families throughout Santa Ana Zegache you will hear similar stories; it is a town full of women, children, and the elderly. Most men have left either to find work in the big cities of Mexico or to traverse the scorching deserts of the Southwest to enter the United States as undocumented immigrants.

Griselda and her family are just a few of the millions who have been adversely affected by NAFTA. Signed in 1994, the agreement created a trade zone between Canada, the United States, and Mexico and sought to reduce barriers to trade and investment between the respective countries through the reduction or elimination of tariffs on exports. The premise behind free trade agreements, like NAFTA, is that through opening domestic markets to foreign competition (market liberalization) and the removal of state subsidies to domestic producers (privatization), a more efficient market economy would be created that would subsequently fuel economic growth and thereby reduce poverty (McMichael 2007; see Lesson 8). However, such agreements had very negative outcomes for smallholder agriculture and the communities organized around smallholder agriculture since they eliminated programs and policies that were vital to enabling small-scale producers to compete against large-scale corporations, including state-backed pro-smallholder land reform, subsidized seeds, fertilizers, fuels, and machines, and state credit and insurance networks, buying groups, and marketing boards. Without these public subsidies and programs, large agriculture companies ignored peasants and smallholders in favor of selling inputs to and buying food from well-financed industrial farms geared toward cash crop exports. The result was that peasants and smallholders were unable to remain agricultural producers and feed locals, an outcome that has undermined long-term food security and exacerbated the root factors producing hunger in small rural farming communities throughout the country.

On top of these problems, free trade policies were selectively applied to developing countries (McMichael 2007). The European Union and the United States, the two actors that were drawing up the rules for the global trade in food, were allowed to continue their protectionist and heavily subsidized agricultural policies while less powerful states in the global South had to eliminate theirs (see Lesson 9). This selective application of free trade policies incentivized and enabled the European Union and the United States to dump—sell below the cost of production—their agricultural surplus on the global South and outcompete Southern producers. Examples of dumping, beyond the case of corn in Mexico, include the destruction of Jamaica's milk industry, Senegal's poultry industry, and Ghana's poultry industry by imports from the European Union and the United States.

In short, the global hungry are those who have been most negatively affected by the push toward a world organized through free trade agreements that benefit well-capitalized large-scale farmers. The rural poor often have little to no access to quality farmland and little to no state supports for agriculture. While this is the reality for many today, it does not have to be their future. Research has found that investments and policies to support smallholder agriculture are quite effective at combating poverty and hunger, more so than investments in resource extraction or manufacturing, and that trade liberalization policies and privatization efforts without supports for smallholder agriculture exacerbate poverty and hunger (FAO 2015). Alongside these programs, a more robust welfare state with strong social protection programs, such as cash transfers, has been found to be a "highly-cost effective way to promote rural poverty reduction and improved food security and nutrition" (FAO 2015, 37). Based on these findings, there is the possibility of a future with less hunger and poverty, but only if there is an investment in smallholder agriculture and rural communities that empowers them to first feed themselves and, second, be competitive with larger agricultural producers.

Conclusion

Hunger is pervasive. The number of hungry may rise and fall with the stock market, but even in good times hunger remains. And while in the United States there is a strong tendency to see the hungry as moral failures, this lesson has taken a structural and historical approach to underscore how hunger is an outcome of how society is organized. In particular, hunger is the result of how the distribution of work and income intersects with the production and distribution of food. Those who are hungry are those who are marginalized from and within the labor market. They are people who either cannot work or cannot find well-paying jobs. Thus, the problem of hunger is not generally caused by the lack of a work ethic, but by the lack of well-payed work and the lack of access to income when one cannot work. While in the United States the relationship between food and hunger points to the current inadequacies of the minimum wage and food assistance programs, and therefore employment policies and the social safety net to mitigate poverty, globally we see that this relationship is a result of international trade policies that have benefited large-scale farmers and harmed the vast majority of smallholders. Such insights reaffirm the need for the creation of economic and political policies that are inclusive and directly strengthen the livelihoods of the poor, because only then will the structural factors producing long-term hunger be addressed.

Discussion Questions

1. Should we be concerned with hunger in the United States? Why or why not?
2. How has your race, class, gender, or geographic location shaped your access to food and your experiences with hunger? What social structures, social institutions, and policies have affected your access to food and experiences with hunger?
3. Think about the tension between short-term and long-term solutions to hunger in the United States. Why do you think there has been a movement in the United States since the 1980s toward short-term voluntarist solutions to hunger rather than long-term governmental programs?
4. Using your sociological imagination, what type of social changes would you advocate for to address hunger?

Exercises

1. Volunteer at an EFN organization or antihunger organization and discuss the pros and cons of their ability to address short-term and long-term hunger. What success is the organization having in reducing hunger? What could the organization do better to address hunger? Why might the organization currently be unable to address long-term hunger? What would need to change to enable the organization to address the structural roots of hunger?
2. Participate in the SNAP challenge. In 2007, Congress members were issued a challenge. They were asked to attempt to live on a typical food stamp budget, that is, to only spend about one dollar per meal, or twenty-one dollars per week. This was called the Food Stamp Challenge and sought to bring the difficulty of avoiding hunger and eating healthy to privileged members of society through direct experience. Since then, hundreds of groups across the United States have participated in the SNAP challenge. Today, the challenge is to live off four dollars a day, or twenty-eight dollars for the week. See http://www.frac.org/wp-content/uploads/take-action-snap-challenge-toolkit.pdf for details.
3. Visit the USDA's Food Environment Atlas and obtain information on your community's food environment, such as access and proximity to grocery stores, restaurants, participation rates for SNAP, national school lunch and breakfast program, Women, Infants, and Children, household food insecurity, obesity and diabetes rates, and general demographic profiles. Then do some research on your community's history and how federal and private practices and policies have shaped this food environment. Compare your community with that of other students in your class and determine any associations between the history of the communities, the demographic profile of the communities, and their access to food.

Additional Materials
Readings

Berg, Joel. 2008. *All You Can Eat: How Hungry Is America?* New York: Seven Stories Press.

Edin, Kathryn J., and H. Luke Shaefer. 2015. *$2.00 a Day: Living on Almost Nothing in America*. New York: Houghton Mifflin Harcourt.

Holt-Gimenez, Raj Patel, and Annie Shattuck. 2009. *Food Rebellions: Crisis and the Hunger for Justice*. Oakland, CA: Food First Books.

Saad, Majda Bne. 2013. *The Global Hunger Crisis: Tackling Food Insecurity in Developing Countries*. London: Pluto Press.

Schwartz-Nobel, Loretta. 2002. *Growing Up Empty: How Federal Policies Are Starving America's Children*. New York: HarperCollins.

Thurow, Roger, and Scott Kilman. 2009. *Enough: Why the World's Poorest Starve in an Age of Plenty*. New York. PublicAffairs.

Walton, John K., and David Seddon. 1994. *Free Markets and Food Riots: The Politics of Global Adjustment*. Cambridge, MA: Blackwell.

Winne, Mark. 2008. *Closing the Food Gap: Resetting the Table in the Land of Plenty*. Boston: Beacon Press.

Films

Adams, Zac. 2014. *Hunger in America*. Skydive Films.

Black, Stephanie. 2001. *Life and Debt*. New Yorker Films.

Jacobson, Kristi, and Lori Silverbush. 2012. *A Place at the Table*. Magnolia Pictures.

Karslake, Dan. 2014. *Every Three Seconds*. First Run Features.

Unknown. n.d. *The Last Hunger Season*. Courter Films.

Websites

Feeding Hunger, http://www.feedingamerica.org/

The Food and Agriculture Organization of the United Nations, http://www.fao.org/hunger/en/

Food Research and Action Center, http://frac.org/

USDA Food Access Research Atlas, https://www.ers.usda.gov/data-products/food-access-research-atlas/

USDA Food Expenditures, https://www.ers.usda.gov/data-products/food-expenditures.aspx

USDA, Food Security in the United States, https://www.ers.usda.gov/topics/food-nutrition-assistance/food-security-in-the-us/

References

Alderman, Liz and Steven Greenhouse. 2014. "Living Wages, Rarity for U.S. Fast-Food Workers, Served Up in Denmark." *New York Times*, October 27, 2014. https://www.nytimes.com/2014/10/28/business/international/living-wages-served-in-denmark-fast-food-restaurants.html.

Althaus, Dudley. 2013. "Despite Obesity, Much of Mexico Goes Hungry." Public Radio International. September 16, 2013. http://www.pri.org/stories/2013-09-16/despite-obesity-much-mexico-goes-hungry

Burnett, Victoria. 2016. "Oaxaca's Native Maize Embraced by Top Chefs in U.S. and Europe." *New York Times*, February 11, 2016. https://www.nytimes.com/2016/02/12/world/americas/oaxacas-native-maize-embraced-by-top-chefs-in-us-and-europe.html

Coleman-Jensen, Matthew P. Rabbitt, Christian Gregory, and Anita Singh. 2015. *Household Food Security in the United States in 2014*. Economic Research Report No. ERR-194. Washington, DC: US Department of Agriculture, Economic Research Service.

Darlington, Shasta, and Patrick Gillespie. 2017. "Mexican Farmer's Daughter: NAFTA Destroyed Us." CNN. February 9, 2017. http://money.cnn.com/2017/02/09/news/economy/nafta-farming-mexico-us-corn-jobs/.

Desilver, Drew. 2017. "5 Facts about the Minimum Wage." Pew Research Center. Last modified January 4, 2017. http://www.pewresearch.org/fact-tank/2017/01/04/5-facts-about-the-minimum-wage/

FAO (Food and Agriculture Organization of the United Nations). 2015. *The State of Food Insecurity in the World 2015*. Rome: UNFAO. Accessed December 5, 2016. http://www.fao.org/3/a-i4646e.pdf

Feeding America. 2015. "Map the Meal Gap 2016." Accessed December 5, 2016. http://www.feedingamerica.org/hunger-in-america/our-research/map-the-meal-gap/2014/map-the-meal-gap-2014-exec-summ.pdf

FCWA (Food Chain Workers Alliance). 2012. *The Hands That Feed Us: Challenges and Opportunities for Workers along the Food Chain*. Food Chain Workers Alliance. June 6, 2012. http://foodchainworkers.org/wp-content/uploads/2012/06/Hands-That-Feed-Us-Report.pdf

FCWA (Food Chains Workers Alliance), Restaurant Opportunities Center of New York, Restaurant Opportunities Center of the Bay, Food First. 2014. *Food Insecurity of Restaurant Workers*. Accessed December 5, 2016. https://www.scribd.com/document/234905417/Food-Insecurity-of-Restaurant-Workers

Gray, Kelsey Farson, and Shivani Kochlar. 2015. *Characteristics of Supplemental Nutrition Assistance Program Households: Fiscal Year 2014*. Alexandria, VA: US Department of Agriculture, Food and Nutrition Service.

Jamieson, Dave. 2012. "Minimum Wage for Restaurant Servers Remains Stagnant for 20 Years under Industry Lobbying." *The Huffington Post*, June 2, 2012. Last modified December 6, 2017. http://www.huffingtonpost.com/2012/06/02/minimum-wage-restaurant-workers_n_1515916.html

Joliffe, Dean, Craig Gundersen, Laura Tiehen, and Joshua Winicki. 2013. *Food Stamp Benefits and Childhood Poverty in the 1990s*. Washington, DC: USDA, Food Assistance and Nutrition Research Report No. (FANRR33).

Liu, Yvonne Yen, and Dominique Apollon. 2011. *The Color of Food*. Applied Research Center. February 2011. https://www.raceforward.org/sites/default/files/downloads/food_justice_021611_F.pdf

McMichael, Philip. 2007. *Development and Social Change: A Global Perspective*. 4th ed. Thousand Oaks, CA: Pine Forge Press.

McMillian, Tracie. 2014. "The New Face of Hunger." *National Geographic*. Accessed August 16, 2016. http://www.nationalgeographic.com/foodfeatures/hunger/

Mills, C. Wright. 1959. *The Sociological Imagination*. New York: Oxford University Press.

OECD (Organisation for Economic Co-Operation and Development). 2014. *OECD Employment Outlook 2014*. Table N: Earnings Dispersion and Incidence of High and Low Pay. Accessed January 15, 2017. http://www.oecd.org/els/emp/employment-outlook-statistical-annex.htm

Oxfam America. 2014. *Working Poor in America*. Oxfam America. June 11, 2014. http://www.oxfamamerica.org/explore/research-publications/working-poor-in-america/

Poppendeick, Janet. 1998. *Sweet Charity?: Emergency Food and the End of Entitlement*. New York: Penguin Books.

Rose, Donald J., Nicholas Bodor, Chris M. Swalm, Janet C. Rice, Thomas A. Farley, and Paul L. Hutchinson, "Deserts in New Orleans? Illustrations of Urban Food Access and Implications for Policy," Presented at Understanding the Economic Concepts and Characteristics of Food Access, conference, University of Michigan National Poverty Center, February 2009.

Shierhloz, Shier. 2014. *Low Wages and Few Benefits Mean Many Restaurant Workers Can't Make Ends Meet*. EPI Briefing Paper No. 383. Economic Policy Institute. August 21, 2014. http://www.epi.org/files/2014/restaurant-workers-final.pdf

Taylor, Anna, and Rachel Loopstra. 2016. *Too Poor to Eat: Food insecurity in the UK*. Food Foundation. May 2016. http://foodfoundation.org.uk/wp-content/uploads/2016/07/FoodInsecurityBriefing-May-2016-FINAL.pdf

Tiehen, Laura, Dean Jolifee, and Craig Gundersen. 2012. *Alleviating Poverty in the United States: The Critical Role of SNAP Benefits*. Washington, DC: U.S. Department of Agriculture.

Treuhaft, Sarah and Allison Karpyn. 2010. *The Grocery Gap: Who Has Access to Healthy Food and Why It Matters*. Oakland, CA: Policy Link and Food Trust.

USBOL (US Bureau of Labor). 2017. "Characteristics of minimum wage workers, 2016" US Bureau of Labor Statistics. Accessed December 5, 2017. https://www.bls.gov/opub/reports/minimum-wage/2016/home.htm

USDA (US Department of Agriculture). 2016. "Definitions of Food Security." US Department of Agriculture, Economic Research Service. Accessed December 5, 2017. https://www.ers.usda.gov/topics/food-nutrition-assistance/food-security-in-the-us/definitions-of-food-security.aspx

Ver Ploeg, Michele, Vince Breneman, Paula Dutko, Ryan Williams, Samantha Snyder, Chris Dicken, and Phil Kaufman. 2012. *Access to Affordable and Nutritious Food: Updated Estimates of Distance to Supermarkets Using 2010 Data*. Economic Research Report No. ERR-143. Washington, DC: USDA, Economic Research Service.

Walker, Renee E., Christopher R Keane, and Jessica Burke. 2010. "Disparities and access to healthy food in the United States: a review of food deserts literature." *Health & Place* 16(5): 876–884

Plastic food containers. (Photo © Carsten ten Brink /Flickr / CC BY-NC-ND 2.0.)

14

Food and Obesity

Melina Packer and Julie Guthman

O ver the past two decades or so, no other food issue seems to have captured more attention in the United States than the so-called obesity epidemic. National health statisticians charted a significant increase in population-wide body mass index (BMI, the metric used to gauge obesity) between the early 1980s and 2000s, generating great concern from a variety of constituencies. Attempts to explain this rise, and obesity itself, have followed apace.

Many pundits argue that obesity reflects a failure of personal responsibility. They see obesity as a lack of self-control and call for changes in "lifestyle," often translated as acceptance of calorie-restricted diets. Others, particularly in the public health and planning professions, recognize that a discourse of personal responsibility is at best ineffective and at worst psychologically damaging. Joining nutritionists, **alternative food movement** activists, farm and food policy advocates, food system researchers, and even popular food writers, they are arguing for a **food system perspective** on obesity to guide policy that will change the social and physical environment that mediates food intake. A food system perspective attempts to look at the entirety of processes, institutions, and regulations that shape the production, distribution, and consumption of food. As it applies to obesity, the food system perspective would take into account the external conditions that shape what food choices different people have, such as the cost of food or the location and design of restaurants and retailers, rather than chastising individuals for making certain choices given a limited menu of options. For example, proponents of a food system perspective often focus on the government policies that have made less nutritious food cheaper than high-quality fruits and vegetables. They also focus on business behavior, noting that many grocery stores strategically place their high-profit, low-nutrient food near the entrance and checkout line, thereby enticing shoppers who may have entered the store for basic groceries such as milk, fruit, and meat to pick up junk food on the way in or out. Proponents of a food system approach to obesity generally shun the shame-and-blame game and instead call for such solutions as more farmers' markets, stronger regulations on junk food, or an end to commodity crop subsidies.

In the name of addressing **health disparities**, advocates of a food system perspective also draw attention to race- and income-based differences in population-level obesity rates. In the United States, black and **Latinx** people tend to have higher BMIs than whites. Size also correlates with income in the United States, albeit along gendered lines; obesity rates are similar among men regardless of income, while wealthier women tend to have lower BMIs than poorer women (CDC 2016). Concerned scientific researchers, health-care providers, and public officials thus often focus their food system–oriented obesity interventions on people of color and lower-income people because these populations appear to be the most affected.

In several respects, the food system perspective comes across as a more ethical approach to addressing the disproportionate burdens of seemingly diet-related health issues than shaming and blaming. And yet, those who embrace the food system perspective, including many critical scholars, still treat obesity as if the connections between food intake and weight are clear and uncontested. For them, the problem lies with how food shopping and eating are mediated. For instance, the **obesogenic environment** thesis, explored later in this chapter, assumes that people who live in neighborhoods that are dominated by fast food restaurants and junk food retailers will tend toward obesity because of the high-calorie food that is available. They may not consider that people metabolize foods quite differently.

This lesson questions the food system perspective, even though it improves on the personal responsibility approach. Although we share many of the concerns raised by the food system perspective, including its attention to public policy and business behavior, we find that current research has not reached consensus on many of the assumptions embedded in this perspective, and therefore has not fully accounted for the (food-related) causes of obesity. As a result, many of the interventions that follow from this analysis may be misguided or unwanted, such as calorie counts on restaurant menus or creating markets that contribute to neighborhood **gentrification**.

For that matter, the extent of the obesity "problem" is by no means a settled question, nor is the relationship between obesity and health. While we do not deny that obesity rates increased significantly in the 1980s, or that obesity correlates with income and race, the significance of those changes and correlations is subject to scientific controversy. As for the relationship between obesity and health, those who contend that obesity indicates ill health often cite a 2004 CDC study that claimed poor diet and lack of exercise was nearing tobacco as a primary cause of death, having contributed to 400,000 deaths in the year 2000 (Mokdad et al. 2004). This study was unusual in that the authors attempted to establish the number of deaths by behavior rather than by condition (for example, the behavior tobacco use as opposed to the condition lung cancer). These researchers used rates of obesity as a proxy calculation of deaths from poor diet and insufficient exercise, thereby assuming that obesity results from such behaviors (an assumption we will examine in this lesson). As it turned out, that figure of 400,000 deaths was revised markedly downward to 112,000 deaths, based on another study, also by CDC scientists, who reanalyzed the same evidence (Flegal et al. 2005). The later study revealed that people who are modestly overweight actually have a *lower* risk of death than those who are of "normal" weight and showed no "excess mortality" for mildly obese people. Flegal and colleagues subsequently reviewed a good number of studies that attempted to measure excess mortality related to overweight and found that adults in the higher BMI category have no greater risk of dying than adults in the normal range (Flegal et al. 2007). Regarding other health issues, although the majority of studies suggest that larger people are more prone to metabolic disease such as type 2 diabetes, a growing body of research reveals that the relationship is not so clear-cut. Scientists are also exploring whether it is type 2 diabetes that causes obesity, given findings that lipids, including fats, *both promote and suppress* inflammation and insulin resistance (Wellen and Hotamisligil 2005). While this lesson does not focus on the obesity and health debate, it is important to note that the entire obesity "epidemic" rests on a deeply fractured foundation of biomedical uncertainties.

Instead, this lesson examines some key assumptions that underpin the food system perspective, some of which barely differ from the personal responsibility approach. We specifically focus on the following four:

Assumption 1. Obesity results from an excess of calorie intake relative to calorie expenditure (the **energy balance model**).

Assumption 2. Obesity results from built environments that encourage consumption of nutritionally vacuous foods (the **obesogenic environment** or **food desert** thesis).

Assumption 3. Obesity results from (US) agriculture policy, which subsidizes commodity crops like corn and soy rather than fruits and vegetables, therefore overproducing cheap, nutritionally inferior foods.

Assumption 4. Obesity results from what people purposely ingest as food, as opposed to other ingestions or exposures.

In what follows, we do not refute each assumption with incontrovertible evidence; rather, we provide countervailing evidence and argumentation to reveal the lack of scientific consensus. Since each assumption tends to unevenly implicate people of color and people with lower socioeconomic status, throughout the discussion we give particular attention to the aspects of each assumption that bear on these populations.

ASSUMPTION 1: OBESITY RESULTS FROM AN EXCESS OF CALORIE INTAKE RELATIVE TO CALORIE EXPENDITURE (THE ENERGY BALANCE MODEL)

Perhaps the most common assumption, repeated by nutrition and policy experts alike, is that people are becoming overweight and obese, especially since the 1980s, because they consume too many calories relative to the energy they expend, perhaps with some allowance for genetic predisposition. At the most basic level, it is not clear that calories are most responsible for fat production. A calorie is not a constituent ingredient of food; it is simply a measurement of heat in burning. The word **calorie** comes from a device dating back to eighteenth-century laboratories, the calorimeter, which measured the heat expended during chemical reactions; this amount of heat was then understood as energy. Calories were applied to food (and, some would argue, have become a stand-in for food) as a way of measuring the amount of heat/energy the average (read: adult white male) human body generated during digestion. Given the true meaning and use of the calorie, defining and measuring food in terms of this unit seems a cognitive jump. Calorie counts are, at best, a rough approximation of food intake and subsequent energy expenditure (see Lesson 4).

Putting aside for now the flawed assumption that all human bodies process foods identically, even if researchers and policymakers simply used calorie counts as a proxy for quantity of intake, it appears that not all calories are created equal. Contemporary scientists remain divided on this complex issue, but mounting evidence suggests that carbohydrate intake, including especially fructose, leads to weight gain and metabolic disorder significantly more than protein or fat intake (Lustig, Schmidt, and Brindis 2012). The United States' leading expert on childhood obesity, for instance, has campaigned publicly and passionately against sugar in particular, condemning this substance as toxic, poisonous, and evil. New research suggests that what matters more is not how *many* calories one consumes, but what *kinds* of calories.

Returning to the claim that people are consuming more calories than in the past, in a thorough review of the literature on caloric intake and expenditure, researchers Michael Gard and Jan Wright (2005) found no definitive proof that food intake in industrialized countries has risen and activity levels have declined, particularly in the years since 1980, the established onset of the obesity "crisis." As they reported, the science on food intake is quite contradictory, with some studies suggesting even a reduction over the past several decades. A more recent (and solely US-based) analysis, combining national food recall surveys and longitudinal household purchasing data, found a significant decrease in all US households' caloric purchases (controlling for socioeconomic differences) between 2003 and 2011, especially in households with children (Ng, Slining, and Popkin 2014). As for claims made based on food availability per capita, they are based on food produced on an annual basis and have little to do with how much people actually consume, which is notable given the huge amount of food that is wasted in the (US) food system. One team of cardiologists even went so far as to suggest that the US Department of Agriculture's "food availability per capita caloric consumption estimates" have remained so invalid over their thirty-nine-year history that they should not be used to inform public policy (Archer et al. 2016). Nevertheless, researchers and pundits continue to use food availability per capita to demonstrate increasing caloric intake.

The **energy balance model** also fails to explain population-level differences in average weight by race/ethnicity and gender, differences that are at the center of concerns about health disparities. With the exception of Asian Americans, people of color and low-income people in the United States tend to have higher BMIs than white people and higher-income people, especially among women. Yet national dietary intake surveys do not show significant differences in total caloric intake by race or ethnicity, while women tend to consume fewer calories than men overall. For example, average daily caloric intake in 2013–14 broke down as follows: 2,080 calories for non-Hispanic whites, 1,853 for non-Hispanic Asians, 2,133 for blacks, and 2,104 for Hispanics; 1,786 for women and 2,382 for men (USDA 2016, per their race/ethnicity categories). National consumption surveys do not show that caloric intake differs significantly by income either, with poorer people reportedly consuming fewer calories than wealthier people on average. In the same 2013–14 USDA study, those earning less than $25,000 per year reported consuming 2,061 calories per day while those earning more than $75,000 per year reported consuming 2,096 per day. Physically active jobs (construction, landscaping, housecleaning, etc.), meanwhile, tend to be performed by those very same low-income populations which are reportedly gaining the most weight. Empirically, then, there is insufficient evidence to attribute population-level weight gain to the energy balance model. And yet, the energy balance model is embedded in another prevalent assumption of the food system perspective: the obesogenic environment thesis.

ASSUMPTION 2: OBESITY RESULTS FROM BUILT ENVIRONMENTS THAT DISCOURAGE EXERCISE AND ENCOURAGE CONSUMPTION OF FAST FOODS (THE OBESOGENIC ENVIRONMENT OR *FOOD DESERT* THESIS)

The **obesogenic environment** thesis, introduced in the late 1990s, is that people are gaining weight because they are surrounded by cheap, fast, nutritionally inferior food and a dearth of opportunities for physical activity. Although this thesis draws needed attention to potential *structural* causes of obesity, it has not held up empirically, especially on the food side of the equation. In addition, it internalizes two critical presumptions that perhaps explain why evidence has not supported the theory. First, and explicitly, it assumes the energy balance model, questioned earlier. Second, and implicitly, it assumes that the environment simply acts on (certain) people, such that (some) people will necessarily eat junk food simply because they are frequently exposed to it.

Studies relating different **foodscapes** to obesity have found inconclusive or inconsistent evidence, even in highly localized settings. Earlier reviews of mostly US studies claimed more support for the thesis. Four of five studies that measured differences in weight status by access to supermarkets found that people with greater access to supermarkets had lower BMI and/or were less likely to be overweight or obese compared to those with less access. Five of eight studies examining access to takeaway food outlets in relation to weight status found that greater access was associated with greater BMI and/or prevalence of overweight/obesity. However, in both sets differences were small to moderate in magnitude. Moreover, associations of access to grocery and convenience stores were found to be mixed, as was access to restaurants and cafes (Giskes et al. 2011). More recent studies have taken into account not only these data limitations but also methodological inconsistencies that made the literature reviews themselves questionable. Individual obesogenic environment studies have been designed so differently from one another that they are difficult to compare or synthesize. Taking account of and controlling for such study design variability, a comprehensive 2014 review analyzed ninety-three obesogenic environment studies from three regions: North America (more United States than Canada), Europe (mostly the United Kingdom), and Australasia. Across the ninety-three studies included in this review, the only environmental factors that seemed consistently associated with adult overweight and obesity were urban sprawl and land use mix, and even these consistencies were found only in North America (Mackenbach et al. 2014). Regarding methodological quality, of the eighty-three studies that were deemed scientifically rigorous (judging by such characteristics as large and representative sample sizes, longitudinal analyses, validity and reliability of measures, etc.), only twenty-nine of these methodologically sound studies found results in support of their obesogenic environment hypotheses. As the review authors conclude, "Although there is a general consensus that the physical environment has an important influence on individuals' weight status (in environments where there is no food, one cannot eat; in environments where there are no cars, public transport or machines, one cannot avoid being more physically active for transport, daily activities or work), a large body of research has failed robustly to identify direct causal pathways between the physical environment and weight status" (10).

It is possible that these obesogenic environment studies remain inconclusive in terms of weight status because spatial analyses by design cannot account for human behavior and individual decision-making rationale. Analyses of space can only indicate *associations* of urban form and rates of obesity and not the *causal* relations between them. Showing the geographic proximity of a household and a fast food restaurant does not tell us, for example, whether members of that household eat at that restaurant, nor does it tell us why or why not. Studies that *do* attend to human behavior have demonstrated that people do not necessarily consume or shop for food near their places of residence, but rather on the way home from work or school.

The mere presence of a grocery store (or absence of a fast food restaurant), moreover, does not guarantee that people's diets will change. A longitudinal study of over five thousand people in four major US cities (Birmingham, Alabama; Chicago, Illinois; Minneapolis, Minnesota; and Oakland, California) concluded that "greater supermarket availability was generally unrelated to diet quality and fruit and vegetable intake, and relationships between grocery store availability and diet outcomes were mixed" (Boone-Heinonen et al. 2011, 1162). In terms of individual agency, the obesogenic thesis also does not adequately explain why in mixed income locales, such as New York City, weight continues to correlate with income even though all residents are exposed to the same environment. In this context, the obesogenic environment theory would seem to suggest that people with less income are somehow making worse shopping choices or are somehow less able to resist junk food than their higher-income neighbors.

Given the statistics that people with lower incomes, on average, have higher BMIs than people with higher incomes, the obesogenic environment thesis has been applied to low-income neighborhoods in particular. Food system and nutrition advocates have characterized certain environments as **food deserts**—neighborhoods where at least one-third of the population does not own a vehicle and lives over one mile from a grocery store or supermarket—which, in turn, seem more prevalent within lower-income census tracts (USDA 2017a) (see Lesson 13). This food desert classification, and its attendant assumptions, remains problematic on several levels. First, the term *desert* can be stigmatizing, and several community-based organizations and food justice activists have indeed responded negatively to this terminology. Second, in addition to the point made above that the mere existence of grocery stores does not guarantee specific grocery purchases, supermarkets are not necessarily the only or the best resource for healthy foods (assuming, again, that consumption of certain foods can cause, prevent, or reduce obesity). Smaller, independently owned food and convenience markets located in so-called food deserts have been found to offer an array of healthy and culturally relevant food items at comparable price and quality (Short, Guthman, and Raskin 2007). Notably, other significant drivers of people's shopping decisions are unaddressed by these obesogenic environment studies regardless of the size or type of grocery; if both small stores and supermarkets pay low wages, for instance, then lacking access to healthy foods, or requiring access to cheap food, remain valid issues for quite different reasons.

Social scientists have also shown that people with lower incomes choose where to shop and eat based on a myriad of factors besides proximity, such as cost, taste, or quality of food (Alkon et al. 2013). Some people travel quite far from their homes to procure culturally relevant foods and maintain a diversity of cooking traditions, while others might strategically visit a variety of markets, collecting coupons and following weekly specials for staple food items. Even nutrition scientists are beginning to abandon the faulty obesogenic environment thesis; one prominent group boldly titled their 2016 study "Where People Shop Is Not Associated with the Nutrient Quality of Packaged Foods for any Racial–Ethnic Group in the United States" (Stern et al. 2016). In terms of obesity specifically, a 2014 study of a Philadelphia food desert intervention concluded that the new grocery store affected neither fruit and vegetable intake nor BMI (Cummins, Flint, and Matthews 2014). In short, both individual studies and systematic reviews of the food desert literature have shown that the evidence is mixed and that the thesis is not well supported empirically.

Accessible and healthy grocery options are certainly important. Indeed, ideally all neighborhoods would offer such amenities. It is worth noting, then, that obesogenic environments appear to reflect the financial resources of those who inhabit such places, and the waves of investment and disinvestment that have produced such disparate environments. In other words, what may be predicting the prevalence of obesity in certain places is, in fact, structural racism and classism (putting aside for now what produces variation in size relative to race and class), with features of the built environment being an *effect* of that spatial patterning rather than a cause. Maybe people of color and lower-income populations are not heavier because they live in places devoid of fresh produce; rather, socially marginalized groups who may be heavier for a variety of reasons are disproportionately located in such spaces because of historic legacies of employment and housing discrimination (see Lessons 13 and 20). People may nevertheless seek out cheap food because of poverty. One additional question is whether agricultural subsidies make food artificially cheap. This is the next assumption of the food system perspective that we explore.

ASSUMPTION 3: OBESITY RESULTS FROM (US) AGRICULTURE POLICY, WHICH SUBSIDIZES COMMODITY CROPS LIKE CORN AND SOY RATHER THAN FRUITS AND VEGETABLES, THEREFORE OVERPRODUCING CHEAP, NUTRITIONALLY INFERIOR FOODS

Another target of food system perspective advocates has been US agricultural policies. The problem, they have argued, is that the **commodity subsidy programs** make crops such as corn and soy artificially cheap, especially in comparison to fruits and vegetables. Since the New Deal, the US government has been supporting farmers who grow basic crops deemed of national importance such as soybeans and other oil seeds, corn, rice, wheat, cotton, and sugar—commodity crops. The means by which they support farmers have included nonrecourse loans, direct payments, and crop insurance—all of which allow farmers to stay in business even when market prices are inadequate. In turn, food manufacturers and livestock producers are able to purchase these artificially cheap ingredients and feeds, making their innumerable products and byproducts artificially cheap as well. Fruit and vegetable crops are not subsidized in this way.

Therefore, according to this line of argument, the government is encouraging the consumption of high-calorie and nutritionally vacuous food relative to lower-calorie and nutritionally superior food. This analysis then suggests ending commodity subsidies so that food prices reflect their real cost of production. While there is much to criticize and reform about commodity subsidies and crop insurance programs, such as their tendency to benefit already wealthy farm operators and discourage ecologically sound farming practices, there are many ideas and assumptions embedded in this subsidy argument that call for more scrutiny.

Today's US household, on average, spends a smaller percentage of its income on food than in the 1950s and a smaller percentage than their European counterparts as well (USDA 2017b). Although this ratio varies by income, it is worth noting that today even the poorest US residents spend only 15 percent of their income on food while the wealthiest spend closer to 10 percent, on average. One central assumption is that it is the commodity programs alone that allow people in the United States to spend a relatively small proportion of income on food. Although subsidies contribute to the overproduction of certain commodities, such as corn and soy, and overproduction brings prices down for those commodities, a much broader set of practices, industrial dynamics, and policies make food in the United States relatively inexpensive. In general, the reason that processed food costs less than fresh fruits and vegetables has little to do with subsidies and much more to do with production procedures. Simply put, many processing ingredients, such as soy, corn, and wheat, are far less costly to produce on a mass scale than fresh fruits and vegetables. Soy, corn, and wheat, all primary ingredients in snack food, can be tilled and harvested by machine, whereas fresh peaches, strawberries, and lettuce, among other fruits and vegetables, require a great deal of hand labor in weeding and harvesting. In short, differential labor costs are a major driver of production costs.

As it happens, fresh fruits and vegetables are subsidized too, albeit in less direct ways. Many of these are grown in the US West and South, in Texas, Arizona, California, and Florida. In most of these places, farmers have depended on federal government irrigation projects for water. They have used the technologies developed through the land-grant universities to manage pests (see Lesson 6). They have also tended to depend on punitive immigration laws and a militarized border to access cheap labor (see Lesson 11). At full cost, without spillover benefits from government-sponsored research, infrastructure projects, labor regimes, and other government investment, fruits and vegetables would be even more expensive to grow and harvest. Thus, to suggest that removal of the corn and soy subsidies would make fresh produce relatively cheaper is overly simplistic.

In light of the subsidy argument, health economists have attempted to model the effects of subsidy removal on caloric intake. Using a highly detailed, multimarket model based on actual US statistics over a ten-year period (1992–2002), they found that removing US subsidies on grains and oil seeds (i.e., soy) would cause only minimal decreases in caloric consumption, while removal of all US agricultural policies, including both direct subsidies like commodity payments and indirect subsidies like import tariffs, would cause an increase in total caloric intake (Rickard, Okrent, and Alston 2013). While this study equates caloric purchases with caloric intake, the analysis nevertheless demonstrates that, on their own, US agricultural subsidies produce minimal effects on food prices and subsequent purchasing/consumption patterns, particularly in comparison to other major, confounding factors, such as international trade policy.

With subsidies a weak explanation for the prevalence of cheap food, the question remains why the empirical links between income and obesity are so consistent. As we have already discussed, more energy-dense foods, like hamburgers and fries, are cheaper because of differential production costs. Arguably, then, people with less income are making a rational, intelligent decision when purchasing a cheaper, more energy-dense food item, given their financial constraints. Yet, the results of national dietary surveys remain mixed and do not neatly correspond with population-level obesity patterns (see Assumption 1). Put another way, the available evidence does not consistently or reliably show that lower-income people eat more junk food than higher-income people, or that black women eat more junk food than white women. Also, those reportedly consuming the most highly processed food are not necessarily the same groups with the highest BMIs. According to industry statistics, white men, for example, eat at fast food restaurants more than other racial groups, and yet non-Hispanic black men have the highest rates of obesity. So, regardless of whether subsidies make certain foods cheap, the assumption that lower-income people tend to eat more cheap food, and that this consumption leads to obesity, still does not hold. Even research that is sympathetic to the ways that poverty constrains choices tends to assume the energy balance model, leaving the lingering questions about this model described earlier. Perhaps, then, the food system perspective is too focused on *food* consumption.

ASSUMPTION 4: OBESITY RESULTS FROM WHAT PEOPLE PURPOSELY INGEST AS FOOD, AS OPPOSED TO OTHER INGESTIONS OR EXPOSURES

A fourth assumption is that people are obese because of what they purposely ingest as food. This assumption ignores the numerous substances people ingest unintentionally or are exposed to or, for that matter, how bodies react under stressful conditions. New science in three areas—**endocrine disruption/epigenetics**, **stress-cortisol**, and the **microbiome**—suggests that weight gain may not be as related to intentional food consumption as commonly thought.

The endocrine system comprises the glands and pathways that emit hormones, such as the thyroid, pituitary, and hypothalamus glands.

Endocrine *disruption* thus entails interference with the action of these hormones. One source of disruption are external agents, often chemicals, that behave like, interact with, or alter the function of hormones produced by the body—mimicking, enhancing, or inhibiting them. These endocrine disrupting chemicals (EDCs) in turn can act on a gene's developmental mechanisms, altering phenotype expression. Scientists are now seeing that the mechanism of these phenotypic changes can be **epigenetic**, meaning that they cause heritable changes in gene function without changing the DNA sequence, that is, without mutation. Put more plainly, EDCs can interfere with genetic expression in ways that permanently transform bodily form and function, and these changes can be passed on to offspring.

A set of animal studies found that maternal exposure to EDCs altered genetic pathways for fetuses in ways that generated adult obesity. Notably, both low and high doses of synthetic estrogens given to mice during gestation and immediately following birth resulted in significantly higher body weight at adulthood than that of genetically identical control groups fed the same diet. Demonstrating an epigenetic effect, this research also found that the genes that direct fat distribution are permanently altered by the exposure, such that the tendency toward high amounts of fat tissue would be passed on to offspring (Newbold et al. 2008). In reviewing these sorts of studies, some scientists have concluded that these epigenetic processes can work independent of caloric intake and expenditure (Holtcamp 2012). Scientists have also noted that EDCs involve multiple modes of action, meaning that there is not just one biological pathway through which chemicals can contribute to obesity. With many possible chemicals and pathways at work, the extent of their contributions to obesity may be difficult to ever determine.

Importantly, many of the chemical substances that researchers have identified as possible **obesogens** are prevalent in the food system, including certain pesticides, bisphenol A, and phthalates (chemicals present in plastics and other types of packaging materials). Food ingredients and processing agents may be part of the mix as well. Soy, also associated with obesogenesis, is not only a major source of livestock feed but also a microingredient in many processed foods. Commonly used food additives have also been found to have hormone-mimicking properties. It appears that obesogens are present all along food supply chains, from farm production, to transportation and storage, to food processing and retail.

These newer scientific findings may help explain some of the gender and racial differences in rates of obesity—or lack thereof. Black, Latina, and white women have seen obesity prevalence increase at similar rates since the 1980 baseline, suggesting similar exposures (Chang and Christakis 2005). Recall also that women show more variance in obesity than men. Because women produce more estrogen and have higher percentages of body fat, they have the physiological propensity to store more fat. Given that women consume fewer calories on average than men, in the United

States, it is possible that other exposures to EDCs, such as from personal care and household cleaning products rather than from food, contribute to women's higher obesity rates overall.

Geographic and class variation in obesity rates may be partially explained by endocrine disruption and epigenetics as well. Although some obesogens are indeed ubiquitous, others tend to be more present in certain environments. For example, obesogenic pesticides are used predominantly in rural agricultural areas, which tend to have higher rates of obesity prevalence than cities, as well as other health problems related to EDCs. As for class variation, the US data provided previously on daily caloric intake do not necessarily support the assumption that low-income people eat more calories or eat more junk food. It is probably demonstrable, however, that low-income people are exposed not only to more EDCs, but also to more nutritional deprivation in utero, which has been shown to predict obesity (Thayer and Kuzawa 2011). Furthermore, chronic stress and disruptions to circadian rhythms are two additional processes that change bodily function.

Physiological processes that tend to be experienced by those in precarious economic situations, such as chronic stress and sleep deprivation, have all been consistently associated with obesity in epidemiological studies (de Oliveira et al. 2014). In the case of stress, this appears to be related to the secretion of stress hormones, not simply stress eating (Incollingo et al. 2015). Stress activates the hypothalamic–pituitary–adrenal axis in the body's effort to maintain homeostasis, which, in turn, provokes circulation of cortisol, a hormone that increases abdominal adiposity. Disruptions in circadian rhythms, or interrupted sleep cycles, have also been shown to cause obesity. Comparing two groups of mice that ate the same quantities of the same foods, one study found that the mice whose sleep was repeatedly disturbed not only gained more weight but also developed metabolic disorders (Hatori et al. 2012). Research exploring the links between weight gain and stress may overstate the supposed ill health outcomes of the so-called obesity epidemic, yet raises compelling questions regarding noncaloric pathways to metabolic dysfunction, particularly for those who are socially disadvantaged and therefore more likely to have disrupted circadian rhythms and be exposed to chronic stress.

In addition to epigenetic pathways, researchers are also looking to the science of the (gut) microbiome to explain rising obesity rates. While by no means definitive or without controversy, newly emerging microbiome studies bring up interesting and important questions regarding the role of environmental factors beyond individual control (Davis 2016; Fändriks 2016). Antibiotics, for example, may negatively interfere with gut microbiomes to cause multiple health issues, including several metabolic disorders associated with obesity. Even if one chooses not to take antibiotics, assuming bacterial infection can be avoided, people are regularly ingesting antibiotic residues through water, air, and food, and may be unwittingly using antibiotic cleansers in public and institutional restrooms. Moreover, similar to the epigenetic effects of EDC exposure, microbiomes and their attendant problems (as well as benefits) are transgenerational; parent microbiomes are passed on to offspring via gestation and birth (Lemas et al. 2016).

Scientists are just beginning to explore relationships between socioeconomic status and the gut microbiome. Thus far results are mixed, though there certainly seems to be an association. For example, one study comparing impoverished and wealthier children living in the same Brazilian neighborhood found that children of high socioeconomic status have *less* favorable gut microbiota than children who live in poverty (Mello et al. 2016). By contrast, a comparative study of adults in the United States found that as neighborhood socioeconomic status increased, so did the diversity of resident adults' gut microbiota (Miller et al. 2016).

In sum, this new batch of scientific evidence suggests causes of the post-1980s increase in size that extend far beyond current assumptions about diet and obesity implicit in the food system approach. Notably, many EDCs were introduced in the 1950s and 1960s, during an era in which the slogan "better living through chemistry" did not provoke incredulity. They then became truly ubiquitous at just about the same time that BMI values began to increase—in the 1980s (Baillie-Hamilton 2002). Likewise, the stressors of economic precarity have certainly worsened over the past several decades, as government assistance has been rolled back and wages have declined. To be clear, this science is emergent and not short of controversy either. Studies supporting these ideas are also based on correlations and/or have inconsistent findings. But this new research nonetheless suggests pathways toward obesity well beyond what people ingest as food, whether in terms of "personal responsibility" or structurally constrained choice.

Importantly, these possible contributors to obesity also implicate the food system, but in ways more far reaching than the current food system perspective encompasses. These potential causes point to the failure of government regulation to ensure that food workers and consumers are not exposed to unsafe levels of toxic chemicals and additives, or to prevent the overuse of synthetic hormones and antibiotics in livestock production that appear to be affecting human metabolic functions. They also point to the unacknowledged biological toll of high-stress and low-wage jobs—exactly the kind that prevail in food and farming work in particular.

Conclusion

It may be reasonable to think that food deserts and commodity subsidies lead (poor) people to eat too much low-quality food and that this overconsumption causes obesity. The four assumptions questioned in this lesson complicate this line of reasoning. First, empirical evidence does not support the energy balance model that nevertheless remains at the center of nearly all obesity research, interventions, and policies. Second, the obesogenic environment thesis stands unsupported, if not invalidated, by the spatial, social, and epidemiological literatures. Third, national-level dietary intake surveys do not show consistent, significant differences in either quantity of calories or quality of foods consumed by different races and ethnicities, genders, or incomes, while commodity subsidies demonstrate minimal effects on caloric intake and food pricing overall. Fourth, noncaloric pathways to obesity are both frequently overlooked and disturbingly ubiquitous. They also appear to affect certain populations more than others. The fact that income, and to a lesser but related extent, race/ethnicity and gender, remains a fairly strong predictor of weight status is worthy of concern. Yet this lesson suggests that these correlations may be less about what people eat and more about chronic stress, disturbed circadian rhythms, and widespread toxic exposures, all of which have been linked to obesity. Obesity, that is, may be far less about food intake and far more about social and environmental (in)justice.

Ideally this presentation of additional and contrary evidence productively questions overly simplistic assumptions embedded in the food system perspective. It thus implicitly calls into question many of the solutions that follow from those assumptions, such as providing calorie counts on menus, building more supermarkets, or eliminating commodity crop subsidies. Despite its claims to look at the entirety of processes and institutions that bring food from farm to table, the food system perspective has been remarkably narrow in its calls to action, perhaps stemming from its close ties to the alternative food movement, which has largely focused on low-hanging fruit (see Lesson 20). Obesity, in other words, may be better treated by even deeper engagements with policy, especially policies relating to environmental toxins and income inequality, among other structural issues. Three areas of policy in particular are of utmost importance: labor rights, antitrust law, and chemical regulation. In terms of labor rights, those concerned about rising obesity rates could support legislation ensuring living wages and safe working environments, including protections for undocumented workers (see Lesson 11). Arguably, higher pay and safer jobs would reduce food insecurity, stress, and on-the-job toxic exposures, all of which have been linked to obesity. Better implementation and monitoring of antitrust laws, meanwhile, could help correct and prevent **corporate concentration** in the food system, a disturbing trend that exerts downward pressure on wages and enables powerful companies to both exploit employees and constrain consumer choice (see Lesson 7). Regarding chemical regulation, public health advocates might call for **cumulative risk assessments**, studies of toxins that explore the adverse health effects of multiple chemicals in interaction, rather than of a single chemical in isolation. Advocates could also demand that regulatory science attend to the effects of chronic, low-dose exposures experienced by nearly all US residents, rather than simply the acute, short-term poisonings modeled by most toxicology studies. Public health officials might also shift their data-gathering priorities to national **toxic body burden** rather than BMI. Citizens could simultaneously demand that the US Congress and the

Environmental Protection Agency and Food and Drug Administration adopt the **precautionary principle**, an approach that assumes chemicals are unsafe, and withholds them from the market, until proven otherwise. A focus on the policy environment would, moreover, build stronger challenges to environmental and social ills, regardless of whether they happen to manifest as fat.

Discussion Questions

1. What are the personal responsibility and food system approaches and what is missing from each perspective?
2. If scientific studies show that greater quantities of food consumed do not necessarily lead to weight gain, then what else might explain rising obesity rates?
3. Given that low-income people do not eat significantly more junk food than higher-income people, then why do you think lower-income people tend to weigh more, on average?
4. Why might it be more effective to reform chemical regulations instead of agricultural policy in an attempt to improve public health?

Exercises

1. Share examples based on your personal experiences that complicate the energy balance model.
2. Explore why focusing on people's weight, or stigmatizing certain foods, might cause more harm than good and why.

Additional Materials

Readings

Bacon, Linda, and Lucy Aphramor. 2011. "Weight Science: Evaluating the Evidence for a Paradigm Shift." *Nutrition Journal* 10(1):9.

Boero, Natalie. 2012. *Killer Fat: Media, Medicine, and Morals in the American "Obesity Epidemic."* New Brunswick, NJ: Rutgers University Press.

Gard, Michael, and Jan Wright. 2005. *The Obesity Epidemic: Science, Morality, and Ideology.* London: Routledge.

Guthman, Julie. 2011. *Weighing In: Obesity, Food Justice, and the Limits of Capitalism.* Berkeley: University of California Press.

Holtcamp, Wendee. 2012. "Obesogens: An Environmental Link to Obesity." *Environmental Health Perspectives* 120 (2): a62–68.

Kirkland, Anna Rutherford. 2008. *Fat Rights: Dilemmas of Difference and Personhood.* New York: New York University Press.

Landecker, Hannah. 2011. "Food as Exposure: Nutritional Epigenetics and the New Metabolism." *BioSocieties* 6 (2): 167–94.

LeBesco, Kathleen. 2004. *Revolting Bodies?: The Struggle to Redefine Fat Identity.* Amherst: University of Massachusetts Press.

Saguy, Abigail Cope. 2013. *What's Wrong with Fat?* New York: Oxford University Press.

References

Alkon, Alison Hope, Daniel Block, Kelly Moore, Catherine Gillis, Nicole DiNuccio, and Noel Chavez. 2013. "Foodways of the Urban Poor." *Geoforum* 48:126–35.

Archer, Edward, Diana M. Thomas, Samantha M. McDonald, Gregory Pavela, Carl J. Lavie, James O. Hill, and Steven N. Blair. 2016. "The Validity of US Nutritional Surveillance: USDA's Loss-Adjusted Food Availability Data Series 1971–2010." *Current Problems in Cardiology* 41 (11–12): 268–92.

Baillie-Hamilton, Paula F. 2002. "Chemical Toxins: A Hypothesis to Explain the Global Obesity Epidemic." *The Journal of Alternative and Complementary Medicine* 8 (2): 185–92.

Boone-Heinonen, Janne, P. Gordon-Larsen, C. I. Kiefe, J. M. Shikany, C. E. Lewis, and B. M. Popkin. 2011. "Fast Food Restaurants and Food Stores: Longitudinal Associations with Diet in Young to Middle-Aged Adults: The CARDIA Study." *Archives of Internal Medicine* 171 (13): 1162–70.

CDC. 2016. "Adult Obesity Facts | Overweight & Obesity | CDC." Accessed January 18, 2017. Last modified March 5, 2018. https://www.cdc.gov/obesity/data/adult.html

Chang, Virginia W., and Nicholas A. Christakis. 2005. "Income Inequality and Weight Status in US Metropolitan Areas." *Social Science & Medicine (1982)* 61 (1): 83–96.

Cummins, Steven, Ellen Flint, and Stephen A. Matthews. 2014. "New Neighborhood Grocery Store Increased Awareness of Food Access but Did Not Alter Dietary Habits or Obesity." *Health Affairs (Project Hope)* 33 (2): 283–91.

Davis, Cindy D. 2016. "The Gut Microbiome and Its Role in Obesity." *Nutrition Today* 51 (4): 167–74.

de Oliveira, Carla, V. L. Scarabelot, A. de Souza, C. M. de Oliveira, L. F. Medeiros, I. C. De Macedo, P. R. Marques Filho, S. G. Cioata, W. Caumo, and I. L. Torres. 2014. "Obesity and Chronic Stress Are Able to Desynchronize the Temporal Pattern of Serum Levels of Leptin and Triglycerides." *Peptides* 51:46–53.

Fändriks, L. 2016. "Roles of the Gut in the Metabolic Syndrome: An Overview." *Journal of Internal Medicine* 281 (4): 319–36.

Flegal, Katherine M., Barry I. Graubard, David F. Williamson, and Mitchell H. Gail. 2005. "Excess Deaths Associated with Underweight, Overweight, and Obesity." *JAMA* 293 (15): 1861–67.

Flegal, Katherine M., Barry I. Graubard, David F. Williamson, and Mitchell H. Gail. 2007. "Cause-Specific Excess Deaths Associated with Underweight, Overweight, and Obesity." *JAMA* 298 (17): 2028–37.

Gard, Michael, and Jan Wright. 2005. *The Obesity Epidemic: Science, Morality, and Ideology.* London: Routledge.

Giskes, K., F. van Lenthe, M. Avendano-Pabon, and J. Brug. 2011. "A Systematic Review of Environmental Factors and Obesogenic Dietary Intakes among Adults: Are We Getting Closer to Understanding Obesogenic Environments?" *Obesity Reviews: An Official Journal of the International Association for the Study of Obesity* 12 (5): e95–106.

Hatori, Megumi, C. Vollmers, A. Zarrinpar, L. DiTacchio, E. A. Bushong, S. Gill, M. Leblanc, et al. 2012. "Time-Restricted Feeding without Reducing Caloric Intake Prevents Metabolic Diseases in Mice Fed a High-Fat Diet." *Cell Metabolism* 15 (6): 848–60.

Holtcamp, Wendee. 2012. "Obesogens: An Environmental Link to Obesity." *Environmental Health Perspectives* 120 (2): a62–68.

Incollingo Rodriguez, Angela C., E. S. Epel, M. L. White, E. C. Standen, J. R. Secki, and A. J. Tomiyama. 2015. "Hypothalamic–Pituitary–Adrenal Axis Dysregulation and Cortisol Activity in Obesity: A Systematic Review." *Psychoneuroendocrinology* 62:301–18.

Lemas, Dominick J., Shanique Yee, Nicole Cacho, Darci Miller, Michelle Cardel, Matthew Gurka, David Janicke, and Elizabeth Shenkman. 2016. "Exploring the Contribution of Maternal Antibiotics and Breastfeeding to Development of the Infant Microbiome and Pediatric Obesity." *Seminars in Fetal and Neonatal Medicine* 21 (6): 406–9.

Lustig, Robert H., Laura A. Schmidt, and Claire D. Brindis. 2012. "Public Health: The Toxic Truth about Sugar." *Nature* 482 (7383): 27–29.

Mackenbach, Joreintje D., Harry Rutter, Sofie Compernolle, Ketevan Glonti, Jean-Michel Oppert, Helene Charreire, Ilse De Bourdeaudhuij, Johannes Burg, Giel Nijpels, and Jeroen Lakerveld. 2014. "Obesogenic Environments: A Systematic Review of the Association between the Physical Environment and Adult Weight Status, the SPOTLIGHT Project." *BMC Public Health* 14:233.

Mello, Carolina S., Mirian S. Carmo-Rodrigues, Humberto B. A. Filho, Ligia C. F. L. Melli, Soraia Tahan, Antônio C. C. Pignatari, and Mauro B. de Morais. 2016. "Gut Microbiota Differences in Children from Distinct Socioeconomic Levels Living in the Same Urban Area in Brazil." *Journal of Pediatric Gastroenterology and Nutrition* 63 (5): 460–65.

Miller, Gregory E, Phillip A. Engen, Patrick M. Gillevet, Maliha Shaikh, Masoumeh Sikaroodi, Christopher B. Forsyth, Ece Mutlu, and Ali Keshavarzian. 2016. "Lower Neighborhood Socioeconomic Status Associated with Reduced Diversity of the Colonic Microbiota in Healthy Adults." *PloS One* 11(2):e0148952.

Mokdad, Ali H., James S. Marks, Donna F. Stroup, and Julie L. Gerberding. 2004. "Actual Causes of Death in the United States, 2000." *JAMA* 291 (10): 1238–45.

Newbold, Retha R., Elizabeth Padilla-Banks, Wendy N. Jefferson, and Jerrold J. Heindel. 2008. "Effects of Endocrine Disruptors on Obesity." *International Journal of Andrology* 31 (2): 201–8.

Ng, Shu Wen, Meghan M. Slining, and Barry M. Popkin. 2014. "Turning Point for US Diets? Recessionary Effects or Behavioral Shifts in Foods Purchased and Consumed." *The American Journal of Clinical Nutrition* 99 (3): 609–16.

Rickard, Bradley J., Abigail M. Okrent, and Julian M. Alston. 2013. "How Have Agricultural Policies Influenced Caloric Consumption in the United States?" *Health Economics* 22 (3): 316–39.

Short, Anne, Julie Guthman, and Samuel Raskin. 2007. "Food Deserts, Oases, or Mirages?: Small Markets and Community Food Security in the San Francisco Bay Area." *Journal of Planning Education and Research* 26 (3): 352–64.

Stern, Dalia, J. M. Poti, S. W. Ng, W. R. Robinson, P. Gordon-Larsen, and B. M. Popkin. 2016. "Where People Shop Is Not Associated with the Nutrient Quality of Packaged Foods for Any Racial-Ethnic Group in the United States." *The American Journal of Clinical Nutrition* 103 (4): 1125–34.

Thayer, Zaneta M., and Christopher W. Kuzawa. 2011. "Biological Memories of Past Environments: Epigenetic Pathways to Health Disparities." *Epigenetics* 6 (7): 798–803.

USDA ARS (US Department of Agriculture, Agricultural Research Service). 2016. "WWEIA Data Tables : USDA ARS." Accessed January 28, 2017. https://www.ars.usda.gov/northeast-area/beltsville-md/beltsville-human-nutrition-research-center/food-surveys-research-group/docs/wweia-data-tables/

USDA ERS (US Department of Agriculture, Economic Research Service). 2017a. "USDA ERS—Food Access Research Atlas." Accessed January 28, 2017. Last modified May 18, 2017. https://www.ers.usda.gov/data-products/food-access-research-atlas/

USDA ERS (US Department of Agriculture, Economic Research Service). 2017b. "USDA ERS—Share of Household Spending Devoted to Food and Calorie Availability Vary by Country." Accessed February 11, 2017. Last modified February 10, 2017. https://www.ers.usda.gov/data-products/chart-gallery/gallery/chart-detail/?chartId=82368

Wellen, Kathryn E., and Gökhan S. Hotamisligil. 2005. "Inflammation, Stress, and Diabetes." *Journal of Clinical Investigation* 115 (5): 1111–19.

FOOD, JUSTICE, AND SUSTAINABILITY

Organic produce at the supermarket. (Photo © Daylen / Wikimedia Commons / CC BY 4.0.)

15

Organics

Brian K. Obach

Y ou have probably seen products labeled *organic*. If you are like most Americans you have probably eaten at least some organic goods as well. In the United States today most of these products include a green and white USDA seal indicating official approval by the federal government. But what does organic mean? The definition of **organic** has evolved over several decades and the particulars of what constitutes organic methods have been debated throughout. Even today, some would say that the organic seal represents the highest standard of healthy sustainable agricultural practices, while others would argue that it is an essentially meaningless marketing term. The place of organic agriculture in our society has also changed dramatically. Once the province of fringe countercultural radicals seeking to subvert the dominant social order, today organic is accepted by the most powerful institutions, from the federal government to multinational corporations. This lesson will trace the evolution of organic and consider some of the debates that continue to shape the social meaning of this agricultural practice.

WHAT IS ORGANIC?

Until recently, most farms were small, and farmers relied primarily on natural inputs produced on the farm itself. But as you read in Lesson 5, over the past 150 years, technologies were continuously introduced that revolutionized the way farming is done. New machinery was adopted, synthetic pesticides and fertilizers were brought to the farm, and hybrid seeds and biotechnology transformed the plants themselves. Most food today is the product of large-scale industrial-style agriculture that bears little resemblance to farms of the past. Many considered these technologies key to feeding a growing population and to human progress generally. But some saw social and environmental problems arising from these new methods. It was in this context that critics of industrial farming technologies consciously sought to define natural methods of growing. This is what came to be called organic farming (Conford 2001).

Farming, by its very essence, involves human manipulation of the natural environment, but organic proponents have always sought to identify methods that more closely mimic natural processes. The specific practices that define organic growing continue to evolve through deliberative and, at times, politically charged processes. It is not surprising that the precise meaning of organic remains elusive. What defines a "natural" farming technique is open to vastly different interpretations. That definition is currently encoded in US law and through international agreements. For a product to be labeled organic in the United States today, it must be certified as meeting the requirements specified by the US Department of Agriculture's **National Organic Program** (NOP). But not everyone agrees with the current rules regarding acceptable organic practices. Many are highly critical of the NOP and believe that the organic sector today is radically different from what early proponents envisioned.

THE DEVELOPMENT OF THE ORGANIC SYSTEM

Organic Pioneers

Understanding the controversies surrounding organic today requires that we consider how the idea came about and how it evolved over time. Concerted efforts to promote a more natural approach to farming began in Europe in the early 1900s. Rudolf Steiner was a prolific Austrian philosopher and author who advocated for farming methods that he considered more consistent with the natural order. He opposed the use of synthetic pesticides and fertilizers and focused on the farm as a self-contained organic unit. Steiner's approach to farming came to be known as **biodynamic agriculture** and some still utilize these methods today.

Another early advocate of natural farming methods was Albert Howard, a British agriculture scientist who, through observing peasant farmers in India, learned that soil could remain productive indefinitely with natural inputs that preserved complex microbial processes. His Indore method of **composting** (named for the region of India where he studied) serves as a basis for much organic agriculture today. Lady Eve Balfour was another important figure in organic history. An enthusiastic proponent of natural farming, she founded the Soil Association in 1946, which is still the most important organic organization in Britain.

The United States found its organic champion in Jerome Irving Rodale, an entrepreneur and publisher. Rodale, whose magazines focused on science and health, became captivated by the potential health benefits of food grown using natural techniques. In 1942 he launched a new publication, *Organic Farming and Gardening*, dedicated to spreading the ideas of Howard, Steiner, and other organic pioneers. At around the same time he founded the Soil and Health Foundation, which would later become the Rodale Institute, a major organic research organization still in operation.

Rodale's publications developed a following among gardeners and some small farmers who were wary of the new technologies and the synthetic fertilizers and pesticides increasingly used in commercial farming. *Organic Farming and Gardening* served as a forum for discussion and debate as advocates of natural growing sought to identify best practices and where boundaries should be drawn between conventional and organic methods.

Although Rodale developed a following through his publications, organic remained on the margins for several decades. Establishment agricultural scientists and nutritionists looked on it with scorn. They considered it a backward-looking devolution advanced by hucksters and quacks opposed to scientific progress. Organic remained largely unknown to most consumers caught up in the onslaught of new processed convenience foods entering the market in years following World War II.

Growth and Organization

While some questioned the virtues of industrial agriculture from the start, it was not until the late 1960s that the concept of organic attracted a more significant following. Counterculture radicals who challenged nearly every aspect of conventional society latched on to the oppositional message implicit in organic philosophy. Activists opposed to the Vietnam War and supportive of civil rights and black liberation struggles questioned everything touted by big business and dominant political and social institutions, including how food should be produced. Organic was especially attractive to members of that segment of the counterculture movement who sought to drop out of conventional society and seek an alternative, more natural way of life. Participants in this **back-to-the-land movement** created communal farms in the countryside and adopted organic growing methods (Balasco 2006).

Most of these communes did not survive long. However, some participants continued with organic farming. Others who remained committed to their countercultural ideals established food coops or opened natural food stores or restaurants. This was an effort to undermine dominant institutions by creating an alternative economic order that participants hoped would ultimately displace industrial capitalism. During the 1970s this network provided an outlet for organically grown goods, but organics remained well outside of the mainstream.

It was at this time that organic farmers began to organize among themselves to share knowledge. They could not count on support from government and university-based agricultural extension agencies that were firmly committed to industrial farming. They were likewise shunned by most in the conventional farming community, where there was considerable distrust between mainstream growers and these *hippie farmers*. Thus new organizations such as California Certified Organic Farmers, Oregon Tilth, and the Maine Organic Farmers and Gardeners Association served as a means of providing mutual support. Similar developments were occurring in Europe. In a broader effort to bring coordination and coherence to organic practices there, the International Federation of Organic Movements was established in 1972 (Obach 2015).

It was through these associations that participants began the process of formally defining organic growing practices and developing **organic certification** systems to distinguish products grown according to these methods. But because these organic associations were spread out across the country and not very connected to one another, they each developed their own definitions and procedures. By 1975 there were eleven organic associations offering certification based on their own unique set of guidelines (Treadwell, McKinney, and Creamer 2003). This would prove to be important to understanding some of the controversies associated with the creation of a national organic system decades later.

Organic farmers were organizing and seeking to formalize the organic system in part to defend themselves against persistent attacks from dominant agriculture interests and their political representatives. Nutritionists, food scientists, and others invested in the conventional food system routinely denounced organic as a meaningless hoax. Earl Butz, the secretary of agriculture under President Richard Nixon, was an outspoken proponent of industrial agriculture. He claimed that the adoption of organic methods would lead to mass starvation as only conventional agriculture could produce the quantity of food necessary to feed a growing population (Duscha 1972).

By creating formal associations, organic farmers were better able to promote their products and to defend their farming methods against attacks from conventional food interests. But the fact that these associations were not unified behind a single definition of organic practices inhibited further expansion of organic sales. The confusing and contradictory standards used in different parts of the country inhibited the development of a national organic market. This was not necessarily a problem for many small growers. They primarily sold their products locally where consumers were familiar with the associations that certified organic farms in their region. Yet during the 1980s organic had slowly gained popularity beyond the counterculture followers that had served as the initial customer base. Some entrepreneurs recognized the potential for expanding beyond locally oriented fresh whole foods that made up most organic sales. Processed items like granola or salsa also had appeal to the growing number of organic consumers. Yet these products required several ingredients that may have to be grown in different parts of the country. Because varying organic standards were used in different parts of the country, no regional organic association would certify the finished product if it contained ingredients that did not meet their own particular requirements. Thus it was very difficult to obtain organic certification for any product except whole foods, like fresh fruits and vegetables, that were produced for local sale. The decentralized, regionally operated organic system limited organic market growth.

Some attempts were made to coordinate the disparate private regional organic associations and develop a unified national system, but none was successful. While these efforts failed, problems within the organic system intensified. Some began to advocate for the federal government to implement consistent, enforceable standards nationwide. While some believed in the need for national coordination, the notion of federal government control over the organic system clashed with the antiestablishment sentiments still held by many organic farmers. After all, the federal government had a long history of hostility to the organic sector, so involving them in organic governance could undermine the whole system. Nonetheless, during the late 1980s several incidents intensified the call for federal oversight.

The Turn to Federal Control: The Organic Foods Production Act

Perhaps the biggest problem associated with the lack of a single legal standard to define organic was that it created opportunities for fraud. With no legally enforceable standard definition, there was no way to prevent unscrupulous operators from falsely claiming that their product was organic and cashing in on the price premium that organic consumers were willing to pay. Organic farmers in California had already uncovered cases of fraud and they were pressuring their state government to enact enforceable rules. But one major incident made bogus organic labeling even more tempting to fraudulent actors.

Food scares always drew more customers into the organic market. Outbreaks of food-borne illness would attract more people seeking a safer alternative to the conventional food system. In addition, synthetic ingredients used in food production would occasionally be found to be carcinogenic, driving even more people to seek a more natural alternative. One such finding drove interest in organic through the roof. In 1989 the Natural Resources Defense Council, an environmental organization, released a study suggesting that Alar, a chemical commonly used on apples, caused cancer. Reports of this finding on the popular television news magazine *60 Minutes* set off a "panic for organic" (Shapiro and Wright 1989). It came as a shock to many that apples, long touted as a natural way to keep the doctor away, might actually be poisonous because of the chemicals used on them. Anxious consumers sent organic sales soaring. Given the increased demand, prices rose and this heightened concerns that opportunists would take advantage of the vague definitions and the weakness of organic oversight to cash in on this lucrative new market.

Consumer groups were already pressuring members of Congress to clarify organic standards, but following the Alar scare, the need for federal oversight of organic became clear. It appeared that federal officials would take action with or without the involvement of organic farmers or others from the organic community. Despite reluctance on the part of many, some organic leaders began working with congressional representatives to craft federal organic legislation (Merrigan 2000).

Developing the legislation was a complicated process that involved much negotiation. Organic representatives from associations around the country worked with legislators to consider how to standardize the diverse rules and practices that they had in place regionally and to agree on a plan for federal oversight. Despite continued skepticism by some organic activists, a legislative proposal was developed. In 1990, with lobbying support from national consumer and environmental organizations, the Organic Foods Production Act (OFPA) was passed into law.

Some have suggested that the passage of the OFPA was an effort on the part of big agribusiness corporations and the government to "take over" organic. Looking at the organic industry today, one could argue that this is indeed what happened. But there is little evidence to suggest that this is what was plotted from the start. Organic proponents pushed the law through over the objections of many conventional food and agriculture interests. At this point it appeared that conventional industry actors were taking a wait-and-see approach. After decades of denouncing organic as a meaningless fad, it was clear that organic products were beginning to attract the interest of mainstream consumers. Yet even with the growth in the popularity of organic, it still represented a tiny fraction of the overall food sector. In that sense, organic did not pose a threat to conventional agribusiness, especially if rules were stringent enough that organic could not feasibly expand beyond its small following. Alternatively, if rules were such that it became possible to mass produce organic goods (as would later prove to be the case), and if organic's popularity continued to grow (as it did), then agribusiness may be able to profit from the new market. But even after the passage of the OFPA, the direction it would go was unclear. There was still a great deal to be resolved. The legislation provided only the general guidelines for how the organic system was to operate, but specific policies would need to be developed.

CONTROVERSIES IN ORGANIC LAW AND POLICY

The creation of the specific rules for organic agriculture proved to be highly contentious. Ironically, the OFPA placed the new NOP under the authority of the US Department of Agriculture, a federal government department where many officials were still very opposed to organic. It took several years and there were many conflicts between the organic community and federal authorities as they hammered out the nuts and bolts of what the rules for organic should be. The biggest battle occurred in 1997 when the USDA proposed a set of rules that was very different from what organic proponents had sought. The USDA's draft proposal included allowances for food irradiation, genetically modified organisms, and the use of sewage sludge as fertilizer, practices that directly contradicted traditional understandings of organic. These major points of contention came to be called the Big Three (Obach 2015). This set off a wave of protest from the organic community. Over 275,000 comments were submitted to the USDA protesting their flawed proposal, a record number in the history of the department. In the face of this firestorm, the draft was withdrawn and a revised version, minus the Big Three, was released later. This new set of rules was ultimately adopted. By 2002, twelve years after the passage of the OFPA, the NOP was finally up and running.

Political battles over the organic rules did not end with the implementation of the NOP. A rift was emerging between traditional organic proponents and organic businesses that were growing in size and influence. Following the fight over the Big Three, organic activists recognized the need to be more organized and politically engaged. The Organic Trade Association was now serving as the primary voice for the increasingly powerful organic food businesses. The regional organic farming associations stepped up advocacy on behalf of small organic farmers. A consumer watchdog, the Organic Consumers Association, had formed following the Big Three battle, and this group became very politically engaged using an aggressive style rare among organic proponents. The seeds of internal conflict were already growing, but all these groups were still coordinating under a loose coalition called the National Campaign for Sustainable Agriculture. Yet this tentative unity was soon to fracture.

This kind of organization and formalization is common as grassroots movements mature into established political pressure groups. But it also creates the potential for more explicit internal division, differences that can be glossed over when a movement is still developing formal positions and political tactics. The fact that the organic sector was rapidly changing also created fertile ground for conflict to emerge. Tensions between traditional small organic farmers and the rapidly growing organic food industry had been building. This reached a peak soon after the NOP went into effect when a conflict emerged over the question of synthetic ingredients in processed organic foods.

The organic law made certain allowances for the limited use of some synthetic materials in organic *farming*, but the use of synthetic ingredients in organic *food* was explicitly prohibited. At the time that the law was being crafted, the organic market consisted almost exclusively of fresh produce. Few had given extensive consideration to processed goods. Organic proponents assumed that there would be no synthetic ingredients in *any* finished product; thus the clause was included in the law.

On the surface, the prohibition of synthetic ingredients seemed obvious and appropriate. But on closer examination, even committed organic advocates recognized that there were circumstances under which certain synthetic ingredients should be allowed. For example, baking powder is a synthetic product, but it had long been used in organic baked goods. It was widely accepted and never questioned. This seemed like grounds for making an exception to the total ban on synthetic ingredients. But then it became clear that there were other grounds on which exceptions should be made. In some instances a key ingredient may not be available in organic form simply because of the slow development of the market for certain products. It made sense to many that there should be a limited number of short-term exceptions made, similar to the allowances recognized for the use of some synthetic inputs in organic farming. In light of this, a list of exceptions for allowable synthetic ingredients and a policy for adding and removing ingredients from the list was created.

There was some flexibility already built into the organic law. The law specified that to bear the USDA Organic label, products would have to be made with at least 95 percent organic ingredients. Other ingredients did not have to be organically grown, provided they were not explicitly prohibited. If a product was made with at least 70 percent organically grown ingredients, it could not bear the USDA seal, but it could be labeled "Made with Organic Ingredients."

While the law included these labeling provisions and allowed for some nonorganically produced content in organic products, it explicitly did not allow for synthetic ingredients. The addition of the list of synthetic ingredient exceptions therefore violated this provision of the law, resulting in a lawsuit brought by an organic blueberry farmer from Maine. Many small organic farmers and some organic associations supported the lawsuit and saw it as an opportunity to rethink the general direction of the organic industry; should it allow for the highly processed goods that were already appearing on the market? Or should organic be limited to fresh produce grown by small farms as was the traditional vision? That question was put to rest when big companies involved in processed organic products succeeded in getting the law changed to officially allow those exceptional synthetic ingredients. With that legal change, the future direction of the organic sector became clear. It was no longer under the control of small organic farmer groups. Big companies would be playing an increasingly important role.

ORGANIC MOVEMENT VERSUS ORGANIC INDUSTRY

The organic sector has undergone significant changes since its adoption by counterculture activists intent on transforming the food and agriculture system. There is deep tension between those involved in the "organic industry" and those who still consider themselves part of the "organic movement." While changes in the organic sector were already underway in the 1980s and 1990s owing to its growing popularity among consumers, the establishment of the NOP provided a legitimacy and a structure that ushered in a torrent of conventional agribusiness involvement (Howard 2009). Some organic companies, started by small, ideologically committed entrepreneurs, had already grown into multi-million-dollar enterprises by the 1990s, but once the NOP was in effect, conventional food corporations wanted in on this increasingly profitable sector. Large natural food retailers like Whole Foods had already proved to be highly successful, putting competitive pressure on small independent organic retailers and the few remaining food coops. Conventional supermarkets then began stocking more organic items and even big-box stores like Walmart and Target started carrying organic products.

Agribusiness corporations like General Mills and Dean Foods also added new divisions specializing in organic goods, what some have come to call Big Organic. They quietly began buying up the most successful independent organic companies, leaving many consumers unaware that they were now purchasing their favorite organic products from multinational corporations (see Lesson 7). These conventional operators usually retained the original brand names or used folksy packaging and images of red barns and green fields to foster the idea that products were still produced by a small farmer down the street. But international distribution systems replaced the alternative networks that had developed among organic farmers, food coops, and other independent sellers.

Organic farming itself also underwent a transformation. With greater demand and conventional agribusiness involvement came dramatic changes in growing practices. Conventional farmers converting some of their land to organic production may be following the letter of the law, but many of these new organic operations bear little resemblance to those created by the natural farming pioneers in terms of scale and the technologies used. This has been referred to as the *conventionalization* of organic (Guthman 2004).

The fact that much of organic law focuses on farming inputs and food ingredients makes superimposing conventional practices over the organic sector relatively easy. Movement founders envisioned small farms growing a diversity of crops and raising livestock such that on-farm composting would generate the fertilizer necessary to create a closed-loop system, a farm that was a sustainable organic whole. Yet when organic philosophy had to be codified into law, the holistic practice of organic growing was reduced to input considerations. Growers not ideologically committed to using sustainable practices could easily forgo composting all together and simply purchase allowable organic material shipped in from anywhere in the world to fertilize large-scale monoculture crops. Products can then be shipped to big distributors and food processors who can exploit exceptions to the ingredient rules to make highly processed goods, which are then sold around the world, mirroring the conventional food system in nearly every way, save the nature of some of the materials used.

These conventionalized organic practices have become dominant. Big Organic now controls much of the market. Today, over 90 percent of organic sales occur at the supermarket or in big-box stores, not at the food coop or farmers market. The number of very small organic farms has continued to grow, but their numbers pale in comparison to the organic acreage now operating under the control of large agribusiness corporations. Most organic growing is not done by ideologically committed small farmers, but by large conventional growers who have converted a portion of their land to organic production to sell to big food corporations. Small-scale, ideologically committed "movement" farmers and other organic activists are oftentimes hostile toward the big industry players. Grassroots groups like the Organic Consumers Association and the Cornucopia Institute regularly call for boycotts of corporate organic brands that they believe are not living up to organic ideals.

Conflicts regularly erupt over additions to the national list of allowable synthetic ingredients. Representatives of Big Organic typically seek to add more exceptions, while those representing traditional organic groups like the National Organic Coalition oppose a further loosening of the rules. Activists have been successful at holding the line in some instances. For example, given that livestock was not a big part of organic production when the law was originally crafted, corporate dairy operations were taking advantage of legal ambiguities to operate large animal confinement operations, a practice antithetical to traditional notions of organic. Using lawsuits and consumer pressure, activists were able to clarify livestock rules to require that animals have access to pasture and that they primarily receive a natural organic diet. But even in victory, activists face an ongoing struggle to maintain organic integrity within the NOP. With regard to dairy cows, it is estimated that half of the organic milk sold still comes from large industrial dairy operations. While required to provide regular pasture access, remaining rule ambiguities and lax enforcement allow Big Organic dairy operators to engage in practices that do not approach the vision presented by early organic proponents.

These debates about particular organic rules are tied to larger disagreements about social change. Some have accepted the involvement of large corporations in the organic sector. They see this as a means of making organic accessible to a broader population. The resources and economies of scale that big firms are able to bring to the organic sector help to lower prices and make organic goods more affordable to low-income communities. They argue that most shoppers are not going to the food coop or to Whole Foods; they are shopping at Walmart. And if Walmart can provide people with organic goods, that is something to be applauded. Likewise, most people do not simply eat fresh produce and whole foods. Financial and time constraints in contemporary society mean that many will be eating processed prepared meals, and those committed to growing the organic market believe that some flexibility in the rules is justified to be able to provide those foods in organic form. Proponents of this approach believe that the hardliners are unrealistic in thinking that we are going to transform the entire structure of the food system. By clinging to this idealism, the purists are limiting organic to a small market of elite consumers and forgoing the environmental and social benefits of expanding organic and bringing it to a broader population.

Critics of Big Organic counter that corporate domination of the organic system is undermining the very ideas at the heart of organic philosophy (Fromartz 2007). The intent was not to simply reproduce the conventional food system with a few different materials. A healthy and ecologically sustainable system was always the goal. The ecological benefits of organic farming are undermined if growers are importing large quantities of inputs, even if they are sourced organically instead of being synthesized. Large-scale monocultures harm biodiversity and require that growers use even more of those off-farm inputs to maintain soil fertility. Movement farmers argue that the original focus of organic on the health of the soil is being lost, as are the health benefits to consumers. Scientific research has yielded some conflicting evidence about the overall nutritional benefits of eating organic. Some studies have found that organically grown goods are more nutritious, while others have found no differences in nutrient levels between organic and conventionally grown goods. Yet, a few things are clear. Eating organic reduces the amount of potentially harmful synthetic chemicals in the human body. The effects of agricultural chemical residues and other synthetic substances used in conventional food are not fully known, and many health experts say it is best to avoid them. While the overall nutritional benefits of organic remain in dispute, certain nutrients have been found to be more abundant in organic produce. But it is also well known that fresh whole foods are more nutritious. Activists argue that we should retain the original ideal of building a truly alternative food system based primarily on fresh healthy local foods, not highly processed goods and produce shipped from around the world. Environmental protection is also advanced not simply by using fewer synthetic pesticides and fertilizers, but also by supporting small diverse farms that protect the soil and water, enhance biodiversity, and reduce "food miles." These debates about the environmental, health, and social implications of the changes in the organic sector continue to rage. In the meantime, those still seeking to improve the system of food and agriculture have adopted a range of strategies.

THE FUTURE OF THE ORGANIC MOVEMENT(S)

The initial development of the NOP is what brought organic proponents from around the country together for the first time. It unified what was a highly decentralized movement. But the creation of this program and the subsequent development of the organic industry have fostered a splintering within the organic community. While there is much overlap and some mutual support, those still committed to advancing a more sustainable food and agriculture system have adopted three discernable approaches: (1) defending the integrity of the NOP, (2) creating independent certification and labeling systems separate from the NOP, and (3) local food advocacy.

Many organic activists have remained focused on the NOP. Groups like the National Organic Coalition, the Organic Consumers Association, and many of the regional organic farming associations concentrate much of their effort on ensuring that official NOP rules reflect traditional organic ideals. While often assuming different positions, representatives of corporations involved in the organic sector are also very engaged with the NOP rule-making process. Although corporate players are clearly seeking to ensure profitability, not everyone affiliated with big business is completely lacking in the commitment to organic principles. Many involved in Big Organic see true environmental and health benefits, and they believe that their pragmatic approach will maximize these improvements in the food industry (Haedicke 2016).

While some remain committed to the NOP, another segment of the movement has focused on creating alternative certification and labeling programs that they believe better advance traditional organic ideals. For example, Certified Naturally Grown is an alternative labeling system that operates similar to organic prior to federal government involvement. Here farmers are organized in networks whereby they inspect one another's production methods instead of relying on federally accredited certifiers. The farming techniques that they use largely reflect organic growing practices,[1] but the system is geared toward small farmers serving a local market. It reduces the paperwork and fees that are required in the NOP, costs and work that many small farmers find objectionable and burdensome. Some long-standing organic advocates have also sought to use new certification schemes to push the industry "beyond organic." The Rodale Institute has developed a Regenerative Organic label that requires growers to meet a host of standards reflective of traditional organic ideals, but not captured by the USDA program.

The organic movement pioneered the use of market-based certification and labeling to try to reform an industry. Since organic paved the way, numerous reformers have adopted the use of certification and labeling schemes (Conroy 2007). Some, like Certified Naturally Grown and Regenerative Organic, were developed directly in response to the perceived shortcomings of the NOP. Other certification and labeling systems address a wide range of practices and products. Today one can find labels such as bird friendly, grass fed, free range, genetically modified organism free, rainforest certified, and dozens of others.

One effort designed to address a major shortcoming of organic rules has to do with worker protections. Nothing in organic law or policy addresses labor issues. There is a well-established fair trade certification and labeling system designed for imported goods (see Lesson 16), but some organic proponents have been active in efforts to create a domestic fair trade system to ensure that farmworkers on organic farms are justly compensated and well treated. Studies have found that farmworkers in the organic sector endure conditions no better than those on conventional farms (Shreck, Getz and Feenstra 2005; see Lesson 11). Organic farm laborers do avoid exposure to some of the most hazardous synthetic chemicals, but aside from some of the smaller organic farms run by ideologically committed farmers, working conditions for farmworkers are poor across the board. The Domestic Fair Trade Association was created to address this issue.

The creation of an additional monitoring system for matters of social justice in the organic sector was particularly important to some. While many consumers focus on the health and environmental benefits of organic, some activists feel that many of the broader transformative goals of the movement have been lost along the way. Aside from the absence of any worker justice provisions in organic rules, organic has at times been denounced as elitist by critics who say that organic goods are too expensive for lower-income people.

---

[1] Despite using organic growing practices, sellers are legally prohibited from calling their products organic unless they are formally certified through the NOP. An exception is made for very small farms that gross less than five thousand dollars in annual sales.

Most organic products cost less than 30 percent more than their conventional counterparts, but some can be over double in price. This can create a real barrier for low-income consumers. Many also note that low-income people often do not have access to venues where organic goods are sold. Food justice organizations, which usually address issues of racial inequality as well as class, have at times sought to make organic goods available to poor communities (Gottlieb and Joshi 2010; also see Lesson 20). But the food justice movement developed separate from the organic food movement, which is predominantly white and has largely failed to incorporate issues of race and class into their work, despite its early ties to social justice movements. Some conceive of organic as a means to aid small farmers, but justice for farmworkers and low-income consumers has not received nearly as much attention. The Domestic Fair Trade Association is one example of how sustainable agriculture activists are seeking to address social justice issues outside the organic system.

In addition to those who have pursued alternative certification and labeling schemes and those who remain committed to improving the NOP, a third trajectory of sustainable agriculture activism can be found in the **local food movement** (see Lesson 17). Although some elements of local food advocacy, such as the slow food movement that originated in Europe, can be traced back to the 1980s, these were mostly geared toward promoting and preserving regional food traditions in the face of increasing globalization. The local food movement that we see in the United States today developed largely in response to the perceived shortcomings of organic under the NOP.

As described earlier, historically, organic food for the most part meant local food. Organic farmers were almost exclusively distributing their fresh whole foods in local markets. Issues of farm size, ownership, and food processing were given little consideration when developing organic policy, because originally the entire organic sector reflected the independent local small farm ideal. Yet when codification of organic practices under the NOP allowed large corporations to capture the bulk of the market, many consumers and sustainable farming advocates shifted their attention. Prominent food writers, such as Michael Pollan, began advocating for a focus on local (Pollan 2006). Local food proponents touted the benefits of reconnecting to the land, to farms, and to farmers, fostering a sense of community not found in supermarkets or big-box stores (Lyson 2004; Obach and Tobin 2014). Seasonal eating creates a sense of place, while yielding ecological benefits through the reduction of food miles, the distance that food is shipped from farm to plate. Similar to organic at its origins, this movement is largely decentralized and not formally organized. It manifests itself in the growth in things such as farmers' markets, which have experienced a fourfold increase in the past twenty years. Interest in local food can also be seen in conventional supermarkets that commonly note when a product is locally grown and in the boom in *farm-to-table* restaurants that promote their locally sourced fare.

Community-supported agriculture (CSA) programs are another development that reflects a new focus on local food (Schnell 2007). These CSAs vary in their specific procedures, but most allow consumers to purchase a seasonal share in a local farm. Members pay one price at the start of the season and then pick up or have delivered a package of fresh produce on a weekly basis. Some CSAs also distribute meat and dairy products. The up-front payment allows small farmers to avoid loans for startup costs. It also distributes the risk among all the shareholders in the face of a bad growing season, thus helping to save local farmers from bankruptcy.

Interest in local food among consumers corresponds to the growth in the number of very small farms catering to a local market. The producers operating CSAs and distributing through farmers markets are more likely to be new to farming. Small local growers tend to be younger and are more likely to be female, relative to the male-dominated conventional farming sector. These farmers often use sustainable growing practices, although many are not formally certified organic.

Conclusion
Organic is now a $49 billion industry in the United States. Over five million acres of farm and pastureland are now certified organic. Over 80 percent of consumers report purchasing at least some organic goods. Every mainstream institution, from multinational corporations to universities and agricultural research organizations, is now invested in the organic enterprise. By most measures this would be considered an immense success. But these gains must be put in perspective. Organic still represents less than 5 percent of total food and beverage sales. In terms of acreage, it is less than 1 percent of total farmland. The broader transformation of the food and agriculture system that organic proponents sought remains a distant dream. The environmental and health benefits that organic has to offer, while still significant, have been undermined by the conventionalization of the organic farming and food industries. In itself, the gains of the organic movement have been limited. But these sustainable farming activists have spurred new efforts.

Alternative or additive certification and labeling schemes may help to advance some of the issues left unaddressed in the official organic system. But some express concern about consumer confusion and fraud as shoppers are inundated with a plethora of vague or unverifiable label claims (Consumers Union 2013). The attention to local food has brought focus back to the preservation of small farms. But unless consumers also insist on organic certification or have true intimate knowledge of farm practices, there is no guarantee that local farms will perform better environmentally. Food miles may be reduced, but this is one small part of the overall ecological footprint of our food. All the while, social justice concerns, once central to the vision of countercultural organic proponents, receive relatively little attention from organic advocates or the various offshoots of the movement.

Organic production, as originally envisioned, offers great promise for a more sustainable farming and food system. It also incorporates social and health benefits. Yet as evidenced by the small size of the organic sector relative to the whole of the food and agriculture industry, the strategies used to advance this vision have come up short. Several analysts attribute this short-coming to the market-based social change approach adopted by organic proponents as opposed to more traditional state-centered politics (Guthman 2004; Obach 2007).

The fundamental strategy for revolutionizing the food and agriculture sector was based on the hope that more and more consumers would purchase organic goods and, in doing so, more and more producers would adopt the desired practices until we arrived at an entirely transformed system. Education and market forces alone would drive reform. Many organic proponents shunned political action or any involvement with the state. It was only out of desperation that organic leaders resorted to government oversight through the NOP, but the basic strategy remained the same. The state would be used to manage the system and guard against fraud, but activists were still relying on the market to advance the organic cause. Farmers were not being *required* to adopt sustainable practices through state mandate; the hope was that they would be *motivated* to do so out of moral conviction or by the promise of greater profitability.

The consciousness of many consumers has been raised and the organic sector has grown considerably as a result of increased consumer demand. This has drawn in farmers and producers large and small who see benefit in meeting that demand. But ultimately the profitability of organic relies on the price premium that only some consumers are willing and able to pay. It is unlikely that all but a small fraction of consumers will cease buying lower-priced conventionally produced goods all together. Thus, some producers will adopt a business model targeting the organic niche market. That market may even have some additional room for growth. But unless laws are passed that impose restrictions on ecologically damaging farming practices, or until policies that subsidize conventional growing are eliminated, organic and other more ecologically sound farming practices will likely remain marginal. Organic proponents have provided a great service in creating a vision and demonstrating that sustainable agriculture is possible. The challenge now is identifying the strategies that can make that vision a reality.

Discussion Questions

1. Do you think it is preferable to modify organic standards to bring down the costs of production and make organic goods more affordable and accessible to more people? Or is it better to maintain high standards even if it means that many will not be able to afford organic goods? Can you think of policies that could make healthy sustainable food available to all people?
2. Do you buy organic products? Why or why not?
3. What are the benefits or drawbacks of purchasing local food relative to buying organic? Do you think it is more beneficial to buy local foods that are conventionally grown or organic goods from another part of the country?

4. What are the strengths and weaknesses of market-based social change strategies such as that used by the organic movement? Could such an approach foster fundamental social change or does it inevitably give rise to a niche market with limited social or environmental impact?
5. Is it feasible to believe that organic growing methods could be mandated by law for all food producers? Why or why not? Is there other state action that could be taken to reduce the harmful ecological impacts of conventional farming? If so what are they and how could they be advanced?

Exercises

1. *Investigating the food industry.* Go to a nearby supermarket and do some browsing. First, choose an organic product and try to identify where the product was made/grown and who produced it. Second, seek out an equivalent conventionally produced product and compare prices and packaging with the organic product. What are the similarities and differences? Third, conduct web-based research to determine who makes each product. Do large agribusiness companies make them both or not? Do the same company or different ones make them? Last, which product would you choose and why?
2. *Debating organic.* Imagine that you are going to be on a television talk show panel about food. The panel consists of three representatives, an executive from a conventional food corporation, the president of a mid-sized independent organic food company, and a small organic farmer who operates a CSA. Write the opening statement/argument for each panelist as he or she seeks to persuade viewers about the benefits of their type of operation, including how each would critique his or her counterparts.

Additional Materials

Films

Food Inc. (2008), documentary on food industry

Websites

Cornucopia Institute, https://www.cornucopia.org
National Organic Coalition, http://www.nationalorganiccoalition.org
Northeast Organic Farming Association, http://www.nofa.org
Organic Consumers Association, https://www.organicconsumers.org
Organic Farming Research Foundation, http://www.ofrf.org
Organic Trade Association, https://www.ota.com
Rodale Institute, http://rodaleinstitute.org

References

Balasco, Warren James. 2006. *Appetite for Change: How the Counterculture Took on the Food Industry.* Ithaca, NY: Cornell University Press.
Conford, Philip. 2001. *The Origins of the Organic Movement.* Edinburgh: Floris Books.

Conroy, Michael E. 2007. *Branded!: How the "Certification Revolution" Is Transforming Global Corporations*. Gabriola Island, BC: New Society.

Consumers Union. 2013. "Greener Choices." Accessed December 21, 2013. http://www.greenerchoices.org/home.cfm

Duscha, Julius. 1972. "Up, Up, Up—Butz Makes Hay Down on the Farm." *New York Times*, April 16, 1972, SM34.

Fromartz, Samuel. 2007. *Organic, Inc.: Natural Foods and How They Grew*. Orlando: Harcourt.

Gottlieb, Robert, and Anupama Joshi. 2010. *Food Justice*. Cambridge, MA: MIT Press.

Guthman, Julie. 2004. *Agrarian Dreams: The Paradox of Organic Farming in California*. Berkeley: University of California Press.

Haedicke, Michael. 2016. *Organizing Organic: Conflict and Compromise in an Emerging Market*. Stanford, CA: Stanford University Press.

Howard, Philip. 2009. "Consolidation in the North American Organic Food Processing Sector, 1997–2007." *International Journal of Agriculture and Food* 16 (1): 13–30.

Lyson, Thomas A. 2004. *Civic Agriculture: Reconnecting Farm, Food and Community*. Medford, MA: Tufts University Press.

Merrigan, Kathleen. 2000. *Negotiating Identity within the Sustainable Agriculture Advocacy Coalition*. PhD diss., Massachusetts Institute of Technology, Department of Urban Studies and Planning.

Obach, Brian. 2007. "Theoretical Interpretations of the Growth in Organic Agriculture: Agricultural Modernization or an Organic Treadmill?" *Society and Natural Resources* 20 (3): 229–44.

Brian Obach. 2015. *Organic Struggle: The Sustainable Agriculture Movement in the United States*. Cambridge: MIT Press.

Obach, Brian, and Kathleen Tobin. 2014. "Civic Agriculture and Civic Engagement." *Agriculture and Human Values* 31 (2): 307–22.

Pollan, Michael. 2006. *The Omnivore's Dilemma: A Natural History of Four Meals*. New York: Penguin.

Shapiro, Laura and Linda Wright. 1989. "Suddenly, it's a panic for organic," *Newsweek*, March 27, 1989.

Schnell, Steven M. 2007. "Food with a Farmer's Face: Community-Supported Agriculture in the United States." *Geographical Review* 97 (4): 550–64.

Shreck, Aimee, Christy Getz, and Gail Feenstra. 2005. "Farmworkers in Organic Agriculture: Toward a Broader Notion of Sustainability." *The Newsletter of the University of California Sustainable Agriculture Research and Education Program* 17, no. 1 (Winter/Spring).

Treadwell, D.D., D.E. McKinney and N.G. Creamer. 2003. "From Philosophy to Science: A Brief History of Organic Horticulture in the United States," *Hortscience* 38, no. 5: 1009–1014.

A member of the Michiza cooperative harvesting fair trade organic coffee, Oaxaca, Mexico. (Photo by Daniel Jaffee.)

16

Fair Trade

Daniel Jaffee

Consumers in North America, Europe, and elsewhere in the global North are facing a proliferation of labels on food products that make claims about supporting fairness or justice in their production. How should we evaluate these competing and often confusing claims? Can our food and beverage consumption choices work to advance social justice in the global food system, rather than immiserating the people who work to grow and harvest the food we consume?

Fair trade, now almost thirty years old, is one important effort to address these concerns. The founding aim of **fair trade** was to remedy the unfair economic conditions faced by small-scale farmers—often called producers—in the global South who grow agricultural products that are globally traded. Fair trade is both a social movement and an alternative market system. It aims to use the structures of global markets to reverse some of the injustices they generate. In the words of the late British fair trade pioneer and author Michael Barratt Brown, fair trade works "in and against the market." This paradox helps to explain not only fair trade's successes, but also its limitations (Brown 1993). Is it possible to transform the injustices of the global market from within, or is that a contradiction in terms? What does a fair trade label really signify?

This lesson begins by discussing the dynamics behind the structural inequity in the global trade in agrifood products. We then take a brief look at fair trade's history, the basic mechanisms of the fair trade model for food products, and the current state of fair trade. Two case studies of fair trade in action will give a taste of the social benefits that participating in this alternative market can generate for producers, as well as the limits to fair trade's impact and the contradictions that can arise. We will also examine some key controversies that have caused major divisions within the fair trade movement and market. The lesson ends with some reflections on the future of fair trade and its ability to transform the global market.

STRUCTURAL UNFAIRNESS IN THE GLOBAL COMMODITY TRADE

One useful measure of the (un)fairness of world trade is the "**terms of trade**": the difference between the prices that nations receive for their exports of **primary commodities** (i.e., unprocessed or minimally processed crops or minerals, such as coffee, cacao, tea, sugar, tin, or copper) and the generally higher prices they must pay to import finished or manufactured goods. For at least the past century, these terms of trade have systematically disadvantaged nations and communities that rely on producing and exporting primary commodities. One of the most pervasive legacies of European colonization for many poor nations in the global South—which endures to the present day— is their continued dependence on the exportation of just a few food crops for a substantial share of national revenue. For example, several east African countries (including Ethiopia, Uganda, and Burundi) depend on coffee sales for over half of their total export revenues.

In the 1960s and 1970s, proponents of **dependency theory**, such as Andre Gunder Frank and Samir Amin, identified this *unequal exchange* as one of the principal mechanisms that perpetuated and deepened underdevelopment in what was then called the Third World (Amin 1976; Gunder Frank 1966). The real (inflation-adjusted) prices for these primary commodities—with the exception of oil—fell steadily through the twentieth century and into the twenty-first, a trend that still holds despite some major commodity price spikes in the past decade.

The world markets for these products are also typically dominated by a small number of very large multinational trading and processing firms (see Lesson 7). In the case of coffee, for example, the top five roasting and distribution corporations (Nestlé, Kraft, Sara Lee, Procter & Gamble, and Tchibo) control 69 percent of the global roasted coffee market. Trade policies also make it difficult for commodity producers to capture more value from their exports by processing them at home. For example, the European Union allows duty-free imports of green (unroasted) coffee, but it charges a tariff of 9 percent on imports of roasted coffee. Proponents of dependency theory viewed these patterns as a hallmark of a **neocolonial** relationship that perpetuates the extraction of cheap raw materials—and cheap labor—from the countries of the **periphery** (the South) to feed the demands of corporations and consumers in the **core** nations (the North).

Even while they have fallen over time in real terms, world commodity prices are also volatile, because they are set by traders on futures markets like the New York Coffee, Sugar, and Cocoa Exchange, based on perceived future supply levels. As I write this (in April 2018), the world price for green (unroasted) coffee is hovering around US$1.15 per pound, but in November 2016 it was over $1.80 per pound. Between 1999 and 2005, during the most severe coffee price crisis ever, it was much lower, bottoming out at 41 cents per pound in 2002, far below the break-even point for coffee farmers (see Figure 16.1). However, these numbers only tell part of the story: most small-scale coffee farmers receive only 25 to 50 percent of the world price because of the many intermediaries (e.g., buyers, processors, brokers, exporters) who take a cut along the way. In many places, small-scale producers have no alternative except to sell to local intermediaries at whatever price they are offering. The creation of fair trade was a response to these exploitative conditions.

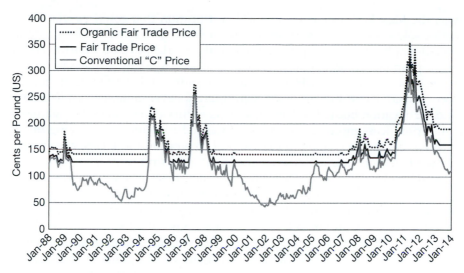

Fair trade and conventional ("C") green coffee prices, 1988–2014.

FAIR TRADE'S HISTORY AND STRUCTURE

The historical roots of fair trade contain two distinct but complementary threads. The first is a *development strand* that grew out of liberal religious charities and development groups such as Oxfam and Bread for the World, which after World War II worked to create markets for the handicraft products of refugees and other economically disadvantaged groups in Europe, the global South, and the southern United States, often organizing producer cooperatives in the process. These efforts matured into an alternative trade movement in the 1960s and 1970s, consisting of networks of *world shops* in Europe that sold clothing, crafts, and sometimes tea or coffee, and church-based organizations in the United States such as Ten Thousand Villages and SERRV. A separate *solidarity strand* arose from activist movements on the political Left beginning in the 1960s, including groups like Twin Trading in the United Kingdom, which created markets for the products of socialist states like Cuba, North Vietnam, and Mozambique that were blocked from international trade. In the mid-1980s, Equal Exchange was founded in the United States and sold Nicaraguan coffee to circumvent the US government's embargo on that country. These various initiatives were referred to as alternative trading organizations.

But it was not until 1988 that fair trade in its current form emerged. The Union of Indigenous Communities of the Isthmus Region (UCIRI), a cooperative of indigenous coffee farmers in the southern Mexican state of Oaxaca whose members were struggling with predatory intermediaries, allied with the Dutch nongovernmental organization (NGO) Solidaridad to create a bigger, fairer, more direct market for their coffee in the north. What emerged was the Max Havelaar label, a social certification that could be placed on coffee sold under any existing brand that abided by its criteria. These criteria included a higher, stable price set above the world price and partial credit or prepayment before the harvest was delivered to allow farmers to escape from debt. Sales of Max Havelaar grew rapidly and the fair trade model soon spread across Europe, with each country developing its own licensing and certification body. The basic goal was to link democratically organized small producers more directly with concerned consumers, removing many of the links in the commodity chain and freeing up more capital to be returned to the producers in the form of a higher, fairer price. Fair trade soon moved beyond coffee to include other commodities—initially tea, cocoa, and bananas and later rice, sugar, honey, wine grapes and other fruit crops, and many more products. In 1997, all of the European fair trade groups came together to create an umbrella certification body called Fairtrade Labelling Organisations International (FLO), and by 1999, fair trade certification had spread to the United States, Canada, and Japan. By this point, the bulk of fair trade sales consisted of coffee and other food products, rather than crafts and artisanal goods. A portion of fair trade sales still took place through alternative trading organizations—including nonprofit groups or worker cooperatives like Cafédirect and Divine Chocolate in Britain and Equal Exchange in the United States—but increasingly the new volumes came from a *mainstreaming* strategy, which aimed to persuade conventional retail corporations to sell fair trade-certified goods. This mainstreaming approach has led to a dramatic increase in fair trade sales, which as of 2018 have surpassed $8 billion worldwide, yet it has also sowed the seeds of the key struggles that have affected the movement over the past fifteen years.

How do consumers know that the products they are buying were produced under fair(er) conditions? Since the Max Havelaar label appeared in Europe, the fair trade movement has relied on labeling, backed by third-party (independent) certification and based on detailed standards, to attest to the social conditions of production. To place the label on their products, retail companies must meet a series of criteria. Buyers must pay a minimum price (also called the floor price) for a given commodity, which protects farmers against fluctuations in world markets, plus an additional *social premium* to fund social development projects for producers. For example, as of 2018, the minimum fair trade price for green coffee was US$1.40 per pound, plus a social premium of 20 cents per pound, totaling $1.60. If the coffee is also certified organic, an extra premium of 30 cents per pound must be added, for a total of $1.90. It is important to note that these amounts are paid to producer organizations, not directly to farmers; the costs of administration and transportation often reduce substantially the price farmers actually receive.

As fair trade expanded into products like tea and bananas, which are often grown on plantations or estates by hired laborers (but also by small producers in many places), fair trade organizations developed a second set of standards for these plantation settings, which are recognized as an arena of highly unequal, often exploitative labor relations. In this context, fair trade certification means that the social premium amount is paid into a fund to be administered by a *joint body* of workers and management for the benefit of workers. It also requires that owners must respect workers' right to form independent unions or associations and that they adhere to national labor laws, including payment of minimum wages.

However, unlike labor laws enforced by governments, fair trade certifications are created by nonprofit, civil society organizations, most of which emerged from social movements, and they are voluntary. Agrifood scholars refer to such certifications as a form of **nonstate or private regulation** (see Lesson 9). While the content of standards and the process of certification might appear to be a dry, technical matter, in the case of fair trade it has proven to be a highly contentious issue, as we will see.

THE SOCIAL IMPACT OF FAIR TRADE

First, however, let's examine whether fair trade lives up to the claims of its advocates. According to the international certifier Fairtrade International (FTI; formerly FLO), "when farmers can sell on Fairtrade terms, it provides them with a better deal and improved terms of trade. This allows them the opportunity to improve their lives and plan for their future. Fairtrade offers consumers a powerful way to reduce poverty through their every day shopping" (Fairtrade International 2016). The US certifier Fair Trade USA claims that its standards "promote safe, healthy working conditions, protect the environment, enable transparency, and empower communities to build strong, thriving businesses. When you choose products with the Fair Trade label, your day-to-day purchases can improve an entire community's day-to-day lives" (Fair Trade USA 2016).

These are big promises. To get a handle on the social impacts that fair trade markets can generate, we will take a brief look at findings from research on two case studies of fair trade in action—one involving small-scale coffee farmers and the other hired laborers on tea plantations.

Smallholder Coffee Producers in Mexico

Approximately 70 percent of the world's coffee is produced by small-scale farmers, who grow it on plots that they own or rent. In Mexico, the world's seventh-largest coffee producer, smallholders play an especially important role: 64 percent of the nation's coffee land is held by peasant and indigenous producers growing less than five hectares (twelve acres) of coffee. Moreover, two-thirds of the producers who grow less than two hectares (five acres)—almost half of all Mexican coffee farmers—are indigenous people.

My own research on fair trade examines coffee producers in the Sierra Juárez mountains of Oaxaca, Mexico's most indigenous state (Jaffee 2014). The Zapotec indigenous communities in this region, who have inhabited the same lands for over a millennium, have only cultivated coffee for about a century, and only since the 1950s has it been a significant cash crop. These communities were greatly harmed by the coffee price crash of the early 1990s and the more severe crisis of 1999–2005 when world prices hit rock bottom, families' incomes from coffee plummeted by as much as 85 percent, and many producers abandoned their coffee plots. In those years, the prices paid by fair trade buyers were much higher than those offered by the conventional market. In that context, this study aimed to answer a seemingly straightforward question: What difference does a fair trade market make? That is, what are the social, economic, and environmental benefits of fair trade for the producers who participate?

I focused on a democratic, indigenous small-producer organization called Michiza, which was founded in 1985 to escape the grip of predatory intermediaries and thus access a fairer price for its members, much like UCIRI. Michiza has approximately one thousand member households in over forty communities across the state of Oaxaca. This mixed-method study (combining ethnographic and survey research) compared two groups of households during the depths of the most recent price crisis: organized producers who were members of Michiza and sold their coffee through the international fair trade market, and unorganized families in the same villages, whose coffee was sold to *coyotes*, local intermediaries who then sold it to the conventional world coffee market.

The study's findings illustrate the complexities and contradictions that can be generated by an alternative market system. The fair trade households in Michiza received four times more *gross* income for their coffee than their nonmember neighbors because of the higher fair trade prices. However, partly because their coffee is certified organic—which requires substantially more labor (including hired labor)—their costs were much higher too. Once their expenses were taken into account, the study found that fair trade households' average *net* yearly coffee earnings were only US$230, after thousands of hours of exhausting family labor. The unorganized households, on the other hand, earned an average of $48 for their harvest—virtually nothing. However, because the Michiza members hired many of their non–fair trade neighbors to bring in their harvest, the higher incomes generated by fair trade prices were spread throughout the community, generating positive economic ripple effects.

In other areas, the benefits of fair trade were clearer. Michiza member families were significantly less indebted than the conventional households and less likely to stay in debt year after year. This was partly because fair trade's preharvest credit enabled Michiza to give its members part of their payment in advance, eliminating the need to turn to local moneylenders. I also looked at issues of hunger and food security and found that fair trade households were significantly more food secure and experienced fewer food shortages than their neighbors who were not Michiza members.

There were also important environmental benefits, mostly linked to the fact that fair trade producers must perform a series of tasks to maintain their organic coffee certification—which for Michiza is the ticket to accessing the higher prices of fair trade (because many buyers only want coffee that is both organic and fair trade certified). Michiza members are required to compost their acidic coffee pulp and to spread the finished compost on their coffee plants; they also have to build terraces to deter soil erosion and trap nutrients and organic matter. Beyond being environmentally beneficial, these practices also led to higher coffee yields than those of the non–fair trade producers. The Michiza members also applied these organic practices to their own food crops.

The qualitative part of the study also identified several less tangible, but equally important, benefits to Michiza member households. These included greater participation by women, both as heads of households making decisions about production and the use of fair trade income, and increasingly as leaders of the cooperative organization, assuming greater power over Michiza's direction. Other intangible benefits for cooperative members included acquiring education and new skills through involvement in collaborative production, leadership in the organization, and greater knowledge and transparency about the markets for their crops. A member of Michiza's leadership council expressed it this way: "The producer says, 'Well, maybe I'm not earning too much money [in fair trade] . . . but I'm learning the kinds of things I didn't have when I was a conventional producer.' They get to know more people, they know that their coffee is being sold for a certain price, and they know where it ends up, and that nobody—at least not within the cooperative—is lining their pockets with the difference. They have more information, they have come to value many things they didn't value before . . . and they say 'Well that is a profit too, right?' That is a profit" (Rigoberto Contreras, quoted in Jaffee 2014, 245).

However, fair trade does not operate within a vacuum: small-scale coffee producers in Mexico and elsewhere are impacted by broader economic and political forces affecting these regions and peasant agriculture in general, something I discuss further later. Also, since this study was completed, the coffee harvests of these Oaxacan farmers (and thus their coffee incomes) have been harmed by weather conditions linked to climate change and, more recently, by a disease known as coffee leaf rust (or *roya*), which has decimated harvests across Central America and has now spread into Mexico and South America.

Waged Tea Laborers in India and Kenya

Of the plantation crops that FTI does certify, tea is the most significant, with 123,000 waged workers. Fair trade-certified tea is produced by hired tea pickers on plantations in Asia and Africa (as well as by small farmers), with India and Kenya the dominant producers. Several researchers have studied what the hired labor model of fair trade means for these workers. Anthropologist Sarah Besky lived and worked on tea estates in the Darjeeling region of northern India, and her ethnographic research examined the struggles for social justice and labor rights that are taking place on those plantations. She found that in the case of India—unlike many other nations—wages and labor conditions are tightly regulated by the government under the Plantations Labour Act of 1951, passed shortly after independence from Britain.

The law mandates that employers provide workers with health care, education, housing, and food, and it also regulates pickers' wages; these protections are reinforced through negotiations between labor unions and estate owners (Besky 2014). According to Besky, these labor rights regulations made Darjeeling tea plantations especially attractive to buyers who were seeking fair trade-certified tea starting in the 1990s. Plantation owners must put the fair trade social premium payments into a fund to be administered by a *joint body*, composed of workers and management, for the benefit of workers. However, Besky found that many Darjeeling plantation owners were using the fair trade social premium to pay for the same worker benefits and wages that they had already been providing as required under Indian labor law for over fifty years. In other words, they did not provide any new protections or income to workers because of fair trade certification.

Sociologist Rie Makita also studied Darjeeling tea plantations and echoes some of Besky's conclusions: she found that the required fair trade joint body did not meet regularly and contained no workers, contrary to FTI standards. She also writes that while workers did receive some financial benefit from the premium funds, these were all in the form of loans, some of which came from a microcredit program personally administered by the plantation's manager (Makita 2012).

Yet there are a few counterexamples in which plantation workers receive more substantial benefits from fair trade. Fair trade wine grape plantations in South Africa, because of the country's legacy of racial apartheid, have a unique requirement that the workers must own at least 25 percent of the plantation (and receive a proportional share of profits), an arrangement that can generate more meaningful financial and labor rights benefits (Jari and Snowball 2015). Some critics argue that this co-ownership requirement should be extended to fair trade plantations in all countries.

Across fair trade plantations in all crops worldwide in 2014, the fair trade premium amount averaged a modest US $117 per worker. According to FTI, 64 percent of these premium funds were spent on housing, education, health care, and other services directly for workers, while 20 percent were spent on community-level projects (Fairtrade International 2015).

Stepping back a bit, what does the academic literature say about fair trade's overall impact on social conditions for both small farmers and waged workers? As the previous examples indicate, the picture is complex. Most fair trade scholars agree that for small-scale, organized peasant farmers, fair trade does indeed make a difference, although usually not a transformative difference. Fair trade rarely brings small-scale producers out of poverty, but it often gives them greater economic stability because of somewhat higher and less volatile prices for their crops. It can also generate important noneconomic benefits, such as better knowledge and transparency about markets and prices, lessening or ending farmers' exposure to pesticides, strengthening their independent organizations, and increased participation and social status for women. On the question of whether the plantation fair trade model (beyond only tea) can meaningfully improve livelihoods for waged workers, the verdict is less clear. Anthropologist Sarah Lyon concludes that "in its current form fair trade certification provides few identifiable advantages to waged agricultural laborers" (Lyon 2015, 159).

Overall, assessing the large body of social science literature that exists, the social and economic benefits of fair trade are much clearer and easier to identify for organized small farmers than they are for hired plantation workers, at least at the present time.

KEY CONTROVERSIES WITHIN FAIR TRADE

Since the late 1990s, several issues have generated substantial controversy among different groups of participants in fair trade. These conflicts have also highlighted the tensions between fair trade's multiple identities: as a social *movement*, as a certification *system*, and as a *market* for agrifood products.

The first major area of controversy involves the role of large agrifood corporations in the fair trade system, especially since 2000. In that year, the specialty coffee giant Starbucks—initially pushed by activist groups such as Global Exchange—started purchasing fair trade-certified coffee. Since then, many large corporations, including Dole, Nestlé, Cadbury, Walmart, McDonalds, and Dunkin' Donuts, attracted by the potential profits, started producing and/or selling some fair trade-certified products. As discussed, this mainstreaming strategy led to a dramatic increase in fair trade sales in North America, Europe, and beyond—which has translated into more income for producers. However, these large corporate players bring much greater power and a very different set of motivations to the table than the small, *movement-oriented* companies and nonprofit groups that originally founded fair trade. This raises the key question of whether the major growth achieved through conventional agrifood corporations is a sign of success for the movement, as some promoters claim, or a threat to fair trade's founding principles, as some critics assert.

The entry of these companies into fair trade was controversial partly because most were only selling very small volumes of fair trade products. For example, Nestlé—which received fair trade certification in 2005 in Great Britain for its Partners Blend coffee label—was by 2008 still only purchasing 0.25 percent of its total coffee supply under fair trade conditions (Howard and Jaffee 2013). Activists charged that Nestlé, which had been the target of a consumer boycott for over twenty years for its infant formula marketing practices in the global South, was engaged in **fairwashing**—a practice similar to greenwashing, in which corporations that sell minimal quantities of fair trade-certified goods use the *halo effect* of fair trade in their advertising and public relations to persuade consumers that they are socially responsible. Put another way, should companies with documented histories of problematic labor, human rights, or environmental practices be allowed to burnish their corporate images with the fair trade seal? If the answer is yes, should they be required to purchase at least a certain percentage of their supply under fair trade conditions to have the right to use the label on any of their products? If so, what should that minimum threshold be, and should it be raised over time?

A second, related issue is the tension between the original, small-producer model of fair trade and the newer plantation mode involving waged laborers. The movement has become increasingly divided over a key question: should international fair trade certification be opened up to plantations in all crops, rather than keeping several of the most important crops for small farmers only, as it currently does? These six crops—coffee, cacao, cotton, rice, honey, and sugar—together account for over 75 percent of world fair trade sales. For example, under the current FTI standards, fair trade coffee—even if it is sold by a large corporate firm like Starbucks—must still be purchased from small farmer cooperatives like Michiza. On the one hand, advocates of opening up certification to all plantation crops, including the US certifier Fair Trade USA and some large retail grocery chains, say that waged laborers in large-scale agribusiness are among the most exploited workers and that they need the labor protections and extra income fair trade could provide (Raynolds 2014). On the other hand, small farmer groups, many fair trade NGOs, and most 100 percent fair trade retailers respond that small producers would be under-cut and outcompeted by cheaper supplies of the same crops from plantations and that large retail chains would switch to buying from large-scale produc-ers instead of organized small farmers if they were allowed to.

It is also worth considering how plantation agriculture fits into the larger forces at work in the global agrifood system. Small-scale peasant farmers around the world are increasingly being driven off their land and into the waged labor force in a process known as **depeasantization.** According to sociologist Philip McMichael, "commercial agriculture and habitat degrada-tion routinely expel peasants . . . from rural livelihoods" (2012, 171). Although monocrop plantations are a legacy of the colonial era, this form of commercial agriculture continues to expand today. The causes of depeasantization also include global trade agreements that have lowered tariffs and led to *dumping* of cheap, subsidized, imported food that undercuts peasant farmers. They also include the phenomenon of *land grabs*, in which investors and some na-tional governments are buying up or leasing massive areas of land (estimated at over one hundred million acres) in Africa and elsewhere in the South, much of it inhabited by rural communities without secure land titles, who are usually displaced from their land (see Lesson 12). The journalist Stefano Lib-erti, in his book *Land Grabbing*, quotes a manager of a land investment fund speaking to a conference of elite investors: "There's no point in trying to fool ourselves. Large-scale agricultural businesses take land, water, and markets from small farmers" (Liberti 2013). Many of these displaced peasants either migrate to cities or become workers on nearby plantations. While exceptions do exist, plantations are typically marked by highly unequal social power between workers and owners, with laborers often exposed to labor rights abuses and toxic agrochemicals; only a tiny proportion are represented by labor unions. Clearly, waged plantation laborers need better tools to protect their human rights and achieve fairer pay. The question currently being debated within the fair trade movement is whether fair trade is the most appropriate model to protect these workers in crops like coffee, cacao, and sugar cane, which are also produced by many economically vulnerable smallholders. As of 2014, there were 204,000 hired laborers in the FTI system—over half of whom were tea pickers—compared with 1.45 million small farmers. Fairtrade International is currently strengthening its standards for plantation workers in the crops it does certify and moving to require living wages and stronger protections for union organizing (Stevis 2015).

This tension over the role of plantations recently caused a major split within fair trade. In 2011, Fair Trade USA shocked the movement when it announced that it would leave the international certification system governed by FTI to create its own certification that allows all crops grown on plantations. Fair Trade USA's chief executive officer, Paul Rice, wrote that "through this more inclusive model, [we] can reach over four million farmworkers who are currently excluded from the system." In contrast, Ryan Zinn of the NGO Fair World Project argued that allowing unlimited plantation crops into the fair trade system "would undermine 25 years of fair trade development" with democratically organized small producers. One effect of this split is that in the United States, the same Fair Trade USA seal now appears both on coffee from plantations and on coffee grown by small farmers, meaning that consumers can no longer distinguish between these two models. Dean Cycon, owner of the coffee roaster Dean's Beans, alleged that "Starbucks, Green Mountain, and other coffee companies will [now] be able to become 100 percent fair trade not because they've changed their business practices one iota, but because Fair Trade USA has changed the rules of the game" (Jaffee 2014).

A third contentious issue involves multi-ingredient products. It is one thing to make the connection between your purchase of a bag of whole-bean coffee— which is a single, discrete product that undergoes only a few changes between harvest and grinding—and the higher price that organized producers will ultimately receive for that coffee. But what about a "composite" product like ice cream or a chocolate bar that contains many ingredients, only some of which are fair trade certified (such as sugar or vanilla)? What is the minimum percentage of fair trade content that a product should contain to be allowed to bear the fair trade label? Should companies be required to purchase all ingredients that are commercially available from fair trade sources, or should they be free to include conventional ingredients in fair trade–labeled products instead? All these issues are addressed by the FTI standards, and they are currently being disputed among producer groups, activist NGOs, and commercial firms.

A fourth and final issue—following Fair Trade USA's departure from the international system—has been the appearance of several new, competing fair trade seals in the United States, each of which encodes different values and supports different sets of social relations (Jaffee and Howard 2016). One of these new seals, Fair Trade America, was established by FTI to certify US products that meet its international standards, which still prohibit plantation-grown coffee and several other crops and contain more rigorous labor rights conditions. Another is the Small Producer Symbol, created by the Latin American and Caribbean Network of Fair Trade Small Producers and Workers (CLAC), which only certifies the crops of organized smallholders, requires companies to adhere to a minimum level of fair trade purchases (eventually rising to 25 percent of total volume), prohibits companies with a history of labor rights violations, and sets a higher minimum price than FTI. Finally, the Fair for Life seal, created by the organic certifier Institute for Marketecology (IMO), allows plantations in any crop, but also mandates a minimum of 80 percent fair trade content in a product to use its seal and requires scrutiny of companies' labor practices not only at the production end of the commodity chain, but also throughout their entire business operations. With multiple options to choose from, several food companies have recently switched certifications.

This proliferation of fair trade labels is a double-edged sword. It means that US consumers can no longer simply look for the label—instead, they must do some of their own research and balance a range of different factors. At the same time, it offers consumers the option to express their preference for alternative models of fairness in the global trading system.

In summary, fair trade standards are a highly contested arena. This is because a lot is at stake: these complex standards determine how much income producer groups and workers will receive for their crops and what markets will be open to them, as well as how much flexibility and profit retail companies will have in purchasing, labeling, and selling fair trade goods.

WHERE NOW FOR FAIR TRADE?

As fair trade approaches the end of its third decade, it is both more successful and more divided than ever. According to the most recent data (from 2014), there were 977 small farmer organizations in seventy-four countries in the international fair trade system that collectively represented 1.45 million producer members—a growth of more than 50 percent since 2010. There were also 229 plantations or estates with hired labor in the FTI system employing 204,000 workers, a growth of 79 percent since 2010 (Fairtrade International 2015). At the same time, consumer demand for fair trade products has not kept up with this growing supply. Across all crops, producer organizations on the FTI fair trade register were only able to sell an average of 39 percent of their total production at fair trade terms. This means that 61 percent of their crops still must be sold to conventional buyers, almost always at lower prices and less favorable terms. Fair trade coffee organizations were only able to sell 28 percent of their total production at fair trade terms; for tea, the figure was a mere 10 percent. In other words, there is still a great deal of work to do in increasing consumer demand for fair trade products and realizing fair trade's potential to improve producers' livelihoods.

Because of the tensions discussed above—especially over the role of mainstream corporations and plantations—fair trade now stands at a fork in the road regarding what its primary mission will be in the future. Should fair trade continue to be mainly a tool to generate greater social and economic justice for structurally disadvantaged small-scale farmers, or should it instead be a device to modestly ameliorate the worst labor rights abuses in global agribusiness? These two visions are different enough that it may be difficult to reconcile them within a single certification system, as Fair Trade USA's recent departure from the international system suggests. They also highlight the divergent values and structural interests of different groups of participants in the fair trade system: small-scale farmers, plantation owners, small fair trade retailers, large corporate firms, supermarket chains, and others.

These differences, in turn, raise basic questions about the tension between fair trade's multiple identities: as a movement, a market, or a system. Most of the statistics about fair trade sales, volumes, and growth in this lesson refer to the certified model of fair trade that since 1997 has been administered at the international level by FTI. For many years, most fair trade participants operated on the tacit premise that this formal *system*, and the certified fair trade *market* it regulated, was synonymous with the *social movements* that created fair trade beginning in the 1980s. However, since roughly 2000, the controversies I described earlier have increasingly challenged that premise. Some fair trade movement pioneers even argue that it is time to move beyond certified fair trade entirely.

However, there is also a countermovement within the formal fair trade system that has pushed back against some of the more controversial policies and achieved some major reforms, including higher minimum prices for several crops and greater representation for small producers within FTI's governance structure. This countermovement includes organized producer assemblies within FTI and advocacy NGOs such as the Fair World Project, which evaluates fair trade certifications and pushes certifiers to adopt policies that are more favorable to small-scale producers.

The past decade has also seen an expansion of fair trade in new directions, beyond the formal certification system and the traditional South-to-North model. These include domestic fair trade initiatives in some nations of the South, notably Mexico, Brazil, and South Africa, which in turn form part of the larger *solidarity economy* movement that links small producers, social movement groups, and cooperatives to build alternative domestic economic networks. Several social movement groups in the North have also adapted this model to link domestic farmers and farmworkers to fairer markets, using certification but without employing the term *fair trade*. In the United States, these include the Food Justice Certified label created by the Agricultural Justice Project and the Fair Food Program created by the Florida-based farmworker organization Coalition of Immokalee Workers.

Some fair trade movement participants argue that this growing diversity of fair trade models and initiatives is a positive development that can help return fair trade to its founding principles. Matt Earley, the co-owner of Just Coffee, a Wisconsin-based coffee roaster, argues that "if we want to build an authentic model of fair trade that lives up to its name, we must work directly with small farmers and transform the term from a marketing device to a real movement based on building economic democracy" (Jaffee 2014).

Conclusion

As this lesson illustrates, fair trade's original aim to operate in and against the market—to create an alternative market system that rectifies the injustices in global agrifood trade—is a challenging task indeed. Fair trade uses many of the existing structures and participants in the mainstream global market, while it simultaneously attempts to redistribute wealth and power within that system. However, because many of those conventional market actors have interests that are quite different from those of the small producers and alternative traders who created this movement in the first place, fair trade has become a highly contested arena.

This raises the much bigger question of the limits of market approaches to achieving social justice. Can market-based tools like voluntary product certification—a form of nonstate regulation—really deliver fundamental social and economic change? Can we shop our way to social justice?

Fair trade has generated substantial social, economic, and environmental benefits for many small producers and their organizations. Nevertheless, these same producers are also affected by the broader structural dynamics in the global economy that continue to disadvantage rural and indigenous communities across the global South. The Indian scientist and activist Vandana Shiva illustrates this point:

> *While so many people in the North are rich, and most people in the South are poor, some fair trade initiatives might survive, in the short run, by trading partnerships between consumers in the North and producers in the South. But as this [neoliberal] economic model unfolds . . . the low, artificially low prices of agribusiness-dominated agriculture will make fair trade such a luxury that it will start to shrink again. (Jaffee 2014)*

In other words, market-based social change initiatives like fair trade are necessary and vital, but alone they will almost certainly be insufficient. The dominant ideology of the past forty years tells us that our primary identity is that of consumers, rather than citizens (see Lesson 1). Fair trade's widespread appeal is understandable because it offers us a hopeful vision that is compatible with the dominant neoliberal ideology many observers call *market fundamentalism*, which holds that the market is the only acceptable venue for social change. However, there is a limitation to our power as consumers in this arena. The British author George Monbiot (2004) captures this tension succinctly:

> *I can congratulate myself for not buying cocoa produced by slaves, but my purchases of fairly traded cocoa do not help to bring the [modern] slave trade to an end, because they don't prevent other people from buying cocoa whose production depends on slavery. This is not to say that voluntary fair trade is pointless—it has distributed wealth to impoverished people—simply that, while it encourages good practice, it does not discourage bad practice.*

What, then, *would* be effective at curbing or ending this bad practice? Part of the answer would likely involve creating legally binding minimum international standards for labor rights and mechanisms for regulating the volatility in global commodity markets. Such large-scale changes will not come from the purchasing choices of even millions of consumers. Rather, they must come from the only institutions large and powerful enough to legally enforce such systemic change—governments and international institutions—who in turn will only act if pressured to do so by organized movements of engaged citizens. What would it mean to operate as citizens, rather than merely as consumers? We would do well to consider how to link concrete consumer actions, such as purchases of certified fair trade goods, to engagement with much broader and deeper social movements that are aiming to change the ground rules of the global economy. Perhaps in this way, fair trade could be a first step toward making *all* trade fair.

Discussion Questions

1. Had you purchased or consumed fair trade-certified products before reading this lesson? If so, what were your motivations for buying them? What attributes or values did/do you associate with fair trade?
2. Do you feel that it is possible to achieve greater social and economic justice through the marketplace? If so, under what conditions? If not, why not?
3. What are the advantages and drawbacks of an individual politics of consumption, of "voting with our dollars?"
4. When alternative markets such as fair trade become mainstreamed, how can they retain their transformative power?
5. Can ethical consumption serve as an entry point to broader or deeper social action or engagement? If so, how could this best be achieved?

Exercise

Trace and compare the commodity chains for two similar fair trade-certified food products—for example, two fair trade chocolate bars or two types of tea, bananas, wine, etc. The two forms of the product could be:

(a) grown/harvested under different production forms (small-scale farmers vs. hired labor/plantations),
(b) distributed/sold by different types of firms (large or multinational firm vs. small/medium firm), or
(c) certified by two different certifiers (e.g., FTI/Fairtrade America vs. Fair for Life, or Small Producer Symbol vs. Fair Trade USA).

In your comparison, aim to identify the multiple nodes or links in the commodity chain for each of the two products, the organizations or companies involved, the physical transformations the products undergo at each node, and, if possible, the prices paid at each node for the crop or product. The goal should be to reveal as much as possible about the social and economic (and possibly environmental) conditions facilitated by each version of this product; to highlight the differences and/or similarities between these different production, retailing, or certification systems; and to discuss the implications of those differences.

Additional Materials

Readings

> *For a Better World*. Biannual publication produced by the NGO Fair World Project on fair trade, labor rights, certification, and related issues, http://fairworldproject.org/resources/for-a-better-world-publication/

Films

> *Connected by Coffee*
> *After the Harvest: Fighting Hunger in the Coffeelands*
> *The Dark Side of Chocolate*
> *Black Gold*
> *Birdsong and Coffee: A Wake Up Call*

Websites

> *Fair Trade Institute*. A comprehensive collection of academic and practitioner literature on fair trade and an excellent starting point for research, http://www.fairtrade-institute.org

Websites for Fair Trade Certifiers

> Fairtrade International, http://www.fairtrade.net
> Fairtrade America, http://www.fairtradeamerica.org
> Fair Trade USA, http://www.fairtradeusa.org
> Small Producer Symbol, http://www.spp.coop
> Fair for Life, http://www.fairforlife.org

References

Amin, Samir. 1976. *Unequal Development*. New York: Monthly Review Press.

Besky, Sarah. 2014. *The Darjeeling Distinction: Labor and Justice on Fair-Trade Tea Plantations in India*. Berkeley: University of California Press.

Brown, Michael Barratt. 1993. *Fair Trade: Reform and Realities in the International Trading System*. London: Zed Books.

Dolan, Catherine S. 2010. "Virtual Moralities: The Mainstreaming of Fairtrade in Kenyan Tea Fields." *Geoforum* 41:33–43.

Fairtrade International. 2015. *Scope and Benefits of Fair Trade: Monitoring & Impact Report*. 17th ed. Bonn, Germany: Fairtrade International.

Fair Trade USA. 2016. "What Is Fair Trade?" Accessed November 26, 2016. http://fairtradeusa.org/what-is-fair-trade

Gunder Frank, Andre. 1966. *The Development of Underdevelopment*. New York: Monthly Review Press.

Howard, Philip H., and Daniel Jaffee. 2013. "Tensions between Firm Size and Sustainability Goals: Fair Trade Coffee in the United States." *Sustainability* 5:72–89.

Jaffee, Daniel. 2014. *Brewing Justice: Fair Trade Coffee, Sustainability, and Survival.* Updated ed. Berkeley: University of California Press.

Jaffee, Daniel, and Philip H. Howard. 2016. "Who's the Fairest of Them All? The Fractured Landscape of U.S. Fair Trade Certification." *Agriculture and Human Values* 33:813–26.

Jari, Bridget, and Jeannette Snowball. 2013. "Is Fairtrade in Commercial Farms Justifiable? Its Impact on Commercial and Small-Scale Producers in South Africa." *Agrekon* 52 (4): 66–88.

Liberti, Stefano. 2013. *Land Grabbing: Journeys in the New Colonialism.* New York: Verso Books.

Lyon, Sarah. 2015. "The Hidden Labor of Fair Trade." *Labor* 12 (1–2): 159–76.

Makita, Rie. 2012. "Fair Trade Certification: The Case of Tea Plantation Workers in India." *Development Policy Review* 30 (1): 87–107.

McMichael, Philip. 2012. *Development and Social Change.* 5th ed. Newbury Park, CA: Pine Forge Press.

Monbiot, George. 2004. *Manifesto for a New World Order.* New York: New Press.

Raynolds, Laura T. 2014. "Fair Trade, Certification, and Labor: Global and Local Tensions in Improving Conditions for Agricultural Workers." *Agriculture and Human Values* 31 (3): 499–511.

Stevis, Dimitris. 2015. "Global Labor Politics and Fair Trade." In *Handbook of Research on Fair Trade,* edited by Laura T. Raynolds and Elizabeth A. Bennett, 102–19. Northampton, MA: Edward Elgar.

Produce market, in California. (Photo by Clare Hinrichs.)

17

Food and Localism

Clare Hinrichs

Y ou buy some apples at the farmers market that takes place on the edge of your campus on Friday afternoons. You stand in line patiently waiting your turn to speak with the farmer selling her apples, other orchard fruit, some cider, and jams. You've seen her here before, although you haven't ever stopped to buy anything. She sells varieties of apples that are different than what you've seen at the convenience store on your block, where it is usually only a few Red Delicious. Her apples sit in rustic baskets with handwritten placards, presenting the price and the name of the apple varieties (Wickson, Pink Pearl, Stayman's Winesap, Macoun). They cost more than you would ordinarily consider spending, but you've seen pictures of this farm on social media and people post that her apples are awesome. On the display table, you notice recipes for apple deserts, soups, and salads. You see a map showing the location of the farm on the far side of the county near a town whose name is new to you. As she bags your apples, the farmer mentions a harvest celebration on her farm the following weekend and slips a flier into your hand. Walking home, you're curious now about this farm. You decide to ask a friend with a car about going over to the far side of the county next weekend to learn more.

In this relatively simple exchange of getting apples at the farmers market, you have participated in a small way in the local food system. Your purchase of this familiar food directly from the farmer inserts you within what many see as a promising alternative set of relations restoring connections between local farmers and local eaters. In this lesson, we explore the rise and appeal of localism in connection to farming and food and note some of the political ambiguities within this food systems alternative. We describe the development, aims, and some outcomes of new institutions and initiatives to reconnect producers and consumers of local food. We focus on two signature direct marketing institutions: farmers markets and community-supported agriculture (CSA) farms. We turn next to efforts to *scale up* local food through institutional purchasing so that more farmers can be involved and more consumers reached. We conclude by reflecting on the evolution, benefits, and limitations of food localism and outline some models that build from a focus on local food and could represent promising approaches for addressing problems in the food and agricultural system.

THE IDEA AND APPEAL OF LOCAL FOOD

Why all the fuss now about local food? If you think about it, for most of human history, food could only be local in origin. As agriculture developed, crops and animals were raised by the households that consumed them or by others in the community or possibly the nearby surrounding region. People's diets depended on nearby resources and lands. But this was sometimes a precarious situation. Crops could always fail because of drought, flood, pests, or disease. Livestock could sicken or fall to predators or thieves. Although human food was necessarily and predominantly local for most people most of the time before agriculture modernized and industrialized, this was not something to call out or label. Local food was simply food.

The inherent localness of food also meant that distinctions emerged in the varieties of food across different places, as people developed unique culinary preferences and traditions based on cultivars and breeds that thrived in particular places. But extreme localness, even adapted to the resources and limitations of different places, could always give way to catastrophe or crisis. If the food supply was largely local and became diminished for any reason, hunger or even starvation could result. That we today might pose *local* as a special attribute of food can be seen as a result of the productivity gains and distributional expansion of the modern industrial food and agricultural system. Some food now receives the adjective local to mark it as special and different from the food status quo in countries like the United States, which centers on products from conventional, industrial supply chains, often sourced globally and therefore from both anywhere and nowhere in particular (see Part 2).

The increasing prevalence and popularity of local as a word now distinguishing alternative food and farming is inextricably bound to the promises, as well as the disappointments of the industrialization of agriculture and globalization of food. Specific attention to local food can also be linked to the rise, commercial success, and standardization of organic food and farming (see Lesson 15). When organic food and farming was still primarily a warm and fuzzy countercultural movement, the domain of hippies, back-to-the-landers, and other sustainable farming visionaries, organics was by default a mostly local alternative. Consumer interest in and commercial sales of organic food have grown rapidly since the 1990s. As battles over the composition of US federal organic standards dragged on for a decade until the final rule was passed in 2000 and as the role of larger-scale farms and agribusiness companies in the growing organic food market became more evident, some who felt dismayed by the *conventionalization of organic* argued that local food and farming offered a new and better alternative—a way to go *beyond organic*. Precisely because it held connotations of conviviality and closeness and was not codified or standardized (as organic had now become), local food had fresh appeal as a marker of alternativeness. For many people, local food became the *new organic*—not dictated by official, centralized rules, but rooted in more authentic community relationships and trust.

In the first two decades of the twenty-first century, local food has become even more prominent as a marketing trend and a lifestyle statement, yet also as an organizing catchphrase for (some) alternative agrifood movements. As one indication of local food's arrival, in 2007, the New Oxford American Dictionary pronounced *locavore* (someone who favors eating local food) its word of the year. Local food continues to elicit nods of excitement and approval, but there remain some who scorn its potential faddishness and point out its political ambiguity. When localism becomes the hallmark of an alternative food and agricultural system, it is not that hard to get on the bandwagon. Knowing when and where the local farmers markets take place, belonging to a popular CSA farm, or dining (assuming you can afford it) at the trendiest new farm-to-table restaurant can serve as a way of signaling one's **cultural capital** (see Lesson 2). For some people, participating in local food systems may be more about cultivating a personal **food identity** than about building a comprehensive local food community or working to change the prevailing food and agricultural system.

Before examining specific manifestations of food localism, we should first consider some wider uses and meanings of the term localism. After all, not only food, but also many other things can be local. **Localism** can be understood as the general view that the interests of local people and places are understood and served best by people near those places. Sociologist and science and technology scholar David Hess (2009, 4) suggests that the local is often understood as under threat, "a disappearing phenomenon as the world becomes more transnational, cosmopolitan, de-territorialized and culturally homogeneous." We might talk about local schools, local roads, local arts, local energy, local media, and so forth. In all these cases, we are referring to infrastructure, resources, utilities, and expressions that may arise from and are intended to serve people in a particular place. In this sense, there is an emphasis on proximity between the genesis of the good or service and its ultimate beneficiaries. As we will see, **proximity** is a central theme in localist orientations to food and farming. However, Hess (2009, 55) also tells us that localism "emphasizes the problems of the corporatization of the economy and the loss of local sovereignty, and it draws attention to the project of building an economy based on economic units other than large corporations, rather than finding solutions that adjust the role of the government in the economy and that address the pervasive growth of within-nation inequality." Hess cites these features of localism as seeds for some tension in how localism reconciles issues of sustainability and justice. These tensions are recurring, important challenges to whether and how food localism can serve as a robust alternative to the dominant food and agricultural system.

One important, yet contradictory feature of food localism is its ability to straddle conventional political divides. British food policy researcher Tim Lang (2013) has observed that "the local is beloved of both the political left and right, and nowhere more so than in the world of food." How can local food be so elastic in its political sensibilities? On the one hand, prioritizing local food corresponds to rejection of corporate dominance and control in a globalized food and agriculture system. It instead favors return to smaller-scale enterprises and local and community-based ownership and control. But on the other hand, prioritizing local food also resonates nicely with more conservative and libertarian ideologies that would reject the influence of governments and administrators who seek to regulate specific farming practices, standardize food safety procedures, oversee food processing, or tax food sales.

It is no accident that in his best-selling book, *The Omnivore's Dilemma*, food writer Michael Pollan (2006) featured Joel Salatin, a Shenandoah Valley, Virginia farmer, as an exemplary local food farmer. The wisecracking, commercially successful Salatin is simultaneously a fierce champion of sustainable local food and farming and community self-reliance and an outspoken conservative-libertarian critic of government intervention in the food and agricultural system or almost any state role that could possibly hamper individual prerogative. In this way, a turn from the industrial, globalized food economy toward locally shaped and serving models has broad ideological traction, not only in the present-day United States but also in many other parts of the world. This political ambidexterity—evident with both progressive *and* conservative impulses in local food—may contribute to the broad appeal of food system localization. However, this very ambiguity in the motivations for food localism has also been a serious source of critique. It may also help to explain why other alternative food framings, including food sovereignty (see Lesson 18) and food justice (see Lesson 20), which offer potentially more politically pointed food system alternatives, resonate now for many people who are challenging the food system status quo.

RECONNECTING FOOD PRODUCERS AND CONSUMERS THROUGH DIRECT MARKETS

Focusing on local prioritizes closer proximity between food producers and consumers as a way to counter the environmental, economic, and social harms of an increasingly industrialized food and agricultural system in an era of neoliberal globalization (see other lessons in this volume). Such proximity has most often been understood as having direct, unmediated market linkages between farmers and food producers on the one hand and food shoppers and consumers on the other, with the aim of creating shorter food supply chains, promoting more direct interactions, and building communal ties. Through such direct interactions, local food then becomes "food with the farmer's face." Two particular forms of direct-to-consumer marketing—farmers markets and CSA—are often seen as signature local food institutions (Hinrichs 2000). Both illustrate the many dimensions of proximity that are part of the idea and appeal of local food. We will come back to these two local food institutions later.

Proximity can be a complicated idea when applied to food. On the one hand, it most obviously references a spatial dimension—*geographic* proximity. This refers to food that is produced *and* consumed within some specific community boundary, perhaps a town or a county, or where those exchanges happen within a certain delimited (and generally close) distance, as measured in linear terms (by the mile or kilometer). But proximity further references social dimensions that may or may not overlap with spatial proximity. For example, for many local food advocates, local has come to imply *relational* proximity, the idea that people within some common physical geographic space will readily hold each other in regard, will like and trust one another, and will respect and support each other's interests. Here, local food is attractive for its promise of new social connections or perhaps reconnections among people in communities where social connections may have thinned or frayed. Related to those assumptions about relational proximity, many local food advocates also see local as a stand-in for various attributes or values that signal quality in the production, processing, and distribution of food. Such values have become more important now to many producers and consumers. Spatial proximity is assumed to confer these additional *values of proximity* (Eriksen 2013) including authenticity, freshness, traceability, or place of origin—in short *good food.* In sum, local food's core and obvious characteristic of spatial or geographic proximity tends to be overlaid with additional, but often more slippery meanings, including assumptions about the nature of social relations and the extent of solidarity between producers and consumers or about the specific values inhering in locally produced and consumed food.

Farmers markets

Since the late 1980s–1990s, **farmers markets** have been recognized as prime venues for buying and selling local food and have generated great public enthusiasm and growing policy support. Importantly, farmers markets are contemporary incarnations of an old model, now revived and reshaped for the exchange of local food. Public markets have had a long history of making food from a region available to shoppers. Periodic markets at town squares or on public greens were also important places where farmers might sell their goods to local residents. With interest in retail farmers markets renewing and accelerating through the 1990s, farmers markets propelled the growing interest in local food. In the United States, by 2014, there were 8,268 farmers markets, an increase of 180 percent since 2006 (Low et al. 2015). For farmers, farmers markets have represented an opportunity to receive a greater share of the food retail dollar by circumventing *middlemen* or distributors and reaching customers directly. For consumers, farmers markets offer the immediacy of encountering one's farmer face-to-face; greater confidence about purchasing fresh, high-quality food; and satisfaction in supporting an independent, local, and sustainable farm economy. For communities, farmers markets are seen as a way to enliven public spaces and foster social and civic interactions.

As farmers markets have grown in number and type and soared in popularity, they have offered new market opportunities and improved farm livelihoods for many small producers, particularly those growing fruits and vegetables. However, they are not a panacea or even a possibility for all types of farmers. And while farmers markets can be a good source of fruits and vegetables, local breads, prepared foods, and sometimes cheeses and meat for customers with the time and money to shop for them, they have also been critiqued for catering more to elite *foodie* interests and overlooking food access concerns of more disadvantaged communities. In a comprehensive study of the spatial distribution of US farmers markets, rural sociologist Justin Schupp (2017) found that farmers markets were more likely to be located in more densely populated places, rather than more sparsely populated rural areas, and that not all poorer and minority neighborhoods were equally likely to have farmers markets.

In many ways, the larger impact of farmers markets may be as much symbolic as it is economic. They have helped showcase dynamic and appealing examples of local, sustainable gardening and farming. This has increased the positive visibility of agriculture, reminding diverse publics that alternatives to mainstream supermarket food exist. Importantly, they provide a setting where food producers and consumers can interact most directly, sharing aspects of the experience of growing, preparing, and eating food. To the extent that farmers markets increase public awareness of the challenges and risks, accomplishments and pleasures of local farming and food, they foster recognition of and perhaps commitment to community-based alternatives to the mainstream food and agricultural system.

Nonetheless, there has been some evolution in the farmers market model, which speaks to both the success and the limitations of this particular direct market institution. First, although many of the most established farmers markets are thriving in terms of number of vendors and customer traffic, farmers markets in general are no longer seen as the only market route for farmers who want to produce and sell locally, as we explore later. Some local farmers may include farmers markets within an overall market mix as part of *branding* themselves for a particular demographic or customer segment, even though the farmers market is neither their most significant nor their most reliable sales outlet. Other local farmers start out with farmers markets, but eventually "graduate" to other market outlets, either because they cannot afford the modest returns or because their business has grown.

Second, many farmers markets have incorporated technological innovations prevalent in other more mainstream food markets. While keeping the rustic, folksy, face-to-face aspect of farmers markets remains a priority, electronic technologies have changed the farmers market experience for both farmers and consumers. Local farmers use email and social media to reach, respond to, and interact with customers. Accepting credit cards as well as Electronic Benefits Transfer for the Supplemental Nutrition Assistance Program (food stamps) in the United States has increased convenience and access for farmers market customers across socioeconomic levels. Third, many farmers market organizers and advocates have worked with government and nongovernmental organizations to broaden access by lower-income communities to farmers markets further through US federal programs like the Farmers Market Nutrition Program and the Special Supplemental Nutrition Program for Women, Infants, and Children or supplemental coupon programs like Wholesome Wave or Fresh Bucks. While none of these interventions completely solves the challenge of increasing access to local food, which depends foremost on locating viable farmers markets in communities with need, such efforts still work to make high-quality locally produced food more available and accessible to populations who have long been underserved and overlooked. Finally, many farmers markets now strive to balance the commercial space of local food sales with community health programming, including nutrition and food systems education. This may mean providing cooking demonstrations, recipe recommendations, and the like, with the best of these efforts emerging from meaningful partnerships with trusted, credible community-based groups, rather than coming from paternalistic concern to get poor people to make "good food choices."

Community-Supported Agriculture

Community-supported agriculture is a second and more recent direct-to-consumer marketing institution that represents food localism. Although there are now variants, the basic model for a CSA farm (or a CSA composed of a group of collaborating farms) is to offer an annual *share* in the farm, where consumers pay a farm-set fee prior to the growing season and in return receive a weekly or biweekly share of the farm produce. In joining a CSA, members agree not only to a share of the bounty, but also to accept the inevitable and unpredictable risks in local farming. The share price and range of products received may vary depending on the particular CSA farm and options it provides. For example, in 2017, one northeastern Pennsylvania CSA offered a twenty-two-week regular produce share for $500, with the option of a twelve-week flower share for an additional $144. Some CSAs have small memberships (perhaps just twenty or fewer individuals or households), while others can be very large, with members in the several hundreds, multiple delivery locations, or even home-delivery for an extra fee.

That first term, *community*, would seem the central principle in CSA. It clearly invokes the social assumptions of benefit through the relational proximity of local food. However, specifying the composition and obligations of this community has been a source of debate among those promoting and studying CSA. What kind of community is the CSA? Are the CSA farmer and members equal partners in the risks and responsibilities of this community? How committed are CSA members to their CSA farms, in terms of staying involved and supporting them through good times and bad, the sweet abundance of June strawberries as well as the late tomato crop that succumbed to hail? Are members reflective of the diversity of residents in the local area or are CSAs ultimately just another food fashion for foodies to try on?

Community-supported agriculture first emerged in the United States in the mid-1980s, inspired by the Japanese farming model of *teikei*, literally meaning "food with the farmer's face on it" (Schnell 2013). The actual number of CSAs in the United States is difficult to know because the federal government only began to collect formal statistics on CSA farms around 2007. Some have argued that early government measures were imprecise and likely overcounted CSAs at about twelve thousand, when less than five thousand may be a more reasonable estimate (Schnell 2013). Measurement is challenging given the lack of an official CSA definition and ambiguities about local farms supplying products to a central CSA farm or themselves dealing directly with local customers. Furthermore, a given farm may run a CSA for season or two and then close down the CSA, while still continuing to farm, but later start the CSA again. Despite the uncertain context for many individual CSAs, CSA and related membership-based direct-to-consumer models have become popular and increasingly publicized local food alternatives in Canada, Britain, many European countries, and elsewhere around the world.

For farmers, CSA can represent an economic benefit because of the reliable income stream (most or all of it in advance of the season) from the sale of local food directly to committed customers. As a signature direct-marketing institution with relatively low overhead, CSA is favored by many new and beginning farmers who wish to tap into the burgeoning consumer interest in local food and like the commingling of community and commerce in CSA ideals. Although it requires good production skills to ensure product through the season and proficiency in managing CSA members, who remain customers, CSA offers farmers opportunities to experiment with locally suited crops and varieties, to practice sustainable farming techniques, and to become part of the local agricultural community and landscape. For consumers, depending on their level of involvement, CSA can provide an illuminating view on the contributions made by and challenges facing local farmers. CSA can bring the seasonality of food into sharper relief. It can introduce some people to quantities and types of fresh produce they have never previously encountered and offer them support and inspiration for eating in new, more healthful ways.

However, as CSA has proliferated and specific models have diversified, reports have emanated from some regions of growing competition among CSA farms for customers. This suggests that this particular local food market may be a more perilous, less dependable option for at least some farmers, who must now work harder to recruit and retain members—in short, to ensure the community foundation, but also the economic viability of CSA. To succeed, some CSA farmers have had to become more businesslike, pricing shares in more accordance with costs and a closer eye on competitors, and catering more deliberately and actively to customer preferences. On the one hand, such changes would seem to undermine some of the original noneconomic values that so distinguished CSA. But on the other hand, these shifts may simply be part of an unfinished story in how this local food institution is evolving.

In the late 2010s, there have been more efforts to address some of these tensions and contradictions in CSAs and reclaim this model in support of a more justice-oriented transformation of food systems. Two examples include, first, the recently proposed International CSA charter (for the United States and Canada), which lays out the principles to which CSA should cohere and, second, the work of the European-based network URGENCI as the source for a more radical solidarity-based vision animating CSA. Both models represent efforts to ensure that CSA does not become enmired or diminished by the more parochial, narrow concerns that can sometimes underlie food localism.

MOVING BEYOND DIRECT MARKETS: ISSUES AND APPROACHES IN SCALING UP LOCAL FOOD

Recognizing that direct market institutions, such as farmers markets and CSAs, by themselves sometimes fall short in addressing the varied concerns and interests of food producers and consumers, local food advocates in the mid-2000s began to talk about a need to scale up local food. They asked whether direct-to-consumer market venues were living up to their billing as the best or only way to organize an alternative food system. How could producing and selling local food better address the needs of small and medium-size farmers who had neither time nor inclination for the customer-intensive interactions at the heart of farmers markets or CSAs? How could high-quality local food, especially the fruits and vegetables so important for healthy diets, be made more accessible to groups for whom regular farmers markets and CSAs were not convenient, affordable, or culturally inviting? **Scaling up local food** to include more and different types of farmers could increase the supply of locally sourced food and give farmers who want alternatives to global commodity markets more opportunities to sell their products locally. Scaling up beyond direct markets would also increase access to local food for a less elite, more diverse set of consumers and eaters. Wider access could reduce the risk that local food, like organics before it, remained mostly a form of *yuppie chow*.

Efforts to scale up local food crystallize several debates discussed earlier in this lesson and demonstrate the growing diversity of local food as one promising food system alternative. Some early critics of local food pointed to the problem of the **local trap**—not just in food and agriculture, but also in other sectors (Born and Purcell 2006). The local trap refers to the assumption that the local scale automatically and consistently confers benefits, rather than harms. The local trap highlights a common tendency to confuse the means (here, organization at a certain scale) with achieving particular goals (such as environmental improvement, economic prosperity, or social justice). Rather than making localism itself the aim in designing and organizing food systems, there is a need to ask how particular levels and scales of organization, for example, small-scale and local or mid-sized and more regional or even large and national or international, actually support or obstruct achieving important food systems goals. The move to scale up local food acknowledges that a strict fixation on means (local in the sense of geographic and relational proximity) may not always be the best or only way to address priorities for improving food systems. As geographer Phil Mount (2011) has observed, scaling up local food does run the risk of affecting perceptions about the legitimacy and desirability of local food, but he also argues that such concerns can be managed by better governance among food systems actors—through what he calls a "negotiation of accommodations."

What then are some examples of scaling up local food? The broad category of **farm-to-institution** sourcing best captures this development. In 2016, the popular US-based food politics blog *Civil Eats* described farm-to-institution sourcing as the sleeping giant of local food. Institutional sourcing refers to the significant food purchasing conducted by schools, hospitals, restaurants, and other private- or public-sector entities that regularly prepare meals in larger than household quantities. Institutional sourcing often involves not direct, but intermediated markets, in which a local farmer's products are handled by one or more *intermediaries* before reaching the final consumer. Sometimes intermediated markets involve the classic middleman, such as a conventional food distributor. Some conventional food distributors now recognize the market opportunity in meeting new customer demand for local food products. However, sweeping industrialization of agriculture (see Lesson 5) and globalization of food (see Lesson 8) in the latter part of the twentieth century have eliminated much traditional food distribution infrastructure in many parts of North America. In the early 2010s, local food advocates pressed for developing new food distribution businesses and organizations, sometimes called **food hubs**, to aggregate and move more local food from nearby farm fields onto more local plates. While some large institutional food buyers like school districts and hospital systems might purchase directly from local farmers, many more have favored buying local food through intermediated markets that provide scale efficiencies and necessary organization to ensure both the quantity and the quality such institutional buyers seek.

Farm-to-school programs are an especially widespread instance of scaling up local food through public institutional procurement. In the United States, building on prior years of activity in this area, the 2010 Healthy, Hunger-Free Kids Act provided a significant stimulus by launching the US Department of Agriculture's National Farm-to-School Program. In 2013–14, almost $600 million worth of local food was purchased by US schools, including every state in the country and the District of Columbia (Low et al. 2015). The majority of local food sourced by schools comes through intermediated, rather than direct markets, but local farmers and their farms may be connected to children in schools via educational programming, farm field trips, or school visits. Supporting small and medium-sized local farms, building new food businesses such as food hubs, and improving the quality and healthfulness of school meals are often central aims of farm-to-school programs, although the specific emphases may vary from region to region.

Scaling up local food has also included developing and responding to demand for local food on the part of restaurants. While some chefs may buy directly and selectively from farmers at farmers markets, others can make more and better use of local food products obtained through a knowledgeable, well-organized, and efficient intermediary, such as a food hub. Important in such arrangements is that information about the provenance of the product (including what variety or species and from what specific local farm or processor) be retained. Here the *values of proximity* are necessary for the local farmer to be rewarded and for restaurant customers to provide that reward. Although farm to table is often associated with the high-end, specialty market for local food, a range of restaurants, up market and down, could conceivably source more local food if they had access to the necessary distribution networks.

Finally, scaling up local food also potentially includes more sourcing of local food products by retail supermarkets. Like restaurants, supermarkets recognize consumer interest in local food and see opportunities to benefit their businesses by carrying and highlighting more local foods. For many supermarket chains, this involves rediscovering their long-abandoned local sourcing practices and determining whether and how local sourcing can align within their current supply chain logistic models. Although some supermarkets may purchase produce or other items directly from local farmers and be glad to market them as local, they may also impose stringent packing or quality requirements that limit which local producers can actually sell into this market. Although eager to enter the market for local food and capable of broadening consumer access to local food, larger food retailers such as Walmart, which rely on standardization, may also in the end genericize local food (Bloom and Hinrichs 2017). Whether supermarkets are more likely to demean or to democratize local food may depend on your point of view concerning the mainstream food and agricultural system. Scaling up local food generally means moving beyond an emphasis on immediate and direct exchanges between local food producers and consumers. While new intermediated markets have the potential to extend the reach and impact of local food for some local farmers and for many more consumers, the actual outcomes and tradeoffs of different pathways of local food from farm to fork should be closely examined.

Conclusion

In this lesson, we introduced you to food localism as one of the many initiatives and agrifood movements that now represent alternatives to the dominant food and agricultural system. Because of its successful dissemination and popular appeal, food localism has become a familiar idea to many people in the United States and elsewhere. At the same time, its very prevalence in public discourse, media, and advertising and the growing interest of agribusiness in local food may dilute or derail some of its more transformative possibilities for increasing environmental sustainability and social justice in the food and agricultural system. For these reasons, it is important to scrutinize both the surface and the subterranean meanings of local, to consider what it contains, what it stands in for, and what it simply leaves out. It could be argued that practicing a more **reflexive localism** (Dupuis and Goodman 2005) is precisely what has led to more experimentation and adaptation by farms, organizations, and networks as they work in different places and regions to build more localized food systems.

Direct-to-consumer markets, most notably farmers markets and CSA, were the signature, feel-good manifestations of local food. Direct markets have been supported and expanded, but also critiqued on social equity grounds, sometimes justifiably, especially if viewed in isolation from the larger webs of alternative and local food markets, institutions, and initiatives that are becoming evident in some communities. In many places, the landscape of local food has become far more interesting, complex, and layered than one of farmers markets or CSAs alone. As local food advocates and practitioners have sought to scale up, many have relinquished earlier rigid notions of what constitutes local—exercising the "negotiation of accommodations" that Mount (2011) says will be vital for more effective and just local food systems governance. A multitude of ventures, enterprises, and initiatives now aim to increase the supply and types of local food from a more diverse set of farmers and food processors, to use new delivery models, and to increase access across socioeconomic groups, but specifically including more disadvantaged and vulnerable populations. Some farmers will focus more on artisanal products for white-tablecloth markets, while others may farm a few of their fields to ensure that nearby food banks and food pantries can offer hungry people more fresh produce. Other farmers will strive to get high-end diners to appreciate previously discarded or disregarded parts of the crop or animal, as American chef Dan Barber promotes in his 2014 book *The Third Plate*. Overall, there has been movement from a focus on niche markets to more realistic consideration of how exactly food supply chains work, how the social relations along the chain matter, and how food system components can be organized to better complement one another within communities and places, not only in terms of the bottom line.

Looking forward, what are some directions and emphases for agriculture and food alternatives that could build from and push beyond local food to address more of our urgent societal goals? Three models come to mind: place-based food systems, regional food systems, and integrated food systems.

Place-based food systems are not new, but are newly poised to advance thinking about local food. In contrast to the emphasis on proximity versus distance in food localism, place explicitly emphasizes the cultural meanings and traditions of food and farming practices as emerging in specific locations. Place requires closer attention to the biological and ecological distinctions characterizing locales and the cultural practices associated with indigenous and traditional foods. Emerging in the mid-1980s in Italy, the slow food movement represents an important antecedent for new approaches to place-based food systems. Emphasizing *ecogastronomy*—a melding of environmental attention and concern with the possibilities for pleasure in producing, preparing, cooking, and consuming food, the slow food movement advocates for local, delicious, and healthy foods and against the homogeneity and control of the modern, industrial food and agricultural system. Place-based food systems more broadly may align with these political aims of slow food, but may further emphasize the role of place-based farming and food in local economic revitalization and renewed community identity. However, although they are promising, place-based food systems also merit some caution. They risk being put under glass, like museum pieces, set, and no longer permitted to change. They can face challenges of authenticity or even appropriation. And they can manifest tensions regarding social inclusion and exclusion that are similar to those experienced by some local food systems initiatives.

Regional food systems concede that a strictly local food supply may be difficult to produce and unable to meet the food needs and preferences of diverse populations in a given area. New economic uncertainties and mounting evidence about the effects of climate change have led some food systems advocates and experts to advise shifting the emphasis from local food systems to work more on promoting and strengthening regional food systems (Clancy and Ruhf 2010). Why? Considering a larger region permits certain economies of scale, captures greater potential diversity in types of foods produced, and allows better for the impact of changing food productive capacity and supply in particular localities. Planning, organizing, and governing food systems at the regional level may offer flexibilities and redundancies that are valuable insurance in times of environmental or economic crisis. By anticipating long-term environmental concerns, regional food systems offer adaptability. They do not eliminate local, but instead situate it: local becomes nested within regional *systems*.

Finally, an integrated food systems perspective explicitly recognizes the cross-sectoral connections of food and agriculture. For example, the HEAL Alliance promoted by the US based Union of Concerned Scientists has pushed for broader, more integrated design of national food and farm policy: HEAL stands for Health, Environment, Agriculture, and Labor, recognizing how improvements in any one area may be supported or thwarted by policies and programs in the others. Local, as we have seen, is a seductively simple, but inadequate metric. Because of the limitations in overfocusing on local, many food and farming advocates have expanded to more nuanced cross-sectoral frameworks to address food system change. Such frameworks recognize that leveraging change in one sector may be necessary to achieve desired important changes in others. In short, the dimensions of the food system are interconnected. Thus, health outcomes of the current food system need to be addressed, as do environmental impacts of large-scale industrialized production systems and the technology-intensive agriculture itself and the conditions of labor across food and farming systems. An integrated food systems perspective represents both a broader and a more nuanced effort to bridge production and consumption than local food ever achieved, when focused more narrowly mostly on having direct connections between food producers and consumers. Producing food is not just a matter of raising crops or livestock. It involves health concerns through environmental exposures in production and processing and through nutritional content and quality of the resulting food. It intersects with the labor and wage conditions not only of farmworkers, but also of food processors, handlers, and servers (see Lesson 11). Focusing strictly on local food becomes inadequate when the food system problems are so complex and interconnected. As we write in 2017, it is unclear how a more deeply integrated approach to food system alternatives will fare in the US national policy context, although there is inspiration to be drawn from initiatives, innovations, and policy changes elsewhere around the globe.

Returning now to our vignette at the beginning of this lesson, what came of your visit to the farm growing apples on the far side of the county? Perhaps you learned more about how the farmer and her family used to sell all their apples wholesale through a large distributor, but rarely got a very good price. That motivated them to try the farmers market, but sometimes, especially on rainy days when sales are slow, the roundtrip drive to the market has not seemed worth it. You heard how the farmer had trouble finding enough help to pick apples and other fruit when they needed to be harvested. She mentioned that she has hired migrant farmworkers originally from Mexico and believes that everyone's documentation is in order. You also learned that the farm growing apples is not certified organic, but instead practices integrated pest management, which uses biological and mechanical controls, only turning to pesticides as a last resort. Finally, you were interested to learn that the farmer and her family have been donating quantities of culls and extra fruit to the county food bank for some years now.

Pondering your own place within this local food system, you wonder whether you could arrange to get the farmer to donate some of her apples to the student food pantry that opened last year to address food insecurity on your campus. You think in new ways about that lecture in class last week on farm and food policy. And then you decide: it's time to text your friends and tell them you're baking a pie with several of this local farmer's tastiest apples. You ask your friends to come by soon—for slices of warm homemade pie.

Discussion Questions

1. When thinking about local food systems, who benefits and how? How might these benefits differ for those who produce, process, distribute, prepare, sell, or consume local food?
2. What are possible drawbacks when people focus on eating local foods? How could or should those drawbacks be addressed?
3. Think of a community where you lived while growing up. Were farmers markets or CSA farms present there? If so, what impact did they have on that community? If not, what explains their absence in that community? Were there other means by which people obtained locally produced food?
4. How would you define local for your college or university? What should be the boundaries of the local food system for your college or university, and why?

Exercises

1. *Eating locally.* Choose a period of time during which you will experiment with local eating. First, you need to define what will constitute your local food system. Second, for your chosen period, obtain as much of your food as possible from your local food system. Third, analyze your experience in eating locally. Questions to consider include the following: Did you have to change your diet and how did you feel about that? Did you eat any new or unfamiliar foods? Where did you obtain your local food? Was eating locally more or less expensive than your usual diet? Did eating locally cause you to meet any new people? How easy or hard was it for you to eat locally and why? How possible is a mostly local diet where you live?

2. *Learning about local food markets through observation and informal interviewing.* Identify a farmers market in your area that you can visit. Spend about thirty to forty-five minutes observing activity and interactions there. What types of farms or other food businesses are present that day and what products are they selling? How much do different products cost? How are vendors similar or different in how they display their wares and the image they present to shoppers? What types of people are shopping at the market and what do you notice about how quickly they move through the market and how they interact with others? Are there other community organizations, artists, or musicians present, and what is their role at the market? If the farmers market is not too busy when you visit, also speak with one or two farmers. Ask them each two to four questions, such as (1) Why do you sell at this farmers market?, (2) How would you describe your typical farmers market customer?, (3) Is this farmers market the main outlet for your products?, and (4) What are your thoughts about ways to improve the food system in this community? After your farmers market visit, analyze your observations and interview findings.

Additional Materials
Films

> *Ingredients: The Local Food Movement Takes Root*, 2009, http://www.ingredients-film.com/

Websites

> Local Harvest, https://www.localharvest.org/farmers-markets/
> National Farmer Markets Directory, http://nfmd.org/
> National Farm to School Network, http://www.farmtoschool.org/
> Strolling of the Heifers Locavore Index, https://www.strollingoftheheifers.com/locavore/
> URGENCI, the International Network for Community Supported Agriculture, https://urgenci.net/the-network/
> Slow Food, https://www.slowfood.com/ and https://www.slowfoodusa.org/

References

Barber, Dan. 2014. *The Third Plate: Field Notes on the Future of Food*. New York: Penguin Press.

Bloom, J. Dara, and C. Clare Hinrichs. 2017. "The Long Reach of Lean Retailing: Firm Embeddedness and Wal-Mart's Implementation of Local Produce Sourcing in the U.S." *Environment and Planning A* 49 (1): 168–85.

Born, Branden, and Mark Purcell. 2006. "Avoiding the Local Trap: Scale and Food Systems in Planning Research." *Journal of Planning Education and Research* 26:195–207.

Clancy, Katherine, and Kathryn Ruhf. 2010. "Is Local Enough? Some Arguments for Regional Food Systems." *Choices* 25(1).

DuPuis, E. Melanie, and David Goodman. 2005. "Should We Go 'Home' to Eat? Toward a Reflexive Politics of Localism." *Journal of Rural Studies* 21:359–71.

Eriksen, Safania Normann. 2013. "Defining Local Food: Constructing a New Taxonomy—Three Domains of Proximity." *Acta Agriculturae Scandinavica B—Soil and Plant Science* 63 (S1): 47–55.

Hess, David J. 2009. *Localist Movements in a Global Economy: Sustainability, Justice and Urban Development in the United States*. Cambridge, MA: MIT Press.

Hinrichs, C. Clare. 2000. "Embeddedness and Local Food Systems: Notes on Two Types of Direct Agricultural Market." *Journal of Rural Studies* 16:295–303.

Lang, Tim. 2013. "How Localism is Changing What We Eat." *The Guardian*. January 7. https://www.theguardian.com/local-government-network/2013/jan/07/localism-food-policy-the-way-we-eat

Low, Sarah A., Aaron Adalja, Elizabeth Beaulieu, Nigel Key, Steve Martinez, Alex Melton, Agnes Perez, et al. 2015. *Trends in U.S. Local and Regional Food Systems*. Administrative Publication AP068. Washington, DC: US Department of Agriculture, Economic Research Service.

Mount, Phil. 2011. "Growing Local Food: Scale and Local Food Systems Governance." *Agriculture and Human Values* 29 (1): 107–21.

Pollan, Michael. 2006. *The Omnivore's Dilemma: A Natural History of Four Meals*. New York: Penguin Press.

Schnell, Stephen M. 2013. "Food Miles, Local Eating and Community Supported Agriculture: Putting Local Food in Its Place." *Agriculture and Human Values* 30:615–28.

Schupp, Justin L. 2017. "Cultivating Better Food Access? The Role of Farmers Markets in the U.S. Local Food Movement." *Rural Sociology* 82 (2): 318–48.

Harvest. (Photo by Hannah Wittman.)

18

Getting to Food Sovereignty (Locally?) in a Globalized World

Hannah Wittman

An average North American supermarket contains over thirty-five thousand items grown by a broad diversity of farmers in communities located across the globe. At the same time, an even larger variety of foods grown and harvested by farmers, fisherfolk, and indigenous peoples constitute a global seed bank for cultural and ecological diversity.

By the time your breakfast or dinner reaches your table, most of the ingredients have likely transferred hands multiple times, crossing local, regional, and international borders. Your meal has also made its way through many different stages within the food system, including seed saving, land preparation, cultivation and harvesting, food packaging and processing, and distribution to a retail center, fast-food outlet, farmers' market, or local greengrocer. Each of these relationships involves questions related to *ecology* (how was your food grown and with what effect on the environment?), *equity* (who benefits and who suffers from food system failures?), and *empowerment* (who decides what the food system should look like?).

Although humans have been cultivating, trading, and sharing food for over ten thousand years, over the past half century agricultural systems have gone through significant transformations in what many are now calling a *confluence of ecological crises*. The globalization and industrialization of agriculture has increasingly contributed to environmental problems, including biodiversity loss, climate change, and the pollution of waterways (see Lesson 12). The social and environmental impacts resulting from this agricultural transition are also unevenly distributed. Let's consider the case of Brazil: In Brazil's tropical savanna ecoregion known as the Cerrado—designated a biodiversity hotspot—large swaths of land have been cleared for cattle ranching and soybean cultivation as international demand for these products has increased. The soybeans grown in Brazil are often destined for export to China or the European Union, but resulting environmental costs and resource pressures are both localized to the *Cerrado* and globalized through the contributions of this agricultural transition to climate change.

The transformation of the global food system has also resulted in concerning outcomes for human health and **health equity**. In 2016, the Food and Agriculture Organization of the United Nations (FAO) reminded us that almost one billion people across the globe are chronically food insecure. At the same time, the **nutrition transition**—the increasing consumption of energy-dense and highly processed foods high in saturated fats, sugars, and sodium in global diets—has accompanied patterns of urbanization, industrial development, and changing employment patterns and household dynamics (see Lessons 3, 4, and 14). Intensive pesticide exposure has both threatened the health of agricultural workers and contaminated waterways and drinking water systems for both rural and urban residents. For example, returning to Brazil, researchers conducted a study of breast milk contamination in the heart of the soybean production zone in the *Cerrado* in 2011. Agricultural pesticide residues were found in 100 percent of breast milk samples, including pesticides that had been prohibited for use for over a decade.

Finally, although much of the world's food is still produced by over five hundred million family farms, unequal power relations, dispossession, and disempowerment related to the ownership and distribution of agricultural land, seeds, and knowledge have never been more acute. Land-grabbing (large-scale foreign acquisitions of farmland), biopiracy (patenting traditional seed varieties and other forms of agricultural and ecological knowledge), and the privatization of communally managed foodlands have resulted in distinct challenges to both local food security for individual farming families and the regional food economies that they supported. For example, in our Brazilian case, indigenous communities and small-scale farmers have been violently displaced from the soybean frontiers, with significant effects on regional food production for domestic consumption as well as implications for equity and social justice.

What are the possible solutions to this confluence of crises? To reference the slogan and goal of La Vía Campesina, a growing global movement for food sovereignty, how can our global food system "feed the world and cool the planet?"

This lesson introduces the concept of **food sovereignty**—defined by social movements as the right of peoples to healthy and culturally appropriate food produced through ecologically sound and sustainable methods and their right to define their own food and agriculture systems. The food sovereignty movement is a response to the common struggles faced by agrarian, environmental, and antihunger movements across the globe in discussions of how to feed the world sustainably and equitably. The food sovereignty framework enables a critical discussion of the pathways toward a more ecologically sustainable and socially just food system and examines the roles of farmers, indigenous peoples, fisherfolk, the state, civil society, consumers, environmentalists—in short, all global citizens—in constructing a new global food system from the ground up. This lesson will examine the idea of food sovereignty and the ways it challenges the current food and agriculture system. After discussing the recent history of the food sovereignty movement (as a transnational advocacy network) and its relationship to the concept of food security, the lesson provides examples of new policy approaches to food sovereignty based on case studies in Ecuador and Brazil.

SETTING THE STAGE: THE GLOBALIZATION OF FOOD SECURITY

Food security as a human right was included in the 1948 United Nations Declaration on Human Rights, and today forty countries include the right to food in their respective constitutions (see Lesson 13). However, there is little consensus on how this right should be achieved. In the past, national food security initiatives tended to focus on ensuring an adequate food supply through domestic production, and many countries were nearly self-sufficient in food. Global food trade (see Lesson 8) was focused on just a few commodities—such as sugar, wheat, and maize—grown in global breadbaskets.

After World War II, when armed conflict interrupted local food production across Europe, international shipments of food aid became a pillar of US foreign policy and paved the way for the disposal of large agricultural surpluses, eventually decried as *dumping*, particularly from North America (selling imported food in less-developed countries below the cost of production, which can undercut and disrupt local production systems). Even so, postwar reconstruction policies also bolstered programs to support local agricultural production systems as part of a strategy to ensure food security within national boundaries and to reduce vulnerability to global price fluctuations.

At the UN World Food Conference of 1974, the FAO defined food security as the "availability at all times of adequate world food supplies of basic food stuffs . . . to sustain a steady expansion of food consumption . . . and to offset fluctuations in production and prices." This vision dovetailed with the intentions of the **green revolution** to rapidly increase food production through public investments in agricultural technologies, crop breeding programs, and knowledge sharing (see Lesson 6).

However, increased food production did not lead to the expected decreases in hunger at a global level. As noted by Nobel Prize–winning economist Amartya Sen (1981), hunger is often present in the face of high levels of food availability. Sen argued that people's ability to access food is related to their *entitlements*—which are a function of rights (based in the legal system) and opportunities (what options are available in terms of employment, having access to land to produce food, etc.). Hunger is thus fundamentally a social and economic problem, not just a technological one that could be fixed by another green revolution to increase crop yields.

Acknowledging that widespread hunger persisted despite all-time records in levels of food production, the FAO began to consider additional drivers of food security beyond the availability of a global food supply. These drivers include the ability for households to access food (i.e., by using cash income to purchase food or through subsistence-level production); the ability of individuals to engage in proper utilization of food (i.e., choosing foods that are nutritious, safe, and culturally appropriate); and stability (i.e., ensuring that households are protected from sudden price shocks caused by an economic or climatic crisis and from seasonal variations in food availability). In 2001, the FAO posed a new framing of the definition of food security, which is still often used today:

> Food security exists when all people, at all times, have physical, social and economic access to sufficient, safe and nutritious food which meets their dietary needs and food preferences for an active and healthy life. (FAO 2015)

Questions remained, however, regarding who ultimately is responsible for achieving food security. Under **neoliberalism**, the private sector was intended to take a greater role in letting markets facilitate better food access. At the same time, governments were encouraged to reduce support for social *safety nets* that had previously addressed market failures. In addition, by the early 1990s, the negative social and environmental consequences of the green revolution and the globalization of the food system were becoming clearer. Rural communities emptied across the globe, with rapid increases in urbanization especially across Latin America and Asia.

FROM FOOD SECURITY TO FOOD SOVEREIGNTY

The concept of food security—that all people should be able to consistently access and utilize safe and nutritious food—has many important merits. However, the food security framework falls short of addressing *how* food should be produced and distributed and *who gets to decide*. It does not address the fundamentally unequal power relations between different economies and societies that have resulted in environmental and social injustice, including widespread hunger and malnutrition. In the global context, this has given rise to crucial points of tension in how the interests of farmers and eaters are represented in decision-making arenas across the world.

Leading up to and throughout the 1970s, most national governments prioritized local food security and regional economic development through policies that supported national food production systems. These policies included agricultural research extension adapted to local cultures and environments, the regulation of food marketing and distribution systems, and the development of food storage and transportation infrastructure. But in the 1980s and 1990s, structural adjustment programs—a set of neoliberal economic policies imposed on developing countries by the World Bank and International Monetary Fund—instead began to focus on promoting *free market* mechanisms, including export-oriented growth as an avenue to debt reduction and economic development. The structural adjustment programs required that low-income countries take measures to (among other things) reduce trade barriers and other protection measures, eliminate agricultural subsidies, and privatize public services. For low-income countries, receiving a loan from the World Bank or the International Monetary Fund was often conditional on following these terms of restructuring, and there were no mechanisms in place for low-income countries to try to renegotiate the terms.

Additionally, high-income countries, which wielded a disproportionate amount of power in establishing trade rules and regulations, advanced neoliberal policies through the development of the World Trade Organization (WTO). An agreement to join the WTO also meant that individual governments were challenged in their ability to unilaterally set their own priorities or policies for food and agriculture. The WTO focused on reducing global trade barriers, but did not sufficiently recognize differences in agricultural systems and further exacerbated unequal power relations between rich and poor countries in trade negotiations.

COMMON CHALLENGES, DISTINCT GEOGRAPHIES

By the late twentieth century, farming and indigenous communities (and their representative organizations across the globe) were experiencing localized versions—particular to their distinct geographic and cultural conditions—of these broadly similar challenges. As markets opened and tariffs were reduced, many farmers in developing countries experienced drops in crop and livestock prices and were faced with a rush of cheap food imports from more developed countries, such as the United States and Canada. Under neoliberalism, conditions proved favorable for high-income countries (like the United States), who now found new markets open for dumping surplus grains grown by their own farmers. Food production systems in these more developed countries had been industrialized in previous decades (see Lesson 5), and government investment in agricultural credit programs, subsidies, physical infrastructure, and research and extension systems continued.

In low- and middle-income countries, imported foodstuffs from high-income countries that continued to subsidize their agricultural systems often ended up being less expensive than domestically produced foods. For example, in Mexico, cheap US corn flooded local markets and pushed many smallholder farmers in Mexico out of business. Many of these families lost their land and moved either to the city or to the United States to work as laborers. And yet, using a food security metric, the increased availability of cheap foreign foods could still, in many cases, be considered a measure of improvement for a country's food security.

Farmers in Europe and North America also faced challenges to their production systems, traditional ways of life, and environmental sustainability. For example, the National Farmers Union was formed in 1969 as a coordinating body to represent the interests of farming communities in Canada. The union worked to maintain farmers' voices in the establishment of farm policy, including the development of a supply-management framework that protected both farmers and consumers from market volatility. In the 1980s, National Farmers Union members established youth exchanges with farmers in the Caribbean and study tours to Nicaragua, China, and Mozambique. These experiences highlighted similar experiences of agricultural globalization, where multinational corporations had begun to consolidate control over agricultural inputs including seeds, fertilizers, and equipment, as well as marketing and distribution systems (see Lesson 7). Known as the *cost–price squeeze*, farmers in Canada, Mexico, and the United States all faced increasing costs of production, while facing declining prices for their products as a result of market liberalization.

Farmers in Latin America, Africa, and Asia faced these same challenges and more: political conflict and violent repression were major concerns for rural social movements, while agricultural export projects dispossessed many family farmers and communities of their traditional lands. These realities led to a plurality of peasant responses in various countries. Let's look at Brazil once more: From the mid-1960s to the mid-1980s, Brazil was ruled under an authoritarian military government that promoted agricultural modernization and privatized large swaths of public land to be developed for export-oriented beef and soybean production. Millions of smallholders were expelled from their farms during this time. To push back against these practices, groups of peasant farmers and rural union leaders formed the Landless Rural Workers Movement in 1984, with the central aim of fighting for the constitutional right to land for sustainable food production. The organization remains one of the most active social movements in Brazil to this day.

FOOD SOVEREIGNTY: A COLLECTIVE RESPONSE TO GLOBALIZATION OF THE FOOD SYSTEM

While **globalization** was at the heart of the problem facing peasant farmers, it also brought new forms of communication, organization, and coordinated campaigns of resistance to the global neoliberal order. A **transnational advocacy network**—composed of agrarian, indigenous, and fisher social movements, nongovernmental organizations, and civil society groups—came together in shared campaigns addressing issues related to agricultural liberalization. The roots of this network drew on strong regional coalitions that were meeting to strategize responses to common challenges. For example, farmers from several South and Central American countries began to meet regularly to discuss the barriers to agrarian reform. These meetings set the stage for what would more formally become the Latin American Coordination of Rural Organizations in 1994 and the Continental Campaign to commemorate "500 years of indigenous, black, and popular resistance." Other rural and indigenous peoples' movements around the world were also finding opportunities to meet each other and share experiences and strategies for finding alternative solutions to the challenges of agricultural globalization. These place-based organizations began to develop a collective identity and goal to protect the autonomy and health of their local communities, cultures, and ecologies that were directly threatened by the increasing insertion of capitalist market logics into their food systems.

These mobilizations—simultaneously but separately occurring all over the world—converged in 1992 as leaders from eight farming organizations from Central America, Europe, and North America met in Nicaragua at a meeting of the National Union of Farmers and Cattle Ranchers. As a founding vision for what in 1993 would become the transnational peasant movement La Vía Campesina, the Managua Declaration aimed to call the attention of the world to the following:

- Neoliberal policies represent a dramatic constraint on farmers throughout the world, bringing us to the brink of irredeemable extinction and further aggravating the irreparable damage which has been caused to our rural environs.

- Farm communities represent the majority in most regions of the world and it is our work that ensures the food base and life of all societies.

- We demand real participation in the formulation of policies which affect the fundamental condition of our sector in order to overcome the injustices which we bear.

- We draw your attention to the lack of respect which has been shown to our productive culture. It is essential that we pay due attention and strengthen our lives as generators of agriculture as the fundamental and strategic base for the survival of all people.

In 1996, La Vía Campesina—now a global network of peasant, indigenous, and rural women's organizations—held their II International Conference in Tlaxcala, Mexico. Building on decades of discussion, mobilization, campaigning, and regional organizing around the meaning(s) and practice of sovereignty, rights, citizenship, rural development, and democratization, the movement articulated the concept of food sovereignty as

> the right of peoples to healthy and culturally appropriate food produced through ecologically sound and sustainable methods, and their right to define their own food and agriculture systems.

This rejection and reframing of food security highlights the dynamics and values of equity (the right to food), ecology (produced in a sustainable way), and empowerment (the importance of having a voice) in a powerful proposal to change the terms of engagement around food security and the globalization of agriculture. Bringing this conversation to the UN World Food Summit in Rome in 1996, leaders from La Vía Campesina challenged the role of multinational corporations and international governance institutions such as the WTO in setting the terms and rules about what local and regional food systems should look like. At the same time, they demanded the restitution of support for diversified food systems and social justice through campaigns for agrarian reform and for regional and alternative food economies. They protested biopiracy and defended the right of communities to save, exchange, and develop locally adapted seed varieties, or what they view as *biocultural heritage*.

Today, La Vía Campesina maintains a formal network involving more than 160 social movements in seventy-three countries, representing more than two hundred million families. These organizations mobilize locally and participate in transnational advocacy campaigns around a range of themes, including biodiversity and genetic resources, agrarian reform, trade rules, gender and domestic violence, human rights, and agroecology.

Since the mid-1990s, the concept of food sovereignty has gained increasing traction with an even broader network of social movements and nongovernmental organizations. The 2007 Nyéléni summit brought together five hundred organizations, including consumer and urban organizations, and identified what have become known as *pillars of food sovereignty*, building on a decade of global conversations around a set of shared values that can be expressed in local contexts. The Nyéléni Declaration expanded on the concept of food sovereignty as

> *The right of peoples to healthy and culturally appropriate food produced through ecologically sound and sustainable methods, and their right to define their own food and agriculture systems. It puts the aspirations and needs of those who produce, distribute and consume food at the heart of food systems and policies rather than the demands of markets and corporations. It defends the interests and inclusion of the next generation. It offers a strategy to resist and dismantle the current corporate trade and food regime, and directions for food, farming, pastoral and fisheries systems determined by local producers and users. Food sovereignty prioritizes local and national economies and markets and empowers peasant and family farmer-driven agriculture, artisanal fishing, pastoralist-led grazing, and food production, distribution and consumption based on environmental, social and economic sustainability. Food sovereignty promotes transparent trade that guarantees just incomes to all peoples as well as the rights of consumers to control their food and nutrition. It ensures that the rights to use and manage lands, territories, waters, seeds, livestock and biodiversity are in the hands of those of us who produce food. Food sovereignty implies new social relations free of oppression and inequality between men and women, peoples, racial groups, social and economic classes and generations. (Nyéléni Forum for Food Sovereignty 2007)*

A CONCEPT, FRAMEWORK, AND SOCIAL MOVEMENT

Ultimately, food sovereignty is a concept, framework, and social movement that aims to fundamentally transform power relations in the food system. As a concept, it emerged from the principles of community and territorial autonomy: the right to set priorities for local and regional food cultures, using the principles of solidarity. These principles of *equitable empowerment* and *reciprocal responsibility* serve as a set of checks and balances that have governed indigenous and localized food cultivation and trading systems for millennia in all corners of the world. For communities in some regions of the world today, self-sufficiency and sovereignty imply growing all food locally; for others, it means participating in market relations based on the principles of a solidarity economy: equity, cooperation, and shared community well-being, rather than the concentration of profit in a few hands.

As a framework, food sovereignty provides us with a common frame of reference and lexicon for analyzing any food system—whether at the local, national, regional, and/or global scale—and the power relations therein. For example, food sovereignty is concerned with gender dynamics at the household level, race and class dynamics at the community and society level, and environmental resilience at the regional and global scales. It thus helps us to consider not only the outcomes of any particular aspect of the global agrifood system, but also the processes and mechanisms by which this system developed and who has a say in creating and/or influencing those processes (and to what extent).

As a social movement, food sovereignty was conceptualized by and has brought together small-scale and family farmers, indigenous peoples, fisherfolk, and their organizations from all corners of the world. Joining with environmental organizations, urban consumer's unions, antipoverty movements, and movements for human rights, the food sovereignty movement has mobilized to put into practice a vision for a more equitable and ecologically sound food system(s) that empowers and values those who cultivate and distribute food, as well as the people who consume it—as defined on their own terms.

FROM PROTEST TO POLICY: INSTITUTIONALIZING FOOD SOVEREIGNTY[1]

Food sovereignty differs from food security in its *definition* (access vs. empowerment), its *demarcation* (food sovereignty will look different at household, community, regional, national, and global scales), and its *design* (who decides?). Initiatives to put the concept into practice take place at the global governance level, at the national level in the form of legislation, and at the community level through grassroots and civil society initiatives.

Strategically, food sovereignty movements have mobilized to demand that states play an active role in developing specific policies that ensure the right of small-scale farmers, fishers, and indigenous peoples to exist both as food providers and as guardians of the global socioecological resource base. For example, land reform is a strategic demand of many national food sovereignty movements, illustrated vividly in the case of the Brazilian Landless Rural Workers Movement, which mobilized the fulfillment of a constitutional provision that mandated the distribution of idle land to small-scale family farmers. Similarly, the food sovereignty movement played an active

---

[1] This section is partially drawn from H. Wittman, "From Protest to Policy: The Challenges of Institutionalizing Food Sovereignty," *Canadian Food Studies* 2, no. 2 (2015): 174–82. http://doi.org/10.15353/cfs-rcea.v2i2.99.

role in the development of the Voluntary Guidelines on the Responsible Governance of Tenure published in 2012 by the FAO in response to rapid growth in land-grabbing by international and corporate actors after the 2007–8 global food price crisis.

For most advocates, food sovereignty is about supporting both individual and community food security and a sustainable (local, national) agricultural sector through policy reforms. This mobilization has led to calls for the institutionalization of the right to food and food sovereignty at the international level and, in a growing number of instances, into national legislative public policy frameworks.

These policy initiatives are diverse and include **redistributive policies** (agrarian reform and food security and social safety net programs), market interventions including the reemergence of grain reserves, public procurement and government price floor programs, and environmental regulation of harmful agricultural production practices. One national example can be found in Brazil's *Fome Zero* (Zero Hunger) policy framework, which connects policies for reduction of hunger in urban environments with strategic supports for small-scale and family farmers using ecological production methods, in a form of *mediated market*. In this example, public nutrition programs delivered by schools, food banks, and hospitals are supplied directly with agroecologically produced food from local family farmers. At the global level, La Vía Campesina is working on a policy platform based on the United Nations Declaration on the Rights of Peasants and other People Working in Rural Areas, under discussion at the UN Human Rights Commission. Many of these mechanisms fall under the umbrella of food system localization (see Lesson 17), aiming to reduce distancing and increase accountability by reconnecting producers and consumers through participatory policy structures, democratically informed regulatory frameworks, and production models adapted to local socioecological conditions.

The idea that most food could or should be produced and consumed within a designated geographic scale (usually a community, region, or nation) is based on the expected positive social and ecological results associated with localization (including stability in the face of food price volatility). Food self-sufficiency has emerged as a principle in emerging food sovereignty legislation, as is the case, for example, in Indonesia, Bolivia, Ecuador, and Venezuela. The food localization approach is challenged, however, by questions about the role of trade and markets (both local trade and globalized food trade) and at what scale (or scales) food sovereignty can or should occur. It is increasingly acknowledged that localization alone does not immediately translate into food autonomy, self-sufficiency, or food sovereignty; food insecurity occurs even in locations of food abundance; and cross-border trade for consumption needs and desires from bananas to coffee, as well as for basic commodities like rice, soybean and maize, is unlikely to abate. The institutionalization of food sovereignty requires moving beyond simple comparisons of food security–food sovereignty and localization–globalization by identifying adaptive and place-specific mechanisms for implementing the principles of food sovereignty and sustainability while considering practical contradictions and limits (Clapp 2014).

As such, most proposals by grassroots actors do not emphasize self-sufficiency as the primary pathway to food sovereignty. Many farming communities see the value in being able to pursue diversified livelihood strategies through socially equitable food trade, such as through a solidarity economy and other mediated market arrangements. In support of these goals, the food sovereignty movement advocates for a broader range of supports to improve both environmental and food security outcomes, such as the initiatives exemplified in Brazil's Zero Hunger framework. This includes new ways of participating in decisions about agricultural policy and market integration through the implementation of local food policy councils that are integrated into policy debates at national and global levels.

In what follows, we will examine the institutionalization of food sovereignty principles in Ecuador as part of its 2008 constitutional reform and the *Sumak Kawsay* or Good Living initiative, and Brazil, where food sovereignty emerges as part of the larger national Zero Hunger initiative.

LEGISLATING FOOD SOVEREIGNTY AT THE NATIONAL LEVEL

Ecuador

Ecuador's 2008 constitution was one of the first to explicitly recognize the goal of food sovereignty in a national legislative forum, which emerged in the larger context of the broad participation of civil society in its process of constitutional reform. As part of widespread opposition to the neoliberal era in Ecuador, civil society and grassroots actors called for the state to put back into place supports for the local agricultural sector, and for small-scale and family farmers in particular, through programs for agrarian reform and agroecology, using the discourse of national sovereignty. A coalition of agricultural movements and organizations—a *Mesa Agraria*—was formed during the constituent assembly by *campesino* and indigenous organizations. This group contributed proposals for rural development, food security, environmental regulation, and agricultural policy couched in the language of national food sovereignty and support for domestic agricultural markets and distribution models.

Article 281 of Ecuador's constitution mirrors many of the items in the International Convention on Peasants Rights articulated by La Vía Campesina under debate at the UN General Assembly—declaring that "food sovereignty is a strategic objective and an obligation of the State in order to ensure that persons, communities, peoples and nations achieve self-sufficiency with respect to healthy and culturally appropriate food on a permanent basis." In 2009, the Ecuadorian legislature passed a food sovereignty law to support a national rural development strategy that includes improving public infrastructure for storing basic food supplies and targeting smallholder farmers to market to the public sector (i.e., institutional food programs and food reserves). A subsequent law of popular and solidarity economy stipulated that 5 percent of the national budget for public procurement programming should be sourced from small-scale producer associations and cooperatives and specifically targets schools and public daycares in a home-grown school-feeding model.

However, while local food procurement programs have been proposed at a pilot scale in some communities, almost no implementation has occurred since 2009, mainly because of a lack of funding and infrastructure. Additionally, consistent tension exists between government support for oil and gas extraction initiatives—which provide revenues of up to half of the federal budget—that directly challenge the principles of food sovereignty. Oil and gas revenues, even when couched in the language of economic sovereignty, are not invested in sustainable agriculture or domestic food security initiatives and are mainly utilized in public works, paying down external debt and strengthening the export sector.

Agrarian social movement leaders suggest that the targeting of technical assistance and agricultural credit to export-oriented agricultural sectors such as aquaculture, banana, cacao, and palm has detracted from the ability of the domestic agriculture sector to service national food security, which continues to depend on imports for 35 percent of grains and almost 100 percent of wheat. In response, agrarian cooperatives are working on consumer education campaigns to promote *healthy eating* and establish farmers' markets in traditional agroexport centers. However, *campesino* leaders note that consumers are not willing to pay the higher costs of foods produced using agroecological production models and some farmers who have experimented with organic production are now returning to the conventional model instead. In addition, while legislation for food sovereignty exists in theory at the national level, municipal and state governments are the ones responsible for implementation; as a result, initiatives to strengthen the position of individual small-scale farmers and more sustainable production models at the community level are uneven across the country. Overall, significant challenges contribute to a *distribution bottleneck* for domestic food self-sufficiency, resulting from the lack of coordination between different government ministries and from a lack of public investment in infrastructure—such as roads, storage and postharvest processing facilities, and irrigation programs—sorely needed by the small-scale farming sector.

Brazil

Brazil, known as an agricultural export powerhouse, has also enacted some of the most advanced national frameworks for food security and food sovereignty through its *Fome Zero* (Zero Hunger) program. While Brazil's 1988 constitution does not explicitly mention food sovereignty, it does highlight the protection of economic, social, and cultural rights, and in 2010 a significant amendment included the right to food. The *Fome Zero* program was formally launched in 2003 by the federal Ministry of

Agrarian Development and the Ministry of Social Development and Fight against Hunger; it includes a series of food security programs that involve public procurement of food from family farmers for distribution to schools, hospitals, and other national food security initiatives. Programs for land redistribution and for agricultural credit targeted toward women, family farmers, and technical agroecological production are also included under the *Fome Zero* umbrella. With the expansion of the *Fome Zero* program under President Luis Inácio "Lula" da Silva's government (2003–11), the right to food movement became more explicitly connected with rural movements for agrarian reform and food sovereignty. A 2006 law on food security acknowledges that "the realization of the human right to adequate food and to food and nutritional security requires respect for sovereignty, that confer on countries the primacy of their decisions around the production and consumption of food." A 2009 education law also stipulated that 30 percent of school meal programs must be sourced from the local family farm sector, with price premiums offered for products grown using organic and agroecological methods.

Brazil's agrarian reform and public food procurement programs are perhaps the most well-developed examples of legislated food sovereignty mechanisms that link the challenges of rural development with the needs of urban consumers, the environment, and national food security. These programs have had some positive results in terms of supporting the marginalized family farm sector to transition to sustainable agriculture and to have access to secure local markets. Yet, almost a decade after implementation, uptake is still relatively small—less than 3 percent of family farmers in Brazil participate in the Food Purchase public procurement program at the national level. Participants express concern about the bureaucratization of enrollment and marketing processes and difficulty in accessing efficient distribution infrastructure. Small-scale farmers also struggle to upgrade farm infrastructure to meet new food safety regulations designed for industrial food producers and are sometimes unable to compete with larger-scale producers who sell globally and nationally traded commodity items like beans and rice at lower prices (Wittman and Blesh 2017).

Principally funded by the Ministry of Social Development, public food procurement programs are a form of compensatory social policy that aims to partially address the concerns of a struggling family farm sector. In contrast, large-scale agricultural investments are made in the agroexport sector by both government and international financiers, contributing to structural inequality in shaping Brazil's agricultural future.[2] Land inequity has not improved

---

[2] Compare the Ministry of Agriculture's 2013–14 budget of R136 billion (US$62 billion), which supports low-interest loans, grants, and capital investment projects for agribusiness, with the Ministry of Agrarian Development budget for family farm sector support of R39 billion for the 2013–14 season for operating loans, crop insurance, agricultural extension, home-grown school feeding, and other public nutrition programs.

in Brazil despite forty years of redistributive land reform, suggesting parallel processes of redistribution and reconcentration. And while poverty and food insecurity levels have dropped, these are primarily related to the dual strategy of an increase in social safety nets and increased employment resulting from economic growth, rather than from strategic investment in the local and regional food systems. On the whole, the *Fome Zero* program has not resulted in a structural reorganization of the national food system, despite adjusting market relations to meet social/ecological objectives at more regional scales.

CHALLENGES TO INSTITUTIONALIZING FOOD SOVEREIGNTY

Much evaluation is still needed on how these national-level policies and programs are implemented in their respective contexts and to what extent they are addressing the principles and goals of the food sovereignty framework (i.e., culturally appropriate food security, equity, democracy, locally adaptive agricultural policies, ecological sustainability). Several challenges to the institutionalization of food sovereignty are immediately apparent. These include how to scale the implementation of food sovereignty principles up and out, without losing connection to the principles of democratic engagement and connection to place, and how to confront an international trade regime that is systematically trying to remove support for domestic food and agriculture programs.

Public procurement programs supporting domestic social and ecological priorities are also contentious at the level of international trade negotiations. Directly challenging many food sovereignty–inspired initiatives to procure sustainably produced food from small-scale and local producers, the WTO's Government Procurement Agreement aims to "mutually open government procurement markets among its parties"—a market that is worth US $1.7 trillion, according to the WTO. Some suggest that placing qualitative criteria on products (ethical, sustainable, ecological, denomination of origin, etc.) to make them "not like" imported products (and therefore to allow discrimination in their favor) will sidestep the fears of trade disputes, as will structuring procurement programs to conform with allowed public policy objectives (for example, for specific environmental outcomes). Similarly, provisions in the WTO that allow for government procurement of products for government purposes without resale (i.e., school lunch programs and meal programs at public institutions) suggest that these programs may be allowed under current trade rules (MacRae 2014).

WHAT'S NEXT: MULTISCALAR APPROACHES?

Food sovereignty is ultimately about changing and decentralizing power in the food system—reducing the influence of the global and corporatized food regime and providing a foundation for diverse, sustainable, and democratic food provisioning systems across the globe. Mechanisms for institutional-izing food sovereignty include *autonomous and localized* initiatives—such as farmers' markets and community-supported agriculture, buying clubs, local food policy councils, land occupations, seed sharing and seed banks, agroecology schools, and farmer-to-farmer training networks. These autono-mous initiatives are supported (and in some cases challenged) by *state actions* including legislative reform and state support for the development of public procurement programs targeting small-scale and sustainable agriculture. Fi-nally, the conversation on institutionalizing food sovereignty is taking place in the *global policy arena*, including at the UN Committee on World Food Se-curity and in international trade dialogues. These fora provide for greater participation by and access of global civil society to global governance dis-cussions. This also allows for the expansion of the dialogue on the distribu-tion of rights and responsibilities for sustainability in the global food system, both up (i.e., in the WTO and other global governance institutions) and down (in regional and national legislative frameworks). The globalization of agri-cultural standards and regulatory regimes has done much, however, to dis-possess the rights of local communities, who are rightly suspect of attempts to *globalize* a regulatory framework—even one based on food sovereignty principles. As such, the internationalization of a more progressive set of standards (e.g., organic, fair trade, environmental certifications) may offer some ability to target and support localized transformations in production systems, but so far has had little effect in redistributing power and resources in the global food system (see Lessons 9, 15, and 16), which is, after all, the ultimate goal of the food sovereignty framework.

Ultimately, the final responsibility for moving from international dialogue to making structural shifts in the *distribution of power* in the food system remains at the national and local levels—from food policy councils down to the household division of labor—where *sovereignty* can be territorialized and enacted. As such, policies and programs designed to institutionalize food sovereignty principles will look very different in places like Indonesia and Venezuela (net food importers seeking to increase food self-sufficiency) compared to Ecuador and Brazil (net food exporters seeking to strengthen the family farm sector while improving domestic food security outcomes). Future work looking at the institutionalization of food sovereignty will need to navigate the multiple definitions of and pathways toward food sov-ereignty and assess the extent to which particular initiatives or programs enable power shifts in the agricultural sector.

Discussion Questions

1. In your own words, how would you characterize the concepts of food security and food sovereignty? Where are some similarities, synergies, and points of divergence? What are the strengths and weaknesses of each approach? Are they mutually exclusive?
2. What is the relationship between food localization, food self-sufficiency, and food sovereignty? Are these one and the same? Why or why not?

3. Food sovereignty emphasizes the need for more democratic and equitable participation in food systems policy development and discussions. What are some practical suggestions for how to include a wider diversity of voices in decision-making processes? Can you think of any examples where this has been done well?

4. Through the case studies of Ecuador and Brazil, you may see gaps between the principles of food sovereignty, the institutionalization of the principles, and the implementation of programs on the ground. In your opinion, can food sovereignty be actualized within a neoliberal economic system, or must it necessarily include transformation of the global economic order? Justify your answer.

5. How would you characterize the state of food sovereignty in your own community?

Exercises

1. *Variation on Question 4, above.* Carry out a modified World Café–style activity, where a class breaks into three small groups. Each group addresses only one part of the question (Where are there gaps? Can food sovereignty be achieved in a capitalist society? Or does it require full transformation?). Each group records their conversation on a piece of flipchart paper. Each group gets ten minutes or so to talk about their question. After the end of the first ten minutes, each group member gets up and moves to a different table with a different question (they do not have to stick together). For another ten minutes, the new groups review the previous group's notes and then build on them, continuing to record new points of discussion. Repeat this process one more time until all students have visited all tables/questions. Once complete, post all flipchart notes and do a gallery walk with the class, thinking through common themes that arose as well as points of contention.

2. *Mock meeting scenario.* Have students imagine that they are different stakeholders with their own interests (ministry/government officials, civil society actors, industry representatives) of [insert country] and are meeting to discuss the development or revision of food and agriculture laws and programming via constituent assembly. For new laws to be passed, the majority of stakeholders need to pass a vote. Have students carry out negotiation rounds until a decision is made.

Additional Materials

Readings

Burnett, Kim, and Sophia Murphy. 2014. "What Place for International Trade in Food Sovereignty?" *The Journal of Peasant Studies* 41 (6): 1065–84.

Claeys, Priscilla. 2012. "The Creation of New Rights by the Food Sovereignty Movement: The Challenge of Institutionalizing Subversion." *Sociology* 46 (5): 844–60.

Desmarais, Annette. A. 2002. "Peasants Speak—The Vía Campesina: Consolidating an International Peasant and Farm Movement." *The Journal of Peasant Studies* 29 (2): 91–124.

Edelman, Marc, and Carwil James. 2011. "Peasants' Rights and the UN System: Quixotic Struggle? Or Emancipatory Idea Whose Time Has Come?" *Journal of Peasant Studies* 38 (1): 81–108.

Knuth, Lidija, and Margret Vidar. 2011. *Constitutional and Legal Protection of the Right to Food around the World*. Rome: FAO. http://www.fao.org/righttofood/publications/publications-detail/en/c/80544/

Martínez-Torres, María Elena, and Peter M. Rosset. 2010. "La Vía Campesina: The Birth and Evolution of a Transnational Social Movement." *The Journal of Peasant Studies* 37 (1): 149–75.

Patel, Raj. 2009. "Food Sovereignty." *Journal of Peasant Studies* 36 (3): 663–706.

Wittman, Hannah, Annette Aurelie Desmarais, and Nettie Wiebe. 2010. *Food Sovereignty: Reconnecting Food, Nature and Community*. Halifax: Fernwood.

Websites

Centre for Sustainable Food Systems at UBC Farm
Food First
Global Justice Now
Institute for Agriculture and Trade Policy
University of California's Global Food Initiative
US Food Sovereignty Alliance
Vía Campesina and Nyéléni Europe

Video Clips

Food sovereignty: Valerie Segrest at TEDxRainier
Hands on the Land for Food Sovereignty and Climate Justice
La Vía Campesina in Movement

References

Clapp, Jennifer. 2014. "Food Security and Food Sovereignty: Getting Past the Binary." *Dialogues in Human Geography* 4:206–11.

FAO (Food and Agriculture Organization of the United Nations). 2015. *The State of Food Insecurity in the World 2015*. Rome: FAO. Accessed May 2, 2017. http://www.fao.org/hunger/glossary/en/

MacRae, Rod. 2014. "Do Trade Agreements Substantially Limit Development of Local/Sustainable Food Systems in Canada?" *Canadian Food Studies/La Revue Canadienne des Études sur L'alimentation* 1 (1): 103–25.

Nyéléni Forum for Food Sovereignty. 2007. "Declaration of Nyéléni." February 27, 2007. https://nyeleni.org/spip.php?article290

Sen, Amartya. 1981. *Poverty and Famines*. Oxford: Oxford University Press.

Wittman, Hannah, and Jennifer Blesh. 2017. "Food Sovereignty and Fome Zero: Connecting Public Food Procurement Programmes to Sustainable Rural Development in Brazil." *Journal of Agrarian Change* 17 (1): 81–105.

An urban farm on the former site of Chicago's Cabrini–Green housing complex. (Photo by Scott Olson/Getty Images.)

19

Urban Food Production

Joshua Sbicca

A s *we make our way to the burial mound, people break off into small groups carrying on conversations until we come upon the site. We form a half circle while Ben Yahola, a food sovereignty activist from the Muscogee tribe, prepares an offering to the ancestors. Taking a large abalone shell, he fills it with white sage leaves. He then asks one of the men in attendance to pass around sweet tobacco. Everyone takes a small handful. Ben proceeds to introduce us to this space. This is the only burial mound left on the Milwaukee State Fair Grounds. The others are where the racetrack resides. Ben expresses that local indigenous people had fought to honor that final burial mound, to keep alive spaces of remembrance and history. He explains that the space is for remembering not just Menominee ancestors, but all ancestors. Given that Native Americans are from a nature-based society, nature is also our ancestor. When clouds roll overhead, he interprets, "They are our elders, old men and old women stooping over to watch after us as they pass." Maintaining that relationship between people and nature is fundamental to understanding our place in the world. Ben continues the ceremony by inviting people to say or sing something while making their offering. Most people silently kneel before the sage and tobacco-filled abalone shell and drop their offering inside. A few speak in their native tongue, voice prayers or hopes, or more ceremoniously genuflect, waft the smoke over their heads and bodies, and firmly grip the ground.*[1]

It was fall of 2011 in the lakeside city of Milwaukee and I was attending the fourth annual Gathering, a conference hosted by the Growing Food and Justice Initiative. Over two hundred food activists, farmers, and gardeners converged around the weekend's theme, Sacred Soil: Cultivating the Seeds of Community Transformation. Embedded in the genetics of the event was honor for the relationship between humans and nature, ecological sustainability and social justice, and the ever-present need to foster relationships between people and plants. Organizers planned workshops, dialogues, field trips, and meals focused on dismantling racism and building multicultural alliances. For this convergence to stimulate ecological and social improvements in the food system, stronger human bonds were necessary.

The focus of the Gathering channeled my thoughts as I encountered my first aquaponics system during one of the weekend's planned field trips. The

---

[1] Personal journal entry from September 9, 2011.

Community Food Center, which was run by the recently dissolved Growing Power, a well-known food justice organization founded by the MacArthur Genius Award winner Will Allen, used urban agriculture to support low-income communities of color. While urban farms throughout Milwaukee were still harvesting much of the summer's bounty, winter was imminent, and with it came the end of the growing season for all but a handful of leafy greens and root vegetables. To encounter urban agriculture innovations that extended the growing season in the face of cold, harsh winters and created spaces for social bonding and economic opportunity was revelatory. When I walked into the Community Food Center and turned right into one of their seventeen greenhouses, the aquaponics system exuded warm, moist air, populating the atmosphere with an aroma that smelled like rain after it falls on soil. Hanging plants lined the perimeter, PVC pipes snaked throughout the space, and a large rectangular tank full of fish bubbled as recycled water pumped into its depths. As Will Allen guided us through this "living museum" and "idea factory," the urban agriculture gizmos and gadgets that tied together a range of living systems struck me. A giant compost pile teemed with earthworms and broke down organic matter used to grow potted plants and plants grown in hoop houses on the property. A closed-loop aquaculture project grew fish and recycled their waste to fertilize and grow vegetables, mainly greens, in low-soil plugs, trays, and containers. Staff facilitated all these connections through educational and skill development opportunities for local residents and visitors wanting to become proficient in value-added product development, food marketing, and food distribution. Never had growing food appeared so revolutionary.

I left Growing Power with sights, smells, and tastes that still linger and a sense that this was a real utopian project amid an otherwise economically and racially marginalized community. Instead of waiting for mass insurrection or the collapse of exploitative social systems, these urban food producers envisioned immediate alternatives that fostered connections to nature and people. Nevertheless, the small scale of the organization and the reality that it will require transforming our food system in fundamental ways to produce socially just and sustainable food that nourishes peoples' bodies and minds left me with many questions. The practice of urban agriculture holds promise for solving social and ecological problems, but cities are socially complex places replete with human bonds and barriers that inform the urbanization process and, with it, human's connection to food.

This lesson draws on almost a decade of research into a variety of instances and dimensions of urban agriculture in the United States. I grapple with some of the food system, ecological, and social implications of growing food in cities. To begin, what does it mean to grow food in cities? Are human and nature relations deepened in cities through producing food? To answer these questions, I offer sociological and historical observations that consider the relationship between food systems and urban development. The insights of Ebenezer Howard on planning garden cities and Karl Marx on capitalism, nature, and urbanization build a foundation to then answer other questions.

Does the political economy of cities facilitate or hinder urban agriculture? What kinds and under what conditions? What is the reach of urban agriculture? Is self-sufficiency at an urban scale possible? I then provide examples from Los Angeles, Oakland, San Diego, Orlando, and Detroit to ask different questions. What are the goals, outcomes, and implications of urban agriculture? I specifically discuss the economic and social values, democratic impulses, and community bonds associated with this practice. No treatment of urban agriculture would be complete without also addressing some of the limitations and challenges of urban agriculture. Who is involved and under what conditions? Who benefits and loses? I focus on the challenges of social boundaries, land use struggles, and labor practices to show how growing food in cities is a contested process. Let's begin.

GARDEN CITIES, URBAN PLANNING, AND UTOPIA

At the turn of the twentieth century in London, heavy pollution lingered in the air; poverty, hunger, and malnutrition were rife; and urban agriculture was unsanitary and marginalized as the industrialization of agriculture compelled farmers to exchange their pitchforks for wrenches in factories. The social restructuring that came with the acceleration of capitalist development, manifest in the process of urbanization, inspired many observers to critique the environmental and social degradation and imagine alternatives. Among these observers was Ebenezer Howard (1902), who wrote the book *Garden Cities of To-morrow*, a vision of urban planning and social reform aimed at eliminating a host of problems.

Central to Howard's concerns was the perception that cities failed to foster human flourishing. Indeed, he viewed them as magnets that attracted people like a moth to a flame, only to extinguish human potential by the social and environmental ills contained therein. His solutions were wide ranging, but in sum, they articulated a desire to decentralize the urbanization process by creating **garden cities**. Howard imagined cities consisting of concentric bands based on the local conditions that included a central park, houses containing gardens, and fair allotments of land to city dwellers that diversified the land use into forests, orchards, livestock pastures, and vegetable farms. Hailing the arguments of anarchists like Peter Kropotkin, these garden cities were not to be subservient to a larger state apparatus. Rather, they would require embedding work in the social operation of cities to supersede capitalism and share in the governance of everyday life. Socially, this would require collectivizing land, maintaining livability by controlling the cost of land and ensuring high wages, and merging ecological sustainability with physical and emotional health. Moreover, garden cities were not to be isolated experiments. Instead, railway lines were to connect them regionally. The utopian endpoint would be a network of socially and ecologically sustainable communities run democratically, through mutual association, and with shared responsibility.

One of the legacies of Howard and his contemporaries is the idea that cities should not produce absolute divisions between humans and nature. While his prescriptions may appear idealistic or antiquated, there are insights still relevant today. Consider, for instance, that when Howard wrote *Garden Cities of To-morrow*, 13.5 percent of the world's population lived in urban centers. Today, the urban population is 55 percent and projected to be nearly 70 percent by 2050, with most of the growth likely to occur in the global South (i.e., poor, economically and politically peripheral, postcolonial, and/or developing countries). We are living during a global historic shift from a closer communion to rural food production to losing that connection and buying our food from a shrinking pool of food producers. The results are cataclysmic, from both an ecological and a sociological vantage point, and far exceed the scale of the problem in 1900. According to the Food and Agriculture Organization of the United Nations, 800 million people grow food in cities, producing about 15 to 20 percent of the world's food. At the same time, there are at least 795 million people living in hunger, most of who are small-scale farmers. In countries with high levels of poverty the pace of urbanization has outstripped the ability of many agricultural sectors to adequately feed those moving into what the trenchant scholar Mike Davis (2006) refers to as *megaslums*. He critiques the current *overurbanization* because it "is driven by the reproduction of poverty" (16). The extraction of natural and human capital to expand cities comes with costs to the agricultural sector and how or whether people access food. Like the critiques of Howard a century earlier, Davis observes that cities are sites of deep structural inequalities that serve to fatten the pockets and bellies of the wealthiest while billions of people lose their historic connection to nature and the land.

Although global trends are important, the remainder of my lesson discusses the United States, which is where I have conducted most of my research. In 1940, roughly 40 percent of the population in the United States was urban, and this figure doubled to 80 percent by 2010. During the same period, the country went from having a little over six million farms (18 percent of the labor force) at an average of 175 acres to about two million farms (less than 2 percent of the labor force) at an average of 434 acres. Nevertheless, as farming has declined as an occupation and people move to cities in greater numbers, urban agriculture is increasing, evidenced by the spread of urban farms and community and backyard gardening. Although there are no regularly collected statistics by the US Department of Agriculture, some research suggests an almost 30 percent increase between 2008 and 2013 to nine million urban households involved in growing food (National Gardening Association 2014).[2] Although these trends do not reflect exactly how Howard envisaged his garden cities, the practice of urban agriculture has stoked the

---

[2] The US Department of Agriculture took the unprecedented step of collecting statistics on urban agriculture for the 2017 Census of Agriculture.

imagination of many and transformed our urban landscapes. To further understand urban human and nature relations, I turn to Karl Marx, who also investigated urban and rural divides and the significance of capitalism as a historic driver of socioecological degradation and separation.

SOCIAL METABOLISM, METABOLIC RIFTS, AND URBAN AGRICULTURE

Although the concepts may appear foreign, **social metabolism** and **metabolic rift** explain how the industrialization of agriculture, as well as urbanization, accelerates social division and ecosystem disruption. Social metabolism is the nutrient–energy cycle between humans and the environment. As developed by the environmental sociologist John Bellamy Foster, metabolic rift is an eco-Marxist concept that explains how industrial capitalism as a system of infinite economic growth breaks this cycle. Humans became alienated from nature, from the product of their labor, and from each other. Marx observed that after large landholders compelled political elites, often one and the same, to pass laws in England enclosing formerly common lands, agricultural production began to intensify. The resulting decline in the number of farmers, their transition into industrial workers, and the increased need for more food in cities disrupted the soil nutrient cycle. Whereas smallholder farmers used to maintain a closer balance between the production of rural waste and soil fertility, cities lacked the infrastructure or commitment to recycle the increased concentration of urban waste back to rural farms.

One of the important takeaways regarding the relationship between food production and cities is that there is a complex relationship between humans and nature that explains the degree of health and vitality of urban populations. With respect to urban agriculture, this framework helps to consider the nature of social metabolism within, and the metabolic rifts disrupting, city life. Take the expansive metropolis of Los Angeles, a place I called home for several years. The city is 503 square miles and contains 3.8 million people, mostly people of color, namely Latinx, Asian, and black. The city also houses a huge diversity of immigrants from over 140 countries. To serve the many **foodways**, that is, the culturally distinct culinary traditions and diets of groups, the city is reliant on a global network of food supply chains. These provide everything from American dietary staples pushed by food processors, like potato chips and soda, to specialty food items like sushi-grade tuna sold in upscale restaurants and blue corn masa to enliven food cart quesadillas. With such diverse tastes and a landmass dominated by concrete, a complex network of roads, high levels of air pollution and soil contamination, and sprawling suburbs, all of which indicate different rifts associated with urbanization, expanding urban agriculture is difficult. But nature (and massive hydraulic projects diverting water to an arid climate) has been kind to Angelenos. Despite increasingly common droughts, one of many rifts associated with the long history of capitalist industrial development, the weather is mild and the water keeps flowing. So while the urbanization of Los Angeles disrupts nature's cycles, fruit trees and gardens are abundant throughout the city. Oranges, lemons, plums, nectarines, loquats, figs, and avocados hang from trees. Tomatoes, peppers, eggplant, squash, and their pollinators interact in sun-bleached neighborhoods. Although as an overall percentage of the city such green spaces are limited, they nevertheless complicate the concrete-heavy landscape, suggesting the interaction between an array of social metabolisms and metabolic rifts.

The metabolic rifts associated with capitalist industrial agriculture, such as dead zones in the Gulf of Mexico caused by nitrogen runoff or the exploitation of immigrant strawberry pickers in the fields of California, compel imagining what might suture human and nature relations. Broadly speaking, healing metabolic rifts require creating alternative social and economic arrangements outside of capitalism. One way that sociologists and other social scientists analyze how urban agriculture can lead to economically just and environmentally sustainable cities is to break down the ecological, social, and individual dimensions of social metabolism. For example, the Oakland-based food justice organization People's Grocery grew food as a strategy to increase access to healthy and culturally appropriate food for the historically black neighborhood of West Oakland. Although this was insufficient to heal ecological rifts, it offered a way to mend social and individual rifts. People's Grocery ran gardens and small-scale urban farms that offered noncommodified relationships to land and labor and nonalienating connections to nature. To combat social rifts, the organization ran community gardens that fostered the values of collective learning and resource sharing where people volunteered their time to contribute to a common cause. To tackle individual rifts, community gardens allowed people to cultivate and eat their own food as well as plant crop varieties reflecting their cultural heritage, like collards and mustard greens. All told, the strategies of groups like People's Grocery show how urban agriculture can challenge capitalism's commodification of land and labor and therefore alienation from food.

REVALUING URBAN AGRICULTURE, DEMOCRACY, AND COMMUNITY BUILDING

Numbers are difficult to obtain, but the preponderance of grassroots initiatives and local city planning efforts to expand urban agriculture suggests that urban farms, community gardens, and home gardens are here to stay. Take gardening as a broad category of such activities. The National Gardening Association (2014) estimates that one in three households are growing food: 50 percent live in suburbs, 29 percent in rural communities, and 21 percent in large cities. They find that gardening is expanding most rapidly in cities, especially among millennials and households with children. According to the same report, thirty-nine million households garden at one's own residence or the residence of a neighbor, friend, or relative and three million households participate in a community garden. In terms of basic demographics, most gardening households have college degrees, but the fastest-growing group of gardening households only has a high school degree. Although most gardening households earn incomes greater than $75,000 (35 percent), there are many households that earn less than $35,000 (26 percent). The large body of literature on community gardens shows that many low-income communities and communities of color are growing food not only to enjoy a closer connection with food and nature and to save money, but also to engage civically, build community, and assert cultural identity. These value-laden practices emerge in many ways, but overall reveal that urban agriculture is forming new social metabolisms.

Gardening often begins at home, which serves as a space for gardeners to develop both private and public values. Gardens run the gamut from isolated oases, where the gardener does not interact with others in the community, to communally organized projects that use private gardens to grow and share food. Research finds that home gardens offer a variety of benefits. It is possible, for example, for families to attain marginal food security improvements and diversify their diets when they grow some of their own food. Moreover, home gardens can be sites of resistance to racial, ethnic, or class marginalization and disinvestment and therefore places to generate culturally relevant horticultural, traditional, and/or spiritual practices. In Oakland, the food justice organization Planting Justice creates living wage jobs for formerly incarcerated men, mostly black and from low-income neighborhoods throughout the East Bay. These jobs have built hundreds of edible landscapes, almost a quarter of which have been free for low-income people who want to reconnect to their foodways and grow food for their families. Growing food can also be an act of opposition to perceived problems with corporate industrialized food supply chains and therefore a commitment to local food systems. Depending on the neighborhood, a concentration of home gardeners sometimes builds community around similar interests and social and ecological knowledge sharing. With respect to environmental benefits, the outcomes vary. Gardens may help diversify the number of plant species in a city and therefore foster more wildlife. There is the potential, then, for greater urban agrobiodiversity if home gardeners are cultivating heirloom plant varieties, experimenting with new plant types, and embedding this in foodways from around the world. However, home gardens may also contribute to polluting storm-water runoff or groundwater from the application of too much fertilizer or nitrogen-heavy compost.

Considering some of the benefits of home gardens, it is no wonder that urban farms and community gardens are also widespread. They hold aesthetic, cultural, health, and social functions. In San Diego at the 2.3-acre New Roots Community Farm, you can find eighty-five families sharing space and growing a plethora of fruits and vegetables. International Rescue Committee runs this farm, which is one of a range of programs used to support people fleeing war, violence, persecution, and human trafficking. In 2009, the organization transformed an abandoned trash-strewn urban plot in the racially and ethnically diverse low-income neighborhood of City Heights into a green wilderness chock-full of unique plants reflective of the community gardeners. Relocated refugees and immigrants are growing crops that they had in their home countries and subsidizing their family budgets with the resulting food. For example, Cambodian gardeners grow winged beans and Kermit eggplants, while a range of indigenous leafy greens like African nightshade and jute mallow ruffle in the breeze of Somali garden beds. Refugees are selling these plants, along with more typical varieties, in small amounts at farmers' markets or to neighbors without garden plots. There are other noncommodified values in addition to the cultural exchange and reproduction of foodways. As one Latina community leader exclaimed, "The most important part of gardening for me is becoming part of nature, you are filled with energy, you can move, you are alive." As this anecdote of refugee farmers suggests, the power of gardening to animate people and nurture strong communal ties reveals that food does more than ensure physical health and survival; it is socially significant.

These trends contend with the **neoliberal** turn in urban governance (see Lesson 9). Many noneconomic values empower and offer modes of resistance for urban farmers with less power than business and political elites. Consider, for instance, that since the 1980s, when political leaders like Ronald Reagan and Margaret Thatcher institutionalized the *laissez-faire* (i.e., neoliberal) theories of economists like Friedrich Hayek, *big government* has dwindled. Whereas prior to this time cities ensured greater social welfare and regulations, they devolved into sites of aggressive real estate development and the privatization of formerly public spaces and services. Additionally, cities have increasingly become sites to invest capital. This has meant that consumerism predominates. Instead of developing cities to increase social connectivity, citizenship becomes secondary to the atomized shopper as cities compete to increase spending by people with high disposable incomes. Shopping districts litter the landscape, while spaces for noncommodified socializing face resistance by real estate developers, their lobbyists, and sympathetic local political officials unless they might increase property values and attract private investment. Amid this shift, some residents, albeit the exception, have sought to carve out zones that are more autonomous and have the capacity to shift urban priorities.

One of the common ways in which participants in community gardens and other forms of urban agriculture have viewed their practices is as a manifestation of civic engagement and democratic participation. Per the sociological imagination of C. Wright Mills, turning personal troubles into public issues requires looking beyond an immediate experience, such as hunger, and connecting it to a structural condition like poverty. Many antihunger, food security, and food justice organizations take such an approach to urban agriculture. In research in Orlando, Florida, I focused on a local chapter of Food Not Bombs, which worked to redistribute food waste and redirect produce from urban farms and gardens to low-income people as well as the homeless. Food Not Bombs is a global, decentralized movement of over one thousand chapters in more than sixty countries that uses food waste as a tool to link capitalism, militarism, and poverty. As a nonhierarchical network, it preferences anarchist principles of freedom and equality to address poverty, hunger, and malnutrition in each location that it operates. In Orlando, the group has resisted neoliberal development strategies around the ritzy Lake Eola Park, which was a long-standing site to hold weekly feedings and build community to challenge economic inequity in the city. Tensions between business and political elites and Orlando Food Not Bombs culminated when the city of Orlando passed an ordinance that banned the feeding of homeless people in downtown parks. This was a social cleansing practice on the part of the city to "beautify" the park and prevent "undesirables" in a gentrifying neighborhood with a lake ringed with newly built expensive condominiums. Although the city ultimately prevailed in preventing feedings, the group continues to operate a few blocks away on the steps of City Hall. On the one hand, a public space where Orlando Food Not Bombs participated in First Amendment–protected assembly and speech to critique neoliberal city priorities no longer exists. On the other hand, as a compromise, the group is now able to occupy the heart of political power in Orlando, although it is in violation of the city ban on public feedings. Orlando Food Not Bombs tied together issues of hunger, poverty, and urban food waste to build community across social divides and stoke democratic participation in opposition to the neoliberal city.

Scaling up to the level of citywide policymaking, there are collective commitments like **food policy councils** charged with improving local food systems. Food policy councils are usually advisory bodies for cities and counties, or in some instances states and regions that convene people to discuss, coordinate, create, and change policies and programming related to food system development. The democratic participation and citizenship that food policy councils offer reflect one way in which people support urban agriculture through political organizing and not just through consumerism. According to the Center for a Livable Future at Johns Hopkins University, as of 2015, there are 282 food policy councils in the United States and Canada, 215 of which are in the United States. Overall, a little more than a third operate at a city and/or city and county level. Interestingly, however, most are independent grassroots coalitions (41 percent) or housed in nonprofits (21 percent), while only a handful are embedded in government (18 percent). Despite this organizational variability, only 23 percent report having no connection to government. There are a few implications. First, food policy councils reflect a grassroots democratic urge to mobilize people and resources across a range of food-related topics to influence the direction of local food systems. Food policy councils throughout the United States and Canada report that they overwhelmingly engage in a moderate to high degree of civic engagement, that is, voluntary action to solve community problems (83 percent). Second, government is vital to the activities of most food policy councils. Seventy percent report that they participate in political actions to influence government at the level of public policy or policymakers.

One of the characteristic priorities of food policy councils, along with healthy food access and education, is urban agriculture. Yet, how advocates go about producing food makes a difference for the long-term sustainability and equity of the practice. For almost two decades, scholars have offered incisive critiques of the food movement for working outside the state to grow local food within cities. In brief, with the neoliberal elimination of state protections and regulations there has been devolution of responsibility to the individual. As people increasingly internalize neoliberal ideologies, this reproduces individualized, apolitical, and self-improvement approaches to solving problems that result from capitalism or other structural forces. This has consequences for marginalized groups with few resources; individual or economically focused actions to produce food privilege wealthier and whiter groups. Given the limitations of strictly neoliberal approaches, urban agriculture advocates can leverage food policy councils as a democratic and government-driven mechanism. Reflecting the power of the state, urban food policy councils around the United States are passing policies that promote urban agriculture, such as the right to raise chickens, bees, and goats as well as preserve land and set up community and school gardens. Along with procurement policies and policies to create greater equity in access to food, local food policy councils have managed to strengthen urban agriculture networks. From institutional mandates like school requirements to purchase certain volumes of local, fair, humane, and ecologically sustainable food to farmers markets programs that accept food stamps to support low-income shoppers, city-produced food is finding its way onto the plates of millions of people.

These grassroots municipal victories are percolating up to greater governing scales that push back against neoliberal social forces. For example, between 2012 and 2014, eleven states and the District of Columbia enacted twenty-two laws related to community gardens, urban agriculture, and small-scale agriculture. Interestingly, eight of these sought to increase access to land for small-scale agriculture, an issue I will return to later. As food activists push cities, states, and provinces throughout North America to integrate urban agriculture into their policy frameworks, advocates are developing networks to share best practices. Through food movement LISTSERVs such as COMFOOD and fpn-clf, urban food producers and their supporters are emulating successes and modifying practices according to local social conditions. For example, fpn-clf LITSERV participants have frequently requested information from others on the benefits and drawbacks of different food policy structures. In January and March of 2017, conversation centered on the question of effective advocacy and democratic participation as it relates to working within government agencies, nonprofits, or independent organizations. These moments of shared learning enrich food politics in that municipal experiences get reinterpreted as part of a larger movement force to alter the food production landscape.

Yet, within this moment of expanding urban food policy, one can observe a range of ideological commitments and socially constructed notions that are at odds. Differences become obvious when considering the deeply entrenched structural inequalities that riddle cities throughout the United States. Poverty, homelessness, weak educational infrastructure, mass incarceration, gentrification, pollution, and health disparities are just a few problems that reflect the failings of capitalism and the ongoing legacy of institutional racism. Given the scale of these problems, the inward-looking focus of some gardeners or farmers who want to reconnect to nature or cultivate more green space may reflect a commitment to self-care or ecology-care that sidesteps the forces reproducing the neoliberal city. When a new community garden or urban farm is built or a policy is passed at a municipal or state level to permit residents to raise chickens or bees, one must ask questions. How are outcomes achieved? Who benefits and who loses? Whose voices are heard or marginalized? I now turn to cautionary tales and critical sociological analyses that propose proceeding with caution before accepting all the fanfare about the flourishing of urban agriculture.

THE TROUBLE WITH SOCIAL BOUNDARIES, LAND USE STRUGGLES, AND LABOR PRACTICES

Three of the major challenges urban agriculture faces are **social boundaries** between groups with different levels of privilege and power, access to land and inequity in who gets to decide what is an appropriate land use, and fair labor standards for urban farmers. In the neoliberal moment, city governments tend to err on the side of the private sector, which reinforces a slew of social boundaries, most commonly along the lines of class and race. In practice, this results in the dispossession of land and resources, the enclosure of the commons, and an ongoing process of commodification that produces new metabolic rifts. Instead of democratically governing and managing a publicly owned resource, many cities see the growth potential of transferring land ownership to a private party. The ramifications of such decisions are evident. Less resourced urban agriculture groups may get short shrift, therefore reproducing economic and racial inequities within urban agriculture networks. One of the implications is that urban agriculture is seen as a leisure practice that does not require offering fair remuneration to urban farmers. In response, marginalized urban farmers are demanding a **right to the city**. As David Harvey (2008) contends, "The right to the city is far more than the individual liberty to access urban resources: it is a right to change ourselves by changing the city. It is, moreover, a common rather than an individual right since this transformation inevitably depends upon the exercise of a collective power to reshape the processes of urbanization" (23). Through an examination of food politics as part of the urbanization process in Detroit, I unravel the obstacles to achieve this collective right and consider what this means for the future of urban agriculture.

Walk down many streets throughout the heart of Detroit and you will see boarded up and abandoned houses, closed factories and warehouses, padlocked schools, and crumbling sidewalks and roads. Pick a random street to turn down and you will likely witness abandoned lots choked with chain-link fences and hardy weeds. The scene may be jarring to the uninitiated, but behind the physical deterioration is a testing reality for many of the city's residents: 80 percent are black, 40 percent live below the federal poverty line, and twenty thousand are homeless. Complicating matters, at least 22 percent of the city was unemployed in 2016. Poverty and racial inequity are central to the social history of this city. Like any city experiencing the rapid expansion of urban agriculture, it is necessary to contextualize this rise within economic conditions, race relations, and the politics of land use. Doing so complicates the boosterism that accompanies discussions of the rise of the urban farmer.

Detroit has experienced many of the historical inequities of cities with large black populations. Between 1935 and 1940, the Home Owners' Loan Corporation, which was a New Deal agency, mapped almost 250 cities to determine credit-worthiness and risk. It was at this pivotal historical juncture that economic inequality dovetailed with institutionally racist practices to set in motion racial segregation and intergenerational poverty in cities like Detroit. At the time, the Home Owners' Loan Corporation defined most of the city, especially its urban core, as either hazardous or definitely declining, attributes that were used disproportionately in communities with large black populations. These categories justified racial discrimination in housing practices. Banks could use these negative connotations with the legal cover necessary to deny black residents loans. Other development practices exacerbated these institutional barriers. With the spread of road infrastructure, cars, and little to no investment in public transportation, blacks were isolated in the urban core while middle-class whites fled to the suburbs. Whites sought to keep their newfound refuge segregated. They engaged in the practice of racial covenants, that is, contractual agreements that prohibit the occupation, lease, or purchase of property by a targeted group or groups, until the Fair Housing Act of 1968 deemed this illegal.

Even the brief flush of resources that came with the car manufacturing economy was insufficient to solve Detroit's social problems. As more black people moved into the middle class, they faced institutional discrimination and disinvestment in their neighborhoods. Moreover, the fleeing of manufacturers to countries with weak labor protection laws dashed decades' worth of unionization efforts as people lost their jobs and no new economic opportunities filled their place. In response, the city started losing its population. Whites and blacks with the means, skills, and/or education to do so left Detroit for the suburbs. Between 1950 and 2010, the city lost over one million people, a 60 percent decline. In the wake of this mass outmigration wallow hundreds of thousands of impoverished and unemployed people. Coupled with citywide mismanagement and corruption, the removal of state investment in basic infrastructure, education, and jobs, and bankruptcy, residents were forced into the hands of ineffectual emergency managers appointed by Michigan governors throughout the 2000s and 2010s. The usurping of control from the hands of locals has infuriated residents who believe that the state is patronizing black communities by undermining their right to self-determination.

Amid these daunting circumstances, residents are navigating how to use urban agriculture to solve real problems. Given the prevalence of abandoned land, there are many projects and businesses hoping to green the city into a postindustrial paradise of urban farms. In 2013, there were around 130,000 empty parcels. Detroit owns 60 percent of these. To put this into perspective, the city is 143 square miles, one-third of which is vacant. The response to these conditions varies. Discourses regarding gentrification, redevelopment, community, ownership, race, and class compete for the attention of local government officials and residents.

On the one hand, there are black-led food justice organizations such as the Detroit Black Community Food Security Network, which runs the seven-acre D-Town farm. Their analysis of conditions in Detroit begins with dissecting power relations, namely capitalism and white supremacy, and ends with advocating for community building, self-determination, and social justice. As such, they reject white-led missionary efforts to "revitalize" their communities through the practice of starting urban farms and gardens that "teach" black people how to grow food and eat healthy. This autonomous ethos challenges historically structured inequalities as well as contemporary forms of paternalism that permeate many branches of government. As their executive director, Malik Yakini, said, "The major problem that we have is that we have concern about large amounts of land being amassed in the hands of single individuals, particularly wealthy white men, and we think that part of the imbalance we see in the world today has to do with large amounts of wealth being amassed by wealthy white men." In response, the Detroit Black Community Food Security Network has worked tirelessly for years to advance food security and urban agriculture policies that benefit low-income black communities. Like the Black Panther Party, they work toward *survival pending revolution*. That is, they are engaging in projects such as a cooperative buying club to make organic and healthy produce more affordable and developing a full-service cooperative retail grocery store to take care of their community until white supremacy is eliminated and capitalism is overthrown.

On the other hand, there are white resource-full people such as John Hantz, who owns several financial services firms who managed to buy almost two thousand parcels of tax-foreclosed land from the city for his corporately sponsored Hantz Farms. In brief, this is an urban reforesting project. There was widespread opposition to this deal. Black Detroiters viewed it as a land grab, namely a way to exploit the financially distressed city in the name of transforming *blight* into green space. This has allowed Hantz to fix capital in cheap real estate in the hopes of creating scarcity and therefore increases to future property values. Instead of working to build community from the grassroots up and revalue the local economy in line with racial and economic justice, Hantz Farms represents the **growth machine** logic. Under this logic, political and business elites (e.g., planners, politicians, and developers) work together to commodify land to increase economic growth within cities. Parts of the public are disposable if they do not enjoy the wealth necessary to direct city development. In Detroit, this process also pits groups against each other through settler colonial language. By referring to the city's vacant lands as no-man's land, entrepreneurs and *creative types* have imagined themselves as pioneers coming to repossess an abandoned city. Together, these groups use urban agriculture as a method for *greening* cities, which may contribute to what some scholars refer to as **green gentrification**. Very simply, this is the social process whereby local governments, economic interests, and even grassroots community groups create or expand environmental amenities, which attract wealthier residents and drive out lower-income residents. But class is coupled tightly with race in cities like Detroit. Therefore, people of color in the United States experience displacement disproportionately and gentrification is a whitening sociospatial process. One of the hidden realities of the growth machine is that real estate speculation, such as Hantz Farms, appropriates the potential environmental value of land, putting profit before people.

Another challenge that urban agriculture faces is the labor that goes into growing food and the forms of remuneration one receives for this work. First, for those urban food producers interested in generating profit, they must develop local supply chains, oftentimes with institutions such as schools or hospitals, restaurants and grocery stores, or direct to consumers through farmers' markets and community-supported agriculture (see Lesson 17). On paper, this appears straightforward. Dig deep, put on your entrepreneurial broad-brimmed hat, and get to work. In practice, however, these producers operate on thin margins and labor is usually one of the biggest (potential) expenses. City land is also usually expensive, and because it is necessary to grow food, a farmer will face more difficulty eliminating this cost than the cost of labor. As a result, there are a handful of strategies. One is to rely on volunteer labor. Usually, this is justified as a form of unpaid work that transfers nonmonetary values to the volunteer, such as urban agriculture skills. Another approach is to self-exploit. In the name of providing good food to one's community, many farmers work long hours for little pay to keep the food as affordable as possible for consumers. Last is a hybrid solution to keep a venture afloat. This can entail a strategy like paying a few people part time to incentivize quality work, setting up an internship program where less-skilled workers exchange labor for skills, and applying for public and private grants to offset labor costs.

Is the exploitation of urban farmers inevitable? Many urban agriculture advocates want to avoid the sweatshop-like conditions of large industrial farms and ensure that people are paid a living wage with comprehensive benefits and work in a safe environment where they are treated with dignity and human rights. But under the logic of capitalism, this labor is still commodified. Thinking back to the work of Ebenezer Howard and Karl Marx, this suggests the need to move toward a postcapitalist future. This would require rejecting the commodification of labor in favor of nonmonetary forms of exchange, say time for fresh produce or working toward a social economy reliant on democratic and participatory decision-making. This does not mean that such methods are free of exploitation. It is quite possible that there is still inequity between what one gives and what one receives. For example, were the Detroit Black Community Food Security Network to open a cooperative grocery store, this would take place within a capitalist context, but reflect the prefigurative impulses of postcapitalist practice. Labor would be commodified, but perhaps not exploited. Conversely, after Hantz Farms prepared their newly acquired land by clearing away refuse, purchasing trees, and planning them for rows, they have held annual tree-planting days, relying on thousands of volunteers to plant over twenty thousand trees. In this case, the labor is not commodified, but it is exploited in that this free labor is used to increase the value of the land, increase property scarcity, and perhaps in time the price of the property. In brief, the range of labor practices in urban agriculture reflects the conflict between the mandates of neoliberal capitalism and whether urban farming can become a way to advance economic and racial justice.

COMING INTO THE URBAN FOODSHED TO RESTRUCTURE SOCIAL LIFE

At the opening plenary of the Gathering in Milwaukee, Ben Yahola offered, "I think this is a sacred moment for us all to be here all at one time and looking to the future to make a change in the world," and then translated from his native tongue, "Your work is so important. This is the way."[3] The core message, especially on those days when participants attended field trips to places like the Community Food Center, was that nourishing ecologically sustainable urban food systems requires bridging social boundaries, especially between differences of class, ethnicity, and race. Social change begins with people. Technological innovations, like an aquaponics system, are only important insofar as people use them to nurture each other. By acknowledging, for example, how capitalism and institutional racism structure contemporary urbanization, participants were emboldened to imagine new ways to tie their food work to equitable urban development. This might include creating green jobs for low-income youth, developing reentry programs that work with formerly incarcerated people, and building urban farms on public land that grow healthy and culturally appropriate crops that also offer spaces to celebrate ethnoracial heritage.

Over the course of the Gathering, *the way* included time spent bridging social boundaries, which participants facilitated collectively through the unbroken tending of a sacred fire. Late into the night, people would huddle

---

[3] Personal recording of plenary made on September 9, 2011.

around the fire, lost in contemplation. Occasionally people broke the silence and offered a reflection or piece of ancestral wisdom. At other times, a group would break into song or strum on guitars. These moments were critical for rejuvenation and recommitment to the formidable task of transforming the food system. They briefly prefigured another society. To extend these social bonds, movement elders offered all the food activists, farmers, and gardeners the opportunity to take home ashes after the closing ceremony as a cue to commit to advancing food justice in one's community. These ashes sit in a small jar on my office desk. When I sit down to write, this artifact reminds me of all those people growing food in their cities, whether to improve their communities, challenge structural inequalities, or just bask in the horticultural glow of green in a gray landscape.

Urban agriculture is more than the production of food within cities. The sociological imagination and analyses I have offered throughout this lesson unpack the conditions that both structure and reflect who grows food, what food is grown, and why and where people grow food. These conditions help explain both utopian longings and a matrix of power relations. Economic and racial inequities present opportunities and obstacles for social change. Cultural traditions manifest in interstitial city spaces. Historical contingencies and environmental conditions complicate the growth of urban agriculture networks. The relationships between humans and nature; people, place, and power; and the built and natural environment evolve and devolve into what appears to be never-ending assemblages that reflect the increasing role of cities as spaces for food production. My time traveling around the United States to learn from urban farmers and food activists has taught me that while urban agriculture is fascinating in its own right, it is also an insightful lens into the struggles and hopes of the people who make up our urbanizing world.

Discussion Questions
1. How do contemporary urbanization processes, such as neoliberalism, impact the development of urban agriculture?
2. What are some connections between gentrification, social inequality, environmental sustainability, and urban agriculture?
3. Can urban agriculture challenge institutional racism within cities? How?
4. Why might socially marginalized groups use urban agriculture as a tool for social justice? Compare and contrast two different cities or two different groups.

Exercises
1. *Build a campus community garden.* In this exercise, you will develop a plan to build a community garden on your campus. First, identify possible plots of land and evaluate their suitability (e.g., access to water, fencing, soil, sunlight). Second, see who controls access to that land. Is it an academic or administrative department, the university, a private donor, or perhaps a public resource? What actions are necessary to

gain access to that land? Are there any restrictions on farming? What about insurance? How long would you have land tenure and under what conditions? Third, identify how you would procure the necessary resources and get volunteers. Consider whether the university has the resources—an academic or administrative department, a faculty member with a grant, or a private donor—or even start a fundraising campaign on campus. Fourth, how will the community garden run? You will need to consider some basics: how to assign plots, the experience level of community garden participants, aesthetic standards, watering schedules, how to compost, whether to have social events and which kinds, and site, path, and garden maintenance. Last, who would get the produce from the garden and why? Make sure to think about food security and hunger issues on campus and in your community as well as the possibilities for building relationships with on-campus dining facilities. This campaign will likely involve taking graduated steps, increasing awareness, building community, and fostering new alliances on campus. Check out the work of the Real Food Challenge for resources on organizing food campaigns on college campuses (http://www.realfoodchallenge.org).

2. *Four corners debate on local urban agriculture.* There are many debates about the kinds of urban agriculture that work best for a community, especially given geographic, historical, and social conditions. Consider this for the community you live in.

(a) A series of statements are presented on slides or written on a board for you to consider. Go one statement at a time. You will repeat the process of taking a position and then debating your position with those who have opposing views. The goal is to use reason and evidence to defend your position.

(b) Decide whether you strongly agree, agree, disagree, or strongly disagree with the statement.

(c) Write down individually a reason or two in support of your position.

(d) Go to one of four corners of the room. Each corner will represent one position: strongly agree, agree, disagree, and strongly disagree.

(e) Within each group, take a few minutes to discuss why you all agree. If a person is in a group alone, the instructor should speak with this person. Make sure that your group can articulate, using as much evidence and logic as possible, why you have taken your position.

(f) The instructor should then facilitate debate between opposing viewpoints. Every group will have an opportunity to defend its position. Make sure that there is ample time to allow groups to go back and forth.

Suggested Statements

Community gardens will fail unless they reflect the diversity of the city.
Local urban agriculture projects are bound to be coopted by free market forces.

Urban agriculture is a necessary environmental amenity to revitalize disadvantaged neighborhoods.

Urban faming and gardening are incompatible with local social movements.

One way to solve economic, gender, and racial inequities is with local urban agriculture initiatives.

Additional Materials

Readings

Ableman, Michael. *Street Farm: Growing Food, Jobs, and Hope on the Urban Frontier.*

Aptekar, Sofya. 2015. "Visions of Public Space: Reproducing and Resisting Social Hierarchies in a Community Garden." *Sociological Forum* 30 (1): 209–27.

Carolan, Michael, and James Hale. 2016. "'Growing' Communities with Urban Agriculture: Generating Value above and below Ground." *Community Development* 47 (4): 530–45.

Cockrall-King, Jennifer. *Food and the City: Urban Agriculture and the New Food Revolution.*

Kato, Yuki. 2013. "Not Just the Price of Food: Challenges of an Urban Agriculture Organization in Engaging Local Residents." *Sociological Inquiry* 83 (3): 369–91.

McClintock, Nathan. 2014. "Radical, Reformist, and Garden-Variety Neoliberal: Coming to Terms with Urban Agriculture's Contradictions." *Local Environment* 19 (2): 147–71.

Pudup, Mary Beth. 2008. "It Takes a Garden: Cultivating Citizen-Subjects in Organized Garden Projects." *Geoforum* 39 (3): 1228–40.

Reynolds, Kristin and Nevin Cohen. *Beyond the Kale: Urban Agriculture and Social Justice Activism in New York City.*

Stone, Curtis Allen. *The Urban Farmer: Growing Food for Profit on Leased and Borrowed Land.*

Wekerle, Gerda R., and Michael Classens. 2015. "Food Production in the City: (Re)negotiating Land, Food and Property." *Local Environment* 20 (10): 1175–93.

White, Monica M. 2011. "Sisters of the Soil: Urban Gardening as Resistance in Detroit." *Race/Ethnicity: Multidisciplinary Global Contexts* 5 (1): 13–28.

Films

The Garden by Scott Hamilton Kennedy
Occupy the Farm by Todd Darling
Plant This Movie by Karney Hatch*Urban Roots* by Mark McInnis

Video Clips

TED Talk: *A Guerilla Gardener in South Central LA* by Ron Finley

Sources

Biewener, Carole. 2016. "Paid Work, Unpaid Work, and Economic Viability in Alternative Food Initiatives: Reflections from Three Boston Urban Agriculture Endeavors." *Journal of Agriculture, Food Systems, and Community Development* 6 (2): 35–53.

Burns, Gus. 2016. "Documentary Explores Hantz Farms 'Land Grab' in Detroit." *Michigan Live.* July 24, 2016. http://www.mlive.com/news/detroit/index.ssf/2016/07/land_grab_documentary_looks_at.html

Davis, Mike. 2006. *Planet of Slums.* New York: Verso.

Essex, Amanda, Douglas Shinkle, and Mindy Bridges. 2015. *Harvesting Healthier Options: State Legislative Trends in Local Foods 2012–2014.* Washington, DC: National Conference of State Legislatures.

Foster, John Bellamy. 2000. *Marx's Ecology: Materialism and Nature.* New York: Monthly Review Press.

Gould, Kenneth A., and Tammy L. Lewis. 2016. *Green Gentrification: Urban Sustainability and the Struggle for Environmental Justice.* New York: Routledge.

Harvey, David. 2008. "The Right to the City." *New Left Review* 53:23–40.

Havens, Erin, and Antonio Roman Alcalá. 2016. "Land for Food Justice? AB 551 and Structural Change." Land and Sovereignty Policy Brief No. 8, Summer 2016. Oakland, CA: Food First/Institute for Food and Development Policy.

Howard, Ebenezer. 1902. *Garden Cities of To-morrow.* London: Swan Sonnenschein.

Johns Hopkins University. 2015. *Food Policy Councils in North America: 2015 Trends.* Baltimore: Center for a Livable Future.

McClintock, Nathan. 2010. "Why Farm the City? Theorizing Urban Agriculture through a Lens of Metabolic Rift." *Cambridge Journal of Regions, Economy and Society* 3 (2): 191–207.

Molotch, Harvey. 1976. "The City as a Growth Machine: Toward a Political Economy of Place." *American Journal of Sociology* 82 (2): 309–32.

National Gardening Association. 2014. *Garden to Table: A 5-Year Look at Food Gardening in America.* Williston, VT: National Gardening Association.

Safransky, Sara. 2014. "Greening the Urban Frontier: Race, Property, and Resettlement in Detroit." *Geoforum* 56:237–48.

Sbicca, Joshua. 2014. "The Need to Feed: Urban Metabolic Struggles of Actually Existing Radical Projects." *Critical Sociology* 40 (6): 817–34.

Taylor, John R., and Sarah Taylor Lovell. 2014. "Urban Home Food Gardens in the Global North: Research Traditions and Future Directions." *Agriculture and Human Values* 31 (2): 285–305.

A worker-owner at Mandela Food Coop. (Photo courtesy of Adrionna Fike, Mandela Grocery Cooperative.)

20

Food and Justice

Alison Hope Alkon

West Oakland, California, has approximately forty thousand residents, but lacks a full-scale grocery store. Historically, the neighborhood was one of a few places in the San Francisco Bay Area where African Americans could buy homes, and though recent gentrification has brought many new residents, it remains predominantly black and low income. Life expectancy here in the *flatlands* is approximately ten years less than in the whiter and more affluent hills. Violence is certainly one cause, but more pervasive, if less dramatic, are the elevated rates of diet-related conditions such as heart disease and diabetes. In addition, there are few opportunities for community-led economic development. The few businesses that are not frightened away by the neighborhood's tough reputation are largely owned by nonresidents. It is hard to find a job, let alone a career.

This bleakness is the result of structural inequalities that have first created and then hamstrung black urban neighborhoods across the United States (see Lessons 13 and 19). **Redlining** refers to a circumstance in which public and private entities refuse services to neighborhoods based on their racial and ethnic makeup. In the decades following World War II, government and private loans were made available to whites, allowing them to fix up existing housing stock or move to newly constructed suburbs. These loans were denied to African Americans, who were left with increasingly segregated, dilapidated communities (Massey and Denton 1993). The deindustrialization of the United States since the late 1970s exacerbated already-existing racial inequalities through massive capital flight, job loss, and economic devastation in the largely black working-class areas of major cities (Wilson 2011. More recently, the 2008 economic crisis has driven black unemployment in these communities to nearly 50 percent, levels last seen during the Great Depression and showing little signs of recovery (Walker 2010), while **differential policing** leads to high rates of incarceration, disrupting families and communities both emotionally and financially. In the Bay Area, gentrification and rising rents create additional barriers to both residential stability and community-led economic development.

Since 2008, Mandela Foods Cooperative has stood as an exception to these trends. A small grocery store, Mandela features produce from regional black and Latino farmers, as well as bulk and packaged foods. It is cooperatively owned by four African American neighborhood residents (though one recently could not afford a rental increase and was forced to move to a neighboring city). Mandela Foods is also supported by Mandela Marketplace, a nonprofit organization, which provides the coop with access to credit, technical assistance and training, and resources that entrepreneurs from wealthier communities can often mobilize through banks and social networks.

Mandela seeks to address **health disparities** by providing neighborhood residents with access to "healthy, culturally appropriate food" that the neighborhood otherwise lacks. It also works to create economic opportunities for community members to participate in the process of supplying that food. In the words of Oakland's Mandela Marketplace's executive director Dana Harvey, "It's not about plopping a grocery store down in a community. It's about engaging and resourcing a community to solve their problems, and own those solutions."

Mandela Foods Cooperative is a prime example of an organization working toward **food justice**. While the movement is still relatively young, and a shared definition of food justice is still emergent, one attempt to delineate the term comes from geographer and activist Rasheed Hislop (2014, 19), who describes it as "the struggle against racism, exploitation, and oppression taking place within the food system that addresses inequality's root causes both within and beyond the food chain." The food justice movement consists mainly of local, community-based projects devoted to increasing access to fresh produce and creating economic opportunities in low-income communities of color. Organizations are also scaling up by working on policy initiatives at the local, state, and even national levels. This lesson will summarize the social and environmental problems that the food justice movement seeks to address, provide some examples of food justice activism, and conclude by highlighting future directions for research and action.

INEQUALITIES IN INDUSTRIAL AGRICULTURE

Attempts to create food justice draw on the many critiques of **industrial agriculture** as environmentally and socially destructive and add that it produces (and reproduces) inequalities such as those of race, class, gender, and national status. As noted in earlier lessons, ecologically, industrial agriculture depends on mechanization, monoculture, and the separation of livestock from fruit and vegetable farming, creating increased reliance on chemical inputs, soil compaction, and fertility loss. Industrial agriculture also increases erosion, through which chemical pesticides and fertilizers can cause ecological harm to nearby waterways. Additionally, fertilizers and pesticides are largely made from fossil fuels, making agriculture responsible for approximately 12 percent of climate change–causing greenhouse gas emissions globally (see Lesson 12). Supporters of food justice draw on environmental justice scholarship and activism, which seeks to rectify the disproportionately high rates of exposure to toxic pollutants among low-income communities and minority communities, to highlight the ways the ecological effects of industrial agriculture are most damaging to these same groups.

Economically, US agriculture has been consolidating small farms into larger agribusiness corporations since the nineteenth century, as reliance on inputs of machinery and fertilizer create economic advantages for those with ready supplies of capital (see Lesson 5). Rather than pass regulation to constrain this trend, the US government created a series of loans and subsidies that primarily aided large corporations. As larger farms yielded increased returns, their owners were increasingly able to influence public policy, ensuring the continuation of government subsidies. Thus, despite a cultural rhetoric depicting farmers as self-reliant and independent, industrial agriculture's dependence on government subsidies provides evidence that the industry is not economically viable. Indeed, through subsidies, farmers are literally paid to invest in agricultural technologies they cannot otherwise afford, undermining their own economic security. Centralization is a key way that industrial agriculture creates class-based inequalities. A few large farm operators become wealthy while many others are put out of business. In addition, US government loan programs have been disproportionately available to white male farmers, leading to class-action lawsuits from black, Latino/a, Native American, and women farmers. The first of these cases, known as *Pigford v. Glickman,* alleged that black farmers were given false information about government programs, denied loans, and given insufficient or arbitrarily reduced loans. Sometimes this racism was **institutional**; the US Department of Agriculture (USDA) required farmers to have credit to receive loans, and this was rarely available to black farmers. Other times it was more explicit, with USDA officials telling a black farmer that disaster relief is "too much money for a n*gger to receive" (Thurow 1998). *Pigford v. Glickman* was settled in 1999, and since that time, over $2 billion has been paid to over eighty thousand black farmers or their descendants, though claims of more contemporary discrimination remain unaddressed (Cowan and Feder 2016).

Economic consolidation has also had devastating economic and social effects on rural communities. In a classic agricultural–economic study, anthropologist Walter Goldschmidt compared two towns in California's San Joaquin Valley with similar geographic and demographic features. The key variable was farm size: one town contained many small farms while large, industrial farms dominated the other. Goldschmidt found that the industrialized farming community lacked solidarity, leadership, prosperity, permanent settlement, and adequate education facilities. Since Goldschmidt's 1947 study, the further widespread increase in industrial farming across the United States has led to increased poverty and class-based inequalities. Today, the San Joaquin Valley is one of the most lucrative agricultural regions in the world, with farmers garnering $6.8 billion in revenues, but it is also one of the nation's poorest, with nearly one in five households living below the poverty line (US Census 2010).

Large industrial farms are also more dependent on nonfamily labor. Agribusiness labor in the United States originally consisted of indigenous peoples, who were replaced by Chinese, Japanese, East Indian, Filipino, and (currently) Latino/a immigrants. The contributions of these immigrants to the preeminence of American agriculture were and continue to be routinely rewarded with racism, economic exploitation, and violence. The 1913 Alien Land Law, for example, which prevented land ownership by Japanese citizens in the United States, was designed to restrict Japanese farm competition in California, and the California Farm Bureau was a strong supporter of Japanese internment, through which many Japanese farmers lost their land. More recently, the Florida-based Coalition of Immokalee Workers has exposed numerous cases of forced labor in which workers were not paid or underpaid, sexually harassed and assaulted, threatened with guns and deportation, and even imprisoned.

Immigrant laborers have engaged in many efforts to organize, culminating in the successful formation of the United Farm Workers Union in 1966. Despite the benefits the union has accrued for those working on unionized farms, the overwhelming majority of farm workers are not unionized and live in substandard housing, are denied welfare and other government benefits, and, ironically, are often food insecure (see Lesson 11). Farmworkers are often particularly vulnerable to pesticide exposure, which leads to many negative health consequences. Industrial agriculture, in contrast, benefits greatly from what Taylor and Martin call "the immigrant subsidy in US agriculture" (1997, 855), as immigration status often inhibits workers' abilities to procure fair wages and benefits. More recently, however, farmworker organizations such as the Coalition of Immokalee Workers have pushed back against human rights abuses, establishing a *fair food program* that seeks to ensure dignity, fair pay, and humane working conditions.

INEQUALITIES IN ALTERNATIVE AGRICULTURE

As noted in earlier lessons, the contemporary alternative agrifood movement draws on critiques of industrial agriculture, as well as the work of health crusaders, the 1960s counterculture, and the environmental movement. Its foundational values include land stewardship, reverence for nature, and cooperative relationships between humans. Participants in the food movement work to create alternatives to industrial agriculture by supporting small farms that eschew chemical pesticides and fertilizers and encouraging local distribution through farmers markets, community-supported agriculture programs, and cooperative grocery stores. However, as the food movement has become more mainstream, industrial foods have taken on many of the trappings of the food movement. Movement rhetoric and, to a lesser extent, preferred practices are often found in the marketing material of large farms and chain supermarkets.

While scholars and activists working for food justice often create and support alternative forms of agriculture, they also claim that the wider alternative food movement has both ignored the needs and desires of low-income consumers, producers, and workers and reproduced many of the inequalities common to industrial farming. In the 1990s, activists working under the banner of **community food security** began to rectify this by pairing economic support for local farmers with increased access to their products among low-income residents. In practice, however, support for farmers, often in the form of demands of premium prices, tended to trump consumer needs. Moreover, the Community Food Security Coalition, the primary organization advocating this goal, was predominantly composed of privileged white activists who, despite a general desire to "do good" were often unwilling to confront issues of racism both within their organization and in the food system at large (Slocum 2007; Bradley and Herrera 2015). Food justice, with its focus on food access in low-income communities of color, arose in response to both the whiteness of community food security and its privileging of producers' needs.

In addition to this chronology, many food justice activists highlight the Black Panther Party's Free Breakfast for Schoolchildren program as among the movement's foundational roots. Amid the political turmoil surrounding cofounder Huey Newton's 1968 arrest and trial, the party turned toward *survival programs* that could meet basic community needs while providing political education. The Free Breakfast program was one of the most successful of these programs, beginning with eleven children in the basement of a West Oakland church and eventually feeding more than ten thousand black children across the country. Indeed, former Black Panther minister of education Ericka Huggins claims that "the government was so embarrassed by our Free Breakfast Program that it started the national free breakfast program" (quoted in Jones 2007). Preventing child hunger may seem a far cry from the local organic produce that food justice activists favor, but both link food provisioning to community empowerment and self-determination.

Food justice is necessary to address the many barriers that make it difficult for low-income people and people of color to access local and organic food as both producers and consumers. In addition to the above-described discrimination by the USDA, farmers of color have endured forced relocation and immigration laws barring land ownership by particular ethnic groups. Native Americans, for example, were often removed from their ancestral homelands and have seen their traditional hunting practices restricted by laws written with recreation, not subsistence, in mind (Norgaard, Reed, and VanHorn 2011).

Despite these obstacles, agriculture has remained a proud tradition in many communities of color, as highlighted through projects like Natasha Bowens's (2015) *The Color of Food*, a photo documentary book and interactive website (http://thecolorofood.com/) created to "amplify, preserve and celebrate the stories of Black, Latino, Asian and Indigenous farmers and food activists working to revolutionize the food system in our communities." One organization she profiles is the Federation of Southern Cooperatives, which has worked for over forty years to develop cooperatives and credit unions to save, protect, and expand the landholdings of black family farmers in the South. They currently support over seventy active cooperative groups with a membership of more than twenty thousand families (Bowens 2015). In addition, *The Color of Food* profiles immigrant farmers such as Maria Catalan, a Mexican-born woman farm owner in Watsonville, California, and May Vu, a Hmong American woman farmer in Fresno County, California, who bring their own multigenerational farming traditions to small-scale California agriculture. Indeed, immigrant farmers comprise the fastest-growing category of farm owner-operators in the United States (Minkoff-Zern, forthcoming). While the food justice movement initially focused primarily on farmers of color, more recently, activists have worked in coalition with farmworker and food labor organizations. Not only are farmworkers often underpaid and mistreated, but ironically, they also often suffer from hunger and diet-related diseases. In addition, assumptions that farmworkers enjoy better conditions on small, organic farms are often unfounded (see Lesson 11).

Marginalized communities also face difficulties purchasing local, organic, and fresh foods, which tend to have higher prices than their conventional and processed counterparts. **Federal agricultural subsidies** were designed to bolster the production of commodity crops such as corn, rice, and soy during the Great Depression and continue to ensure a cheap supply of the ingredients necessary for processed foods. Fruits and vegetables, ironically referred to in agricultural parlance as *specialty crops*, receive minimal subsidies, and there is no federal subsidy for organic production that could help to offset the higher labor cost associated with these foods. The sustainable agriculture movement has largely privileged the economic needs of producers—small organic farmers—and has therefore argued that the price of their goods should be high. This helps to ensure stable livelihoods for sustainable farmers, but is contrary to the needs of low-income consumers (Allen 2004).

As highlighted in the lesson on hunger (see Lesson 13), another barrier to marginalized communities' lack of consumption of fresh food is the relative lack of available produce—let alone locally grown and organic options—in low-income and communities of color. These areas are often referred to as **food deserts** for their lack of fresh produce or **food swamps** for the ample supply of fast-food and liquor stores, though many activists argue that these ecological labels connote a sense of naturalness about what is clearly a human-created problem. But parlance aside, the lack of health food options in low-income communities of color remains real. Beaulac, Kristjansson, and Commins (2009) conducted a meta-analysis of forty-nine studies and found that areas with a high proportion of low-income people, African Americans, or both contain fewer large or mid-sized supermarkets and that the markets that do exist in these communities sell very little fresh food and tend to charge higher prices for similar items. While the location of stores certainly makes shopping for fresh food more difficult, interviews with low-income people of color identify price as the primary obstacle preventing the purchase of fresh produce (Alkon et al. 2013). Moreover, activists have argued that the focus on geographic proximity places too much emphasis on the presence or absence of supermarkets and results in the offering of incentives to chain grocery stores rather than addressing root causes such as racism and poverty (Holt-Gimenez and Shattuck 2011). Nonetheless, there is a fair amount of agreement that the lack of available fresh produce is one obstacle to its consumption. This lack of availability is the result of the long-standing processes of disinvestment in communities of color, including redlining and urban renewal, that were described at the beginning of this lesson. Food justice activists in these communities seek to develop spaces where they can procure high-quality food as a way to push back against these long-standing processes.

A third barrier to the consumption of fresh produce by low-income people and people of color can be found in the language of the sustainable agriculture movement itself. Scholars have argued that farmers markets and other spaces where sustainable agriculture is practiced are **culturally coded as white**, not only because they are primarily and disproportionately frequented by whites, but also because of the discourses that circulate through them. Cultural geographer Julie Guthman, for example, argues that phrases common to the sustainable agriculture movement, such as getting your hands dirty in the soil and looking the farmer in the eye, all point to "an agrarian past that is far more easily romanticized by whites than others" (2008, 394). Given the disenfranchisement of so many African American, Native American, Latino/a, and Asian American farmers, as well as associations these communities hold between farm work and slavery and other forms of exploitation, Guthman argues that it is likely these phrases do not resonate with communities of color in the ways intended by their primarily white speakers. This cultural barrier can suggest to low-income and communities of color that the food movement is not for them, especially when combined with the lack of available organic and local produce in their neighborhoods. Activist-chefs and writers such as Bryant Terry, Breeze Harper, Luz Calvo, and Catriona Esquibel, who identify as black or Latino/a, have responded by attempting to recast sustainable food systems in ways they feel are more culturally resonant to their communities. Bryant Terry's (2009) *Vegan Soul Kitchen*, for example, features recipes "conceived through the prism of the African Diaspora—cutting, pasting, reworking, and remixing African, Caribbean, African-American, Native American, and European staples, cooking techniques, and distinctive dishes to create something familiar, comforting, and deliciously unique." (For more on the relationship between food and identity, see Lesson 2.)

THE MOVEMENT FOR FOOD JUSTICE

There are now thousands of nonprofit organizations and activists across the country working toward food justice. Many, like Mandela Marketplace profiled at the beginning of this lesson, have created farmers markets, community-supported agriculture programs, grocery stores, and community gardens in these neighborhoods. Recognizing that geographic access and cost are both barriers to the consumption of this kind of food, many of these organizations have worked to make it more affordable through subsidies, work exchanges, and a variety of other strategies. Community groups have convinced some private foundations, as well as the USDA, to provide funds for *market match* or *double bucks* programs to extend the purchasing power of federal nutrition assistance benefits like Electronic Benefits Transfer (formerly food stamps) and Women, Infants, and Children at farmers markets and participating health food and grocery stores. When an individual uses his or her food assistance at a farmers market or other approved store, matching funds allow them to receive double the value, offsetting the more expensive costs of fresh food. For those with the most dire food needs, food banks and other emergency food projects have moved toward offering local and organic food, sometimes by creating partnerships with local farmers or nonprofit organizations.

Among food justice activists, particularly those working at the local level, there is considerable debate about the degree to which these alternative food systems should be led by people from the communities most affected by racism and other inequalities. Many white-led food organizations have realized that there is a need in communities of color and have sought to expand their work in this area by, to use one of their common phrases, inviting others to the table. These organizations tend to be more well established and well funded and have greater connections to policymakers than those led by people of color, and this is a source of significant tension among movement leaders (Reynolds and Cohen 2016). Activists of color often argue that when policy and programmatic goals are shaped by "outsiders" who do not live in affected communities, they are less effective. Further, they believe that communities are more likely to be interested in healthier food, and thus to begin to see themselves as part of the food movement, when the leadership looks like them and shares their life experiences. However, it is not clear whether this **demographic matching** can overcome the many barriers presenting communities of color from accessing healthy foods. Leadership from communities of color is necessary to create framing that will resonate with these communities, but does not by itself address the geographic or economic barriers to fresh food.

One strategy that does address these barriers, at least in part, is **farm-to-school programs**. Food movement activists have long supported these programs, but they have largely been voluntary and donation based and thus are disproportionately found in wealthier areas. More recently, however, large urban school districts such as Los Angeles Unified and Oakland

Unified have created school food programs. Oakland, for example, spends 27 percent of their food budget locally, including antibiotic-free, sustainably raised chicken. Their California Thursdays program highlights freshly prepared school meals sourced entirely from California growers and producers. In addition, every school has a garden, and the district is about to launch a farm that will grow produce exclusively for school food. For the district's roughly forty thousand students, nearly three-quarters of whom receive free or reduced-price school lunches, this is an important way to access fresh food. The far larger Los Angeles Unified School District has adopted the Good Food Purchasing Program guidelines crafted by the LA Food Policy Council. Aiming to "do for the food system what LEED certification did for energy efficiency in buildings" (Center for Good Food Purchasing, Nd), the Good Food Purchasing Program provides clear, measurable standards for institutions in the areas of local economies, environmental sustainability, valued workforce, animal welfare, and nutrition. In addition to schools, the USDA funds a host of **farm-to-institution** programs that support the purchase of fresh, local food in cafeterias at hospitals, senior centers, and city offices. These kinds of programs allow individuals to access fresh food without having to opt in through their purchasing decisions. Moreover, this sort of local institutional purchasing provides small farms with an important source of revenue.

Food justice activists work to transform not only the food system, but also the social, political, and economic systems in which it is embedded. Accessible local and organic food becomes a means to address not only the health disparities described at the beginning of this lesson, but also disparities in economic development and political power. With regard to economic development, many food justice projects seek to provide jobs for residents of communities that have been underdeveloped by redlining and urban renewal. This can include hiring individuals for a variety of jobs in the food justice sector, including gardeners, educators, nonprofit staff, and employees at restaurants making use of local and organic produce.

Oakland's Planting Justice is a nonprofit organization that raises funds through several social enterprises including a landscaping company and a commercial nursery (see Lesson 19). They employ thirty-five people, roughly two-thirds of whom are people of color. In addition, 60 percent of their employees are formerly incarcerated individuals who face significant barriers to employment beyond their demographic and economic circumstances. Jobs with Planting Justice provide living wages, health benefits, and peer mentoring opportunities, which are likely responsible for the complete absence of recidivism among employees (the average rate of recidivism in California is 65 percent). Other food justice organizations enable community ownership of food assets, such as the worker-owned Mandela Foods Cooperative grocery store. According to worker-owner Adrionna Fike, community ownership "matters for reasons of representation. It matters for reasons of community development that the developers look like us. That we are developing our own. It matters in terms of self-determination; expressing it, demonstrating it, teaching it . . . It matters when the black people are trying to do that and they have examples of black people who are doing it already!"

Food justice activists have also begun working in coalitions to improve labor pay and conditions in the industrial food system. Organizations have been supporters of the Coalition of Immokalee Worker's Fair Food Campaign, engaging in direct action to pressure restaurants and retailers ranging from Taco Bell to Trader Joe's to sign agreements with the farmworker organization. In addition, the Restaurant Opportunity Center, which advocates for restaurant workers, has directly appealed to food justice activists, arguing that support for sustainable food must include fair pay and equitable working conditions throughout the food system. And food workers have been at the forefront of efforts to raise the minimum wage to fifteen dollars per hour, which has resulted in raises in many states and cities across the countries, as well as efforts to unionize Walmart, the nation's largest food retailer (Lo and Koenig 2017). These efforts are important because food and farmworkers are among those most heavily harmed by industrial food systems.

Food justice activists also use local food system development as a means to build political power, pursuing shifts in policy at the local, state, and federal levels. Locally, activists have worked to revise city zoning ordinances allowing for the sale of homegrown produce, particularly in neighborhoods that are otherwise lacking in access. Across California, in addition to the previously described market match program, food justice activists have lobbied for the recent increase in state minimum wage, as well as bills to assist family farmers and ranchers to conserve water and capture carbon and to protect grocery store workers from being fired when ownership changes hands. At the federal level, the USDA and the Department of Health and Human Services seek to address the absence of fresh food in low-income neighborhoods through the Healthy Food Financing Initiative, which offers financing and marketing support for grocery stores, farmers markets, and other food sources to enter these areas. The USDA also offers Community Food Project grants to programs that meet the food needs of low-income individuals. In addition, food justice activists increasingly enter coalitions working to restrict industrial agriculture's most harmful practices, including pesticides and biotechnologies like genetically modified organisms (Alkon and Guthman 2017).

Last, food justice activists work to shape the discourse surrounding the relationship between racial and other inequalities and industrial and alternative food systems. Perhaps the best known of these endeavors is the Growing Food and Justice for All Initiative (see Lesson 19). Hosted by Milwaukee's Growing Power, a well-known food justice organization whose mission is to support people from diverse backgrounds by providing equal access to high-quality produce, the Growing Food and Justice for All Initiative provides resources for training on how to dismantle racism in the food system and hosts monthly phone calls, a LISTSERV, and an annual conference where activists share strategies and build a collective platform.

Even more radical in its stance is the newly formed Black Land & Liberation Initiative, which trains young people in political education covering black liberation, land reform, and ecology as well as agroecological skills and direct action (http://blacklandandliberation.org/). Organizations like these have done much to highlight the ways that racism and other inequalities structure both industrial and alternative agricultural systems and to argue for local, organic food systems rooted in communities of color as an essential part of the food movement.

FUTURE DIRECTIONS

In the past two decades, food justice has emerged as a concept through which activists push for greater social equity through the formation of community-based food systems and policies that support them. The movement's initial focus was on access to local and organic food among low-income consumers. As the movement has grown, there has been additional emphasis on the potential for food justice organizations to create community-based economic development, to guarantee just wages and working conditions, and to take on the most deleterious effects of industrial agriculture such as toxic pesticides, genetically modified organisms, and labor exploitation.

Recently, the Movement for Black Lives' policy team produced a comprehensive "Vision for Black Lives" (https://policy.m4bl.org/) that lays out a way forward for food justice activism. This platform includes the increased availability of healthy food through the provision of high-quality breakfast and lunch for K–12 students and the institution of a universal basic income. Community ownership of food systems is addressed through invectives to divest from industrial agriculture and guaranteed access to public financing for decentralized, community-controlled food hubs, cooperative organizations, and land trusts. Support for and encouragement of black agriculture is highlighted through the institution of tuition-free agricultural education for colleges and universities, a halt to the foreclosure of black farmland, and reparations for the wealth extracted from black communities by the industrial food system. The platform addresses workers' rights as well, calling for full protections for farmworkers and incarcerated workers (who often work in food production for private companies for pennies on the dollar) and an end to the privatization of prison labor and services, including farmwork and food services. In sum, while it is aimed specifically at black communities, this platform puts forward a broad vision pursuing racial equity through community-based food systems, in short, of food justice.

Another important future direction is the incorporation of a gendered analysis into the food justice movement. Food has traditionally been considered women's work, and kitchens and gardens are often cast as women's spaces. The feminist movement encouraged women to leave the kitchen for professional pursuits in the workplace. For this reason, feminists have often been critical of the alternative agriculture movement's emphasis on a return to the kitchen and the idealization of nonindustrial foods and techniques, which often require more planning, skill, and time. On the production end, women in food businesses, including farmers, crafters, and chefs, often face discrimination from investors, coworkers, customers, and the general public, and thus, women are underrepresented in these industries. Moreover, women are disproportionately poor, and low-income communities of color that lack access to fresh food contain many woman-headed households. Academics have long analyzed gendered dimensions of food systems, particularly food cultures and home spaces, and have more recently begun to draw connections between food systems and sexuality. However, the food justice movement has not really drawn on these to articulate a feminist food justice politic that embraces LGBTQIA communities. These are important dimensions for future work.

Last, food justice activists are increasingly creating ties to other movements for social and racial justice. Beyond labor activism and the Movement for Black Lives platform, activists have begun to make connections with those advocating for prison abolition and immigrant rights. These are necessary and important because both incarcerated people and immigrants are heavily involved in the production of food, with wages far below what would be offered to nonincarcerated citizens. These kinds of connections push food justice activists beyond the creation of alternatives and toward the development of broad coalitions and strategies. Transforming the food system into one that is ecologically sustainable and socially just is an important task, but it is also a means toward transforming our social, economic, and political systems.

Discussion Questions

1. How have inequalities of race, class, and gender affected food systems in the United States? How has the food justice movement responded to this?
2. How has the food justice movement changed over time? How has it affected the sustainable agriculture movement?
3. What are the barriers that low-income communities and communities of color face in purchasing fresh produce? Are there other barriers that the lesson does not mention?
4. What other future directions for food justice activism seem necessary? What are the potential challenges for these kinds of activism?

Exercise

Market survey. As a class, design a basic shopping list including staples such as meat, eggs, cheese, bread, and produce. In pairs or small groups, students will visit stores in various areas near the university. Instruct them to write down the price of each item and the total cost of all items on the list. They should also note the general quality of the store, including access to public transportation, general cleanliness, and customer service. Students can then compare the stores with regard to price, convenience, and overall customer experience.

Additional Materials

Readings

Alkon, Alison, and Julian Agyeman. 2011. *Cultivating Food Justice.* Cambridge, MA: MIT Press.

Alkon, Alison. 2012. *Black, White, and Green.* Athens, GA: University of Georgia Press.

Bowens, Natasha. 2015. *The Color of Food: Stories of Race, Resilience and Farming.* Gabriola Island, BC: New Society Publishers.

Broad, Garrett. 2016. *More Than Just Food.* Berkeley: University of California Press.

Gottlieb, Robert, and Anupama Joshi. 2010. *Food Justice.* Cambridge, MA: MIT Press.

Reynolds, Kristin, and Nevin Cohen. 2016. *Beyond the Kale.* Athens, GA: University of Georgia Press.

Films

A Place at the Table
Food Chains
Food Inc.
La Cosecha (The Harvest)
The Hand That Feeds

Websites

Black Land and Liberation Initiative, http://blacklandandliberation.org/
Food Chain Workers Alliance, http://www.foodchainworkers.org
Growing Food and Justice Initiative, https://www.facebook.com/growingfoodandjustice/
Mandela Marketplace, http://www.mandelamarketplace.org
Planting Justice, http://www.plantingjustice.org
Restaurant Opportunity Center, http://www.rocunited.org
Vision for Black Lives, https://policy.m4bl.org/

References

Alkon, Alison Hope, Daniel Block, Kelly Moore, Catherine Gillis, Nicole DiNuccio, and Noel Chavez. 2013. "Foodways of the Urban Poor." *Geoforum* 48:126–35.

Alkon, Alison Hope, and Julie Guthman. 2017. *The New Food Activism.* Berkeley: University of California Press.

Allen, Patricia. 2004. *Together at the Table.* University Park: Pennsylvania State University Press.

Beaulac, J., E. Kristjansson, and S. Commins. 2009. "A Systemic Review of Food Deserts, 1966–2007." *Preventing Chronic Disease.* 6 (3): A105. http://www.cdc.gov/pcd/issues/2009/jul/08_0163.htm

Black Land and Liberation Initiative. n.d. "About the Initiative." Accessed March 14, 2017. http://blacklandandliberation.org

Bowens, Natasha. 2015. *The Color of Food.* New York: New Society Press.

Bradley, Katie, and Hank Herrera. 2016. "Decolonizing Food Justice: Naming, Resisting and Researching Food Justice. *Antipode* 48 (1): 97–114.

Cowan, Tadlock, and Jody Feder. 2013. "The Pigford Cases: USDA Settlement of a Discrimination Suit by Black Farmers." Congressional Research Service. May 29, 2013.

Goldschmidt, Walter. 1947. *As You Sow.* San Diego, CA: Harcourt Brace.

Growing Food and Justice Initiative. https://www.facebook.com/growingfoodandjustice

Guthman, Julie. 2008. "'If They Only Knew': Color Blindness and Universalism in California Alternative Food Institutions." *The Professional Geographer* 60 (3): 387–97.

Hislop, Rasheed. 2014. "Reaping Equity across the USA: FJ Organizations Observed at the National Scale." Master's thesis, University of California–Davis.

Holt-Giménez, Eric, and Annie Shattuck. 2011. "Food Crises, Food Regimes and Food Movements: Rumblings of Reform or Tides of Transformation?" *The Journal of Peasant Studies* 38 (1): 109–44.

Jones, Brenda Payton. 2007. "The Black Panthers Still Making a Difference: The 40th Anniversary of the Party Brings It Back to the Forefront." *Ebony Magazine*, February 1, 2007.

Lo, Joann and Biko Koenig. 2017. "Food Workers & Consumers Organizing Together for Food Justice." In *The New Food Activism.* Edited by Alison Alkon and Julie Guthman, 133-156 Berkeley, CA: UC Press.

Massey, Douglas S., and Nancy A. Denton. 1993. *American Apartheid : Segregation and the Making of the Underclass.* Cambridge, MA: Harvard University Press.

Minkoff-Zern, Laura-Anne. Forthcoming. *The New American Farmer.* Cambridge, MA: MIT Press.

Movement for Black Lives. 2016. "Vision for Black Lives." Accessed April 30 2018. https://policy.m4bl.org

Norgaard, Kari, Ron Reed, and Carolina VanHorn. "A Continuing Legacy: Institutional Racism, Hunger and Nutritional Justice on the Klamath." In *Cultivating Food Justice*, edited by Alison Alkon and Julian Agyeman, 23–46. Cambridge, MA: MIT Press.

Reynolds, Kristin, and Nevin Cohen. 2016. *Beyond the Kale.* Athens, GA: University of Georgia Press.

Slocum, Rachel. 2007. "Anti-racist Practice and the Work of Community Food Organizations." *Antipode* 38 (2): 327–49.

Taylor, Edwin J., and Paul L. Martin. 1997. "The Immigrant Subsidy in US Agriculture: Farm Employment, Poverty, and Welfare." *Population and Development Review* 23 (4): 855–74.

Terry, Bryant. 2009. *Vegan Soul Kitchen.* New York: Da Capo Press.

Thurow, Roger. 1998. "Soiled Legacy: Black Farmers Hit the Road to Confront a 'Cycle of Racism'—Many Lost Lands, Dignity as USDA Denied Loans Whites Routinely Got." *The Wall Street Journal*, May 28, 1998.

US Census. 2010. "San Joaquin County, CA." Accessed 5/1/2018. https://factfinder. census.gov/faces/nav/jsf/pages/community_facts.xhtml?src=bkmk.

Walker, Devona. 2010. "The Unreported Economic Depression in Black America." *Alternet.org*. November 29, 2010. http://www.alternet.org/ speakeasy/2010/11/29/the-unreported-economic-depression-in-black-america

Wilson, William Julius. 2011. *When Work Disappears: The World of the New Urban Poor*. New York: Vintage Books.

Conclusion: Toward More Sustainable Food and Agriculture

Maki Hatanaka and Jason Konefal

Having worked your way through the twenty lessons in the *Sociology of Food and Agriculture*, you are now aware that the contemporary food and agriculture system is highly globalized, industrialized, and corporatized. There are many benefits to this system. Agricultural productivity is at an all-time high, and thus there is more food than ever before. Seasonality and national boarders are increasingly less of a barrier in accessing food. In much of the world today, consumers have seen a reduction in prices as well as an expansion of the range of food products available to them. Moreover, many of the most appalling food safety problems have been minimized or eliminated in much of the world.

However, as the preceding lessons in this book presented, these benefits also come with costs. To highlight just a few, the costs include persistent poor working conditions and labor exploitation, environmental degradation and resource depletion, and uneven accessibility to healthy and nutritious foods. Moreover, these problems are often unevenly distributed across race, class, and gender and are experienced differentially by social groups.

Increasingly, national and multilateral organizations, academics, practitioners, and activists have begun to use the idea of (un)sustainability to link together the problems facing the current food and agriculture system. In an effort to address these problems, they urgently call for, and are working toward, greater sustainability in food and agriculture. Indeed, sustainability has become a buzzword not only in food and agriculture, but also in society more generally. However, what is *sustainability*? Who gets to decide what sustainable food and agriculture entails? How can sustainable food and agricultural practices be implemented? And last, what role do you think you can play in fostering greater sustainability in food and agriculture?

In wrapping up this volume, we provide you with a broad overview of efforts to transition the food and agriculture system toward greater sustainability. Ultimately, these efforts and movements are shaping and reshaping the future of our food and agriculture system. Building on the discussion of sustainability, we end with suggestions of how you can become involved in making the food and agriculture system more sustainable.

SUSTAINABILITY: A CONTESTED IDEA

Prior to presenting an overview of current efforts to foster sustainability in food and agriculture, let's first look at what sustainability means. While the idea of sustainability seems fairly straightforward at first blush, in reality, it is a highly contested and increasingly politicized idea (Thompson 2010). Indeed, academics, farmers, industry, corporate leaders, and activists all concur that the sustainability of food and agriculture is vitally important; however, there is no agreement as to how we should conceptualize this tricky idea.

Broadly defined, sustainability means ensuring the resilience of people, communities, and ecological systems over time. For example, the United Nations Food and Agriculture Organization defines sustainability as "ensuring human rights and well-being without depleting or diminishing the capacity of the earth's ecosystems to support life, or at the expense of others well-being" (FAO 2017). Given the very open-ended way sustainability is defined, there are several points of tension in trying to put sustainability into practice. Among the most prominent include what level of resilience is sufficient for ecosystems and communities and how we can address equity in protecting and improving livelihoods and social well-being over time. Furthermore, to make things more complex, the idea of sustainability is a multidimensional concept—it is commonly broken down into three dimensions: environmental, economic, and social.

Let us briefly explain the three dimensions of sustainability and their contested character. The first dimension of sustainability is environmental. Environmental sustainability refers to the maintenance of ecological systems over time. While environmental sustainability is widely supported, there is disagreement as to the level at which ecological systems need to be maintained. On the one hand, some advocate that conserving just the necessary natural resources to maintain human welfare is sufficient. On the other hand, others argue that ensuring high biodiversity and intact ecosystems is also necessary (Neumayer 2003).

The second dimension is economic. Economic sustainability refers to whether an economic sector is able to ensure sufficient economic productivity and development. A sustainable economy would need to be able to provide people with the jobs and goods that they require. However, similar to the environmental dimension, there are different interpretations of economic sustainability. For instance, how much economic development is necessary to ensure adequate economic productivity? Is a steady state economy sufficient or is continual economic growth necessary (Daly 1996)?

The last dimension is social. Social sustainability refers to the maintenance of social systems over time. A society that is socially sustainable would provide a quality life for all people, guarantee civil rights and liberties, and have democratic governance.

Thus, social sustainability can be closely related with, and some would argue consistent with, the idea of justice. To make things more complicated, the idea of justice is also quite complex. For example, building a just society entails balancing individual and collective needs and rights. To what extent should people be able to pursue their self-interest? What if such attempts harm other societal members who are in precarious positions (Thompson 2010)?

In addition to tensions within each dimension of sustainability, there are also tensions between the three dimensions (Gould and Lewis 2015). Namely, how should the three dimensions—environmental, economic, and social—be balanced? For example, prioritizing economic sustainability might lower environmental sustainability and vice versa. Hence, depending on how each dimension of sustainability is understood and the ways the three dimensions are balanced, what constitutes sustainability will considerably vary.

Before moving on to current sustainability efforts in food and agriculture, think about what constitutes a sustainable food and agriculture system for you. For example, is agriculture environmentally sustainable if it ensures a sufficient natural resource base to continue to produce food, or are greater commitments to environmental conservation necessary? Do people have the right to food that is culturally acceptable, or is it sufficient for people to just not be hungry? Should efforts be made to ensure the livelihoods of small farmers or is it fine to have an agriculture system increasingly made up of larger farmers? What is a sufficient living wage? In the United States, the Fight for $15 movement advocates raising the minimum wage to fifteen dollars an hour. However, many business owners counter that a fifteen-dollar wage will make it hard for them to stay in business. Note that these are not only important sustainability questions, but also political and ethical questions.

SUSTAINABILITY APPROACHES IN FOOD AND AGRICULTURE

Today, there is little objection that our food and agriculture system is at a crossroads and sustainability is a pressing need. Reflecting the different understandings of sustainability, there are a multitude of efforts working to increase the sustainability of food and agriculture. Primarily, these efforts can be divided into three approaches: (1) community-based initiatives, (2) standard, metric, and certification initiatives, and (3) intensification initiatives.

Community-based sustainability initiatives are rooted in alternative agrifood movements, such as localism, food sovereignty, and food justice. They largely reject today's globalized, corporatized, and industrialized food system as unsustainable. Generally, community-based initiatives seek to (re)localize food and agriculture through building direct relations between producers and consumers. In other words, these initiatives seek to "socially embed" food and agriculture in particular places. This embedding is seen as having numerous benefits, including increasing social capital, local economic development, enhanced food sovereignty, and less environmental degradation (Kloppenburg, Hendrickson, and Stevenson 1996; DeLind 2002). Community-based initiatives are often understood as "something done by people, but not something done to them" (Hines 2000, 31). Such initiatives tend to be bottom-up efforts that emerge from local people in communities. Examples of community-based sustainability initiatives include farmers markets, community-supported agriculture, community gardens, farm-to-school projects, and cooperatives.

Sustainability standard, metric, and certification initiatives first emerged in late 1980s and have continued to proliferate (see Lesson 9). Typically, in such initiatives, standards and metrics are developed through a multistakeholder processes (e.g., academics, professionals, civil society and environmental organizations, producers, and industry representatives). Third-party certification is then used to verify producer compliance and to communicate product attributes to consumers. In general, standard, metric, and certification initiatives are a market-driven approach. The underlying assumption is that the more products that are sustainably certified and purchased by consumers, the greater the incentives will be for producers to shift their operations toward more sustainable practices. Today, there are numerous prominent examples of sustainability initiatives that use this approach, including organic, fair trade, the various sustainability roundtables (e.g., palm oil, sugar cane, soy, and beef), and stewardship councils (e.g., fisheries, aquaculture, and forestry).

A third sustainability approach, sustainable intensification, has emerged in recent years (Garnett, Appleby, and Balmford 2013). Sustainable intensification is the idea that greater sustainability in agriculture is possible with increases in productivity and ecoefficiencies. Grounded in the belief that the world faces further increases in population and resource scarcities, proponents of sustainable intensification argue that agriculture will need to undergo significant intensification and, at the same time, be sustainable (Clay 2011). A key component of such ecoefficient intensification is technological innovations that enable farmers to do more with less. Examples of sustainable intensification include precision agriculture and the use of crop-management software programs, soil and water sensors, geographic information systems, and genetic technologies.

As you can tell, these are very different approaches to making food and agriculture more sustainable. Furthermore, these approaches conceptualize sustainability differently, adopt different methods for achieving it, and are likely to generate different outcomes. Consider whether you think one approach is better and why. Can community-based agriculture systems feed the world? To what extent can the market shift the food and agriculture system toward greater sustainability? Is intensification through technology capable of sufficiently tackling the challenges facing food and agriculture? In all likelihood, sustainable food and agriculture will need to include elements of all three approaches. If that is the case, can commonalities be found across the three approaches? Is it possible for proponents of the different approaches to negotiate and work together?

MOVING FORWARD: WHAT NOW?

The preceding lessons in this book have introduced you to a variety of issues that characterize the food and agriculture system. They have presented how our food and agriculture system has developed into its current form, issues and problems associated with it, and ongoing efforts to enhance the sustainability of food and agriculture. They have also offered you sociological perspectives on power and inequality as they relate to food and agriculture. At this point, you might ask, what now?

Indeed, our students often express feeling overwhelmed after having been exposed to the challenges facing food and agriculture today. They claim that the problems are too big, serious, or complex and that it is impossible to address these problems because they are just one person or a small group of people. Do you happen to share this position and feel helpless? Do you also think that the business-as-usual practices and structures are too entrenched and there is not much you can do to make a difference in food and agriculture?

This book has sought to engage you in critical thought and discussion regarding the food and agriculture system. In the tradition of public sociology, we would like to leave you with some ways that you can bring the lessons of this book beyond the classroom and participate in debates and decision-making over the food you eat and how it is produced. While our suggestions might not result in major changes overnight, they do offer vital ways to make your voice heard and actively contribute to more sustainable food and agriculture in your community. As history demonstrates, action at the local level always has the potential to grow into a regional, national, and even global, movement. Moreover, such activities may also lead to personal transformations in terms of how you view yourself and your capabilities.

Our suggestions are organized around some of the roles most of you play in your everyday lives: students, citizens, and consumers. These roles offer various opportunities to participate in decision-making over the food we eat and how it is produced. Because most of you are probably reading this book for a university class, let's start with the role of student. Universities are large organizations that purchase a lot of food, especially universities with tens of thousands of students. This means that getting your university to commit to fair trade, organic, and/or local foods can have a sizeable impact on the sustainability of food and agriculture. While some universities already have made commitments to be more sustainable in their food procurement, many have not. This indicates that significant opportunities exist for you to get involved at the university level. One place to start would be to join a campus organization that is working on food and agriculture issues. You could also work with organizations that have overlapping interests, such as environmental or community-service organizations. If such organizations do not exist, then this may be an opportunity to start a new organization. To give one example from our university, Sam Houston State University, students and faculty jointly mobilized to establish a campus food pantry a few years ago. This food pantry assists food-insecure students and their families. Just this past year, this initiative expanded to include a community garden. While this is a small initiative, it is making a difference in people's lives on our campus.

A second role that many of you occupy is that of a citizen. In democratic countries, citizens have the right to express their views and have their voices heard. Through voting, contacting your elected representatives, and participating in public meetings, you may be able to affect policies concerning food and agriculture. Thus, while corporations and interest groups may have greater power in shaping food and agriculture policy, citizens also have the ability to counter corporate power if they disagree with it. Particularly, this is the case as we move down in scale from the national to the regional and local levels. Indeed, we see many examples where citizens have become involved in regional and local politics—whether it is pressuring local leaders or serving on government and community boards—and have made a difference with respect to a host of issues, including food security and food justice. For instance, cities around the world have established municipal food policy boards that advise their city governments on food policy. To give just one example from Texas, where we currently reside, the Austin–Travis County Food Policy Board was established in 2009 to "address health disparities; increase local sustainable food production; end food injustices; ensure the community has a voice in policy decisions that support a healthy and equitable food system" (AustinTexas.gov 2018).

A third way you can contribute to making a difference in food and agriculture is through participating in social movements. Needless to say, social movements and activism have long been a crucial source of social change. As Lessons 15 and 16 clearly demonstrate, the emergence and growth of both organic agriculture and fair trade owe much to social movements and activism. Today, the food sovereignty movement (Lesson 18) is a critical movement in the global South fighting to counter many of the negative consequences of corporate industrialized agriculture. The food justice movement (Lesson 20) is taking on a variety of forms of inequality that plaque food and agriculture. All these movements, as well as a host of others, could use your support. There are numerous ways to get involved in such movements. These include donating money, volunteering, and taking part in protests. In particular, at the local level, many grassroots food and agricultural advocacy organizations are in need of volunteers. There are also opportunities to band together with your fellow community members to advocate local changes and initiate programs, such as farmers markets, farm-to-school programs, and community gardens.

A fourth way that you can influence the food and agriculture system is as a political consumer. That is, you can exercise your views and make your voice heard through what you choose to buy and consume. As some of the contributors in this book have highlighted, political consumption by itself often has limited efficacy. However, if combined with some of the other activities discussed here, political consumption can be part of a powerful repertoire of tools to bring about change. Possibilities include joining a community-supported agriculture program, shopping at farmers markets, and supporting local restaurants. These all benefit not only the local food system, but also the communities that you live in. You can also support small farmers through buying fair trade products and more sustainable practices through purchasing organic foods and sustainable seafood. Although such purchases will unlikely transform the food and agriculture system on their own, they will certainly make a contribution to improvements in people livelihoods, your local community, and the environment.

As the preceding lessons in this book have illustrated, food intersects with all our lives in a myriad of ways. Our hope is that this volume has not only provided you with a sociological understanding of how the food and agriculture system is structured and operates, but also motivated you to critically think about the food you eat, talk about it with your family and friends, and take action to build a more sustainable food and agriculture system. As members of society who are—like it or not—part of the food and agriculture system, it is crucial for all of us to think critically about the implications of our actions. In the end, it is our society, our food, and our future.

References

AustinTexas.gov. "Austin-Travis County Food Policy Board." Last modified April 2018. http://www.austintexas.gov/sustainability/foodpolicy.

Clay, Jason. 2011. "Freeze the Footprint of Food." *Nature* 475:287–89.

Daly, Herman E. 1996. *Beyond Growth: The Economics of Sustainable Development.* Boston: Beacon Press.

DeLind, Laura B. (2002) "Place, Work, and Civic Agriculture: Common Fields for Cultivation." *Agriculture and Human Values* 19 (3): 217–24.

FAO. 2017. "Sustainability Pathways." Last modified March 2018. http://www.fao.org/nr/sustainability/home/en/

Garnett, T., M. C. Appleby, A. Balmford, I. J. Bateman, T. G. Benton, P. Bloomer, B. Bloomingame, et al. 2013. "Sustainable Intensification in Agriculture: Premises and Policies." *Science* 341:33–4.

Gould, Kenneth A., and Tammy L. Lewis. 2015. "The Paradoxes of Sustainable Development: Focus on Ecotourism." In *Twenty Lessons in Environmental Sociology,* edited by Kenneth A. Gould and Tammy L. Lewis, 330–52. New York: Oxford University Press.

Hines, Colin. 2000. *Localization: A Global Manifesto.* London: Routledge.

Kloppenburg, Jack Jr., John Hendrickson, and G. W. Stevenson. 1996. "Coming into the Foodshed." *Agriculture and Human Values* 13 (3): 33–42.

Neumayer, Eric. 2003. *Weak versus Strong Sustainability: Exploring the Limits of Two Opposing Paradigms.* Cheltenham: Edward Elgar.

Thompson, Paul B. 2010. *The Agrarian Vision: Sustainability and Environmental Ethics.* Lexington: University of Kentucky Press.

Index / Glossary

ABCD firms, 125
AB InBev, 129
accumulated profits, 53
actors, private, 151
adulteration: A set of systematic practices by
  food processors to increase the palatability
  of highly processed foods, but also to
  increase shelf life, make processed foods
  cosmetically more appealing, and lower the
  manufacturer's cost to produce them, 40, 40*f*,
  53–54
advertising: food, 11; mass, 44
agency: A sociological concept that refers to the
  ability of people (and nonhumans) to act, xxix,
  xxvii–xxviii, xxxii, xxxiii; individual, 245
agrarian capitalism, 43
agrarian question, 89–92
agrarian societies, early, 41–42
agricultural industrialization: Describes a
  set of technologies and practices that aim
  to maximize agricultural productivity and
  profitability and minimize the challenges
  that nature or the environment poses,
  typically by substituting industrial for
  biological processes and human labor.
  Agricultural industrialization occurs
  through extensification and intensification,
  79–92; agrarian question, 90–92; agrarian *vs.*
  industrial ethics, 90; agricultural revolution,
  81–83; agriculture's basis in nature, 205;
  agrifood system, 79; chemification, 85–86;
  Civil War, 84; definition, 205; early 20th
  century, 84–85; emancipatory question, 92;
  on environment, 205–212; environmental
  question, 89; extensification, 79, 206–209; farm
  structure, 88–90, 89*t*, 90*t*; food question, 92;
  genetically modified organisms, 87; great
  transformation, 83; green revolution, 91;
  historical overview, 79–80; industrial animal
  production, 87–88; Industrial Revolution, 79;
  intensification, 79, 209–212; mechanization,
  85; Paleolithic to Neolithic, 80–81; post–Civil
  War, 84; selective breeding, 86–87; World War
  II and Cold War, 85
agriculture policy, obesity, 241, 246–248
agriculture's basis in nature: Agriculture and
  food production depend on the environment
  for their biological and ecological attributes
  and processes, such as plant genetics and
  evolution, pollination, and photosynthesis,
as well as place-based resources like water
  and expansive, high-quality soil and
  suitable climatic conditions within seasonal
  cycles. These characteristics of agriculture
  have influenced patterns of food systems
  development and their environmental
  effects, especially through agricultural
  industrialization, 205
agrifood system, 79
agroecology: The process of applying ecological
  principles and concepts to agriculture to
  improve agricultural system (agroecosystem)
  function. Agroecological production systems
  can enhance organic matter accumulation
  and nutrient cycling, soil biological activity,
  natural control mechanisms (e.g., disease
  suppression, biocontrol of insects, weed
  interference), resource conservation and
  regeneration (e.g., soil, water, germplasm),
  and agrobiodiversity and synergisms
  between components. Agroecological
  engagements and applications have grown to
  increasingly consider social relations, 217
Albertsons, 120
alternative agricultural. *See also* organic:
  inequalities, 354–357
alternative agrifood governance, 158–159
alternative food movement: A collection of
  advocacy groups and programs that seek to
  change the globalized, industrial production
  of food to smaller-scale, less chemical-
  dependent methods, largely through market-
  based, locally scaled approaches, 158–159, 239
American Farm Bureau Federation, 85
Americanized ethnic foods, 25–26
animal genetics, 128
animal production, industrial, 87–88
antibiotics, 250
antitrust: Efforts to achieve fair competition in
  markets, such as by breaking up formal or
  informal combinations of large firms (e.g.,
  cartels), xxx; cases, 119; laws, reinterpretation,
  118–120
appellations, 27
appropriate technologies: Technologies that
  are relevant and suitable for particular social
  contexts, 101
aquaculture: The cultivation of aquatic animals
  in natural or controlled marine or freshwater
  environments, 165–166, 171–174, 173*f*